American Icons

Routledge Research in Cultural and Media Studies

American Icons

The Genesis of a National Visual Language

Benedikt Feldges

Routledge
Taylor & Francis Group
New York   London

First published 2008
by Routledge
270 Madison Ave, New York, NY 10016

Simultaneously published in the UK
by Routledge
2 Park Square, Milton Park, Abingdon, Oxon OX14 4RN

Routledge is an imprint of the Taylor & Francis Group, an informa business

© 2008 Taylor & Francis

Typeset in Sabon by IBT Global
Printed and bound in the United States of America on acid-free paper by IBT Global

Library of Congress Cataloging in-Publication-Data

Feldges, Benedikt, 1964–
    American icons : the genesis of a national visual language / Benedikt Feldges.
      p. cm. — (Routledge research in cultural and media studies ; 13)
    Includes bibliographical references and index.
    ISBN 978-0-415-95635-2 (hardback : alk. paper)   1. Motion pictures—Semiotics.
2. Television—Semiotics.   I. Title.

PN1995.F397 2008
791.430973--dc22   2007021205

ISBN10: 0-415-95635-8 (hbk)
ISBN10: 0-203-93784-8 (ebk)

ISBN13: 978-0-415-95635-2 (hbk)
ISBN13: 978-0-203-93784-6 (ebk)

Contents

Acknowledgments

The many turns and twists on the way to publishing this book may often have been the products of coincidence, possibly also of individual choices and decisions, but were certainly influenced by the efforts of many. From the beginning of the project as a PhD thesis, my mentor, Professor Paul Rutherford at the University of Toronto, has guided me. Professors Ivan Kalmar and Marcel Danesi steadfastly provided semiotic advice and Paul Cobley from London Metropolitan University finally paved the way for reworking the thesis into a Routledge publication. What started at the University of Basel with the fledging idea to use early pictorial advertising for historical research crossed the Atlantic twice before being finished in Basel again, and the project has been infused with the sense of a great distance traveled. Realizing the difficulties involved when attempting to interpret pictures as something other than art, I resorted early on to semiotics, at first without much success. North American popular culture, with its many cross-references, inspired me to understand that the search for communicative logic in pictures can only aid historical perspective as long as historical perspective is also applied to the theoretical conception of pictorial signs, the significance of each building upon the other. From that point onward, shifting back and forth between the history of television and the etymology of American pictorial language, the project led me farther and farther into uncharted territory.

Many thanks are due to Fred MacDonald, who generously invited me into his treasured archive of countless historical reels and tapes, and to the staff of the Museum of Television and Radio, who patiently explained how to screen broadcast history in their dark room. Anne Blonstein and Elizabeth Tucker greatly helped not only with the translation from pictorial into written history, but also with editing Swiss-German into North American English. Friends, among them Martin Cafasso and Felix Stalder, and family, including my wife, Catherine Sokoloff, and my parents, Uta and Mathias Feldges, have seen to it that expert advice also came from close by.

Besides my wife and my family, the University of Toronto and the Swiss National Science Foundation also gave financial support to the project, for which I am very grateful.

Introduction

The ascent of pictorially based communication constitutes one of the most intriguing historical phenomena of the twentieth century. The still picture in newspapers and magazines, as well as the moving picture of the cinema, rose triumphantly from the shadow of the letter that had governed Western civilization for the past several centuries. By midcentury, with the maturation of broadcast technology, pictures were spreading cultural and social communication in a steady, unbroken stream, day in and day out.

From the very beginning, broadcasting's novel pictorial format offered every American citizen with access to a television set the intriguing potential to see any possible sight at any given moment. If this potential could be realized, historians also would have the luxury simply to resee the various manifestations of American life of the past decades. Instead of having to reconstruct past events or circumstances, a historian could simply ride the "video time machine."

A historical documentary that offers to take viewers back in time to (re)witness more than half a century of American history is merely continuing to extend powers and privileges similar to those touted at the very beginning of the implementation of television broadcast technology. On his first public affairs show *See It Now,* in 1951, renowned radio journalist Edward R. Murrow introduced "the control room of Studio 41," a television studio configuration stacked with monitors supposedly able to mirror all relevant life occurring at any moment, anywhere in the nation. With such a technological panopticum, reality as it unfolds could be recorded, "controlled," and then relayed to television audiences.

Today, it is the Museum of Television and Radio in New York that offers its visitors a viewing room stacked with monitors, now designated to mirror the reality of the past. In this panopticum of history, the promise of broadcast technology to capture reality with photographic accuracy also carries a hint of the mythical notion of time travel. In order to assess this promise, we need to ascertain what is seen in historical pictures. Contemplating an early photograph of John F. Kennedy taken, for example, at his twentieth birthday, the professional as well as the amateur historian can glimpse the later president in pictorial contours framed long before his political career took off. In the place of referencing the historical reality of an unknown young man on his twentieth birthday, as it must originally have done, the photograph seems to have changed, and now projects the contours of an icon that is known to millions and familiar even to those who were not even born at the time when it first became a household image. Instead of the historian, it is thus the icon that travels back in time, thereby changing both the reality reference of the photograph and the significance of the pictorial shape at its center.

The icon and the man who provides its contours seem to hold two different positions in history. Such detachment between the man and his appearance contradicts ingrained habits of seeing, because it suggests not only different timelines, but also differently evolving trajectories of significance: instead of reflecting the biography of a historical personality, the picture suggests another narrative, a pictorial one that accounts for the journey of the two-dimensional icon on its way to the spectator's eyes. This pictorial history would consequently account for the significance of an icon first according to the chronology in which spectators came to know and to understand the pictorial term, based on the context provided by previously seen pictures.

In hindsight, so to speak, it is possible to diverge from the traditional mode of seeing and to develop a new understanding of pictorial broadcast media. To do so, it is necessary to dissolve the media's photographically grounded basis in reality, and to conceive of the pictorial shapes on screen as symbols, the significance of which develops in the context of communication. Already in the early 1960s, Reuven Frank, renowned producer of television documentaries and former president of NBC's news division, knew that "the picture is not a fact but a symbol."[1] In his words the screen turns "a real child and its real crying" into a "symbol for all children"; thus real people in front of a camera are transformed into what Nelson Goodman described as a "symbol system," and their agency is replaced by convention as the driving force of signification.[2]

In pursuing the factor of historicity in such a pictorial symbol system, a new dimension of visual communication can be explored. As indicated in the example of Kennedy, visual symbols of people, called "icons," acquire characteristic contours through repetition that distinguish them from others. Over time and depending on the degree of exposure they are granted on the public screen, such icons consequently also aggregate semantic depth. Similarly, symbols of objects, such as the Golden Gate Bridge or a bottle of Coca-Cola, henceforth called "emblems," accumulate a pictorial biography with new layers of meaning added by each pictorial narrative in which they appear, be it an ad, a movie, or news show. These pictorial narratives successively aggregate to form sophisticated pictorial terms, which together form a vocabulary. The concept of collective visual literacy, elsewhere described as a knowledge base that enables comprehension of visual information, can thus more specifically be described as a collective knowledge of icons, emblems, and other generic visual symbols.[3] In order for such a collective, even national vocabulary of visual terms to be generated and cultivated, two conditions need to be met: Pictures must be disseminated to a large, nationwide audience, and they must repeatedly feature a number of icons, emblems, and other generic symbols, so that audiences can recognize and share in the process of developing their significance.[4] Because the broadcast medium came to surpass all previous media in the fulfillment of these two conditions, it can thus be seen as the main generator of national visual literacy.

Starting with a tour through New York's Museum of Television and Radio, this study explores how television pictures and their main visual symbols have become collectibles not only in the mind of American spectators, but also in the showrooms of museums, which present them as national heritage. In comparing the historical, the artistic, and the economic value of broadcast pictures, and in demonstrating how they are organized according to a collector's logic, which first develops categories and then highlights the special among more common collectibles, the study comes to consider the particular, often spectacular status that some icons develop within national visual literacy.

The subsequent analysis of the television documentary *History of the 20th Century* proposes an etymological ride through visual literacy collected over more than half a century of American broadcasting. The nine volumes of the documentary itself comprise a collection of prominent icons, such as Richard Nixon, Marilyn Monroe, Muhammad Ali, Lyndon B. Johnson, James Stewart, Jacqueline and John F. Kennedy, and so forth. Its vocabulary of pictorial terms thus offers an opportunity for reflecting on the visual literacy of the addressed audience and on the historical trajectories of its main icons and emblems. In focusing on the broadcast spectacle as one of the most important generators of national icons, the etymological approach to the documentary's (re)dissemination of pictures further attempts to characterize their status. The symbolic dimension of visual literacy that balances typical with atypical elements of meaning, as it is confronted by "unified," "controversial," and "exotic" icons, is particularly highlighted. This process of typifying visual symbols continues with every new exchange of icons, including their staging by the documentary in the limelight of history.

Having addressed the intriguing phenomenon of visual symbols moving back and forth in time, the discussion moves to their ability to shift without apparent boundary between fictional and nonfictional pictures.[5] If Marilyn Monroe's icon matured in the artistic world of fiction and Edward Murrow's was cultivated in the realm of journalism, what then is the pictorial message conveyed when both visual symbols meet in the same frame? Can such a two-dimensional sight be considered fictional or nonfictional? And what is the meaning when John Wayne, the hero of so many Hollywood movies, appears on the stage of Lucille Ball's television show "playing himself"? Is he then (en)acting his fictional or his nonfictional icon or may it even be said that his icon has begun to speak on its own, based on its collective status in national visual literacy?

Early television's circulation of celebrities of all provenances is discussed as an "iconic carousel" that propelled a discourse of "hyperrealism." [6] Through case studies of the iconic careers of early television celebrities, such as Jack Webb in *Dragnet,* Lucille Ball in *I Love Lucy,* the two journalists Edward R. Murrow and Walter Cronkite, as well as sportsman Muhammad Ali, the television medium's inventive ways of accentuating the reality reference of its screen is scrutinized from various angles. Not so much an artistic style as an overpowering discourse, the medium's hyperrealism is finally characterized as a historical mindset that put belief in the technology of broadcasting before the highly symbolic nature of its picture-based language.

The seamless ease with which television claimed from the beginning to handle the fictional and the nonfictional picture within one screen curiously conflicts with the basic notion of pictorial communication. From Marshall McLuhan's famous observation of the medium being the message to Ann Mary Doane's resolute statement that the "only context for television is itself—its own rigorous scheduling," many scholars have noticed television's predisposition for logical contradictions, but to this day there is little consensus on how to diagnose it. [7] The approach developed here is the first one to concentrate almost exclusively on the pictorial base of television. It shows how this pictorial base develops into a particular kind of symbolic language, and how these symbols acquire historically (diachronically) typified significance, which has the power to engulf any other content presented on screen. Photographically recorded reality may certainly provide helpful pieces of information to the historian, but only when the external context can be reconstructed on site, as done, for example, with the famous "Zapruder film" of President Kennedy's assassination. [8] Onscreen, such pictures, including those that display the reconstruction of the historical pictures' creation, replace the external context with a communicative one, which constructs significance based on the intention of those conveying content, as well as the understanding of those receiving it. Trying to extract content from the pictures' original reality reference, which was in one way or another at odds with the transmitters' intentions, enmeshes the historian in speculations that can never be confirmed in front of a television set. For this reason, the pragmatic solution is first of all to search for the intention of those who present us with pictorial content. This approach to pictorial communication, however, requires not only positioning oneself behind the back of the "evil demon of the picture" (as Jean Baudrillard called the photographic anchor in reality), but also facing the task of identifying traces that transmitters have left in the pictures' content. [9]

To better locate and describe the communicative transmitter-receiver context of pictures, a model of a split pictorial transmittership is introduced and developed throughout the study. Following Barbara Zelizer's observations on the collective nature of authorship in television news, the model proposes to differentiate between creating a picture and presenting it to spectators.[10] The act of taking a photograph often has its own story, one that can sometimes even seem to contradict the mediated content, as in the shot of the famous flag "raising" at Iwo Jima, which actually depicts a moment when the American soldiers were taking the flag down. This act of picture making is also often accomplished by a different person than the one who selects the picture for presentation to an audience.[11] The act of presentation also has its own history, which always involves selection and a decision made in anticipation of a particular audience. While the first act already infuses significance based on the decision to use a camera and to select the shot, translating a three-dimensional view into a two-dimensional frame, the second act performs the further adjustment to a communicative context, designating the shot's significance to be received by an actual audience. As such, this second act of presentation metaphorically expresses the gesture of pointing with the index finger, which gesture has the ability to emphasize pictorial aspects that were not necessarily intended or evident when the shot was created.

In differentiating these two acts of transmittership, it thus becomes possible to locate a shift: from a coincidental production of significance that is still very close to reality, to an intentional significance produced whenever pictures are presented to spectators. If, for example, an amateur video captures a scene such as a plane crash, the coincidental aspect of these pictures—which may also help in reconstructing what happened—is turned into intentional communication, when a television producer selects and edits the pictures in anticipation of his audience's interest in the message and/or in the pictorial spectacle of the scene. Thus, according to the relation between the two components of split transmittership, the pictures will be worked into different categories. For example, there are those more anonymous pictures that have lost touch with the intention of their creators, as is often the case in the broadcast spectacle, and those for which the act of creating and presenting is done by one and the same person, as is often the case with family photography.

In order to pinpoint content in a picture, however, a minimal consensus is required as to how such content is coded (semantics), how it can be combined to form a message (syntactics), and how it adapts to the particular character of those involved in the exchange (pragmatics). If the transmitter-receiver context of pictures provides the first step in shifting pictorial meanings and significance from unmediated to mediated origins, the second step concerns the conventional forces of signification that arrange the two-dimensional shapes into comprehensible pictorial narratives. Combining these forces in the concept of the visual sign, the appendix offers a theoretical outline of how a sign-based logic can be applied to pictures, which always feature novel visual characteristics in novel visual contours. In proposing four principles or codes of visual language, a model is introduced that synthesizes previous attempts at defining visual signs, such as the work of Umberto Eco, and provides the foundation for defining icons and emblems as conventionalized terms of a language that maturates over time.[12] The model is summarized in a kind of glossary at the end of the appendix. It is intended to close a gap in modern theory through defining the pictorial entities needed to understand visual literacy as based on a differentiated vocabulary. Only with this model in place can research be made into the terms' historicity, and thus can a novel type of pictorial etymology be investigated.[13]

The research into the discourse of hyperrealism is thus complemented with the exploration of a new logic for pictorial communication, at the core of which a new understanding of icons emerges. Icons were generally defined by Charles Sanders Peirce as signifying based on their resemblance to a model in reality ("iconicity"); as Umberto Eco noted, this iconicity can never be complete. Here, the factor of iconicity is applied to the process of "iconization," whereby a sign is developed with enough visual characteristics to be recognized in another picture.[14] This small but influential shift in their definition serves as the starting point for comprehending the icons on screen not so much as an "imagined community," but as the material manifestation of the networking of American society via the national idiom of a sophisticated visual language.[15]

Part A

Icons in the Museum

1   Collecting Pictures

Every day hundreds of thousands of pictures are broadcast by any given television channel. At the end of a year, a decade, or even a century, the number of pictures produced by American television alone reaches a dimension that is difficult to comprehend. Yet, such mass production appears to have little impact on the commercial value or the cultural status of the broadcast picture. After only four decades of broadcasting, faster than for many art forms, television has made its way to the museum. Dignified as a national treasure by the Museum of Broadcast Communications in Chicago or by the marble halls of the Museum of Television and Radio in New York, those billions of broadcast pictures of the twentieth century thus add up to compare in some ways with other, distinct art forms.

Evading the ordinary in spite of their overwhelming number, broadcast pictures seem to retain their cultural and commercial significance in the face of time. Nostalgic retrospectives, historical documentaries, candlelight biographies, entertaining year-end reviews, daily CNN snippets of what happened on "this day, this century"—pictorial history on television has become popular enough to sustain its own genres, even its own channels. With the History Channel, A&E, TLC, ESPN Classic Sports, or Nickelodeon, the media has ultimately institutionalized historical pictures within its daily flow of visual entertainment and information.

In discovering its past through reusing its own reels and tapes, television's approach to history differs vastly from that of the movie industry, which has developed its own brand of historical imagery. Unlike film, which uses artistic imagery as dramatic setting, as in the highly decorated Steven Spielberg productions *Schindler's List* and *Saving Private Ryan*, television most often proposes viewing the past in the much more direct fashion of restaging old photographs or rerunning old reels. Trying less to find a new pictorial language for past worlds than to borrow the documentary's aim of showing it "how it really was," the old pictures are deployed as if history were an unchanging property. What sustains this phenomenon of "visual history" on television, it appears, is its ability to stir curiosity. The exotic views into a two-dimensional past, in light of the mythical promise to see history with one's own eyes, seem destined to find the interest of large audiences, thus rejuvenating their commercial value.

By the late seventies and early eighties of the last century, most major networks had begun to invest in state-of-the-art archives, allowing them access to historical pictures whenever needed. Before the big networks discovered the full economic potential of pictorial archives, however, the reels and tapes of three decades of broadcasting were left scattered in the cellars of producers, local stations, and a handful of private collectors. It is hardly a coincidence that Fred MacDonald, a renowned scholar of television history, holds one of the most substantial private collections of television sources.[1] Originally compiling the Chicago-based archive for his academic research, which resulted in several major works on the history of American television, MacDonald retired from teaching in favor of maintaining and enhancing his archive for commercial purposes. The lucrative sale of a shot of Priscilla Presley to the locally produced Oprah Winfrey show, which needed the footage overnight, became the kernel of his business. In the 1990s, the demand for historical footage allowed ABC's Video Source to charge a producer a minimum of $600 per minute of video. Retooling the reels of the past for the present has indeed become a profitable business.

Such commodification of historical broadcast pictures presents a number of problems to those interested in an academic approach to the visual past of the nation. First of all, unlike art historians, scholars of history are not really used to working with sources that have maintained or even increased their value over the years. History should be of current relevance and could possibly be popular, but the case of television appears extreme on both counts. Furthermore, the sheer quantity of historical pictures is baffling to the selection process and this problem of access is complicated further by the excessive value of the source material, particularly if a scholar needs to obtain copies for detailed analysis. And beyond all this lies the question of the nature of these ephemeral broadcast pictures.

What exactly is it, after all, that allows these electronic pictures to generate, despite their mass, time and again, the power to capture the eye and to establish their social and economic significance? By comparison to art, the mass of television pictures defies Walter Benjamin's famous bond between the originality of an art work and its "aura," since the reels can be copied, rerun and resampled without apparent loss of significance.[2] A preliminary hypothesis concerning the particular aura of the broadcast picture involves the following assumption: Since any of the billions of broadcast pictures can hardly beat the ordinary on each single occasion, the mass must involve a measurement of controlled accessibility and selection that regulates which shot is special and which only serves to contrast with the extraordinary. It is thus presumed that not all broadcast pictures have an aura of their own, but all, or to the least those that are not forgotten, are woven into relations that together contribute to the aura of each single shot. Such a web of contrasting relations would thus not only involve those pictures sequenced in a narrative that highlights the extraordinary sight, but also a large pool of absent pictures, with associative characteristics provided by producers and spectators alike. Thus the significance of one television picture would be engaged through a process of collecting, sorting, and arranging many pictures, which, ordered in relations of similarity and difference, provide the basis for a purposeful selection of those characteristics able to attract the gaze of large audiences and to inspire their interest. In this mode, the extraordinary pictures thrive on those in the background, and vice versa, thus furnishing each other on any given occasion with significance and aura. The hypothesis is thus that it might just be the mass of pictures itself that grounds not only the significance but also the aura of television pictures, as it assembles pictorial significance in ever more relations, whenever presented on new occasions and in new narrative contexts.

And there is more difference within the similarity: Unlike that of Benjamin's work of art, the aura of television pictures appears not limited to the unity comprised by canvas, color, frame, and content, but can also hinge on pictorial fragments. Visual symbols of popular personalities or of well-known objects appear to develop significance which provides them autonomous status within a picture. As these sights within the sight move from one picture to the other, and as they commence to differ from other, more general visual symbols within a picture, such as, for example, a passerby, a car, or a tree, they gain, rather than lose, aura by means of repetition. In this dynamic, pictorial fragments, such as visual symbols, receive more pointed significance the more they are staged. Thus, repeated presentation of visual symbols in more or less different contexts not only makes their contours more recognizable than other similar symbols, but also adds layers of significance to their content, shaping icons, such as Elvis Presley or Muhammad Ali, or emblems, such as the White House or the Golden Gate Bridge. The collecting, selecting, and presenting of television pictures thus extends beyond the picture as a whole—unlike the case with plastic art—to include as well single pictorial elements. In consequence, the shaping of contrastive relationships interconnects not only pictures or shots as entireties, but also visual symbols, icons, and emblems within them. Based on this second hypothesis, an otherwise perfectly ordinary picture can gain special significance, and thus acquire commercial value, should it contain one particular fragment, such as an icon. And, following this observation, a picture can also gain such significance and value long after its creation, as indicated by the example of the television station that explicitly asked Mac Donald for a particular visual symbol without regard to the setting of the shot as a whole.

Based on these observations, the large mass of pictures and of pictorial fragments circulating in popular culture provide at each moment and from any given angle a background that regulates the cultural significance, the commercial value, and the aura of those sights presented on screen. The professionals who produce and present the shots and the spectators who see and respond to them consequently combine to manage this wealth of pictorial significance. Both the intention of the producers as well as the response of spectators can initiate the shaping of favorites, thus allowing a select few symbols to acquire more profiled significance as icons that are henceforth recognizable in their unique contours.

The assumption so far is that producers, actors, and audiences all have a part in managing the wealth of pictures produced every day, thereby contributing to the shaping of icons and emblems, to marking the unique among the ordinary, and thus to fueling what has been called "collective visual literacy."[3] Unlike other models of visual literacy, the one here introduced has command of a pool made of small visual terms and pictorial fragments as well as complete shots, the significance of which interconnects in a dynamic fashion. The more pictures are traded, according to the third hypothesis, the more coherent the significance of single pictorial elements becomes, and the higher their potential to establish meaningful visual communication. It is at this point that linguistic dynamics intersect with commercial ones in an uncommon fashion that challenges the attempt to use pictures for historical analysis. While icons such as those of John F. Kennedy or Marilyn Monroe appear as part of history, they also continue to carry an aura that is as mysterious as it is potentially valuable. While history in general remains an abstract product of the rational mind, visual literacy can not only carry the icons of the past into the present, it can also change them according to the logic of its continuous processes of selecting, comparing, ordering, and disposing of characteristics. Visual literacy thus develops its own temporality of collecting and networking pictorial significance, which is distinct from the timeline of general history.

THE COLLECTOR'S LANGUAGE

Objects from the past reach the present in many different forms. Collecting often assumes a central role in this process, for example, in the case of objects considered as art, goods judged to contain elements of material value, such as jewelry, or more generally, all commodities that for one reason or another carry enduring cultural meanings, such as antiquities, baseball cards, stamps, and possibly also icons and other visual symbols. All such collectibles have in common an identity defined within culturally and socially acknowledged rituals of selecting, assembling, and trading, rituals responsible for maintaining, but also for developing and at times even changing, their original circuits of meaning and significance. Once part of the dynamic process of collecting, their value often begins to change according to the economic but also the cultural parameters that determine their exclusivity and scarcity in relation to comparable items. Parallel to the economic factor of the collectors' market, the transition of the object from its original purposes, uses, and meanings to the present also negotiates the invisible boundary that invests the collectibles with historical status. Socially acknowledged collections are able to introduce their collectibles into new discourses with the power to establish both novel commercial value and novel cultural status for their objects, although often without that boundary between the past and the present becoming visible or explicit. It is in this context that the dynamics inherent in the process of collecting, following Krzysztof Pomian, often involve the shaping of a "new language" adjusted to the changing status of the collectibles.[4] However, when such new language marks the film reel's transition into history, what is the impact on its immaterial content, the visual symbols, icons, and emblems, which already carry the signs of a language?

Indeed, it appears that collecting, with its fluid boundaries between the past and the present, as well as its general drive to assemble objects based on their typical and atypical, generic and extraordinary characteristics, has as much in common with the framework of a visual language as it does with that which ascribes commercial status to historical pictures. If the fascinating logic of collecting can allow baseball cards of mediocre players to assume more value than those of other, much more proven players, the same may be true for all pictures and thus for all icons. While visual literacy involves the dynamic of establishing relations of similarity and difference to order the content of visual terms, it may also extend to define their significance by measurement of scarcity, rendering the rare, the forgotten, or the exotic as more valuable and significant than a more common pictorial sight of, say, the nation's president. Such mechanisms combine a largely anonymous dynamic whereby the function of visual literacy as a whole emerges as more than the sum of its parts.

While there is hardly any limit on what can become a collectible and how and for what reasons it can become valuable or significant at any time, within any culture, there nevertheless appears a certain system inherent to the social processes of collecting, a system that Pomian characterized as having the following four stages.[5] In the first stage, an object drops out of its original economic, cultural, and social circuit and temporarily loses value and significance. In the second stage, the object becomes desirable for all sorts of reasons ranging from pure nostalgia to clever entrepreneurship, as this transitional phase already involves the economy of exchange. The most decisive factor for the future value of an object thereby involves whether or not there are other collectors willing to trade, or whether or not there is sufficient interest in the items. At the same time, the interaction based on the rule of scarcity and abundance helps to establish the scope of a collection and to clarify which collectible obtains the defining role as the exceptional, outstanding item that governs the new network of significance of the whole collection. In the third stage of Pomian's model, the collection irrevocably heads toward the limelight of an exhibition, seeking to prove its new raison d'être through the approving gaze of an audience. While the exhibition is the ultimate test of the collectibles' new economic value and cultural meaning, it also occasions a last effort to refine the collection, to improve its comprehensiveness, and to insure its cohesion. Objects of different eras, of different provenances, of different functions and status are now pitched together in ways never intended by their original manufacturers, or their original users. These objects are orchestrated by impresarios in anticipation of an audience's response. The spotlight of such presentations may thus mark the most visible aspect of their transfer into history and reflect that "new language" responsible for networking their semantic fields in newly established relations of difference and similarity.

Each collection draws its own boundaries scripted by criteria that balance general with particular characteristics among the collectibles. A collection of Italian pottery might, for example, build on such criteria as being handcrafted, belonging to a certain region, containing a special clay, featuring color tones characteristic of special burning techniques or displaying motifs of decoration that reference local traditions. While such characteristics define the extent of a collection in broad categories, variations in the individual collectibles add to the process of signification a dynamic element that balances more outstanding with more general characteristics for each item. As a result, items bearing a rare mélange of characteristics emerge as the highlight of the collection and thereby assume a second, contrasting function in defining the collection's meanings and significance, beside that of its general extent. At the end of such a process, it appears entirely possible to exhibit an extraordinary water pot with a rarely found form as the outstanding symbol of Italian handcraft, thus influencing also the significance of the more usual pots, even though no one can know anymore whether the extraordinary pot was only the result of unique experiment or whether it had been rejected as imperfect by its maker.

In this third stage, the value and significance of a collection's single pieces have become interconnected, and collectors will usually strive to keep the collection together. Rather than exchanging items, collectibles are now bought to complete the whole, the value of which tends to outweigh the sum of its parts. In achieving an acceptable measure of completion, the collection has established a new network that inseparably bonds the unique and the general, the jewel that attracts the gaze, and the banality that offsets the exceptional characteristics of the jewel, that builds its stage.

The underlying economic dynamic recreates the object's value according to the classic rules of the market, which speculates on the future value of these artifacts based on their partially self-determined balance of what will be available and what will be scarce. Because of the similarity to operations on the stock exchange, an increasing number of potential collectibles defy, at least to some degree, the usual transition from one economic circuit to the next. Baseball cards, for example, were produced from the beginning as collectibles although very likely at first without full understanding of their future value. So was, for example, a new kind of Swiss watch, the Swatch, introduced by Nicolas Hayek in limited design editions. For more than a century now, art too has been changing to the point that artists work with the knowledge of the potential market value of what they are making. Once their creations are able to attract collectors, a selective few can share in the economic dynamic of collections. In each case, the process of collecting preserves what is otherwise destined for the dustbin of history and eventually commences to seek the approval of a larger audience, which, if granted, further increases the collection's cultural significance. Yet at the very height of a collection's cultural success, the collectibles' newly achieved commercial value often begins to descend again.

The fourth stage of a collection, finally, is defined by Pomian as what is more or less the end of its road into history. In most Western cultures, the institution of the museum defines this fourth and final stage of collections and often presents the economic sarcophagus of the collectibles. At this point in the life of a collectible, a whole new network of social and cultural meanings has replaced the object's original significance and the terminology used to describe its new status bears historical, and often national, connotations.

If these four phases apply to all objects that attain the dynamic of collecting, then they might also apply to each and every person's process of acquiring visual literacy from the pictures encountered day in and day out. In a nutshell, Pomian's four stages would define how the visual signs in pictures become symbols that carry accumulated content and significance. The logic behind selecting, sorting, trading, and selecting again for the purpose of public exhibitions would thus not simply be accompanied by a "new language" created by the collectors of old objects, but would represent the very generator of a visual language, whose terms are traded by most Americans. But if true, what kind of museum could possibly place the lid of a sarcophagus on the terms of this language, which are as active and dynamic as the icons of, for example, Marilyn Monroe or John F. Kennedy?

THE DARK ROOM

The power of the museum rests in the public position from which it can "show and tell." In Tony Bennett's assessment of the historical formation of museums, this power is applied not only to informing visitors, but also to reforming their behavior and manners.[6] Through bundling a wide range of cultural and social discourses, the museum came to represent, in the words of Germaine Bazin, a "fundamental institution of the modern state," the status of which reflects upon the significance of its collectibles.[7] In theory, the transition from Pomian's third to fourth stage not only disconnects the collectibles from their original economic value and their original set of meanings, but also marks them as significant to national heritage. Bazin thus concludes that since the late nineteenth century museums took up where churches left off and nations became the "subject and object of a new cult of collecting."[8] In the wake of the Enlightenment, the discourse responsible for attributing significance to collected objects succeeded a predominantly religious approach to the past that had refrained from distancing it as history. Museums carried forward Christian educational motives and a ritualistic preference for exhibiting the past in impressive showcases, and at the same time initiated the secular discourses of cultural heritage and national history. Similar to churches, museums indeed often house themselves in prominent architectural structures at central urban sites, thus assuming a dominant position in the public sphere.[9]

In the 1980s, the original Museum of Broadcasting in New York ultimately established itself by relocating to a new building and reopening as the Museum of Television and Radio on 52nd Street. While additional museums followed, such as the Museum of Broadcast Communication in Chicago and Washington and a sister institution in Los Angeles, these new museums drew little state funding, instead drawing support from the broadcast industry itself, and a few private donors.[10] In this way, the successfully invented museum for television pictures represents less a public than a commercial institution, nevertheless pursuing the ultimate intent of collecting: to make visible to a general public what had appeared destined to become invisible.

Cultivated by Robert M. Batscha, the Museum of Television and Radio radiates a classic aura. At least on first sight, the demeanor of a classic museum is taken up on the inside; as well, visitors are invited into a screening room to watch a professional presentation of a "selected collection within the collection," reminiscent of the guided museum tour. With the collectibles already dignified by their incorporation into the museum's holdings, such presentations in front of audiences further elevate their status. Yet, while these screenings underline the institution's stated mission to conserve and manage the memory of past American broadcasts, the fourth floor of the museum offers the visitor a much less centralized and much more unassuming view of its holdings. Each visitor has access to a computerized database, which allows her to survey the complete holdings and to select up to five collectibles for personal viewing. In this organizational format, the museum refrains from prescribing the visitor's gaze with any contextual significance. Instead of constructing its visitors as passive admirers of the collectibles' aura, it transforms itself on the fourth floor into a library, inspiring the visitor to make her own choices, to create her own, individual collection out of the vast holdings, and to find her own jewels to marvel at. Thus, each visitor is allowed to act as a collector or historian and to select the footage according to her own special interest and purpose. On this floor, the public actively participates in the process of shaping the general signification of the collectibles and of identifying the extraordinary among the defining elements of the collection.

This unusual concept for exhibiting collectibles creates a peculiar field of tension with regard to the very traditional structure of the museum's first floor. The contrast between the entrance of the Museum of Television and Radio and its actual exhibition rooms is striking. Once visitors have passed the threshold of an entrance equipped with columns fashioned according to the nineteenth century's longing for classical grandeur, they enter a two- to three-story entrance hall decorated with marble. The hall induces a typically restrained atmosphere, prompting visitors to lower their voices and assume the ritualized behavior of respectful and duly interested guests. To those who have not yet begun to appreciate the dignified nature of what they are about to see, a series of signs lay out the usual rules: shirts and shoes are a must, eating and drinking are prohibited, and so, of course, is taking pictures of the pictures. The properly assimilated visitor, having forfeited ten dollars, may then proceed to the computer room on the fourth floor. Although less impressive in its architecture and decoration, the room still retains some of the entrance's dignified atmosphere, if only through the presence of scores of personnel ready to assist the visitor in handling the database on one of the numerous computer terminals. But once his selections have been made, the guest is on his own and makes his solitary way to a dark, low-ceilinged screening room packed with dozens of small viewing consoles. Other visitors at their consoles are not entirely concealed from view, but the screen and headphones soon absorb all concentration, were it not for the substantial background noise. The visitors to the dark room have turned into an audience and they do what all audiences do: they comment on what they see, they laugh and scream, they unwittingly perform Karaoke while joining in with the favorite tunes of an old show, they cheer for their preferred baseball team, even though they most likely already know the outcome of the game long past. Unlike all other museums, the central exhibition room reveals a carnivalesque, at times utterly grotesque atmosphere.[11] Since one cannot hear and can hardly see what others are watching, periods of eerie silence linger between sudden outbursts of unaccountable response. Visitors interact directly with the exhibits they have chosen to see and on occasion also with one another, as when rewinding a scene to let a curious neighbor participate in the viewing. Gone is the high-minded atmosphere of the traditional museum.[12]

In bringing together the spectators at a fairground of the past, the dark room thus allows for an aura that breathes new life into the old pictures, demonstrating their vividness and currency, rather than their sacrosanct status as objects of history.

2   Collecting Language

When museums picked up where churches left off, they retained the role of a public clearinghouse and continued to regulate with socially accepted standards the status and significance of their collections, thus marking each of their exhibits with a particular discursive claim. In the words of its founder, the collectibles of the Museum of Television and Radio present a "national memory" of America's past, which recalls the broadcasts' original function of "recording" socially and culturally relevant events.[1] In her study *Tangled Memories*, Marita Sturken created the term "cultural memory" as specifying an in-between of individual recollection and social discourses of the present. From her perspective, pictures of the past evade pure historical status, since individual arrangements of memory are always entangled with the present. According to her outline, the ground floor of the television museum comprises a "technology of cultural memory," because, like all museums, it represents a society's handling of the past through a restaging of selected collectibles in showcases, thereby also regulating everything that should be forgotten.[2] But as much as Sturken's concept of cultural memory explores the grey area between individual and collective memory, and as much as it suits the nature of the museum's collectibles, it cannot account for their full potential. There can be no doubt, for example, that pictures of past news and other television shows are also understood and enjoyed when seen for the first time. There is thus a difference between recollecting an act of past television watching and the notion of reseeing or even seeing and understanding for the first time what was broadcast decades ago. Furthermore, the concept of memory implies that pictures stimulate significance the way reality does. But although television may feed individual recollection in similar ways to experience gathered in everyday life, the very possibility of manufacturing and presenting pictures to people also points to the difference between memory and visual literacy. Unlike memory, visual literacy accounts not only for a passive recollection of pictures of the past, but also for an active managing of pictorial terms, and thus for the very possibility to understand the narrative structure of pictures in the first place.

It is at this point that the museum's role of collecting and exhibiting objects as epitomes of cultural memory and national history intersects with the symbolic code of a visual language that is itself built on the logic of collecting. To understand the symbolic function of pictures, we collect visual symbols, order them in categories, differentiate them according to their more general and their more particular characteristics, and compare those characteristics for each new symbol that we encounter. When re-viewing visual symbols of the past, we therefore apply a different eye, one that has been informed by the ongoing process of organizing symbolic meaning encountered in all intervening pictures. This dynamic structure of visual language implies that some visual symbols may indeed drop out of their original circulation in collective literacy and may therefore have indeed reached the fourth stage of sacrosanct cultural or historical status. Other symbols, however, never actually drop out of circulation, but remain an active part of society's visual literacy, and thus still influence the significance of other symbols within the continuously changing fabric of visual language, a fabric that aims at contrasting the special and the extraordinary in ever new relations. While the semiotic dynamic of visual literacy befits the spectacle of the dark room, it consequently also challenges the collectibles' potential to reflect an unmediated account of history.

Against this background, the dark room of the Museum of Television and Radio defies the institution's own claim to treasure the television imagery of the past as national memory or heritage. Storing content that is itself collectible in the immaterial sense of visual literacy, the museum prompts the individual visitor to install his own collection within the marble halls. The popular setting of the dark room stages the sharing of individual literacy as a public act that nurtures a national visual language. By no means a sarcophagus of history, this institution perpetuates the significance of its icons and emblems, adding depth to those that are still popular and current, and guarding others in the mode of an etymological dictionary of American visual language. Albeit thus far without the authority held by an institution like the Académie Française, if only because the museum actually fails to see its collection as a treasury of visual language, it nevertheless proposes to complement individual visual literacy with a unifying, national frame.

THE MUSEUM'S SHOP

Comprising more than half a century of American broadcasting, the number of single pictures stored by the Museum of Television and Radio is almost beyond imagination. It is therefore clear that not all of these visual records of the past can possibly be commercially valuable. The museum nevertheless protects the copyrights of all of them and even refrains from handing out copies for research purposes—it is definitely not a public library. The economically motivated protection of what is also appreciated as the pictorial heritage of the nation hints once again at the still active nature of this collection: The dynamics of collection playing on the principles of scarcity and abundance give rise to an ongoing transformation of currency, rendering some shots desirable on one day, while dropping the favorites of another day. As long as there is television, this collection is far from being finished, and as long as new pictures nurture the process of fermentation, nobody can know which of the pictures will gain and which will loose value. Against this background, the museum shop, residing in one corner of the marble hall, is anything but a typical store.

In light of Pomian's scheme, such museum markets could be defined as the "fifth stage" of a collection, one created by clever entrepreneurs to circumvent the collectibles' sarcophagus through (re)producing memorabilia of the act of paying homage to sacrosanct culture. Often relying on the translation of the most spectacular exhibits into visual language, henceforth iconized on T-shirts and coffee cups, such shops could be described in Baudrillard's terms as selling a simulation of both the cultural and the economic value of collectibles, provided that they have actually reached the end of their active life in society.[3] From Eco's perspective, such iconic reproduction of rare collectibles corresponds to a voyage through a "hyperreality" that fabricates the absolute fake in order to attain the "real thing."[4] In terms of visual literacy, such reproduction of extraordinary cultural assets of historical, artistic, or even religious provenance feeds "iconization," because it heightens the public recognition and the semiotic significance of selected visual symbols. In any case, market logic augments the processes that shape icons such as, for example, that of Mona Lisa, and therefore a museum can contribute simultaneously to their collectibles' cultural signification, as well as to their commodification. Mona Lisa exemplifies the entangled patterns of the economic and linguistic logic of collecting, the dynamic of which is powerful enough to replace the aura of the singular object with the glow of a reproducible icon that is no less spectacular or less economically valuable than the original. Touching again on the delicate borderline between those pictures considered art and those not, the standards of originality and uniqueness of the former seem undiminished when subjected to television's mode of heightening a symbol's significance through mass production. But while the collecting of both types of pictures contributes to their economic, as well as their as cultural value, it is only television imagery that proposes time and again to contain a reflection of reality and thus the opportunity to look back to the nation's past. It is from this perspective that the shop of the Museum of Television and Radio, which awaits visitors who have just disembarked the time machine of the dark room, proposes to offer for sale not a mere simulation, but something very close to the "real thing"—or then to the "absolute fake." If the difference between a sight in reality and a picture of the same sight already seems negligible, the difference between the original camera shot and its copies or between its historical and its current broadcast becomes truly insignificant. Unlike a poster of Mona Lisa, which can hardly be mistaken for the original, videotapes, which offer the opportunity to resee at will, for example, past broadcasts of the moon landing, popular sitcoms, news reports from the Vietnam War, or an Oscar night long past, retain only a very sophisticated difference—one as potentially imperceptible as between a work of art and a perfectly crafted copy. As opposed to the difference between the real and the fake, the difference between an original broadcast and its rerun appears much less spectacular even though it marks the boundary between the past and the present. This boundary, like the one between the picture and reality in front of the camera, begins to dissolve when the mass production of pictures commences to interweave pictorial significance, to produce emblems and icons, and thus to fuel visual literacy as the main source of pictorial signification.

Thus stopping at the shop to purchase a number of made for television documentaries on American history, perhaps at first with the instinct of a consumer historian, the realization was made that here at the end of the visit another entrance ticket had been purchased, a ticket to the historical evolution of the American visual language.

When choosing between documentaries, such as *The History of the 20th Century, Yesteryear, The Fabulous Sixties,* or *The Sensational Seventies* (the commercial success of which apparently lasted for two or more decades), the consumer historian can purchase original television footage, which may very well also be a part of the museum's holdings. Similar to the museum's own showings of selected reels, these compilations offer historical imagery that is the product of distinct processes of collecting, selecting, and ordering shots of the past. One can thus buy a commercially manufactured exhibition of collectibles after having seen a personally assembled selection of the same or similar clips in the dark room. In other words, at the end of the visit one can buy a second entrance ticket to the museum, possibly even to the real one that can be seen in the privacy of one's own home.

Part B
Kaleidoscopic Spectacles

3   Pictorial Historiography

Historical documentaries on television have forged a new genre based on presenting pictures as records of the past, an innovation that became popular in the 1970s and 1980s. With the new genre, television became the first medium that, on a regular basis, restaged as historical records pictures it had produced in the past. At least with respect to the moving picture, the rebroadcasting of old clips thus established the novel format of what could be called pictorial historiography.

The rebroadcasting of pictures within the same channels of their original publication, however, tends not only to conflict with the academic principle of distanced, methodological handling of historical sources, but also with questions concerning that invisible element responsible for disconnecting the past from the present: Even should it be true that (photographic) pictures hold a moment of reality, it appears not at all obvious how and at which point such reality would become history and, correspondingly, what would have changed within the pictures. Yet, because none of the documentaries surveyed addressed such latent conflicts behind the concept of pictorial historiography in any direct way, the new format carries the implicit claim that the presented pictures document history the way they documented reality when shown for the first time. The inadequate presentation of pictorial history as a product of mere repetition of the same frames thereby implicates every type of historical documentary: "Serious documentaries," such as the PBS-produced *Vietnam: A Television History* or the *Cold War* series by CNN, claim historical substance for their imageries as easily as more "popular documentaries," such as *The Fabulous Sixties* and *History of the 20th Century*, but also, for example, any number of broadcasts on ESPN's Classic Sports. Certainly, the first category of "serious documentaries" generally uses a verbal corset to place the pictures in an extended historical context. Occasionally, such productions also reflect on the nature of the selected historical footage, as when interviewing the original producers of the footage or discussing a second pictorial perspective on the same event. But, although generally produced with the intent to inform objectively, they rarely reflect on the nature of their sources, leaving it to their audiences to establish a connection between the verbally outlined perspective on history and the one unfolded by the pictures themselves. As a result it is up to the spectator either to take the pictures as a mere confirmation—if not proof—of the verbally communicated facts or to evaluate the historical substance of the presented pictures by individual measurement. In this sense pictorial historiographies of the "serious" and the "popular" kind come together, the main difference remaining that the latter category reduces verbal commentary to a minimum: With little concern for any academic reflections, popular documentaries such as *History of the Twentieth 20th* or *The Fabulous Sixties* set free the historical potential of the old frames not so much to inform, but to entertain their audiences. With the emphasis placed on the visual, these documentaries have no qualms about announcing that pictorial historiography enables viewers to "see it as it was" or to experience the sensation of riding a "time machine."[1]

While the "serious documentaries" certainly appear more restrained in their self-descriptions, they are no more so in their tendency to compile pictorial sources that went through many hands. Rarely distinguishing the original context of the pictures' production or that of the pictures' original presentation to audiences, they almost never explain who was responsible for sequencing the clips in the past, nor, for example, whether or not the pictures were additionally edited to suit the rhythm of their new presentation. Since the historical documentaries rarely take the time to present the full context or introduction of the footage as shown in their original broadcast vehicles, such as newsreels or television news, the historical clips often appear shortened at will and at times seem also to have been arranged to create new visual narratives, for example, to bring closure to a verbally discussed aspect of a story. Because of such arrangements and the impression of an often quite coincidental use of sources, the pictorial part of these documentaries tends to appear rather as a visual anthology or even as a collage of historical sources, than as a visual historiography that develops its own visual narrative.

The more popular documentaries seem even more to take the collage as their model, using visual sources for their power to attract the eye without much concern as to why one shot is followed by the next. The most extreme examples of this can be found in the year-end retrospectives that compile highlights of the past broadcast season, a genre that became popular around the same time as the documentaries. While such year-end retrospectives claim to mirror the most defining moments of the past in anticipation of the footage's future historical significance, popular historical documentaries could be described as following the destiny already inscribed in the source footage by its original producers.

As discussed in the previous chapter on the pictures in the archive, these types of historical collages also contribute to an ongoing circulation of footage on television, raising questions about their historical status. Having analyzed and thereby memorized most of the scenes compiled in the documentary *History of the 20th Century*, produced in the early 1980s, I couldn't help but notice that many of its historical clips are continuously used in contemporary television productions. A shot of Fidel Castro dating presumably from the late 1950s or early 1960s, showing him from behind gesticulating wildly with his right arm, was broadcast in the same week by a historical CNN documentary and an A&E biography on Ernest Hemingway. Interestingly, all three of these "pictorial quotes" were presented without the original sound, thus emphasizing the visual plane of the historical footage. When such glimpses of pictorial information are recycled through almost half a century of television broadcasting, it challenges the very concept of history by perpetuating what was most likely the statement of one American cameraman. Such repetition furthermore influences the evolution of the historical code behind the icon, whose bearer is still active in Cuban politics: If one such visual quote about an icon is repeated more often than others, rather than showing history as it was, it influences the significance of the icon—that is not yet history—in quite disproportionate fashion. Rather than presenting a visual statement of direct historical value, such an instance of rebroadcasting an old clip appears first of all to influence the visual literacy of audiences, and if it does, the clip, be it historical or not, influences the understanding of the same icon in all other pictures, be they modern or old.

This first example from the documentary indicates the necessity of careful methodological consideration, before such a thing as "pictorial history" can take shape at all. In the following, the nine-volumes-strong *History of the 20th Century* will be taken less as a pictorial historiography or an anthology of pictorial sources, than first of all as a depository of the visual terms of a language in the making. Rather than as a study of the real John F. Kennedy or the real Marilyn Monroe, the documentary will be seen as an exercise in the etymology of their visual symbols; only as such can it be taken as a historical source. The documentary, first presented on television in the early 1980s and in the following two decades marketed on videotape, will be considered as the accumulation of a typical sediment of American visual literacy.

A COLLAGE OF AMERICAN SPECTACLE

Like many other historical compilations, such as *The Fabulous Sixties, The Sensational Seventies, Yesteryear,* or *The Class of the Twentieth Century,* the documentary *History of the 20th Century* reflects the popularity pictorial history enjoyed during the 1970s and 1980s.[2] It was produced and aired between 1980 and 1985 in a series of nine volumes covering the eight decades between the turn of the century and the end of the 1970s, with the 1960s occupying two volumes, during which time the makers of the documentary, among others Richard Klein and David Thaxton, pursued the ambitious task of mapping out the imagery of national history. Using material from several archives, including those of the ABC network and the

National Archives, they created a collage of historical clips and still pictures that is typical of the more popular side of the genre, not least because it does not add background information to distinguish the original context of the records or their original vehicles of publication.[3] Republished on videotape in the 1990s, the documentary apparently generated enough interest to continue being marketed, thus still finding an audience beyond the turn of the century. The commercial success of the documentary reflects not only the popularity of the genre, but also the continuity with which pictorial history is being pursued. Moreover, its place on the shelves of educational institutions across the nation, side by side with most of the previously mentioned historical documentaries of both "popular" and "serious" scope, but also with the traditional, written body of work on history, reflects the widespread acceptance of the new format of presenting history, and of its proposed standards of objectivity.

Each of the nine volumes of *History of the 20th Century* commences with a rapid fire of still pictures that offer glimpses of past icons and emblems, mixed with various historic shots of streets, passersby, and other symbols of past everyday life. The still pictures are sequenced along the historical timeline and therefore parallel the development of photographic technology and convention, thus providing an ascent from nineteenth-century black-and-white to modern colored, magazine-style photography. After this photographic race through American history, all volumes but one start with footage exclusively concerning an American topic, immediately presenting its focus on American history. Once the flow of historical pictures is set in motion, the compilation leaves no doubt about its belonging to the genre of popular documentary. In sequencing almost exclusively historical footage, without interrupting the window to the past, for example, by inserting any modern pictures of experts, eyewitnesses, presenters, or even of the man whose voice provides a verbal guide through the imagery, the ride through the visual past remains free of visual reflection from the present.

Loosely structured by the voice-over, each decade is divided into seven chapters titled "Focus on the 1950s" ("Focus on the 1960s" and so forth), "Focus on How We Lived," "Focus on Sports and Games," "Focus on People," "Focus on Science and Technology," and "Focus on Lifestyles." The first chapter is always concerned with the national and foreign politics of the actual decade and centers on the role of the president at the time. Although the titles of the chapters that follow imply a stronger emphasis on cultural history, commentaries on major national or international political events resurface in all chapters. In some cases, issues such as the Vietnam War are pursued through many chapters and thereby presented in various contexts, as when for example "Focus on Sports" re-presents Muhammad Ali's refusal to serve in the army. Focusing predominantly on the four volumes that cover the three decades between 1950 and 1980, the years that parallel television's rise to becoming one of the nation's most dominant media, the following chapters perform a simple statistical analysis, which may help to acquaint the reader with the corresponding imagery of about 2500 narrative fragments. [4]

Rather than providing any factual proof, this survey first of all aimed at supporting the semiotic assessment of the structures that underlie this pictorial historiography. However, even this first attempt to count and categorize those historic topics given more or less comprehensive visual coverage, arriving at approximately 250 topics, divided into 140 political and 110 cultural, proved quite ambiguous. [5] Although offering a broad impression of the documentary's general selection and arrangement of historical records, the basic statistical categorization could not be used for any more detailed analysis of the footage's arrangement. While the topical arrangement may add context to single clips or still pictures within the documentary's chapters, revealing the pursuit of a theme with proper introduction and closure, the footage's combined planes of verbal and visual information, more often than not, run on different paths. For example, when commenting on reactions to the "fairytale" wedding of Farah Dibah, the voice-over claims to summarize a cultural facet of the 1950s, while the pictures could as well be speaking in symbolic language of the diplomatic political marriage between Iran and the West.

Although secondary to the aim of entertaining spectators, the endeavor to create a historical narrative that meets textbook standards shines through the compilation at every turn. While the voice-over refrains from any sharp or even provocative statements, the selection of topics dutifully covers the conventional "big events" of the century. From the Korean to the Cold War, from the Civil Rights Movement to Watergate, from the Great Depression to the oil crisis, from the rise of suburbia to the moon landing, from the assassination of John F. Kennedy to the Iran hostage crisis, all the "musts" of American history are duly featured. By the same standard, the documentary also compiles pictures of those who are not only generally considered the most significant personalities of the past decades, but also whose physical features are still remembered. Taking first place are the icons of American presidents, followed by their wives, a couple of national politicians, and a few foreign heads of state. In the volumes covering the three decades between 1950 and 1980, I counted twenty-three icons that found multiple representations in different times and contexts, eight of which referenced Presidents Truman, Eisenhower, Kennedy, Johnson, Nixon, Ford, Carter, and Reagan.

Indicating the primacy of the visual plane for the documentary's presentation of historical footage, only four presidential icons (those of Kennedy, Johnson, Nixon, and Carter) can be heard speaking for more than thirty seconds. By contrast, no foreign heads of state are presented with the original audio and only three (Khrushchev, Castro, and the Shah of Persia), or four including Britain's queen, are featured on multiple occasions. The only other historical personalities given as much visual and audio representation

Number of Repeated Instances of Icons and Emblems[6]

Icons	Clips	Icons	Clips
Richard Nixon	30	John Lennon	3
John F. Kennedy	27	Fidel Castro	3
Lyndon B. Johnson	19	Nikita Khrushchev	3
Jacqueline Kennedy	15	Marilyn Monroe	3
Dwight D. Eisenhower	12	Elvis Presley	2
Jimmy Carter	11	Shah of Persia	2
Martin Luther King, Jr.	9	Farah Dibah	2
Harry Truman	7		
Lady Bird Johnson	7		
Gerald Ford	5	*Emblems*	*Clips*
Ronald Reagan	5	American flag	47
Robert Kennedy	5	Vietnam chopper	23
Queen Elizabeth	5	White House	12
Hubert Humphrey	4	Capitol building	7
Adlai Stevenson	4	American eagle	7
Muhammad Ali	3	UN building in New York City	6

as the presidents are Martin Luther King, Jr. and Jacqueline Kennedy, the latter not presented in a classic political role. Thus, the visual representation of historical personalities reveals a strong emphasis on the icons of fifteen American men, of whom five are allowed to speak for more than thirty seconds from the tribune of visual history. Together with the selection of political events, the frequency of presentation of historical figures characterizes the historical program of the documentary's imagery as arrested by the traditional historiography of "big" events and personalities.

If the presentation of political issues generally appears bound up in the reverberating significance of a few events and personalities, the arrangement of topics pertaining to the cultural history of the nation apparently offered more leeway. When quoting scenes from cultural life, ranging from footage of past sports spectacles to excerpts from popular movies and television sitcoms, from fashion shows to suburban lifestyle footage, from advertising spots to celebrity weddings, the choice of representation seems not destined to draw any politically motivated criticism: while common sense may expect a featuring of the "big" events and all presidents in due form, the vast bounds of popular culture simply require choices that select some special events and some popular celebrities in favor of others. However, although there is little ground for interpreting any personal preferences, let alone rational intentions behind the general selection of cultural issues, the choices made by the documentary still appear to operate following a similar protocol to that governing the treatment of political history: meta-icons, such as Elvis Presley, Marilyn Monroe, or Frank Sinatra, are dutifully put on the historical stage, as are a number of celebrities from the world of sports, such as Muhammad Ali, and from television itself, such as Lucille Ball.

In total, the imagery of the three decades projects 189 icons of all provenances, which, give or take a few, could all be recognized by the documentary's audience in the 1980s.[7] Reminiscent of Kurt Tucholsky's exclamation "always these same two hundred persons," this body of 189 icons compares in size to the social networks in which people usually interrelate, while comprising a collective of known personalities on the stage of macrocommunication.[8] In the absence of any other explanation, the lasting familiarity of these 189 visual symbols may thus reflect the only reason for their selection. However, since these icons have traveled through history alongside most of the documentary's spectators, the mere restaging of their visual features first of all functions to engage visual literacy, as with the restaging of emblems. Symbols such as the White House (featured on twelve occasions), the Capitol building (seven), or the American flag (forty-three) signify via a merging of the bygone with the present. Although each picture of the flag, the single most featured emblem in the compilation, can certainly be seen as the sign of one particular piece of cloth that has been hung at a particular time and place, the sign of the flag in general first of all communicates based on a symbolic field of meaning that has accompanied the spectator into the present, continuously altering its place in collective visual literacy depending on each individual pictorial representation. The result is an imagery of the past the symbols of which are still in use, and the historical status of which is consequently anything but self-evident.

The documentary's producers not only fail to reflect on the historicity of their actual sources, they also treat the visual information of the footage without proposing any binding historical perspective. In this mode, the significance of icons and emblems as outstanding terms of a collective visual literacy assumes a peculiar kinship with the "big" outstanding historical events, creating a kaleidoscopic order in which a shot of Marilyn Monroe fits naturally beside pictures of events such as the Bay of Pigs, the first American flight into outer space, Muhammad Ali's conversion to Islam, or the inauguration of John F. Kennedy.

Like the beads in a kaleidoscope that fall into perfectly ordered patterns with every turn, the historical pictures of the documentary seem automatically to arrange their historical status from one topic to the next. The succession of historical highlights recalls studies of the spectacle's power to homogenize the traditional separation between news, advertising, and fiction, such as those by Guy Debord and other scholars, including Daniel Dayan and Elihu Katz, Douglas Keller, Peter Rollins, and Christoph

Türcke.[9] As the spectacle captures the eye and diverts the attention, so the documentary's presentation of historical footage precludes interpretation along the classic lines of objectivity and subjectivity, if only so that the perspectives and intentions of its modern authors remain hidden behind the spectacular sights. The kaleidoscopic rejuvenation of past broadcast spectacle thus recalls Erik Barnouw's assessment of the nonfiction film, in which he concludes the term *objective* is "meaningless" in the face of the "endless choices" made in the production of documentaries, and the difference between fictional productions and nonfictional documentaries is not at all evident.[10]

However, while the notion of endless choices challenges the conventional concept of authorship and the related standards of objectivity and subjectivity, it also returns to the previously discussed logic of collecting. Collecting, as it strives for exhibition in a public showcase, necessitates many rounds of selection and thus choices that continuously change the character of the single collectibles, privileging some as the jewels of the collection, while reducing others to the background. In this light, the imagery of the spectacle corresponds with the logic of a collectively maintained visual literacy, which develops the significance of its ordinary, as well as of its special visual symbols, i.e., icons and emblems. The following analysis will focus on the tension between the documentary's claim to view reality through the "never erring" eye of the television camera and its simultaneous dependence on visual literacy, which endows the pictures with historically dynamic significance.

4 The Insignia of the Spectacle

The *History of the 20th Century* introduces each decade, as well as each of its chapters, with the animated graphic of a camera, its lens enhanced by light reflections styled after sunrays. The camera then zooms to the foreground, bringing its lens face to face with the spectator, letting his eyes meet the mechanical eye. An animated hand adjusts the focus, which zooms out again to reveal the first historic picture, most often a still photograph chosen to represent the topics that follow.

In the absence of any trace of the documentary's producers, the animated graphic provides the only visible sign of the present. The visual symbol of the technical device of the camera and the human hand that adjusts its focus reflects the faceless authorship of the documentary's imagery. With the hand in the role of a mere servant of technical magic, the animated introduction to the documentary states its program: rather than individual intent, aesthetic creativity, or professional authority, it is the apparatus itself that projects historical content.

THE CAMERA AS WITNESS

Coming face to face with the discursive eye of the camera, one notices a graphically styled sheen emanating from the lens. It is the sort of luster that cinematographers like to play on a knight's armor, or that advertisers choose to illumine the showcased product. Such a self-conscious shine thus intends to incite a sense of awe at the magic of the camera or at the *deus ex machina* responsible for offering the following pictures as a time-traveling device. However, while the shine confers favorable connotations on the graphic symbol of a camera styled in the present, this symbol in turn introduces historical imagery, which will also contain many more representations of itself. In each of the four volumes between 1950 and 1980, there are on average seventeen distinct clips that center on one or more cameras as their dominant visual information.[1] In some of these frames, a dozen cameras mounted on tripods cluster on little hills or on the deck of a stadium without any operator discernible in any detail. In addition, there are another forty single photo, film, or television cameras in the background of both stills and moving pictures. These images further enhance the magic of the apparatus as creating, reflecting, and simultaneously participating in visual history.

Additional visual reference to the presence of cameras at the scene of historic events is evident in a very particular technologic signal of the past: the flashes of photographers. These appear on more than a hundred occasions between 1950 and 1980. By stopping the VCR, those flashes can sometimes be captured as an almost blank, white frame, and sometimes just as a smaller white patch within the picture. Challenging the theory of visual language at the very beginning of this analysis, the pictorial imprint of these simple white patches conflicts with the communicative structure of visual signs and symbols. Defying the dialectic principle that all visual entities of a picture connect to establish significance in mutual dependence (see the section "The First Code of Visual Language" in the appendix), the white patches instead recall the concept of Gestalt, and, following Seward Barry, would seem primarily to address the emotional realm of the brain.[2] But then again, they also "signal" to the media-literate the presence of another photo camera at the scene. Because the flash of a photo camera remains generally invisible in the still pictures it helps to produce, the white frames represent a curious instance of one technology inadvertently leaving a residue on the product of another technology. In moving pictures, this residue testifies that photographers were present at an event—even when they are actually not visible—which can therefore, albeit by detour, still add pictorial significance in a dialectic way. Less as signs than as impersonal signals, the flashes—almost literally—"highlight" the other signs and symbols, marking them as part of a scene that was apparently worthy of the attention of (press) photographers.

The only other comparable communicative structure in the documentary's historical pictures can be found in the form of historical fireworks, as recorded on the occasion of America's bicentennial anniversary celebration in Washington. These colorful spots on screen are also essentially linked with the technique of their production, although their production was first meant to address the attending audience and was then congenially framed by a camera to re-create an impression of both the event and the artistic display in the sky. Nevertheless, both the colorful spots of the fireworks and the camera flashes function without visual significance, in that they have not accumulated layers of meaning in the way of visual symbols, emblems, and icons. Curiously, the colorful spots together with the flashes appear to present what is arguably the most pure historical residue on the reels used by the documentary, although neither convey any specific meaning. Able to be repeated without gaining additional semantic contours, they function as historical signals of the ritualistic frame of societal events.

The flashes, in addition, are the only instances in which the significance of the material part of the pictures, the celluloid, coincides with the immaterial projection of content. Documenting the interaction of a photographic with a motion picture camera, they leave an imprint, without humanly coded content, that nevertheless carries historical significance. The one hundred flashes counted may therefore be best described as a type of "emblematic signal" that locates the imagery of an event as coextensive with a spectacle powerful enough to attract more than one documenting medium.

Signaling from the depths of history, the imprints left by these flashes mark a counterpoint to the previously discussed animated cameras, which mark the footage from a modern point of view. As the emblematic signals of flashes and the emblematic symbols of cameras combine, the eye of a modern camera is bathed in historical light, enabling the present transmission of a past reality.

If the graphic emblem of the camera stands for those who produced the historical footage, as well as for those who edited the footage into historical imagery, and if the flash signals the technical context of a historical media spectacle, then the past and the present meet at a point where technology appears to be the author of the documentary's visual content. Yet, if so, cameras are not only the subject but also the object of visual history, with regard to all those instances when they themselves appear in the historical footage. In terms of visual language, all the shots that feature the symbol of the historical camera reflect choices made by the original cameramen and the original editors, as well as by the documentary's editors. The seventeen clips that exclusively focus on other cameras, the forty-two pictures that include the symbol of the camera as circumstantial information, and the hundred flashes stand as the visual statements of past cameramen, which, renewed by the choices of the modern editors, comment on all the other visual symbols in their vicinity. In other words, any symbol featured in a shot related to the sight of many cameras mounted on a hill or any icon shown face to face with a historical newsreel or television camera is highlighted as significant, at least with regard to the media itself, the same media that also re-presents such shots as evidence of history.

Following McLuhan's famous observation that the medium itself constitutes the message, the camera within the historical picture symbolically speaks not only of the significance of the presented sights, but also of its own. [3] In rather curious logic, the documentary thus presents modern and past symbols of cameras not only in the role of objective authors of history, but simultaneously as part of that history, and gives them the task not only of witnessing an event, but also of ascribing significance to it, and thus of creating instant history in a truly impersonal fashion.

THE SPECTATOR AS WITNESS

Between 1950 and 1980, almost 300 shots feature spectators and audiences in one form or another. One hundred and fifty, or about every fifteenth shot, feature spectators and audiences as their subject or as their main pictorial content. Of these, sixty-three shots exclusively shape the visual symbol of an "audience," ranging from a couple dozen spectators at a golf match to the packed ranks of a baseball stadium, from a couple hundred at a political speech to a quarter of a million at the March on Washington. Shots focusing exclusively on individual spectators outnumber clips centered exclusively on audiences, with a total of eighty-seven instances.

The historical footage also features numerous occasions of a panoramic shot combining both, wandering from packed tribunes to an individual spectator or the other way around. In general, these shots most often embed in direct sequence a close-up of their main protagonists (for example, a baseball player hitting a home run or a speaker gesticulating) in a snippet of the unfolding action. In such narrative alignment, the shots of spectators and audience frame the visual commentary on an event by symbolizing its ability to attract not only the camera, but also the eye of the crowd. The frequency with which the mise en scène quotes the attendance at an event implies a convention at the root of historical television broadcasting that compares oddly with any other form of journalistic coverage. Even if the footage allows following the original words of a politician's speech, to which this documentary on average allocates only twenty-five seconds or roughly four to five sentences, such coverage places an emphasis on visual content that communicates in an inherently different fashion from a radio or newspaper account. Not only would verbal or written reports rarely engage in describing the appearance of single spectators, they would generally also try to convey factual information about the size of an audience. The cameraman, however, is limited to presenting a general, quite symbolic visual expression of the audience's size in one of two ways, either by choosing an open or a closed frame. Most of the documentary's footage reflects the first option: the symbol of an audience is made by a "sea of heads" that extends up to the frame without being limited by a boundary in the form of other visual symbols, such as houses, streets, trees, and so forth.

Based on the dialectic and conceptual codes of pictorial communication, such shots inevitably imply that the crowd continues beyond the frame and establish the symbolic information for a "large" or even "huge" audience.

The Dialectic Code	The Conceptual Code
This first principle of visual language specifies that all single entities within a picture interconnect their significance with each other. (See also the glossary in the appendix.)	The second principle of visual language differentiates chains of significance that bundle small signifying entities as belonging to a generic concept, such as "house," "forest," or "man." (See also the glossary in the appendix.)

Transcending the banal information that there actually was an audience, the choice of frame shot symbolizes a subjective assessment, the cameraman's estimate of the audience's size and thus of the general significance of the event. The historical value of these pictures, insofar as they might neglect to portray empty last rows, therefore would rest entirely on the role of the cameraman as putatively objective reporter. However, because his agency in making a symbolic assessment of an event's attendance cannot rationally be qualified, not least because his personality remains unknown to the receivers of the pictures, such a notion of his visual editorial power remains veiled. In similar fashion, any historical perspective on the pictures' content in terms of the intention behind selecting and editing these shots into historical imagery can at best unveil the conventions of the original mise en scène. In the place of any impartial information, the many cuts to audiences simply shape a visual symbol of crowds that begins to belong in emblematic fashion to the imagery of "big events."

Those shots that single out individual spectators accentuate the symbolic dimension of this footage even further.

While the dialectic and the conceptual codes establish their belonging to the audience of the featured events, the symbolic code demands the classifying of their appearance, for example, as young, white, female, blonde, well-dressed American, and so forth. Together, the codes initiate what Wolfgang Haug called a "symbolic transfer" amongst all the featured signs and symbols, that is between the portrayed spectator, the audience in general, the protagonist(s) of an event, and the event itself.[4]

The individual receivers of the resulting message may then evaluate whether or not the spectator stands in a typical relation to the event, based either on personal experience or on general visual literacy. In the case of a historical sports event, such as a football game, a female spectator would consequently relate atypically to an audience expected to be predominantly male at the time. In each case, however, the cameraman's choice of focus inevitably shapes a relation between the symbol of a spectator and the character of the audience, as well as, consequently, of the event. Atypical relation between symbols thus stands out as a statement or a commentary

The Symbolic Code	The Iconic Code
The third principle of visual language demands that the significance of bundled visual entities is typified so as to balance their generic concept with their unique visual appearance. (See also the glossary in the appendix.)	The fourth principle of visual language specifies that once typified, entities of significance accumulate further significance whenever encountered. (See also the glossary in the appendix.)

that conveys significance enhanced by the cameraman's choice of focus. Similarly, the behavior of such a spectator symbol may reflect a segment of reality, but also must communicate within the bounds of the dialectic and symbolic principles of visual communication. When, for example, the spectator displays gestures of discontent, the receiver at home has little basis for connecting that expression with either a particular detail of the event or with its general reception. The receiver thus depends almost completely on the objectivity of the pictures' authors.

By the same standards, the visual symbol of an applauding audience can be only loosely associated with one particular play or, in the case of a speech, with one particular line or argument, and needs therefore to be taken as a symbolic commentary about the general response to the event. When the historical footage contains a clip featuring an applauding audience that is held for a couple of seconds before cutting to a different shot, the time frame of the picture creates a second type of open or closed information. Similar to the spatial alignment of a "sea of heads," the temporal rhythm of motion pictures inscribes on each frame a significance that is controlled by the transmitter. (See also the section "The Verbal, the Written, and the Visual" in chapter 9.) When applause is not covered in its complete extension, including its rise and fall, its portrayal signifies in terms of the frame's length in relation to the general rhythm of the visual narrative. Besides certain unmistakable gestures, such as a standing ovation, and given that most audiences are likely to clap at an event on one or another occasion, if only for ritual reasons, the only way of knowing whether such a shot of a clapping audience was actually intended to illustrate a favorable response ultimately rests on a viewer's familiarity with the conventions and style of the pictures' actual authors. Thus in terms of general visual literacy, the time frame of such a shot adds to the symbolic typifying of audience response, by comparison to other instances of applause and their time frames. However, because the convention of pictorial narratives changes over time, and because the behavior of actual audiences also develops, the documentary's imagery that does not acknowledge such evolution obstructs a clear perspective on the historical content of these pictures. In each case, the conventions underlying the visual portrayal of spectators and audiences of past events, including the rhythm assigned to the mise en scène of their response, commence to project content that is less connected to the events' own, often ritualistic background in society, than to habits of broadcasting that have come to nurture their own ritual of pictorial presentation: a ritual of visual mass-communication that has not yet become history, at least with regard to the documentary's own mode of presenting the historical spectacle.

Together, the symbols of audiences, individual spectators, packs of reporters, photographers, cameras, microphones, spotlights, flashes, and so forth frame an event in a mode that merges its place and status in society with a pictorial display that unfolds its own ritualized conventions and

The Insignia of the Spectacle

Symbols	Clips
Audiences (at the center of the focus)	63
Individual spectators (at the center of the focus)	87
Audiences or spectators (as one of several visual symbols)	148
Cameras (at the center of the focus)	17
Cameras (as one of several visual symbols)	42
Photographers (in general)	38
Flashes (in general)	113

shapes its own place and status in media history in symbolic fashion. In this form, the pictures appear as a two-dimensional spectacle of the three-dimensional spectacle. The protagonists of the second spectacle are illuminated by the shots presenting symbols of the media's presence, which mimic the agency of the pictures' transmitter, and by the shots of attending spectators or responding audiences, which mimic the captivated presence of the receiver at home. Like the self-referential symbol of the camera, those of anonymous spectators and audiences symbolically anticipate or even reference the response of audiences at home. All eyes, those presented as visual signs and symbols within the picture, as well as those of the audience designated to receive the created pictorial messages, are focused on the main stage of the event. The visual message asserts not only the objectivity of the camera as a symbol of the transmitter, but also the receptivity of the audience as a symbol of the receiver, as both parties witness the event and endow it with significance.

If the shots of extensive media presence, cheering fans, and applauding audiences convey to the individual receiver the overpowering significance of media and public interest, they also construct her as a participant in the spectacle who contributes to its significance through the mere act of watching it on screen. If a spectacular event can generally be defined as a sight that attracts the eyes of beholders in overwhelming fashion, these pictures seek to share symbiotically in the event's attraction and, in Althusser's words, to hail the individual receiver as a participant in the event, or at least, to simulate his participation, as Baudrillard would characterize it.[5] The insignia of the broadcast spectacle therefore emulate the significance of an event, not only by symbolically incorporating the transmitter-receiver context into the visual message, but also by asserting a unity between the event's potential as a spectacle and the spectacle of the broadcast pictures themselves.

This unity between the spectacle of the event and that of the broadcast picture tends to contraindicate the attempt to qualify the pictures as communication, because it renders the search for a conscious transmitter rather difficult.

5 Pictorial Genres

While the insignia of the media spectacle symbolically render the early broadcasters as both the transmitter and the content of their own footage, the documentary's producers present a voice-over which effects to demonstrate their participation in the broadcast spectacles of the past. Lines such as "we saw," "we witnessed," "millions watched on TV," or even "the whole world was watching" accompany on numerous occasions the presentation of those clips, the visual plane of which arrays the insignia of the broadcast spectacle. The use of "we" fashions a symbolic dimension that complements the language of the pictures: in the way the pictures symbolically integrate their own transmitter-receiver context via the insignia of the spectacle, the first person plural verbally incorporates the spectators into the historical footage.[1]

However, while the insignia of the spectacle reflect the work of the footage's original creators and presenters, the voice-over apparently addresses this work as recollected by modern audiences. Catering to the widespread convention of associating pictures with memory, as discussed in the sections on collecting historical footage, the commentary encourages reception of the pictures as memories of the past, the only author of which is the individual recollection of the receiver herself. The absent differentiation between memory and visual literacy, or between having seen the original broadcast and having actually witnessed the original event, further corroborates the documentary's treatment of the footage as a self-contained vessel of historical truth. The documentary's producers hide their own role as subjective transmitters of sign-based content, preferring to allow the television compilation of "television memories" to spiral between contradictory facets.

In commenting on hearings held in the late 1960s about the increase in violence on television, the documentary retreats to footage that features its own representatives and was possibly produced by its own network. Growing discontent with the portrayal of violence on screen led to a public discussion about the way television news shows commented on the war in Vietnam and the demonstrations at home. The historical clip features an ABC spokesperson, in the limelight of media attention, defending the network by citing the First Amendment. He declares to the reporters present that television news is obligated to report truthfully: "We must tell it and show it like it is," and not "close our eyes to the realities of our time." In selecting the clip as historical document without challenging either its verbal or its visual message, the documentary traps the content of both the record's verbal and visual messages in what amounts to a communicative meltdown of extraordinary dimensions. To begin with, the footage reveals what at this point have become the familiar signs and symbols of a spectacle, only this time it is television itself that stands in the center of the signaling flashes. From a pictorial tribune, the ABC representative verbally asserts the imperative of objective reporting by claiming the right to issue subjective statements as protected by the First Amendment. Ultimately, he combines the imperative of impartial journalism with the discourse of pictorial reality: in the way that "we" should not close our eyes on reality, the camera should not close its eye and must show the "realities of our time"—as it shows, among other things, his own appearance in the act of self-justification.

It is thus as if the ABC representative speaks from within the picture about the picture of himself, both as a newsman and as a participant in the hearings. Simultaneously, by using "we," he extends the voice of his utterance to include television receivers: he speaks both as a journalist inside the picture and, like the spectators outside the picture, as a witness of the "reality of our time," which, given the occasion of the event, springs from the pictures broadcast by "objective" media journalists like himself.

The paradox at hand concerns once again the discursive convention that merges the role of the creator with that of the presenter of the pictures. This merging ultimately hides the communicative agency and its mediated content behind the notion that the communicated picture reflects unmediated reality and, by consequence, cannot be anything other than an objective account. This concept of pictorial journalism recalls Barbara Zelizer's analysis of journalistic practice in American television. The construction of "proximity" or a sense of "nearness" between journalists and events, according to Zelizer, appears as a typical means for conveying "to audiences a sense of authorship and authority for the stories they cover."[2] In the example at hand, however, the construction of such nearness, "regardless of the actual proximity of reporter to event," is carried out not only by the journalist in the spotlight, but also by the cameraman and the modern presenter of the footage. Expanding on Zelizer's take on television journalism as based on a "collective authorship," it becomes possible to distinguish (at least theoretically) three parties involved in transmitting visual content to audiences: First of all, there is the creative side, the cameramen and all who help them, including not only technicians but also those who assigned them a place at an event. Secondly, there are all those involved in receiving, editing, and selecting the pictures for broadcast, together forming the presentational side of the conveyed content. And thirdly, there are the journalists who speak from within the picture. Their role actually poses the most complex questions with regard to their actual contribution to the conveyed content. Because the perspective so far concentrates on the visual part of the broadcasts, we will first of all focus on the relation of creative and presentational transmittership, before returning in the third part to the problem of journalists appearing within their own reportage.

In the case of the ABC representative surrounded by the insignia of the spectacle, the apparent proximity between the journalist and the event also applies to the relation between the journalist and the cameraman, who can be considered analogous to the "wedding photographer," whose task, in the words of Dayan and Katz, is to be "faithful to the ceremony as organized." [3] This deferential attitude is evinced not only by the creators of the pictures, but also by those who collect and select them for exposition to audiences. Although the presentation process also offers many opportunities to add to a statement, if not to form a new one from scratch, the presentation of the ABC representative appears in Zelizer's words "as near to the event as can possibly be." Similarly, the modern presentation of the clip within the documentary appears much in line with this deferential attitude. Thus the second time these pictures are collected and selected for publication, this time as a view into the past, proximity to the event is still being proposed as a guarantor of objective pictorial commentary.

When the historical clip thus shows an ABC representative who is asserting the media's objective attitude towards the realities of our time at the same time as he is invoking the right under the First Amendment to state one's personal opinion, the search is on: not only for the objectivity of pictorial commentary, but also for the presence of the subjective.

THE IDIOMATIC AND THE CREATIVE CAMERA

When the documentary's original footage is divided between the camera of the spectacle and the individual or creative camera, roughly 57% of all themes pertain in one way or another to the broadcast spectacle, while the remaining 43% could be broadly associated with an individual or inquiring agency on behalf of their producers.[4] This 43% includes footage of such diverse phenomena as family life, the development of interstate highways, the rise of suburbia and the creation of shopping malls in the 1950s, the escalation of the Vietnam War and the developing counterculture in the 1960s, and spreading drug consumption and the worsening plight of Southeast Asian refugees in the 1970s.

Free from the previously described insignia of the spectacle, these kinds of pictures contain a certain element of arbitrariness, an accent on happenstance that marks the significance of their visual signs and symbols. The houses, families, cars, shopping mall consumers, individual protesters, drug users, soldiers, or refugees that ultimately made it into the imagery of the documentary not only underwent multiple processes of selection in order to represent a historical record, they were also sought by the original camera because they were symbolic in the first place, leaving millions of other possible symbols hidden from visual history. Once again, we recall Erik Barnouw's warning, cited earlier, of the uselessness of the classic categories of objectivity and subjectivity in the face of the "endless choices" made in the production of documentaries. [5] However, those pictorial signs and symbols that survived all the rounds of elimination offer the possibility of analyzing, at bare least, the element of coincidence inherent to the logic of all collecting, which was also active during their compilation.

Against the concept of split transmittership, the creative side, including those who send a cameraman to a given event and the cameraman's own focus, represents the first round in the spiral of endless choices. As close as the cameraman positions himself to reality, his decision to use the apparatus already compromises the potential of the picture to reflect untainted reality, and guides the coincidence at the root of the pictures' creation. The transition from purely "coincidental record of reality" to consciously mediated content follows with the decision to present some or even all produced pictures to others. Constituting a second act, such presenting involves its own context that necessarily changes, if ever so slightly, the content of the pictures in question. Comparable to the act of pinpointing significance with the index finger, the choice to present a picture includes at least the invitation "to see." It is in the move from creation to presentation of pictures that the element of coincidence or happenstance is relativized by the agency of the presenter: If there is objectivity or subjectivity in the pictures it could thus be found in the relation between these two sides of their transmission.

In this theoretical approach, one possible relation between the two acts of transmittership is that of harmony, which can, but does not have to be the case, when the creator and the presenter of the pictures is one and the same person. The documentary actually provides such an example when turning to a family's everyday life in the 1940s. Citing some data on rising salaries and low costs of living, the verbal context of the pictures shapes the visual signs and symbols as an example of a typical American family, not least by using once again the "we" form. The sequence is then juxtaposed first with a picture of Hitler's icon and then with black-and-white footage of the Second World War, hints of things to come, both in history and in the documentary's narrative outline. Although the footage is sequenced as an introductory comment—and as such, a very symbolic one—the combined verbal and visual context still specifies "typical historical family life" as the main historical content.

What can be seen are a woman and children vacationing on a beach, skiing, and playing on a porch. While the principles of visual language (see the theoretical sections in the appendix) construct the visual symbols as a "mother," with her "children," and the porch as their "home," the clips also feature a couple of men without, however, offering sufficient symbolic interrelation to allow identifying one of them as the father of this family. The external context of the presented signs and symbols therefore suggests that the father is operating the camera—which, however, is a speculation based on the assumption of a "typical" genre of family pictures. The pictures were taken with a film camera able to produce color, but their grainy display betrays at best semiprofessional quality, thus further anchoring their origin in the realm of private, family photography. So does their content: the symbols of smiling faces, playing children, joyful interaction on a beach, skiing, and so forth propose the visual narrative of an intact, happy family life at home and on vacation. To this extent, the intention and purpose that transcend the message allow for characterizing these pictures as a typical visual account of a family who recorded some special moments over a certain period of time to forge a self-created, but also self-contained visual commentary on their life.

To whom, however, do such pictures communicate significance? Presented by the documentary as a typical record of American family life in 1940, these sights were never meant to find the anonymous eye of mass audiences, yet, similarly to the presentation of the spectacle, their visual content pertains to the extraordinary moment. Albeit not catering to the rituals of a nation, but to those of the family that initiated the use of the camera, the act of creating these pictures inscribes significance in their visual signs and symbols and anticipates the second act of presenting them to a select audience. This conditioning marks the genre of these pictures, as it belies the documentary's act of presenting them: First of all, the majority of American families emerging from the Great Depression could hardly afford the semiprofessional equipment used to produce such family pictures. And, secondly, without the background of their original presentation to selected spectators by either the cameraman himself or somebody close to the family, the pictures can hardly document the family life of those persons portrayed, because the possibility to evaluate them as typical or atypical in comparison either to other pictures of that family, or to knowledge acquired in real life, is missing.

What is typical about these pictures, however, is the ritualistic background of their production, their relation to the widespread genre of family photography. Within microcommunicative bounds, family pictures can circulate and signify based on an "idiomatic" network of shared visual literacy. Referencing the family's own language, such an idiomatic network engages a play of anticipation, on behalf of both the producer/presenter and the audience, of how the signs and symbols are to be understood. The signs and symbols, circulating within such an idiomatic network, thus accumulate shades of meaning only recognizable to those who participate in the network's communicative interaction on a regular basis and who know about the specific preferences of the pictures' creator, for example, with regard to one particularly disliked family member. By the same standard, such a microcommunicative network also develops a particular brand of icons and emblems. Only recognizable to those who participate in the idiomatic network, those symbols repeatedly featured thus acquire iconic characteristics, and consequently start to signify not only based on their either typical or atypical relation to the knowledge of a person's behavior in real life, but also in typical or atypical relation to the other pictures that one has seen from that person. All this, however, is lost to the overwhelming majority of the documentary's audience, for whom the sight of these symbols is new and thus communicates without enriched idiomatic meanings. Put differently, the original communicative network in which these symbols circulated marks a visual literacy particular to the microcosm of family members and friends that share their "own language," the Greek word "idiom."[6]

When transferring the idiom of their original creation and presentation to an anonymous context in macrocommunication, the signs and symbols of these family pictures may still hint at their intimate significance and thus inspire curiosity, but historically, they can ultimately only communicate as a genre-typical example of American middle-class family photography. The presentation, directed to the general visual literacy of distanced audiences, therefore effectively eliminates most of the pictures' communicative potential, as well as their historical substance, the way it also conceals pictures' origins in subjective creation and presentation.

The rupture of these pictures' original transmittership and their transfer to a macrocommunicative presentation of visual history actually carries an additional twist. When studying the credits at the end of the volume, it becomes evident that the footage stems from the family of one of the documentary's producers, thus implying that one of the depicted children may very well represent one of the pictures' modern editors. If true, the transfer of genre not only extinguishes the pictures' original significance, it also calls out the claim of objective pictorial content: Similar to the ABC speaker in the spotlight of instant history, this footage from the realm of microcommunication also provides a peculiar idiomatic context that projects its modern transmitter as interrelated with the very content of the historical signs. But despite such methodologically problematic self-quoting in visual terms, the pictures' status as objective, historical records nevertheless seems unchallenged, at least in the eyes of their presenters. In the end, the two examples of historical pictures are marred by similar logical problems, despite being produced by two very differently motivated cameras and despite being originally presented in completely different communicative contexts. In the place of any subjective source of significance within these pictures, it is thus not objective significance that takes over, but rather a type of discourse, which in the place of the missing idiomatic context between original transmitters and receivers, presents the pictures as signifying without another source than the technically created reference to reality.

THE JOURNALISTIC AND THE ARTISTIC CAMERA

In the two chapters dedicated to the 1970s, the documentary turns on several occasions to the plight of refugees in Southeast Asia. The pictures used to document the fate of civilians in times of war can suggest that camera crews focused on specific scenes based on individual decision and journalistic intention. In what is verbally referred to as the extension of the Vietnam War into Cambodia in 1971, the footage reveals an older man whose face bears an expression of agony, before cutting to a little girl who carries a baby on her back, walking alongside a ditch. When methodically inferring the position of the camera from the visual signs and symbols, one detects once again an element of the arbitrary: why these pictures and these refugees and not any others? The close-up on the facial expression of the man and the portrayal of a lonely child carrying a baby shape a visual message that is inseparable from the coincidence of a camera crew having been there and not at another place in order to create a pictorial statement about the dark face of the war. The subjective nature of these pictures appears especially evident from the perspective of the receiver: first, to infer any objective information, the receiver has to assume that the cameraman did not, for example, consciously exclude other people in order to make the girl appear as if she is on her own. Second, the receiver has to ignore the cameraman's existence—and thus the creative author of the pictures, who, after all, was standing close to the girl—in order to accept the statement about the lonely fate of a small girl in times of war.

Indeed, for a brief moment, the girl looks up and meets the camera's eye before pursuing her path. While such a glance would point to an interactive role of the cameraman with the subject he is visually commenting on, the resulting pictures nevertheless differ from those produced both by the camera of the spectacle and the intimate family camera: the visual statement about the girl contains a distance that demands ignoring the camera's presence, while simultaneously excluding the possibility that the child could have influenced the creation of the visual message in any conscious way. The characteristics of such a distanced camera thus reduce the communicative significance of the girl's gaze to a symbolic gesture that, paradoxically, suggests to the spectators on another continent a proximity that would enable both meeting her eyes and confronting her fate.

The very possibility of seeing a lonely child looking back for a brief moment thus stands intrinsically interwoven with the conditioned tendency to accept that what is being shown is reality—or here, history—as it unfolds.

The result is that although created as an individual, subjective commentary about civilians in a time of war, the presentation of these pictures' symbolic message ignores that subjectivity, even presumes its objectivity, in order to be understood in the first place.

In the example, the quality of distance could thus be described as having two aspects: firstly, the distance between the camera reporter and his subject, and secondly, that between the presenter and the motif of the shot. Although the camera reporter was certainly close to the girl, the creation of the shot nevertheless maintains a certain distance, which is characterized by his endeavor to construct a pictorial message without his subject participating in any conscious way. The second relation of distance measures the gap between the creative and presentational authors of the clip, who operate at not only an impressive geographical but also an extended temporal distance. If historical pictures are thus still able to radiate a sense of authentic immediacy decades after their production and their first airing, such an effect may be due to the paradoxical constellation of a broken idiomatic context: the pictures appear to retain an element of immediacy expressly because their presentation is distanced from the date and place of their creation, from the subjective intention of their creator to create a visual commentary, and ultimately also from the actual fate of the child that served as the motif of the shot. In this reading, the timelessness of these pictures is quite directly comparable to the production of a fictional message that is artistically designed to shape a lasting impression without, however, making the claim of objectivity. [7]

Of the types of compiled historical footage, one carries creative, subjective authorship in a more distinctive fashion than these journalistic reportages. This type consists of all those instances in which the documentary's producers illustrate cultural life with pictures taken from Hollywood movies, advertising spots, or television shows. Almost always properly introduced and contextualized in their genre by the documentary's voice-over, these historical pictures are set apart from the presentation of all other pictures, if only because their original intention and context is for once made explicit, apparently in order to inform spectators that these pictures are neither objective, nor pertaining to reality in any direct form. Most of these snippets from movies, sitcoms, television shows, and advertising spots are thereby presented by the documentary in a mode that fashions a distinction between entertaining and informing rather than between fiction and nonfiction. Whether the pictures reveal one of the curious monsters of 1950s horror movies, feature animated images of benevolent Ajax dwarfs, or show a scene from the popular sitcom *I Love Lucy*, they primarily serve to reflect cultural rather than political history. The presentation of these shots also provides one of the few occasions when the intentions of the makers of the documentary harmonize with those of the pictures' creators, as well as one of the few occasions when the discourse of pictorial reality is not invoked. Although the documentary's transmitters only occasionally refer to the authors of these creative pictures, they generally leave no doubt of their artistic origin and subjective content. The presentation of these fictional narratives differs from the previously discussed, nonfictional journalistic pictures mainly in that the original, creative intention of their makers is still present, whereas that of the journalists is made to seem unimportant or nonexistent.

When these fictional narratives are compared to the genre of family pictures, however, some similarities emerge. In the same way that ritual typically unites the intentions of all those involved in posing for the picture, producing the picture, presenting and responding to it, the set for a fictional production usually gathers the intentions of all those involved under one roof. On the side of the transmitters, the idiomatic network of producing visual significance is thus intact, and the relation between the camera and its object, whether an actor or a product being advertised, is close, in some sense as harmonious as between family members or friends. The element of distance emerges in the relation between the presenting and the viewing of the fictional account: Firstly, unlike for family pictures, the viewing is specified by a macrocommunicative context, since these pictures are made for anonymous eyes. And secondly, they are open for criticism—as should also be the case for journalistic pictures.

In each case, the documentary's presentation of the fictional accounts of movies, television shows, and advertising spots also adds novel contextual significance to the selected pictures. Although the pictures were originally produced as individual artistic expressions, the compilation elevates their historical significance, positioning them as examples of all comparable fictional productions of the 1950s and 1960s. Yet, similar to a series of pictures of houses meant to document the construction boom of the 1950s, the compiled fictional accounts can not provide a context for each other that would allow them to comment visually, concerning, for example, why these symbols have been chosen and not others, or whether or not these pictures indeed provide a typical account of that time. It is simply implied by the documentary's transmitters that the short excerpts adequately characterize the 1950s style of television show or the 1960s style of advertising. The second presentation of these excerpts, years after the first, adds a layer of meaning that emphasizes their representative, historical status, without providing any basis—or conscious directive—for establishing in what sense they might be typical of past times. The act of rebroadcasting these pictures not only projects their main symbols to the individual recollection of modern spectators, but also inspires a renewed process of typifying and classifying their meanings in the present. Thus, the selected pictorial symbols are simultaneously elevated to the status of exemplifying national history and rejuvenated by the ongoing process of shaping their semantic field in national visual literacy so as to inspire, for example, renewed interest in seeing the complete series of vintage shows.

FOUR GENRES

This first survey of the documentary's imagery can be completed by considering four pictorial genres. Besides the microcommunicative family or "idiomatic" picture and the "creative" picture, which category can be further split into the "journalistic" and the "fictional" or "artistic" picture, there are two further genres, the "presentational" picture and the "scientific" picture. Based on the concept of split transmittership, the presentational picture, previously introduced when describing the insignia of the spectacle, designates all those pictures for which the traces of individual creation are lost or overpowered by the context of their presentation. As a result of the intention of the presentation, the camera work generally appears deferential, if not purely technical, to the point that it seems negligible. The element of distance enters between the creative and the presentational side of these pictures, while the relation between

Four Pictorial Genres

Genre	Example	Relation between camera and object	Relation between creation, presentation, and spectators (idiom)
Idiomatic picture	Family picture	Intimate	Integrated, intact (idiomatic) network
Creative picture	Journalistic picture	Distanced, detached	Integrated (provided the journalist is known)
	Artistic, fictional picture	Intimate	Integrated (depending on teamwork)
Presentational picture	Spectacle	Intimate/ deferential	Disrupted (personalities of the cameramen and/or the presenters, apart from those within the picture, are irrelevant)
Scientific picture	Documentation	Deferential	Intact (picture's context can be reconstructed)
	Inquiry	Experimental	Intact (creation of picture can be repeated)

the presentation and the spectators appears close. With the producers' agency veiled, the relation between the presentation and the content of the picture, as well as between the content and the spectators, tends to appear closer as well.

The fourth type of picture is the scientific picture. The intention of this pictorial genre could be defined as the trading of knowledge and information that can be either verified or disproved. Similar to the fictional pictures, the pictures catering to science are set apart in the form of separate chapters dedicated to technological achievements particular to each decade. Among the footage illustrating scientific progress, an animated graphic explains the basic workings of the first satellite, the Russian Sputnik. This animation of the Sputnik's trajectory into outer space avoids any assumption of direct reference to reality, as would conventionally be made for photographic pictures. Therefore, such a visual account of history carries creative authorship. At the same time, the signs radiate a factual, scientific objectivity that does not seem to account for any individual authorship. The implication that their historical content is factual or objective is therefore again disconnected from the pictures' original transmittership, but in contrast to other (photographic) historical pictures is also disconnected from an essential reference to reality. In the place of such reference then, the scientific concept of verification, or falsification, appears to regulate the pictures' historical significance. When selected into the documentary's compilation of visual history, the content of such pictures depends on evaluation by their modern transmitters, who are responsible for contextualizing the pictures' information, more specifically, the scientific principles being conveyed. If the pictures explained the flight of the Sputnik in any false way, it would thus be up to the pictures' modern transmitters to pinpoint the error and explain its historical significance. In each case of scientific pictures, the documentary's transmitters imply that the pictures' content has been verified, if not by their decision to present them, then by a scientific paradigm that is still current. The animated graphical pictures thus present a set of signs, which arguably contain a more conclusive reference to reality in comparison to the documentary's much more plentiful photographic imagery. At the same time, however, they also exhibit rational content that cannot yet be qualified as historical, since they convey information that is still current. In the documentary as a whole, the animated depiction of the Sputnik's flight appears to be the only type of visual communication able to convey content rationally, without the modern presentation significantly altering the original information.

Most other pictures meant to document technological or scientific progress, however, carry the distinct characteristics of their presentational transmission. Pictures taken from the first space walk may have been originally intended for observing the experiment for scientific purposes, but when mass-communicated they assume a different significance.

In many cases, pictures used to document progress in space technology reveal less a scientific perspective than the media's anticipation of audiences' interest. For this reason, it appears hardly coincidental that these clips often also display the familiar insignia of the spectacle in the form of watching audiences, cameras, and so forth, albeit carrying the implication of an originally scientific intention.

Based on the concept of split transmittership it becomes possible tentatively to categorize the documentary's pictorial sources according to four genres:

Idiomatic Pictures

The first genre is characterized by the use of pictures in microcommunicative settings and includes, for example, family photography, amateur videos, and children's paintings. Often used to introduce a receiver to the idiomatic network of a group, a family, or a small community, the genre specifies acts of communication in which creative and presentational authorship often reside in one and the same person, or at least in persons who are part of the same idiomatic network. (A professionally taken wedding picture would therefore not qualify for this type of picture, not least because it anticipates an anonymous audience, emphasizes a presentational context, and usually projects a professional style of arranging visual signs and symbols.) However, all such pictures with intact idiom assume discursive characteristics once they are presented in a macrocommunicative context. Once having crossed the boundary to anonymous communication, these pictures' signs alter their significance and their idiom is replaced by discourse.

For example, when using family photography for documenting 1940s life in American homes, a new presentational authorship overrides the microcommunicative background in order to present the pictures to an anonymous audience as unmediated—and thus discursive—vehicles of objective historical significance.

Idiom	Discourse
That part of the signs' and symbols' significance that participates in a communicative network, the members of which know and anticipate each other's understanding of the traded terms. (See also chapter 18, "Notes on the Pragmatics of Visual Language," in the appendix.)	That part of the signs' and symbols' significance that participates in an anonymous network, which according to Michel Foucault generally involves a societal institution. (See also chapter 18, "Notes on the Pragmatics of Visual Language," in the appendix.)

Creative Pictures

The second genre comprises all creative modes of art and entertainment that are designed for macrocommunication. All pictures in this genre retain at least style-related traces of their authorship. These traces tend to anchor subjectivity, to counteract any unmediated reference to reality, and to suggest an interactive idiomatic network of signification, often also making some reference to the teamwork and the technical tools used to produce pictorial narratives. The dynamic of such an idiomatic network is furthermore specified by the audience's role in evaluating and defining significance, as well as by the role of the presentational transmitter, who ideally negotiates the picture's context between artists and receivers. The fairly enhanced role of the presentational transmitter in comparison to, for example, editors of literary works, is apparent in all cases in which the audience's response to pictures addresses less their creators—or for that matter any models or actors—than those who exhibit or publish them. Characterizing the discursive side of the genre, the particular split between creative idiom and presentational context often leads to complete omission of the names of artists, as, for example, in advertising or whenever the credits of a show or a movie are cut off on television. However, culturally established art or entertainment generally assumes discursive characteristics, which often appear magnified by the particular nature of visual language. For example, once a work of art such as Leonardo da Vinci's Mona Lisa is visually quoted within a photograph, a movie, or a television show, the complete picture is rendered as one visual symbol, signifying as an emblem of art or, with respect to the smiling lady, as an icon. In such a context, the presentational transmittership together with the iconic code overpowers the picture's original idiomatic context with the discursive effect of allocating social and cultural status.

Presentational Pictures

The third basic genre, the presentational or spectacular picture, is meant to qualify all those pictures that project their significance by hiding their creative or subjective authorship in a more or less conscious attempt to render visual significance as immediate or even as factual to spectators. Pictures of natural phenomena, ranging from beautiful sunsets to devastating tornadoes, as well as those of all types of social events, demonstrate the main characteristics of this genre, projecting visual signs in terms of a social or cultural relevance that transcends the subjective intention of their creator. But because the use of technical actants such as brush or camera appears consumed by a visual context coextensive with reality, as in, for example, a sports spectacle, such pictures highlight the idiomatic role of their presentation. In place of the creative transmitter, however, it is an anonymous presenting transmitter that anticipates the audience's response, and this anonymous presentational anticipation governs the signs' idiomatic significance. Thus, pictures produced by video cameras installed and operated for surveillance also fall into this genre, in which pictures tend to be infused with an unmediated aura of objectivity, although this aura is broken once they are actually presented in an act of communication. The discursive quality of these pictures appears especially accentuated once their presentational transmitter-context is hidden or even suppressed. Examples of such suppression can be found whenever the names of creative and/or presentational transmitters are not disclosed or whenever these transmitters are portrayed as an integrated part of a spectacle when, for instance, the visual symbol of a cameraman or a commentator becomes part of the visual narrative created about an event. The proximity of this genre to the conventional discourse of pictures as mirrors of reality indicates not least the ease with which a spectacular shot can travel between micro- and macrocommunication in the practice of visual communication. For example, an amateur video of a catastrophe such as a plane crash may or may not anticipate publication to larger audiences, but once presented in the new idiomatic context of macrocommunication, the video tends to project an unmediated eyewitness account of reality, although the voice of the actual witness has been lost.

Scientific Pictures

The fourth and last genre is characterized by the most rational use of pictures in the context of scientific exploration. Visual signs can be defined as rooted in such a use insofar as their pictures contain an experimental character, rather than providing an objective method of showing what might actually exist. Within the context of an experiment, contrast relations are visualized and interpreted. The visualization process requires that creation and reception of visual forms occur within one and the same scientist (or community of scientists), and the interpretation process necessarily involves some reference to the characteristics of the technical actants used to produce these visual forms. The interpretation of these forms thus concerns less the symbolic than the empirical code of perception, whereby a concept is allocated by means of an analytical process. While highlighting the rationality of the dialectic and conceptual logic involved in demarcating contrast lines—and while indicating the capacity to draw boundaries in service of rational recognition—the experimental character of scientific pictures also necessitates the concept of verification or falsification. To serve as scientific proof, these pictures need to be repeatable in similar form, which relativizes any possible reference to a particular moment in reality. Such repeatability, however, not only specifies the very nature of signs in general, but connects the symbolic and historical codes of visual language in particular, as well as it also concerns the idiomatic reference of signs. Once such pictures are presented to others or published in a scientific journal, their forms turn into signs that include a reference to the reputation of their creator. At the same time, the contours of, for example, a particular cellular structure assume the status of a visual symbol or even an emblem and as such become part of a community's visual literacy. As long as they circulate within an integrated idiomatic network of significance and as long as they are based on scientific principles, this genre of pictures appears the most resistant to any alteration in the wake of transgressing the boundary between micro- and macrocommunication. However, the visual signs and symbols of scientific communication also carry discursive elements in the form of conceptual paradigms, as described by Ludwik Fleck or Thomas Kuhn, for example.[8] Especially when beginning to leave their original, scientific network, they tend to be subjected to new presentational transmitter contexts that often alter their idiomatic significance in favor of contextualizing their signs as mirroring factual information. In this mode, they tend to project objectified knowledge discursively, while simultaneously trading their innovative, conceptual logic for the symbolic codes of visual language. The more distant the signs' original idiom, the more symbolic appears the significance of their visual variables, such as color, size, and so forth, in any standardized representation of scientific knowledge: a discursive phenomenon that is also evidenced by the occasional attempts to present colorful depictions of crystalline structures as a kind of art.

This tentative classification of four pictorial genres may not apply to all possible uses of visual language. It is first of all designed to trace the vast potential for conflict that arises when comparing the proposed theory of a sign-based language with the practice of visual communication, not least because signs and symbols always imply a transmitter-receiver context. Yet, once the documentary is probed for sources of authorship and possible responses of audiences, such analysis collides with both the spectacular character of its imagery and the exploited tendency to see pictorial significance formed by reality, rather than by men and women of the media. As much as the attempt to apply the four categories to the documentary's compilation of pictorial sources, which, with few exceptions, fails to contextualize their original transmission, may at first appear to be an artificial exercise, it can nevertheless contribute to an understanding of the conventional standards used to present pictures as records of reality. When the reality aspect of pictorial information is emphasized, it is at the cost of differentiating the complex interaction at the basis of the pictures' creation and presentation—not to mention the audience's part in responding and thereby influencing the communicated significance. Against this background, the concept of split transmittership and the four genres are not only designed to differentiate between micro- and macrocommunicative settings, but also to pinpoint the transfer from coincidence involved in the creation of photographic pictures to communicative significance in the hands of those who present them to an audience: while there may still be considerable coincidence involved in taking a picture, its selection for presentation to an audience replaces all such happenstance with communicative agency. According to this logic, the additional process of selecting the pictures once again for publication, as has been done by the makers of the historical documentary, should definitely dominate their significance. The opposite appears to be the case, however, given the ease with which the documentary projects its imagery as an untainted account of reality and embraces coincidence as a part of the camera's faithfulness to objectivity and neutrality.

6 The Narrative of the News Spectacle

When differentiating the documentary's imagery based on the four genres, about 56.4% of the original shots could be assigned to the presentational genre of past broadcast spectacles, about 42% to the creative genre of either journalistic origin (about 28%) or fictional origin (about 14%), with the remaining 1.6% devoted to the microcommunicative context of scientific pictures and idiomatic pictures taken by amateur cameramen.[1] The documentary's producers, however, approach the historical pictures with few exceptions in the presentational mode, suppressing the pictures' creative origins in favor of accentuating their faithfulness to reality. This tendency also underscores the sources' ability to evoke an immediacy that typically complements the spectacle's power to attract the gaze. Both aspects of presenting pictorial information appear anchored in the world of newsreels, which television had early on started to integrate. In fact, NBC directly adopted the Camel-sponsored Fox Movietone Newsreel in 1948 before establishing the fifteen-minute-long *Camel News Caravan*. Eventually, all three networks established the nightly fifteen minutes of news, before switching to the thirty-minute format during the 1960s. By the late 1960s, when the depiction of "too much violence" on American home screens led to a lively controversy about the public role of television news, the moving picture was well established as one of the nation's most important sources of information and the role of objectively mirroring the nation's "public sphere" was hardly ever questioned.[2] It is the triumphant advance of the moving picture to the omnipotent status of grounding almost all the nation's cultural, social, and political events that the documentary's compilation ultimately comes to reflect some decades later, when it presents the fragments of past news by and large in the same editing order, thus drawing on their original narrative matrices as if they were free of bias and opinion.[3] Searching for the bias and opinion of past and modern broadcasters, one first notices the quite standardized, newsreel style, a format that shaped the typical characteristics of the broadcast news spectacle and that continues to leave an impression on contemporary broadcasting.

In general, the archetypical newsreel narratives as reflected by the documentary often start with an opening or "establishing shot" that features the spatial parameters of an event, for example a convention hall or a stadium, taken from an elevated camera position. The first shots most often already include the first insignia of the spectacle, when, for example, panning and/or zooming in to concentrate on the presence of audience members. The following shot usually takes the focus to the center of the stage, zooming in to present a close-up of the main protagonists of the spectacle, for example, a politician giving a speech. The pictures then switch back and forth between shots of the audience, of individual spectators, and of the main protagonists while one can occasionally hear excerpts from their original speech. This format of presenting the spectacle in the short form of news represents what can be called a historical news matrix of the broadcast spectacle. Its basic editing format, in relation to the quoted insignia of the spectacle, is used not only for the presentation of political events, but applies as well to cultural or sport events, with the latter featuring scenes of a game in play in the place of an orating politician.

The coherence and continuity in which this matrix surfaces, especially throughout the representation of the 1950s and 1960s, reflects on the roots of the news format in the classic newsreel style.[4] The segment about the 1950s still caters to the classic newsreel style: it features the spectacles in a fast cut-rhythm, often including shots that exclusively depict cameras mounted on tripods. In the later segments, these particular shots eventually vanish, while the visual symbols of cameras appear more often as an integrated part of the spectacle, for example, as the result of a camera pan or a zooming out from the center of an event's stage. The time frame in which the documentary presents sequences typical of the broadcast spectacle, especially when accompanied by the original audio of a speech, often appears to correspond with the original format of delivering a short summary of an event, although there are also cases that indicate the documentary's own choice in selecting and editing a quote.[5] Generally speaking, for each event, what modern and likely also past presenters found representative or noteworthy has been reduced to an average of twenty-five seconds of verbal audio, which often carries through the visual narrative. In this mode, the audio merges with the focus on a protagonist, which is most often intersected with cuts and pans to the event's audience, to its media attendance, and often also to the faces of single spectators.

The conventionalized matrix of news-style broadcasting accentuates the presentational genre of these pictures, since the news cameramen are held to a standard of deferential recording and any traces of individual agency are ultimately erased at the editing board. Any bias would therefore stem from the original, as well as the second presentation of these narratives by the documentary's producers. With the intention and agency of the creative side obscured, the narrative matrix produced at the editing board would consequently be the likeliest carrier of traces of political opinion. When comparing the presented narratives, it can immediately be noted that some of the highlighted personalities are presented with the original audio, while others remain mute, and there are considerable differences in the duration allocated to those who are heard speaking. On the visual plane alone, it can furthermore be observed that not all of these conventionalized narratives feature the insignia of the spectacle in full array, including applauding audience members or cheering spectators, photographers, flashes, and cameras pointing at center stage. Those presentations that integrate all these factors are often verbally complemented by the documentary's voice-over with lines such as "the attention of the nation turned to," "millions watched when," and the use of "we." When the verbal and visual presentation, including excerpts from original speeches, feature such congruence, the broadcast spectacle appears in particularly harmonic narrative outline. This archetypal form of narrating a news summary resonates with Guy Debord's assessment of the spectacle as an "instrument of unification," because it appears not only to level the intention of an event's protagonists with their attendants, but also with that of television audiences.[6] It can be observed that such unified narratives, indicating a general convergence in attitude toward the status of an event that is shared by the past as well as the modern presenters of these pictures, are used exclusively for depicting national occasions and rituals, such as presidential inaugurations and other presidential speeches, as well as party conventions, albeit with the partial exception of the coverage of the Democratic convention in 1968. Apart from three instances concerning American diplomacy—President Kennedy's visits to Paris, Berlin, and Greece—not a single visually and verbally unified narrative depicts an event that stages a foreign politician on foreign soil. Apart from the aspect of original speech excerpts, a similar broadcast style also applies to traditional cultural and sports events of unchallenged national stature, such as the opening night of a Hollywood movie, the Oscar celebrations, the Super Bowl, or the World Series. There is one exception, however, in which the unified narrative of the spectacle is used to depict a foreign event: an English horse race, the broadcast of which incorporates a close-up of the queen as celebrity spectator. There are also a couple of similar, but much shorter narratives of Olympic games held in different countries, which, however, focus exclusively on the display of American athletes.

In contrast, a different type of broadcast spectacle can be identified in the documentary with regard to both footage left more or less in its original cut and material apparently edited by its modern presenters. This type of spectacle almost never features the original audio of speeches and never the voice of the original commentator, as provided in some of the unified sport spectacles. Interestingly, this type also rarely features those symbols of the media that consciously or not reference the participatory, deferential attitude of the camera to the main stage. An example of such a different narrative is footage about a military parade on Red Square that is cut to introduce the leaders of the Soviet Union waving from the balcony. In contrast to the unified spectacle, these pictures allow glimpses of the audience, but without the distinctive symbols of applause or of general approval by individual spectators. Thus, their visual narrative lacks those symbols of appreciation that ultimately reference only the transmitter's point of view, as it also lacks those symbols of other cameras that highlight the media's flirtation with the event and its significance. Nevertheless, the resulting visual narrative still indicates that the parade reflects an established ritual of another society, apparently powerful enough to attract the attention of foreign media and achieve inclusion in the documentary's historical compilation. Although the pictures reference the event's power to attract the eye, the narrative presentation proposes a distance that radiates discontent in comparison to the previously characterized nationally unified broadcast spectacle. Since military parades tend to create a similar kind of spectacle wherever they are staged, this element of presentational distance belies the notion that a deferential camera suffices to guarantee at least some measure of objectivity. Although the basic difference between the two different types of mise en scène can only be found in the picture's content through comparing the manufactured insignia of the broadcast spectacle, the transmitters' distance from what is portrayed can also be corroborated from another angle. In the documentary, parades on Red Square appear twice, first to present—and thus familiarize—the visual appearance of Stalin, and later that of Brezhnev. In place of other possible occasions to introduce a new face at the top of a nation's political system, the spectacle of the parade is twice used in a way that contradicts its original agenda, as well as presumably the will of its main protagonists. Although their icons were very likely originally introduced in a different fashion to American television audiences, the documentary's presentation of the military parades performs their "iconic inauguration" for modern viewers and thereby indicates the producers' capacity to use the eye-catching power of a broadcast spectacle for their own purposes. The documentary's particular use of the footage also further reveals a visual predisposition toward the presented event. Rather than commenting on the role of these parades in terms of the Soviet Union's historical traditions or explicitly to explain, interpret, or critique the parades' original agenda, the pictures further serve as somewhat symbolic introductions to a chapter on the burgeoning war in Korea, and a chapter on the general topic of the Cold War. The visual signs and symbols of the same type of event are therefore twice rendered as a predisposed broadcast spectacle, which not only distances the event from the agenda of its main protagonists, but also disconnects it from its actual place in history, albeit claiming frame by frame to show it as it was. While the parade thus still serves as an eye-catcher, its editing into a pictorial spectacle marks the distance of the presenters, as opposed to the symbiotic display of a unified transmitter-receiver network in the previously discussed narratives. Participating only halfway in the protocol of action proposed by the event, these distanced pictures carry characteristics of predisposition in the sense that they include an invitation to audiences for dissent or controversy, although such an invitation would be difficult to prove in a frame-by-frame analysis.

FROM THE NATIONAL TO THE CONTROVERSIAL SPECTACLE

When differentiating between a unified and a distanced, controversial mediation of the spectacle, it is important to keep in mind that the camera itself is generally positioned in advance of an event and thus preconditioned to record its course of action from a particular angle. The arranging of such a camera tribune already implies an anticipation of the event's protocol that reduces to some degree the leeway of the camera's operator to shape individual messages. The power to assign a place to the camera often carries over into the resulting visual narrative. In some cases, the placement of the mechanical eye even resembles the mounting of fixed surveillance cameras. The very act of placing the camera involves an expectation of what it can record, and as the first step of a communicative act it initiates a process that relativizes the element of contingency in favor of establishing the interactive potential of signs. As a shot is transformed into a message, the selecting, editing, and conveying of the recorded pictures finalizes the disconnection of contingency, establishes visual percepts as signs, and constructs intended idiomatic or discursive content. In a comparison of the surveillance camera and the historical camera of the spectacle, the transmitter concept appears only slightly different: the creation of pictures by the surveillance camera is directly related to an intention to present the pictures to others, which intention defines their signs' purpose. The almost perfect control over the process of creating and presenting visual content compares with the broadcast spectacle in so far as it reduces the creation of pictures to a deferential act characterized by the technical potential of the camera in relation to its assigned perspective, although the human handling of the broadcast camera obviously contains more individual leeway and agency with regard to moving the focus. Yet in terms of the control involved when a camera is invited to record a predesigned course of action, the symbiosis between the selection of a sight and its monitoring appears to reduce individual agency to a minimum. In the sports spectacle in particular, the controlling or framing of contingency necessitates camera angles that correspond with the context, rules, and tradition of the particular game and reflect its self-declared highlights. Should the event's display contain unexpected elements, these generally correspond to the purpose of the game in terms of, for example, which side wins for what reasons, or the taste of the pictures' presenters, who may welcome the gesture of a funny fumble even when it was not anticipated or intended by the protagonists of the game. Thus, the concept of the deferential camera does not exclude a cameraman's individual agency, or ignore that accidents can happen in front of the camera, but rather it illustrates a communicative setting that mediates the individual handling of the camera and eradicates chance events once material has been selected and edited for broadcasting. In terms of the symbiosis between announcing, inviting, mounting, and controlling a camera's focus, as well as presenting the resulting picture as a unified account of the broadcast spectacle, it is therefore not surprising that such visual commentaries rarely feature any gestures that are unstaged, or even unfavorable to the agenda of both the protagonists of the event and those responsible for rendering it as broadcast spectacle.

An example of the extraordinary symbiosis between media and events is provided by the party convention designed to nominate the frontrunner for an upcoming presidential election. Featuring a tight protocol that specifies the behavior of the delegates as a homogenous audience, this ritualized event attempts to control its translation into a pictorial spectacle in part precisely by anticipating the deferential attitude of cameramen, who are held to "objective" reporting. Once a candidate is selected, any previous dissent is expected to be overcome, if only to demonstrate closed party ranks and to avoid any controversial symbolic messages when portrayed visually. In such cases, the possibility of creating an individual statement with the camera is limited by the event's power to exact from the media a sensible, neutral, and thus ultimately deferential portrayal, in order to receive the same treatment as the other party. For this reason, all fifteen depictions of the conventions of the two big parties feature, with the exception of the Democratic Convention of 1968, similar imagery and the same type of visual narrative. In fact, the similarity is so extraordinary that the historical footage levels any significant differences between the two parties, and fails to register any shifting style in the event's organizational display on screen in the three decades between 1950 and 1980, apart from the switch from black and white to color. While this extraordinary continuity in the display of visual information may owe much to a heightened sensibility for media objectivity when covering the central democratic processes, it also reflects the participatory demeanor of the intimate, deferential camera with regard to the convention of the unified spectacle: few other events could have demanded such strictly regulated symbolic typifying of their visual enactment.

In light of such conventionalized visual reporting, the Democratic Convention of 1968 stands out as truly atypical, even though most of the footage taken inside the convention center still documents the typical enacting of unified enthusiasm for the elected candidate. What makes the mediation of this spectacle different is that its protagonists lost control of its agenda, tempting the media to "hijack" the convention's display, as Dayan and Katz put it.[7] However, the scripted course of action broke down not so much because of any action on the part of the events' protagonists or its actual participants, but due to the context of a second spectacle: the demonstration outside the hall proved spectacular enough to deflect the attention of the camera. On screen, the presentational juxtaposition of these two events thus forges interrelated symbolic messages, although the pictures were rooted in two different kinds of broadcast spectacle, which involved radically different agendas, intentions, and interests. In general, demonstrations also feature ritualized aspects designed to render the collective agenda of its participants publicly visible. Like all organized and announced spectacles, they are designed to attract attention, and thus also the eye of the camera. But in contrast to more settled events, demonstrations have much less tradition, are often designed to highlight controversial issues, are much less controlled in their protocol of action, and can thus rarely rely on deferential media coverage. In fact, the documentary's footage about the demonstrations in Chicago centers on visual commentaries on the eruption of violence between protesters and police forces without attempting to trace the original protocol and agenda of the organized protest, other than quoting its famous slogan "the whole world is watching." At least, assuming that being beaten bloody by the police was not the main intention of most of the protesters, the pictures ignore the staged part of the spectacle and focus solely on the uncontrolled part of the spectacle's course of action: the blue lights of police vehicles, the sirens, scenes of violence erupting between protesters and policemen, and the flashes and spotlights of the media amid the chaos. Unlike the unified spectacle, such a demonstration never appeared powerful enough to dictate the positioning of the camera. On the contrary, the television camera moved freely through the ranks of the protesters at the price of losing a spatially ordered perspective for its visual commentaries. The editing and presenting of the pictures furthermore virtually exclude the possibility of understanding the pictures in their original temporal order. Ultimately, the pictorial narrative neither follows the timeline of the event, nor allows for spatial orientation, thus making it impossible to understand the background to the portrayed outbreaks of conflict and violence. The scenes of erupting chaos were certainly a defining part of the event and thus needed to be part of any reporter's commentary. But unlike a verbal account that can differentiate between the event's motives and the reasons why violence broke out, and can reflect on who provoked whom, the visual account of the camera appears simultaneously objective in scope and slavishly attracted to visual symbols of violence and chaos. Unlike the surveillance or the deferential camera, this camera was free to roam the event and to choose its angles within the scene: the chance nature of the captured gestures of violence, which lack a larger context to explain what instigated them, therefore owes much to choices made by both the cameramen and the picture's presenters. In this outline, the coincidental aspects themselves found the interest of the pictures' producers and are responsible for generating the spectacular, attention-demanding display on screen. Overriding any attempt to portray the intentions and agency of single protesters or policemen, or those of the event's organizers, the mise en scène of unplanned violence and chaos therefore reveals a distance that characterizes the media's approach to controversial events. The pictures communicate a coincidental collage of symbolic gestures of violence, emblems of the attention-demanding blue light flashes of ambulance and police vehicles, as well as original audio featuring screams, sirens, and the one verbal quote of the event's protagonists, "the whole world is watching," which eerily reflects the camera's insurmountable longing for capturing these out-of-the-ordinary sights. Invited to the spectacle, but without following any prearranged script, participating, but without distinct motives, the resulting pictures construct happenstance as the kernel of a broadcast spectacle that may satisfy the curious, voyeuristic eye, but fails to declare either the intention behind their creation and presentation, or the political character of the event. The coincidental context of these pictures is intensified by the fact that the incidents at the Republican Convention in Miami that same year, considered "more serious" "in terms of injuries and life lost," did not influence the media's coverage of that convention, mainly because they occurred far from the networks' cameras.[8] Hence, the element of happenstance appears in many ways to be the author of the spectacular pictures of the 1968 Democratic Convention. By comparison to the usually controlled, participatory coverage of such events, however, the pictures also project a distanced attitude on the part of the broadcast's transmitters, and construct if not a politically biased, then at least a controversial pictorial message.

The broadcast pictures of the unified and the controversial spectacle within and outside the Democratic Convention contain a very peculiar convergence of two very different modes of the spectacle's conventional mise en scène. With the deferential mode of traditional convention reporting breaking down, the agenda of the Democratic congregation shifted towards the controversial spectacle taking place outside the hall. The demonstration outside never had the traditional background and the unified status that would have allowed its protagonists to control or influence the event's display on screen, but in conjunction with the other event it succeeded in grabbing a national spotlight usually preserved for the unified spectacle. It may have been in the interest of the protest eventually to influence the ordered protocol of the unified spectacle, but it is hardly a coincidence that the outbreak of tumultuous scenes filmed inside the convention hall had less to do with the actual agency of protesters than with protagonists of the media themselves, namely Dan Rather and his crew. The controversy on the floor may have matched the controversial spectacle outside, but only in a symbolic fashion that had much to do with the media's own agency. The event outside ultimately provoked the media to import the distanced camera inside the hall and abruptly to terminate the traditional accord of deferential convention reporting.

Many of the memorable pictures of the convention appear to owe much more to the atypical, extraordinary mise en scène of its display in comparison to the traditional broadcast style than to any visual information that would actually corroborate the Democratic Party's being in a controversial state. In the symbolic dimension, however, the events come to be judged as not only a reflection of political dissent and conflict within the party, but also in the nation as a whole. Instead of discussing both events separately and illuminating the reasons behind the actions of their protagonists, namely the nation's involvement in Vietnam, the spectacular pictures convey the message of higher forces at work without differentiating individual motives, nor, for that matter, disclosing the role of those responsible for converging the events into one, controversial broadcast spectacle.

Not only did television magnify the chance aspects always involved in outbreaks of violence and chaos into a controversial spectacle, the broadcasting of such scenes had already become institutionalized on the screens of the late 1960s. The "violence at home and abroad" is subsequently featured by the documentary as the main visual narrative for the period between 1965 and 1970. By the time the voice-over concludes that "there was a lot we watched on television that made us anxious and the violence broadcast to our living rooms was difficult to escape," the historically interested spectator has also seen uncountable shots of demonstrations gone awry, including, for example, an advertisement for the Nixon campaign that sequences some thirty still pictures of a similar spectacular, controversial character. Thus, the documentary restages the pictorial media discourse of "violence at home and abroad" by reusing spectacular pictures from its past broadcasts. In the case of the presentation of the Democratic Convention, the same discursive attitude of presenting an objective picture is maintained, while convention activities are juxtaposed with scenes of violence, which have been selected because they appear as contrastingly coincidental in their reference to reality as possible. Thus, the pictorial convention of the broadcast spectacle itself is permitted to shape an imprint of chaos and violence at home. This fashion of visual reporting had also begun to dominate the mise en scène of the "violence abroad," as the television spectacle commenced to write history as a superhuman force into its visual message.

VIETNAM FRAMED BY THE SPECTACLE

When documenting the events that led to what scholars describe as the escalation of the war in Vietnam, the documentary starts with a series of still pictures of elite troops exercising. Overlaid with dramatic music, the still pictures reveal training drills that are verbally described as preparation for a yet unclear mission in Vietnam. Cutting to moving pictures, the camera then zooms in on one soldier, to focus on a skull sewed onto his sleeve. The next cut presents a series of shots of helicopters flying over tropical vegetation, and the voice-over provides information on how many soldiers had already been stationed in Vietnam and how experts believed victory to be "around the corner" in 1963. Further footage of a helicopter dropping American soldiers in a rice field is set to the music of Carl Orff's *Carmina Burana*. Stating that Vietnam was a "divided country," the voice-over prepares the next cut to pictures of Buddhist monks protesting in the streets of Saigon.

The camera focuses in on one monk, who has set himself on fire, being watched by a crowd that has formed a circle around him. The voice-over identifies the action as directed against the "corrupt and repressive Diem regime" and remarks that the "pictures shocked the world." The next cut reveals an Asian woman checking her make-up with a hand-held mirror. The voice-over proceeds to inform us that the woman is Diem's sister-in-law, "Madame Nhu," who had dismissed the Buddhists' protests as "barbecue shows." When she is then seen speaking at a lectern equipped with microphones, the voice-over explains that she toured America hoping to rally support for her brother-in-law's regime.[9] It furthermore adds that President Kennedy had already "reviewed" his Vietnam policy and ordered a thousand soldiers back home. Only at this point can some original audio of Mrs. Ngo Dinh Nhu's speech be heard. But taken out of context, her words such as " . . . and then whispering in our ears our shortcomings in finding a solution . . ." convey little sense to the documentary's receiver. Still over the same pictures of Nhu, the voice-over finishes the opening sequence on the history of the Vietnam War with the information that a bloody overthrow of the Diem regime was soon to take place and then the documentary starts a new chapter on sports and games.

This sequencing of historical footage, including the choice of music, is perhaps the documentary's most explicit presentation of a subjective visual narrative which, rather than simply restaging the pictures of the past, conveys the producers' opinion and perspective. At the same time, however, the edited footage contains multiple aspects of the spectacle. The footage of a burning monk includes what appears to be a small crowd of spectators, but is also labeled as having "shocked the world." What actually shocked the world—and possibly still rattles modern viewers—concerns the suicide of the monk and questions about his personality and the motives behind the radical execution of his protest. Setting oneself on fire as a means of political protest is certainly meant to draw attention as a highly unusual action. But the fact that it is able to attract a camera cannot possibly suffice to determine the resulting pictures as historical, at least not without the provision of a distanced perspective, one that would also overcome the emotional force of these pictures. The names of the Buddhist monk and of those who created and published the visual commentary about his action apparently did not make it into history. As shocking as the visual signs of a burning human being may be, those who presented them to the world cared neither for the person's background nor his specific motives. Instead the pictures serve as a symbolic commentary that vaguely speculates about the monk's action as exposing the "corrupt and repressive" regime of South Vietnam. The visual narrative subsequently proceeds to juxtapose the spectacle of the burning monk with that of a press conference held by Diem's sister-in-law in America. Contextualized by the voice-over as intending to rally American support for Diem, the press conference was apparently designed to attract the attention of the media and the American people to what Nhu had to say.

As with other press conferences, the documenting presence of the cameras was preplanned. Only in this case, the attraction of the media resulted not in an interest in Nhu's words, but in how she looked and comported herself in the public spotlight. Whether or not Nhu anticipated the cameras capturing her gesture of applying make-up, she certainly did not control either her own role in the spectacle, or the outcome, the presentation of a symbolic visual message that corroborates a notion of her actively veiling the corruption beleaguering her husband's and brother-in-law's regime.

The narrative juxtaposition of these two spectacles, the one protesting, the other defending the regime in South Vietnam, is therefore used to contextualize the footage by creating the visual expression of a highly unusual, exotic, and rather controversial leadership in South Vietnam. Similar to the juxtaposition of the Democratic Convention with the spectacle of street protests, the historical footage facilitates such interrelations of visual messages because it was produced in the mode of the spectacle without disclosing any specific journalistic intent other than to record what appeared to the broadcasters as attractive, curious, out of the ordinary, or simply exotic. Through discounting the original agenda of both the Buddhist monk and Diem's sister-in-law, the pictures concentrate on their gestures' general symbolic quality, the particular characteristics of which ultimately stand as the only reason why these visual messages were created and published in the first place. The interrelation between the two different spectacles, further accentuated by Nhu's metaphor of "barbecue shows," functions similarly to the previously discussed conjunction of the unified and the controversial spectacle. Only in this case, the combination is more glaring, given the spatial and temporal distance between the two linked events. Yet in both cases, the act of arranging different spectacular sights into one message seems to veil rather than disclose the subjective intentions of the pictures' presenters, which effect raises questions as to the historical factuality implicitly ascribed to each shot. While the pictures could be contextualized, for example, by referring to the fact that the Diem regime was helped to power—as well as bloodily overthrown—with substantial contributions from Washington, or that it reflected the rule of a Catholic minority in Vietnam that had previously served the French colonizing authority, their visual message communicates in another dimension. If it indeed had been the intent to summarize the political background of Vietnam in journalistic fashion, such pictures are unlikely to have been created in the first place. Why, after all, should it be up to one monk or one woman to display the political history of a country? Furthermore, even if these two persons convey a symbolic message that is relevant to the country's history, why choose these pictures that reflect their ability to stage an event, but not to control the camera's portrayal of their agendas? In order to assert a truthful portrayal of what really happened, this treatment of the broadcast spectacle replaces the potentially biased transmitter with a higher power responsible for disclosing the symbols' real message.

Using these controversial spectacles to narrate the onset of the war in Vietnam, the documentary turns to equally eclectic pictures to narrate the closure of the violent conflict. After commenting on "more bad news in 1975" and the plight of refugees in Cambodia and Vietnam, including the previously discussed double casting of some pictures of refugees, the voice-over states that "television and its new satellite technology carried the last days of a free South Vietnam to millions of American homes." What follows is footage of American citizens leaving Saigon or "frantically rushing for the last helicopters to freedom" and a white American man uttering some barely audible words of confusion and desperation into a reporter's microphone. After that, the documentary embarks on a lengthy sequence of pictures of helicopters crashing into the sea, their pilots barely saving their lives by jumping out at the last second. One of the clips still bears the original caption "OFF VIETNAM—BY SATELLITE." The footage is used to indicate the "panic" of those moments, and its content is explained as "stolen helicopters" flown by "Vietnamese refugees" trying to reach the safety of American warships. Accordingly, mention is made that the ongoing arrival of "fleets of choppers" caught the Navy by surprise. However, the verbal explanation appears rather thin in view of the action-loaded pictures. If the rush to safety was a completely spontaneous act, it is hard to see how so many of these "refugees" could all individually arrive at the same time, and individually decide on the same perilous method of landing their helicopters. Because the pictures only show choppers with empty cargo space, one wonders why these refugees did not just use one chopper, which would have had the additional advantage that only one of them would have had to execute the dangerous act of diving at the last second. A more logical explanation for the unfolding spectacle would be that these South Vietnamese pilots were not only trained by American instructors, but generally also operated the American choppers only under American orders. In this scenario, American officers could very well have initiated the spectacle of helicopters crashing into the sea in attempt to prevent the machinery's falling into the hands of the North Vietnamese. However, thus identified by the documentary as depicting action carried out by South Vietnamese soldiers and prompted by "panic," the pictures are contextualized as an ominous spectacle. The visceral immediacy of the pictures, the vivid sensation of the peril of diving to safety amidst crushing rotor blades, appears to owe much to the accidental aura of the imagery. While the agenda of the protagonists remains subject to speculation, any traces of individual agency on the part of the cameraman are also missing. Again, it is as if the unfolding scene attracted the camera's focus rather than having appealed to his opinion. Although there is a reference to further spectators at the scene—the choppers crashed "before the eyes of the Navy"—the main reference to the audience rests in the caption "OFF VIETNAM—BY SATELLITE." Not only does the reference to satellite technology add to the notion of a technological apparatus creating the pictures, it also implies two central elements of the broadcast spectacle. First, no matter what has caused a network to switch to a "live broadcast," the live broadcast event necessarily appears to the audience as more significant than the program it replaces, so significant, in fact, that it can tolerate no deferment in being relayed to the nation. Second, and interwoven with the first observation, not only does such a "live broadcast" anticipate national interest, but in the three-network era large audiences could be guaranteed as witnesses to the spectacle. This format especially caters to extraordinary, unexpected, and consequently nonstaged events and is still evident in broadcasting today. Without a protocol, such events can indeed be defined as truly coincidental spectacles. One of the main properties of their visual narrative is that both the cause of an event, as well as the individual role of the camera, can only speculatively support the understanding of the visual signs provided by the pictures, since the coincidental nature of the event obstructs provision of informed, nonspeculative background to its cause, its course of action and, consequently, the pictures' message. In general, such footage often finds rational explanation beyond the speculations of the moment only after they have been broadcast live. Without an agenda that would inform the camera's pictures, the footage of the crashing choppers constructs such a coincidental spectacle, of which the immediacy and emotional power attracts the curious spectator at home in basically the same way as it invited the camera's focus in the first place. The choices made to create these pictures may have stemmed from the intention to record what happened, but the resulting visual signs and symbols remain utterly void of information because their presentational "live" context asserts their significance without being able properly to contextualize their content.

However, in line with the documentary's objective of presenting narrative closure to the American involvement in Vietnam, the pictures also find a distinctive, symbolic agenda. Together with the idiomatic pictures of suffering refugees, the visual narrative conveys the message of human plight, chaos, and panic in South Vietnam. A breakdown of order is solely attributed to the South Vietnamese, with the implication that the American forces had already left, and not that they were leaving in disarray. In this way, the documentary not only commences but also ends its historical narrative of the American involvement in Vietnam with spectacles featuring South Vietnamese protagonists, the motive for whose actions appears emotional or obscure, and in no way a rational response to a situation that was at least partially the result of American agency. The concatenation of controversial and coincidental spectacles ultimately only conveys a sense of radicalism with respect to the monk's martyrdom, of weirdness with respect to Diem's sister-in-law, and of chaos and panic with respect to the unexplained action of the Vietnamese pilots. Symbolically, the visual message of these pictures only leaves a very broad sense of a South Vietnamese "mess" caused neither by North Vietnamese action, since the enemy is never visually referenced by the pictures, nor by American action, since these protagonists remain in the background. As presented, this chapter of American history finds a narrative frame of visual commentaries that, on closer inspection, dissociates both the causes of the war's outbreak and its end from American activities or, for that matter, North Vietnamese agency. The narrative sequencing of past spectacles thus utilizes pictures without reference to either their historical context or their individual authorship to construct history without identifying individual human agency, while at the same time asserting their historical relevance and objective validity as comments about the past.

TYPIFYING THE BROADCAST SPECTACLE

If the visual narrative of the documentary fails to convey a distinct perspective on the causes that led to the outbreak and the end of the war in Vietnam, such a failure is apparently related to the documentary's ingrained notion that these visual records can unfold history on their own. The somewhat kaleidoscopic sequencing of past broadcast spectacles may create a new narrative context and thus a novel historical perspective, but it cannot completely release the pictures from their confinement to the style and intention of their original presentation. But while reference to their original presenters would reflect the pictures' most consistent historical value, the documentary not only fails to indicate the character of these pictures as past instances of communication, but also, through perpetuating their power to attract the eye and to stir up emotional responses, it commences to participate in their (historical) intention. In the same mode, the modern transmitters also appear to propagate the political overtones of the historical pictures, at least to the extent that they fail to reflect on the original intentions behind mediating the spectacle. Although one cannot ultimately discern whether or not the documentary's producers were aware of carrying political discourses into the present, since they seem to rely on the records as objective windows into the past, many of the compiled clips simply restage the predispositions of past broadcasts. One of the more obvious examples of such unfiltered transfer of past politics into modern times involves footage of a speech given by one of the leaders of SNCC and the so-called Black Power movement, Stokely Carmichael.[10] His speech became a historical spectacle because the media arguably had anticipated its controversial status, perhaps already when positioning its cameras and certainly when presenting a biased visual summary to the nation.

Partially cut in the standardized format of an established spectacle, the original footage alternates the focus between the speaker and the responding audience before twice singling out one particular spectator, a black woman who rises from her seat in ecstatic response to Carmichael's speech. While her gestures are reminiscent of those of a Beatles fan, the shot stands out as the only visual commentary of its kind by comparison with all other mises en scène of political events. Based on the dialectic and symbolic codes of visual language, the pictures of that woman transfer their symbolic message to the event itself, as well as to the characterization of the speaker, creating a controversial, if not defamatory, impression. The question is thus why the camera sought out this particular spectator and why this shot appeared twice in the final cut of the event's broadcast. Because the shots also reveal the presence of a much calmer audience around the woman, the visual characterization of Carmichael's audience could have easily remained within the standardized portrayal of more typical spectators. However, the incited spectator apparently attracted the camera simply because of her atypical gestures. While such shot selection could still be qualified as an individual, creative act of shaping a visual message by the cameraman, the presenters appropriate the picture's symbolic message through staging it twice within the short visual narrative of the event. It has furthermore to be assumed that the cameraman was in each case instructed to focus on individual spectators to provide the editor at the cutting board with the shots needed to construct the conventional narrative of the spectacle. When thus singling out that incited spectator twice as an insignia of the event, the presentational transmitter turned the atypical Carmichael follower into a typical one. Albeit entrenched in the discourse of pictures without authorship, the divergent use of the insignia of the spectacle nevertheless reflects a distinct discontent with the event's character and the intentions of its main protagonists. Due to the symbolic dimension of visual language, it may be difficult to pin such discontentment on any single visual sign, let alone to assert that all television spectators actually received the spectator's unusual gestures as a negative message. But even if the pictures' predisposition is not easily verified, it can be assumed that this mise en scène was not intended by Carmichael and thus constitutes a visual perspective that is distanced from the event's agenda. The historical footage may therefore not inscribe a defaming characterization of Carmichael's speech in any objectively readable fashion, but it offers a symbolic message that at least invites controversial response.[11] In restaging this controversial presentation, the documentary reiterates the predisposition of the pictures' original broadcasters through simply recasting their messages.

At this point, three categories of the opinionated broadcast spectacle can be tentatively worked out on the basis of the documentary's imagery:

- *The unified spectacle.* The attraction and status of an event is highlighted by symbols of other cameras, press corps, the audience, individual spectators, and so forth, in ways that reveal a harmony or even symbiosis between the event's agenda and the resulting visual commentary of the media. The ritual tradition of such events provides a protocol of action that asks for a deferential positioning of the camera, which predetermines the outcome of the visual commentary—thus similar to conditions on a movie set. Because the visual signs of such commentaries shape a self-sufficient internal context that cannot conclusively indicate what was external to their frame or explain what transpired before the moments visually portrayed, a knowledge of both the event's own rules and protocol as well as the media's convention in creating its visual narrative adds the external context needed to understand the signs in their full symbolic significance. Without knowledge about the traditional context of baseball games, presidential inaugurations, party conventions, Oscar celebrations, and so forth, the visual signs provide minimal historical information and obstruct assessment of their main communicative function. With knowledge about their external context, however, the pictures create the phenomenon of "instant history," which merges the social setting of an event with the public significance of the broadcast pictures. The pictures, which cannot easily be ignored and which refuse to reveal individual authorship, seem to attain their power to attract the eye sheerly through their reference to reality. Hence, the claim of objectivity inheres in the combination of a deferential, intimate camera and a presentational transmittership that hides its bias in favor of asserting the self-evidence of the depicted event and implementing the discourse of reality.

- *The controversial spectacle.* This category comprises those events that were able to attract the camera, but were not powerful enough to command symbiotic participation in their protocol of action or the political agenda of their protagonists. The disharmony between the intention and the mediation of these events is often subtle in character, because the resulting pictures tend to feature some of the standardized insignia of the unified spectacle, such as shots of the audience, spectators, microphones, and other symbols of the press, although rarely integrating all of them. In fact, none of the examples of the controversial spectacle are actually cut with an exclusive shot of other television cameras, as can be found in seventeen cases of the unified spectacle—in light of this symbol's previously discussed role as an insignia of the spectacle, its absence indirectly symbolizes the nonparticipatory role of the broadcasters. The distanced camera positioning may indicate more leeway in framing and communicating pictorial narratives, but such subjectivity appears countered by the media's own, almost normative quest for presenting special, out of the ordinary material that is able to catch audiences' attention, which in turn veils the agency of those responsible for creating and presenting these pictures. In each case, the disharmony between an event's attempt to control its display and the media's distanced mode of constructing its pictorial representation forges a broadcast spectacle that invites controversial responses. Albeit potentially more objective than the unified spectacle insofar as it involves an individual subjective, rather than deferential, camera handling and applies a certain distance to the event being portrayed, the resulting symbolic commentary defies such categorization. The irrelevance of the "journalistic paradigm of objectivity and neutrality" in the face of the spectacle as observed by Dayan and Katz is here a product of the opposition between the symbolic content of the communicated messages and the implied discourse of reality in pictures. When an event's portrayal is offered for controversial response, the selection and syntactic arrangement of visual symbols almost always appears in a presentational mode: a mode that effaces any distanced or even predisposed attitude by characterizing the pictorial commentary as directly originating in the event itself, rather than being added by the agency of visual reporters or journalists. Once the discourse of pictorial reality has been filtered from their general context, the mise en scène of Cold War ideology within the example of the Red Square parade, the symbolic defaming of the South Vietnamese regime, or that of Carmichael's role in the Civil Rights movement provide few historically relevant clues to what actually happened in the past, but many indications of the historical predisposition of the broadcast media.

- *The exotic spectacle.* Often accidental in character with respect to the nature of an event, as well as to its recording from often improvised camera positions, the exotic spectacle is meant to designate footage of particular, extraordinary scenarios including all sorts of accidents, mishaps, disasters, and catastrophes that have no apparent agenda or protocol of action, but generate the power to attract the camera and keep it focused. Unlike the controversial or unified spectacle, these events are not announced, nor is the camera invited on the basis of an agenda, protocol, or intention. The positioning of the camera is thus fortuitous with respect to both the event's course of action and the attitude of the cameraman toward the unfolding scene. Once a camera is present, it is attracted to the scene out of more or less spontaneous curiosity, which shapes an essentially uninformed account that is limited by the unpremeditation of both the camera's positioning and its operator's intentions. When these pictures are presented to audiences, a lack of information about the immediate context of a scene and/or the larger background of the complete event often mar their interpretation. An example of the exotic spectacle is the descent of the choppers into the South China Sea. Without contextual background, the presentation leaves its curious account open to speculation that could only be verified if the complete event, including the camera angles, could be reconstructed by consulting an array of different sources. The attempt to emphasize these decontextualized pictures' immediacy, reality, or authorless objectivity places an even greater corresponding stress on the emotional significance of their signs and symbols. In each case, it is the media that decides whether the spectacular status of such an event is sufficient to deserve the attention of its audience. Once broadcast as spectacle, it is consequently the presentational transmittership that controls the event's display, that pinpoints what it deems characteristic, typical, or atypical, and that ultimately endows its coincidental aspects with communicative significance. Although based on a curious, rather than on an intimate or distanced camera, the exotic spectacle also reveals aspects of the other two spectacles: with regard to the media's own power to characterize the status of an event, it is comparable to the controversial spectacle, while it is also akin to the unified spectacle in so far as its broadcast is able to generate a unifying response. As atypical, out-of-the-ordinary accounts of "instant history," accidents, disasters, and catastrophes in particular aspire to a nationally shared emotional response that unifies the event with its pictures, and the transmitters with their receivers.

This categorization of the broadcast spectacle serves two causes: first, as a methodological approach to interpreting historical footage, the symbolic content of which transcends the possibility of verification or falsification, and second, as a preliminary conclusion about the subjectivity that can nevertheless be traced in the symbolic messages of the documentary's compilation of historical footage. However, the above categories are not meant to limit the many possible ways of receiving the message of these pictorial spectacles. They are also not meant to be exclusive, and the documentary's examples furthermore reveal many instances where the three categories partially overlap. The footage of the protests at the Democratic Convention, as well as, for example, the shot of the incited Carmichael spectator, previously discussed as representative of the controversial spectacle, also contain coincidental aspects of the exotic spectacle, which renders the chosen symbols as exotic, atypical, and thus interesting and attractive by comparison to more general, conventional mises en scène. In each case, differentiation between the intimate and deferential, the distanced and controversial, and the coincidental and curious camera serves not only to deconstruct the supreme power behind the historical footage's ability to attract the eye, but also to expose the agency of the media that produced and presented this power as a factual mirror of reality, while nevertheless incorporating their own perspectives and opinions into these spectacles. In the following, the usefulness of these three broad categories will be further tested on the presentation of icons, be it those featured at center stage of the established broadcast spectacle, or those whose presence on screen dominates the nonspectacular picture in such a way as to transform it into a spectacle.

7 Iconic Lecterns

The documentary offers snippets of original speeches by politicians and celebrities of all sorts, whose words were considered interesting for historical perspective. With few exceptions, the verbal excerpts of past speeches occur in combination with the presentation of icons. Providing these historically dynamic symbols with what can be termed an "iconic lectern," the documentary's compilation most often underlines the significance of their words by presenting them among the typical insignia of the broadcast spectacle. One exception to this standard of presentation is a speech by the actor James Stewart, whose icon is given a different, less spectacular (re)introduction to the documentary's audience. Apparently, the symbol's ongoing popularity, rooted in the fictional world of Hollywood narratives, was enough reason to support the icon with an iconic lectern from which to make a political statement against McCarthy's witch-hunt. Unlike in most other cases, the footage was filmed in a studio, and so presumably it was the camera that invited the icon and not the other way around (i.e., the icon attracting the camera). Apart from that difference, however, it is nevertheless the unceasing potential of a well-known icon to attract public interest that motivates the selection of this clip. In general, such iconic potential reflects an additional symbolic plane in the narration of the broadcast spectacle. This additional symbolic plane is not grammatically constructed by a complete pictorial narrative, but is tied to the history of one pictorial term.

In the case of the Stewart clip, the actor's icon found a participatory camera, indicating that the actor could rely on a favorable creation and presentation of his appearance in a mode that resembles a movie set. Such setting implies that the actor shared in the general aspiration behind producing these pictures, as did their creators and presenters. The pictures' central function, however, is the communication of the semantic background of Stewart's popular icon. This background, encompassing content from such movies as Frank Capra's *Mr. Smith Goes to Washington,* certainly contributes to a suitable narrative lectern for speaking out against McCarthyism.[1] At least, the selection of this icon, with its signification built in the context of such and other popular movies, indicates the anticipation of past broadcasters that their audiences would find it suitable to speak for this cause.

The rebroadcast within the documentary, finally, leaves no doubt about the modern presenters' intention to transport the unified status of Stewart's icon and with it the content of the selected words into the present.

When searching the documentary's compilation for similarly unified iconic lecterns, a comparable congruence between visual and verbal signs applies with few exceptions only for American presidents. While the documentary allocates an average of twenty-five seconds to the speech of each icon, it can first of all be observed that those clips associated with the controversial spectacle, featuring the icons of Stalin, Khrushchev, Brezhnev, Nhu, or Carmichael, for example, are either without original audio, or else the audio has been cut to short excerpts between five and a maximum of sixteen seconds. By comparison, the unified spectacles feature original audio which on several occasions exceeds one minute of speech, as in the case of several presidents and Martin Luther King (twice), as well as Jacqueline Kennedy and Alfred Hitchcock. There seems to be a direct relationship between the length of speech allocated to an icon and the status of that icon or that icon's historical personality. The documentary returns to the icons of the past as a reflection of the nation's most well-known personalities, the way it also restages the broadcast spectacles of historical events. Thus, little concern is shown for how the icons achieved their social status, what characterizes their potential to attract interest, and what denotations and connotations governed the original process of their iconization. More broadly, the media's function in broadcasting the spectacle can be considered to include that of singling out personae for iconization on screen; once accepted by audiences, these icons comprise another aspect of the spectacle, and in self-referential mode accumulate eye-catching significance in every new presentation. Thus, in seeking to analyze the documentary's mode of showcasing historical icons, the following concentrates less on the actual historical contribution of individuals, than on the historicity of their icons as they came to be mediated on screen.

ICONS IN THE HISTORICAL LIMELIGHT

The documentary introduces most personalities from the worlds of sports, movies, television, science, and politics through pictures of spectacular events, or else it declares their celebrity status by means of the voice-over, before cutting to footage meant to illustrate their particular achievement and their historical significance. Such an introduction serves as a substitution for the historical process that elevated their visual symbol to iconic status in the past. In time-lapsing fashion, the status of symbols is contextualized for all those modern viewers who are not familiar with or might have simply forgotten the iconic contours of some of these symbols. With few exceptions, such as for Richard Nixon, General MacArthur, or Muhammad Ali, the re-formation of these symbols' icons proceeds in harmonic relation to the original response of American audiences, which congruence appears to reflect the continuous historicity of visual language's iconic code.

An example of such pictorial reshowcasing of a person's ascent to iconic status is offered by the documentary's visual introduction of the astronaut John Glenn. The documentary's voice-over glosses the first presentation of his icon on the occasion of his safe return from outer space with the words: "In the next week, the hero was decorated, photographed, cheered, and idolized." The following historical pictures support the verbal introduction sign by sign. A cut reveals half a dozen cameras mounted on tripods, as well as a couple of photographers, before consecutive pictures show President Kennedy honoring Glenn with a medal. Then follows the depiction of a parade, at which a "quarter of a million Americans" celebrated his successful mission. So far, his icon is established in the mode of the unified spectacle: it is presented as the media's focal point, significant enough to be juxtaposed with a well-established icon (that of the president), and powerful enough to draw the gaze of hundreds of thousands of spectators. This assessment of Glenn's presentation, as well as the following observations, are not intended to challenge the comprehensibility of according Glenn a place in history, nor to qualify his popularity as simply based in spectacle, but rather to focus on the way the documentary (re)constructed his visual symbol as a unified icon of national visual language. Glenn's rise to stardom is followed by shots of newspapers thrown down one by one, so that viewers may glimpse their headlines, concerning the space program of the Soviet Union. The next cut takes modern spectators to the sight of a rocket being launched, and then to close-ups on the helmeted faces of two astronauts. The voice-over informs us that the Russians had sent two men into orbit and comments, "we had to admit, an impressive achievement." Immediately after this statement, the narrative returns to America with a "class photograph" of the NASA team chosen for the daring undertaking to land on the moon. In contrast to the icon of John Glenn, the Russian astronauts are not presented in the context of the spectacle, and although the pictures allow a glimpse of their faces, their significance is not further contoured either verbally or visually. Because of such cursory presentation, it is likely that most of the documentary's modern spectators, who cannot recollect the appearance of the Russian astronauts from past broadcasts, will again forget the characteristic patterns of their faces and thus ignore their potentially iconic status. This comparison between the mode of refreshing the pictorial history of John Glenn and that of the Russian astronauts reveals first of all the difference between the symbolic and the iconic code of visual language. Also, the missing continuity and repetition that would have been necessary to render the general visual symbols of Russian men as specific icons also indicates the documentary's national predisposition. The different modes of using visual language therefore carry inherently political, Cold War–era implications, albeit exclusively on the symbolic plane of national visual literacy. While the presentation of Glenn's historical icon supports the general classification of the nationally unified broadcast spectacle, the specific way in which his icon's characteristics have been initiated and nurtured warrants a second look.

In accordance with the proposed theory, any picture of an icon enacts a symbolic transfer to other symbols portrayed at its side or in adjacent shots. The rocket's launch and the Russian astronauts thus translates into the syntactical content that the astronauts were starting into outer space—although only for those whose visual literacy is familiar with such a symbolic constellation. But the voice-over not only translates the pictures' message ("The Russians had sent two men into orbit . . ."), it also adds a new aspect when stating that they were being "sent." By contrast, the selected footage of Glenn's space adventure narrates a successful homecoming in combination with a set of established rituals, a public parade and a public decoration. While his return in public favorably juxtaposes his visual symbol with the unified icon of the president and with the emblematic insignia of the spectacle, including the national flag, it also contains a reference to the personal, private ritual of homecoming. One shot is dedicated to his wife, who had waited anxiously for his return, as the voice-over testifies. Reminiscent of similar pictures that show family and friends welcoming Vietnam soldiers, but also recalling the intimate pictures of refugees discussed earlier, the footage of Glenn and his wife blurs the distinction between personal and public. Qualifying for the category of the journalistic—or artistic—camera in so far as such a scene cannot simply be assigned to the realm of the spectacle, these pictures verge on a realism that stands and falls with the emotional participation of spectators. The truthfulness of the depiction appears to depend on the assumption that Glenn and his wife neither acted the welcoming, nor that their actions were influenced by the public circumstances. However, since neither assumption can be verified or falsified using the visual records alone, a second possible line of questioning involves whether the journalistic camera was invited or welcomed, or whether it appeared uninvited and unannounced in "paparazzi" style. Accordingly, the picture shows characteristics of the deferential, participatory camera of the unified spectacle, adding to it a quite intimate angle. Without being able to determine whether the two were indeed "overwhelmed by their emotions"—which once again indicates the similarity in aura between fictional and unstaged pictorial symbols and gestures—it appears reasonable to presume that they neither objected to the camera's presence, nor to the corresponding presentation of their personal moment in the public spotlight. Nevertheless, the authorship of the portrayed gesture shifts ultimately into the hands of those who edited the pictures into a broadcast spectacle of Glenn's homecoming. The intention behind showcasing the rather intimate, personal gesture as part of a national broadcast thereby complements the unified spectacle perfectly. The verisimilitude of the couple's private joy not only appeals to the participating spectator, who identifies with the characters' personal emotion, but also extends to comprise the nation's collective emotion in terms of celebrating a nationally significant event. In this form, the private and public angles on Glenn's homecoming converge in a pictorial narrative of the nation's history that is broadcast to millions, placing an emotionally and socially unified icon within national visual literacy.

RITUALISTIC ICONIZATION

A similar example of how the documentary reintroduces icons of the past in ritualistic, narrative fashion, merging private and public background, intimate and spectacular characteristics, can be found in one of the most illustrious careers of the early television era, the ascent and tragic end of President John F. Kennedy. The documentary's introduction of Kennedy's iconic persona starts with a still picture of a family sitting before a 1950s television set, gazing at his televised face. A cut takes the spectator to the Democratic Convention at which Adlai Stevenson has just been nominated to run against the incumbent, Eisenhower. At the convention, Kennedy was given the honor of presenting the party's choice to the delegates and, at the same time, to the media and to national audiences. As discussed earlier, broadcasts of these conventions usually feature all the aspects of a unified spectacle, since the camera is advised strictly to observe protocol in order to comply with standards of neutral reporting. The nomination of the frontrunner has become an occasion to present to the media and national audiences the harmonized imagery of jubilant delegates in symbolic con-junction with the face of the newly selected standard-bearer. The ritualistic congruence between these conventions and their media coverage thus gives the parties the unique chance to propel the iconization of their candidate in a partially self-determined pictorial display. For similar reasons, the parties also began to use the opportunity of national limelight to introduce to the media new recruits selected for future roles in national politics. As a ritual within a ritual, the honor of presenting the nominee thereby reflects a sec-ond selection that enables a new face to become nationally recognized in symbolic relation to the event's main icon. Hence, when the documentary introduces the historical icon of Kennedy in the role of the party's hope-ful, not only does it follow the original agenda of that unified broadcast spectacle, it arguably also more or less accurately re-presents the process of his historical iconization. Yet, as a result of this focus on the history of Kennedy's icon, that of Adlai Stevenson actually takes second place. The focus of the convention footage remains on Kennedy for eighteen seconds of speech, and the actual candidate is only later given fifteen seconds of speech, in the more modest setting of a television studio, without an audi-ence and without conjunction to other insignia of the typical broadcast spectacle. It is thus as if the power of Kennedy's icon has shifted back in time to overshadow Stevenson's historical moments in the limelight of media attention.

By the time the documentary turns to the 1960 election and the famous first showdown of presidential candidates in front of television cameras, both Nixon and Kennedy have been introduced to modern audiences as established national icons. Both have been presented in the ritualistic context of their respective conventions, as well as while campaigning on the street. Over a shot of Kennedy and his wife Jacqueline, the voice-over then proclaims that "it wasn't so much what he said, as how he said it"—not that he has actually said anything up to this point in the narrative, other than the eighteen seconds proclaiming Stevenson's nomination at the convention four years previously. The next shots feature a television studio, where Kennedy and Nixon are seen shaking hands while illuminating flashes signal the presence of photographers. Two further shots show a picture of each candidate within the rounded frame of an old-fashioned television set, the screen flickering with interfering black stripes. While these images symbolize the original perspective of television viewers, the voice-over behind the screen-within-the-screen declares that "70 million were watching, more than would vote in November."

The footage only indirectly addresses the well-known and well-debated issue of whether it was the verbal or the visual content that decided Kennedy's victory by a razor-slim margin.[2] Through its provision of visual excerpts without their accompanying audio, the documentary's narrative ultimately does suggest that the television debate favored visual over verbal information, but this message only appears as a circuitous result of restaging the iconization of Kennedy in a series of historical broadcast spectacles. The modern viewer is asked to accept the significance of an icon based on a purely visual portrayal of his features in symbolic conjunction with jubilant delegates, cheering masses, deferential television cameras, and a verbal allusion to seventy million pairs of eyes. In this mode, the restaging of Kennedy's iconization aims from the historical beginning, and thus from before he was actually elected, to show an archetypal icon of unified, national significance without adding any political contours. By the same standard, the person behind that visual term, his political convictions, his character, his motivations, and so forth, disappear beneath the symbolic content of the pictorial mise en scène. The voice-over contributes little additional information, with its description of the "youthful," "good-looking" man and the "beautiful" wife at his side. In the subsequent coverage of the Bay of Pigs disaster, the voice-over consequently identifies that "youthfulness" as the main reason for his ill-fated attempt to initiate a civil war in Fidel Castro's Cuba. By this point in both the compiled historical footage and the documentary's verbal narrative, it is an icon of American visual literacy that acts, and no longer an individual flesh and blood person, or, for that matter, that group of persons who were actually involved in the government's decision making.

By the time the documentary reaches Kennedy's assassination in Dallas, it has showcased the icon in twenty-seven clips, second only to the thirty times it presents Nixon's icon, whose public career lasted many years longer. What emerges from the compilation of Kennedy's pictures amounts to a collage of single pictorial messages that oscillate between the unified spectacle and visual commentaries on his family life. A series of shots is dedicated to his children, who are seen welcoming their father on an airfield and then playing at the seaside in the typical display of a family vacation. With the camera in both series of pictures showing a somewhat intimate, deferential attitude, the boundaries between the public/political and the private/personal converge, as do the genres of the idiomatic family video and journalistic reportage. In fact, only when assigning the pictures a reference to reality, and thus to history, can the boundary between the public/political and the private/personal be maintained. When considering who created these pictures, the first question concerns whether or not the camera was invited and what intention it followed when forging a symbolic message about the icon's private life. Since the footage emulates the genre of family pictures, which typically reflect joyful, ritualistic occasions, it seems to emerge from an invited camera that was expected to comment deferentially on the scene. The resulting pictorial message about harmonious family life therefore indicates a very particular transmittership, which poses as an integrated part of the family's idiomatic network, as in the case of the previously discussed home movies, while at the same time anticipating the interest of a nationwide audience—an audience who cannot possibly know the usual demeanor of the portrayed actors or, for example, distinguish typical from atypical gestures. As a result, the picture's presentation attempts to meld two different genres of picture and to unify private and public aspects in such a way that the visual content is ultimately disconnected from both. The central conflict concerns the impossibility of reconciling "personal" content, which can only be fully understood within the microcommunicative setting of family idiom, with the journalistic conception of conveying content to an anonymous public. But if the pictures cannot possibly comment on or construct a direct reference to the family life of the Kennedys, what can they say that would be of public significance?

The icons of John F. and Jacqueline Kennedy are established with visual commentaries that merge their private and their public personae into pictorial symbols semantically loaded to such a degree that they lose reference to the real character of the two persons they represent, and also begin to blur any objective assessment of these persons' political status. Thus, the emotions stimulated by the narrative's account of Kennedy's assassination in Dallas appear to oscillate between personal and collective sympathy, as well as between empathy for his family and concern for the nation's political system, without finding any middle ground. It is fitting that the documentary closes the pictorial narrative on Kennedy with a lengthy piece of footage showing his widow answering condolences, the visual content of which scene accentuates the dilemma in the presentation of historical records between the personal impact and the public significance of her husband's death.

The restaging of Kennedy's iconization reveals structural aspects similar to those present in the case of Glenn. In both cases, historical footage of the unified spectacle is combined with pictorial gestures that are usually reserved for the private realm. Visual commentaries on small rituals, such as a homecoming, a vacation, or even a funeral, which, although already bordering on public acts, still address themselves to the confined idiomatic network of a family within its local community, complement broadcast spectacles of big events, which address themselves solely to society at large. As a result, the transmittership of the pictures appears submerged by the ritualistic mise en scène of icons in symbiosis with a socially unified, as well as politically relevant, spectacle. The private and public realms are symbolically merged in these nationally unified icons, whose aura owes much to their implied reference to real personalities. The main objective of the transmitters, correspondingly, is to apply these icons to the spectator's real emotions.

CONTROVERSIAL AND EXOTIC ICONS

The documentary's implicit rerun of the historical iconization process most often starts, as in the discussed examples, with footage that fulfills at least some of the outlined characteristics of the broadcast spectacle. This observation also applies to icons of non-American provenance. Icons such as Khrushchev, Castro, De Gaulle, and Brandt are all given such introduction by the documentary, although, as mentioned, without featuring the complete array of characteristics of the unified spectacle. While they are placed on center stage so as to prompt internalization of their visual contours, symbolic reference is never made to these foreign icons' private lives. By contrast, all the icons of American presidents from the 1950s on are pictured at least once beside their wives. The marriage between the deferential camera of the unified broadcast spectacle and the intimate, participatory camera especially typical of the 1960s news magazine is never implemented in the casting of non-American symbols. Even Britain's queen is never seen in conjunction with her husband or in any reference to her private life. The effect of these missing shots is never to evoke emotions that would facilitate viewer identification with these icons. When the historical footage is emotional, the emotions are controversial, as in the case of Khrushchev pounding his fists on a table at the UN or of Castro swinging his arm in an impassioned oratorical gesture. The latter shot, which marks the first casting of Castro's symbol in the documentary, is furthermore taken from an unusual angle that presents the politician from behind. From this perspective, revealing the audience he faces but no other insignia of the spectacle, the visual restaging of his icon therefore starts with an extravagant hand gesture, suggesting a speech driven by emotions that have been deflected into the political arena. Without audio reference to the actual speech and without background information on his well-known rhetorical skills, the visual message is marked by a distance that also characterizes the three subsequent purely pictorial representations of his icon. None of the three shots attempts to narrate any personal or historical aspects of Castro. In terms of the documentary's visual perspective on history, the icon may reflect not much more than a symbolic reference to the foe behind the Bay of Pigs and the Cuban Missile Crisis. In terms of the historicity subtending visual language, however, the introduction of his icon cannot correspond with the actual history of the symbol's first presentations on American screens, to say nothing of the icon's place in any visual literacy particular to Cubans. The documentary's use of the icon apart from historical context indicates, rather, the term's semantic significance in the early 1980s, including all the content it has accumulated since the original shots were taken. Analyzing the icon another twenty years later further disconnects the retrospective focus on Castro's swinging arm from its photographic anchor in history, given that the very same clip could be seen in a CNN documentary, as well as in an A&E biography of Ernest Hemingway, made in the late 1990s. On all these occasions, the pictures were used for the same purpose, as the first visual reference to the Cuban leader. The picture has thus became a symbol *in toto*, almost in the fashion of a famous verbal quote—albeit one without an identified author—that has continuing currency in its reference to a politician still alive and in power. This visual quote leaves no doubt about a predisposition toward the icon that has been written into its iconic contours for more than four decades.

The documentary stages another icon of a still living personality and suggests its semantic status through a very particular representation of its iconic career on American screens. This time concerning an American icon, the pictorial characterization of Muhammad Ali centers on footage taken from a press conference at which the boxer explained his refusal to serve in Vietnam. Although he is shown offering religious and political reasons for refusing to accept the Vietnamese people as his foe, the camera focus on his appearance makes a different argument. The camera repeatedly captures Ali, dressed in oriental clothing, awkwardly and childishly scratching his nose. The focus on this repetitive gesture is held for almost one-third of the clip's length. Since we are trained to control this type of behavior in public, there is a sense that Ali himself is responsible for his own unfavorable impression. However, the scene could have easily been edited out in the typical fashion of the unified spectacle, which would, for example, cut to the audience, media representatives, or single spectators present while letting the speech continue in the background. As in the case of Nhu's press conference, the implicating gesture may indicate the failure of an event's protagonist to control its display, ultimately only referencing those who control its translation into visual language and subsequent publication of what is conventionally hidden from public sight.

In all these cases, it could be argued that Castro indeed uses gestures to emphasize his words, that Ali was generally known for idiosyncratic behavior in front of the camera, and that Nhu must have applied her make-up in full consciousness of the camera's presence, but the historical use of these pictures by the documentary further highlights the gap between the

picture's symbolic message and the convention to see people as self-control-
ling agents. Or, to be more precise, broadcasters exploit this convention in
order to shade icons with their own meaning and significance. Certainly
not intended by those whom the icons represent, these pictures differ from
unified presentations not because they provide any information that could
be objectively isolated as predisposed, but through offering the possibility
to extract negative connotations. Although it is therefore problematic to
attempt any more specific evaluation of the messages' possible reception by
individual spectators, the predisposition can nevertheless be pinned on the
transmitters' side: with extraordinary consistency, historical personalities
such as Khrushchev, Castro, Ali, Nhu, and Carmichael are staged in visual
narratives that leave their visual symbols without individual depth, and render them as either controversial, or exotic, or both. With either missing or
controversial symbolic reference to the private, emotional sides behind their
public, professional appearance, their icons appear utterly devoid of familiar
characteristics that might allow assumptions about their personal motives
and intentions. As a consequence, these icons appear to speak less with
a personal voice, than with one driven by general, discursive convictions.
Unlike the icons of Glenn or Kennedy, which begin to stand not so much
for any particular political function, but for the idea of the extraordinary
individual, these icons remain distanced, curious, or even exotic in the contours of their appearance, as well as in their political motivation. Unlike the
unified mode that harmonizes the agenda of an event and its protagonists
with their visual mediation, including anticipation, if not determination,
of a generally positive response from audiences at home, the predisposed
form disperses the iconic lectern through anticipating a negative or at least
mixed response. The predisposed, controversial icons may still be significant
enough to attract a camera to their event, but they cannot command the deferential one that would endow their verbal argumentation, as well as their
personalities, with particular symbolic weight.

The very fact that the historical documentary is unable to transcend the
past predisposition toward these icons indicates the lasting effect of iconization, which once anchored in a controversial context seems to predispose
its term to attract further unfavorable angles of presentation. With regard
to symbols of foreign provenance, it should therefore be kept in mind that
while there may not be such a thing as a Cuban face in reality, there may
well be one in the two-dimensional world of American visual literacy (at
the same time as Castro's icon projects different semantic shades to eyes
informed by Cuban visual literacy).

THE AMBIVALENT FALL FROM GRACE

The documentary provides two historical accounts of personalities, Richard
Nixon and General MacArthur, who at one time found unified iconization,

before sliding into controversy. In both cases, the initial iconization evolves within the parameters of the unified spectacle, and in both cases, the documentary provides no pictures that would reveal the predisposed camera in the fashion of the previously discussed examples of Ali, Carmichael, or Castro. In the introduction to MacArthur's visual symbol, a participatory, "journalistic" camera presents him interacting with his military staff in the field, presumably a demonstration of his professional proficiency. His success as a general is then narrated in the form of rebroadcasting the pictures of the ticker-tape parade he received in New York upon his return from Asia. The historical footage features almost all the typical insignia of the unified spectacle and also allows a glimpse of his wife, who accompanied him at the parade. It is at this point that the documentary's voice-over commences to add a controversial note to the visual narrative of the hero's homecoming. Citing his insubordination to President Truman's orders and subsequent removal from command, the documentary cuts to footage of street interviews conducted by a journalist. The selected excerpts from the responses of some passersby, however, only reveal mild reservations about the general's conduct and furthermore include President Truman's handling of the situation in their critique. Criticism may thus be verbally expressed both by the voice-over and indirectly by the words of some selected contemporary citizens, but the presented visual narrative contains no controversial angle that would support or even anchor the verbal commentaries. None of the pictures features any of the bold, invasive symbolic predispositions of the camera toward the icon, as in the cases of Castro, Nhu, and Muhammad Ali. The questions of whether or not the general was actually responsible for an act of insubordination, and whether or not he thereby influenced the course of the war in Korea, are furthermore distanced from historical imagery that stages his icon in conjunction with favorable, unified symbols, which all point to his widespread public acceptance. In other words, both the original verbal and visual information of the historical footage itself, as well as the footage's recasting in the verbal context of the documentary, opens a peculiar divide between visual and verbal information that obstructs drawing any rational conclusions about the intention of the pictures' past and modern transmitters.

In the history of Nixon's rise and fall from the status of a unified icon, the documentary actually features two instances of slips into the mode of the controversial spectacle. Beside the Watergate scandal that initiated the end of his presidency, an early campaign finance scandal almost stopped his political career at the beginning. Aspiring to be Eisenhower's running mate in the early 1950s, he faced controversy over his handling of gifts and funds for the campaign. In what became famous as the "Checkers speech," Nixon went on television to seek the exoneration of the public. Presenting himself at home in the company of his wife, he succeeded in "privatizing" the scandal, using both visual and verbal language. While his wife remained the silent partner at his side, his verbal argument built on a metaphor that equated campaign contributions with personal gifts, in particular a dog given to his daughter by a well-meaning donor. This footage is outstanding, not only in that it actually succeeded in diverting the public's attention from the scandal and further accelerated the process of his iconization in unified fashion, but also in that these pictures constitute an example of controlled self-staging usually only possible in advertising and fictional productions. In place of the media's camera, a cameraman acting exclusively on Nixon's orders constructed the visual narrative of the Checkers speech. Yet, although he also paid for the broadcast of the footage on national television, the pictures' presentational context retains the status of communicating from a position of public relevance and significance generally ascribed to television broadcasters. Such implicit genre crossing, it appears, owes much to what has previously been termed the iconic lectern, generally assigned to unified icons. From this perspective, the ability of icons to attract public interest is thus paired once again with their potential to anchor verbal messages in a visual appearance that suggests unmediated, individual agency and authorship. It is as if the favorable mise en scène and the very fact that television presents him on the nation's screens not only enhance the significance of what is conveyed, but also contribute to the impression that he is addressing the public in direct, unmediated fashion.

When the documentary's visual narrative reaches the end of Nixon's political career, more than twenty years after the broadcast of the Checkers speech, spectators have undergone the process of becoming familiar with Nixon's icon based on thirty contexts of re-representations. Most of these settings—party conventions, presidential speeches, diplomatic encounters, receptions on gangways, and so forth—qualify for the category of the unified broadcast spectacle. While the icon of his wife makes a couple of further, albeit rather cursory appearances, there is only one other shot that presents Nixon from a "personal" side, which, however, is twice presented by the documentary. The shot dates back to the fifties and features Nixon and Eisenhower fooling around with a fishing rod. Apparently, the press was asked to join them at a fishing cabin and invited to document at least the beginning of the two icons' "private trip," which it did in a deferential fashion: the pictures construct a visual message that presents the two as "buddies" who are about to share some intimate days outdoors. While the two politicians are thus portrayed in a fashion symbiotic with their own agenda by making "public" a "private" ritual of friendship, there is little reason why the symbolic message of staged intimacy should extend to become a factual record about these historical personalities. However, the documentary recasts the footage in the segment on the 1970s in what appears to be a summary of Nixon's historical background for those who have not seen the previous segments, before turning to the topic of Watergate. While then offering a quite reasonable outline of the course of events by means of a carefully tuned verbal commentary, the subsequent footage never projects a controversial perspective on Nixon's icon that would in any way counter the preceding process of familiarizing spectators with his unified visual symbol. The most visually critical moment comes in footage commenting on his final parting from the White House: Nixon, climbing aboard a helicopter together with his wife, looks back to the camera for a "last time," before raising his arms in a typical victory gesture.

At this point, the documentary's verbal narrative and the visual narrative of the compiled historical footage on Nixon have reached opposing ends, given the selection of a picture that visually conveys a victorious icon. The discrepancy between the visual and the verbal at this point can only be harmonized by interpreting the gesture as a true reflection of Nixon's agency and character before the camera.[3] Here, it would thus be less the original transmittership responsible for selecting the gesture for broadcast, or the verbally outlined context of his fall from grace, but his own—either unconscious or ironic—admission of failure that speaks directly to viewers. That visual gesture, however, can ultimately only be interpreted in light of the previous restaging of his iconization in the unified mode. But this restaging included many positive pictorial messages, such as the self-manufactured and disseminated portrayal of his family life, many pictures taken in the context of broadcast spectacles, and many other media pictures that claim to present a consciously acting politician who speaks directly to audiences. In other words, while the documentary uses many historical clips to reconstruct an active iconic lectern for Nixon's public personality, that last clip suddenly asks spectators to see behind the icon and its reflection of an active public persona, in fact even behind the pictures themselves, to understand the significance of that victory gesture. In order to interpret the gesture as an unconscious reflection of Nixon's personality, spectators would ultimately have to ignore not only the role of those who selected the shot, but also Nixon's own part in the authorship of the visual message. In any case, the pictorial presentation of his career ends the way it began, that is with a focus on the person behind the public man. In this way, the pictorial narrative about the end of Nixon's career builds on an emotional relationship with his icon that might allow speculation about his character and motivation, but leaves aside any critical interpretation of either his private or his political personality. The selected pictures enhance the emotional aura of the icon by focusing on the fate of an individual person, rather than on the ramifications of corruption at the top of the nation's two-party system.

Similar to the unified icon of Kennedy, MacArthur's and Nixon's icons ultimately never encounter the predisposed camera typical of the controversial spectacle. Comparison to the mise en scène of other icons appears once again as the only way to negotiate past the symbolic message of these pictures and to identify the inherent predisposition in the handling of visual language. The documentary never constructs controversial icons with any direct reference to a private personality behind their professional image, which effectively limits not only the semantic depth of their visual symbols, but also the possibility of viewer identification. Or, when turned around, the pictures of Nixon's "misplaced gesture" can only be fully understood in their symbolic potential as a direct reference to his mind and character, which reference demonstrates a different type of iconization than could possibly be at work in the representation of moral or political complicity. As a consequence of these observations, it can be concluded that political motivations effect the status initially afforded to an icon, and that the politically influenced contours of an icon's first appearance into visual literacy will have a continued effect across its entire iconic career.

The documentary's narratives of both Nixon's and MacArthur's rise and fall from the national stage appear dominated by pictures of the unified spectacle, which develop their icon's semantic status so as partially to obstruct their degradation to the controversial, predisposed type. Unlike the controversial icons, they not only retain traces of their originally favorable iconic initiation, but also continue to apply these traces to their referent personality, which application influences the communicative potential of any other pictures in which they are cast, including the re-presentation of historical ones. As the only two cases in which the documentary attempts to cast a controversial shadow on unified icons, these examples also give further indication of a divide between visual and verbal information. This divide both points to the particular symbolic workings of visual language's historical codes, and also suggests that these historical pictures still contain original traces of their transmitters' opinion. The mode of their original mediation apparently inscribes denotation and connotation on the visual terms, and this inscription influences their further use to the point of impacting even a historical perspective on them.

Beyond the nationalistic discourse that is active in the presentation of either unified or controversial icons, another discourse also acts to shape icons' semantic contours.

GENDERED PERSPECTIVES

The documentary presents not one female American icon that could definitively be termed controversial. There are, however, a couple of instances of visual symbols of women, such as the spectator singled out in the footage on Carmichael's speech, which are disposed to reflect controversially on an event and its main icon. The only controversial icon of a woman in the period between 1950 and 1980 is the exotic "Madame Nhu," whose husband and brother-in-law, the Catholic leaders of South Vietnam's minority government, were assassinated by the CIA. Her brief moments in the limelight of American cameras, however, are given a treatment in the documentary that merges more than one discursive angle. Close to the predisposed, controversial spectacle, the iconization of her appearance seems not only incomplete, but also marked by the curious gesture of publicly applying make-up. It is no longer possible to reconstruct whether Nhu intended her action, in some ways appropriate to the spectacle, since make-up is designed to attract the gaze, in some ways not, since its application is supposed to be private and discreet to influence the resulting visual narrative. In any case, a curious cameraman jumped at the occasion, as did the documentary's presenter, who presumably used the shot to underline symbolically a verbal statement about corruption reigning in her husband's and brother-in-law's government. There is a tendency, in American visual histories of Vietnam, not to introduce any icons of its male leaders in either the North or South; the documentary's presentation of Nhu's icon is therefore an isolated, exotic symbolic representation of that country's politics. While controversial icons have so far referenced politically active personalities, the only female icon of such background is presented in a gesture dedicated to the passive function of appearing. Obstructing, furthermore, any emotional sympathy with her quite tragic personal fate, the constructed visual message deflects any political reading of her visit to America into a focus on her unseemly "appearance" in public. John Berger's conclusion dating from the early seventies that women are believed to appear rather than to act thus seems inscribed in the predisposed perspective on her icon, which renders a private gesture made public as a commentary on her female political persona.[4]

The general, rather archetypal notion of women as appearing rather than acting in the public sphere appears as an integrated, almost generic motif of the broadcast spectacle. Visual symbols of female spectators were apparently a favorite focus of the historic camera when commenting on events. On many occasions, shots that either entirely focus on the audience as a crowd, or at least include it as a major symbolic theme, are accompanied with pans that single out female spectators as the pictures' main rheme (what is said about the theme). Particularly in the realm of 1960's sports, the footage appears almost destined to showcase selected visual symbols of women wearing the latest fashions, including sunglasses. To the innocent viewer, these visual symbols would begin to communicate the general identity of the crowd according to the rule of symbolic transfer. To all those familiar with the broadcast conventions of the 1960s, they certainly did not indicate the typical character of predominantly male audiences, but a typical facet of the broadcast spectacle. Attracting the gaze and simultaneously emphasizing another, female gaze at the main, mostly masculine protagonists of an event, the trope of the female spectator writes gender discourses into the typical, self-evident imagery of the broadcast spectacle. When trying to assume the perspective of the women behind their visual symbols, such narratives follow the pattern of "the surveyor and the surveyed," which according to Berger are "the two constituent yet always distinct elements" of female identity in the public sphere.[5] Such an assessment of the historical discourse on gender identity applies even more forcefully for the pictures used to recall exceptional female icons, such as Marilyn Monroe. In the documentary's compilation, Monroe is seen posing in front of cameras, photographers, and reporters, as well as in conjunction with the only non-American icon of nearly unified status, Queen Elizabeth, but she is never heard speaking.

Queen Elizabeth is actually the second most represented woman in the documentary, behind Jacqueline Kennedy, but like Monroe she remains mute.
Among the shots restoring the queen's iconic contours are the television
spectacle of her coronation in 1953, two instances where her icon is singled
out as a celebrity spectator of sports events, and two shots of handshakes,
one with the first black woman to win Wimbledon, the American Althea
Gibson, and one in a truly iconic meeting with Marilyn Monroe. Having
completed the process of the queen's iconization for the modern spectator,
the documentary actually uses the shot of her handshake with Monroe to
initiate the restaging of the actress's iconization. In this fashion, one solely
pictorially presented woman introduces another silent female icon to the
visual history books.

Almost without exception, the documentary introduces female icons in
purely visual fashion, whether in a unified or more controversial perspective. Betty Friedan is mentioned but not visually identified or iconized, and
apart from Eleanor Roosevelt, who can briefly be heard speaking in a political ad supporting Kennedy's campaign for presidency, there is no female
speech on political topics—leaving aside, for the moment, the incomprehen-
sible snippets taken from Nhu's press conference. In the unified spectacle,
many presidential wives may find visual coverage in the ritual role of "First
Lady," but beside Claudia ("Lady Bird") Johnson's icon, which appears
on seven occasions, only that of Jacqueline Kennedy is supported by an
iconic lectern and thus granted unified status in national visual literacy. Yet
although she is the second most represented visual symbol in the segment
between 1960 and 1965, her icon is never presented in conjunction with
words that would indicate her political thinking. She can actually be heard
speaking twice, once in Greek on the occasion of a reception in Athens, and
once for a respectable sixty seconds in which she thanks the public for its
response to her husband's death. The second speech comes at the end of a
lengthy portrayal of her engagement in restoring the White House. For the
occasion, the footage presents her as an admiring beholder of Leonardo
da Vinci's Mona Lisa. The painting, which carries its own universal icon,
is being lent to the White House by André Malraux, France's minister of
culture. The focus ignores the little-known French guest, and centers on the
juxtaposition of the two icons "Jacqueline" and "Mona Lisa." Marking
the center of Jacqueline Kennedy's iconization in the documentary's narrative, the pictorial content of this iconic encounter once again plays with
the camera's gaze at a woman spectator, whose own gazing at Mona Lisa
thereby converts her from the surveyed to the surveyor. Furthermore, visual
language's rule of symbolic transfer is once again implemented to amplify
the aura and significance of both icons. As part of the process of iconization,
similar iconic conjunctions have already been observed in the case of Glenn
honored by Kennedy and of Nixon and Eisenhower fishing. However, the
conjunction of male with female icons in particular figures the symbolic
transfer as a "marriage of icons," which figure was consistently utilized by

the broadcasters of the historical footage. The documentary presents many of its female icons as wives of political leaders, and also dedicates plenty of footage to celebrity weddings, such as those of Grace Kelly to Prince Rainier, of Farah Dibah to the Shah of Persia, of Pricilla to Elvis Presley, and of President's Johnson's daughter, Luci Baines to Patrick John Nugent. Either initiating an iconic career or accentuating the status of an established one, the pictorial content of such footage not only provides the documentary with the chance to stage an "instant iconization" for all those who may have forgotten a particular set of iconic contours, but also places the icon in the favorable context of a culturally embraced ritual. Yet, at the same time as the context of a marriage anchors these icons within a particular community, it also transfers the ritual's display into the anonymous limelight of society in general. Transcending the classic distinction between the private and the public sphere in the genre of the unified broadcast spectacle, these pictures also demonstrate the severe limitation of the accepted role for women on the public stage.[6]

In summarizing these observations, the presentation of female icons within the compiled historical footage differs from that of men in that women almost exclusively appear in the passive role of attracting the gaze. With the exception of Eleanor Roosevelt in her appearance in the political advertising spot, they also remain without a distinct lectern for political argumentation. Women are implemented as the perfect symbolic complement to the spectacle in the role of spectators who are themselves observed. Maybe best illustrated in the shot of the queen as a celebrity spectator of a horse race, but also evident in many pictures that single out fashionable young women in various audiences, the female gaze at the male protagonists of an event appears an institutionalized part of the broadcast spectacle in the 1950s and 1960s. Similarly, the few female icons in the realm of national politics are all cast in the passive, supporting role of first lady, again with the exception of the footage of Eleanor Roosevelt, who continued her political work after the death of her husband. With public references to the private life as the sole indicator of the female unified icon, only Jacquelyn Kennedy's symbol would qualify for such iconization. Moreover, the documentary characterizes her as the "beautiful wife at the side of Kennedy" rather than as the mother of his children. The footage of her Greek address and the juxtaposition of her symbol with the ominous smile of Mona Lisa combine to present her icon as an exotic or inscrutable object of admiration. Thus her icon is given difficult ground for unified identification, at least by comparison to that generally accorded to male icons.[7]

While the reflexive status of female icons as both admiring and being admired adds to the significance of the past broadcast spectacle and its predominantly male protagonists, the passivity inscribed on these symbols through their staging deposits aspects of discourse on gender within the terms of visual language, as the term "mankind" does in written language, or for that matter the term "cameraman," often used here.[8] One of the main differences as compared to such verbal or written deposits of historical discourse, however, is visual language's more direct incorporation of society's current themes into its vocabulary, at least when taking the documentary as a fairly typical and recent collection of symbols and icons of American visual literacy.

EXOTIC VIEWS

Against the background of a visual literacy marked predominantly by the display of American events and American icons, it is certainly no coincidence that spectacles and icons of foreign provenance never find as dense a symbolic tapestry of meanings as those categorized here as unified. For this reason, the visual symbols of foreign personalities, such as France's De Gaulle or Germany's Brandt, may not even be classifiable as icons, but if they are recognized, carry rather curious and exotic aspects for similar reasons to those at work in the presentation of Jacqueline Kennedy's icon. De Gaulle and Brandt are neither iconized in any private context, nor presented in any active role at the center of a well-known event, but appear in the supplementary "female" role of hosting the male icon of Kennedy, who is touring Europe on a diplomatic mission. Emerging through this contrast between a national, unified icon and a foreign one, is therefore a relation between a more active and more passive mise en scène, which leaves a deposit on the grammatical mechanism of symbolic transfer: When the most well-known symbol marks the focal or starting point of a picture's message, it also sets the theme to which all other featured signs and symbols contribute information. If some icons are only featured in the vicinity of a more well-known, more actively placed icon, they also tend toward the passive end according to the grammar of symbolic transfer, meaning that the more radiant icon casts his connotations on the lesser-known, even if these can also contribute to further enhancing the glow of their superior.[9]

Between the oppositions assumed by nationally unified and foreign exotic status, active and passive footing also concerns the controversial icon. In terms of the gendered perspective, the only female symbols presented by the documentary in ambiguous context are those of the spectator at Carmichael's Black Power event and the notorious one of Nhu. Typically, the female icon of the latter is not juxtaposed with an (either male or female) admirer, while the former's ecstatic gestures relate strangely to the political agenda of the male icon at center stage. Nhu's gesture of applying make-up appears as an atypical and exotic act against the background of political appearance on America's public stage. The pictorial reference to her actions, similar to the example of the black spectator at Carmichael's speech, is ultimately turned against her intentions and comments not so much on her personal and political motives as indirectly on the agency of male politicians. According to Joan Scott, the mise en scène of such female agency in the public not only casts a predisposed angle on femininity, but also in a mirroring effect mobilizes characteristics of masculinity.[10] In the conventional scheme of such a mirror effect, female activity projects male passivity and vice versa. Edward Said also characterized the classic Western discourse toward the Orient in terms of this mirror effect, and both gendered and colonialist discourses are evident in the pictorial representation of Nhu.[11] In the absence of any attempt to iconize Diem or, for that matter, Ho Chi Minh, the mise en scène of Vietnam is composed of pilots who crash their helicopters "in panic" as well as the exotic, beauty-conscious "Madame Nhu." These pictures not only satisfy the curious eye but also stage Vietnamese masculinity as driven by emotion, rather than by reason, and, with regard to Nhu as the sole pictorial portrayal of the country's leadership, even as effeminate in terms of classic stereotypes.

By the same standard, the curious behavior of Carmichael's female fan also does little to stage his masculine agency in a flattering symbolic perspective. Unlike the many white female spectators in footage of unified broadcast spectacles, the only colored female admirer gazes at her idol not through expensive, fashionable sunglasses, but through normal, horn-rimmed glasses. Out of all the documentary's footage of the Civil Rights Movement, only Martin Luther King receives a unified iconic lectern. Presented when holding a speech before a quarter of a million spectators at the March on Washington, his icon is staged with the typical insignia of the historical broadcast spectacle but, nevertheless, is not fully contoured in the typical fashion of the unified male icon, since angles on his private life as well as (positive) symbols of the admiring female gaze are missing. Besides Carmichael, the other icons in the area of black American politics, those of H. Rap Brown and Muhammad Ali, are never given the private angle, nor the symbolic transfer to passive female beauty that would symbolize their masculinity in conventional fashion nor is there any pictorial support for Ali's repeated, quite ironic, proclamations of his own, male beauty. Among the some two hundred historical icons featured by the documentary, barely 5% are of black American provenance, and even the two most prominent ones, those of King and Ali, are not as often featured as the average "meta"-icon.[12] Arguably corresponding with the general presence of black American symbols on historical screens, the effect with regard to general visual literacy is thus a more thinly woven net of symbolic characteristics for the part of white American visual literacy pertaining to black culture. In view of visual language's historical codes, the rare presence of black American symbols on historical screens may be reason enough for the documentary to stamp these with atypical, curious, if not exotic vectors of meaning.

An example of the exotic presence of black symbols on historical screens is provided by the footage of a baseball game recorded in the 1950s. The historical cut presented by the documentary is edited in the typical fashion of the unified spectacle, switching back and forth between the audience and game action, cutting twice to spectator shots of a quite young, well-dressed black spectator with a cigar, who stands up from his seat to cheer the action on the field. Like the female spectators in their fashionable sunglasses, the black spectator standing in the ranks of a predominantly white audience, wearing a fashionable suit, and smoking a cigar, must have been aware of his power to attract attention, of being a surveyed surveyor of the game. Whatever his intention and motives, his assigned role compares directly to that of female symbols in the public sphere: both attract attention in accordance with the limited role assigned to them in public places. At a time when many states still regulated the presence of black people in the public sphere, the very presence of the black man's symbol in the ranks of predominantly white spectators suggests a misplacement that parallels the traditional female limitations to act in public and highlights the discursive relation between gender and the exotic.

The exotic view of the black spectator allows an atypical mediation of a unified event of predominantly white male provenance. But while the shot's atypical and rather curious relation to the classic insignia of the spectacle may accentuate the pictures' somewhat coincidental projection of (exotic) significance, it could also be argued that the young man's action was originally intended to make a controversial, political statement directed, for example, at the slow desegregation of baseball. Yet whether or not such intention determined the man's action, the pictorial narrative obstructs such an interpretation through emphasizing the power of an exotic symbol to attract attention, rather than through proposing any identification with the individual character of the agency and motives of the man. Thus, any political dimension in this shot resides in the symbol itself as it falls within visual literacy's triangle of the unified, the controversial, and the exotic: a triangle of signification that accords the unified symbols and icons with active, self-determined agency that gradually dissolves in the case of the controversial and then the exotic symbols and icons.

Although the documentary generally appears quite cautious when verbally commenting on black American history and dedicates much attention to the Civil Rights Movement of the 1960s, as well as to its most well-known icon, Martin Luther King, Jr., such attentiveness is contrasted by the visual narratives of the selected historical footage and the often controversial or exotic status of black icons and symbols. When covering the government's "war on drugs" in the 1970s, the footage visually identifies the problem with a series of cuts featuring black soldiers smoking marijuana or fixing heroine in their tents in Vietnam, before sequencing two further cuts to document increasing drug use by white middle-class students. The editing of these pictures could carry the symbolic message that the drug problem was imported by the Army, but the symbolic emphasis on drug-using black soldiers who wear their uniform improperly draws the narrative in another direction. This last example demonstrates that not only the presentational transmitter, but also the status of the presented symbols in collective visual literacy can override a "journalistic commentary," that verbal and visual messages can venture in opposite directions, and that visual symbols can smooth such contradictions when seen as an unmediated reflection of people's agency. When asking why these men let themselves be filmed consuming drugs in their tents, any reference to in-front-of-the-camera reality appears disconnected from the pictures' communicative potential. The conventional assumption that their symbols represent acting individuals also dissolves: As in the case of Nhu's act of applying make-up, it simply appears nonsensical to see these soldiers as an active part of a visual message that can only negatively reflect on their agency and personality. On the one hand, the conventional construction and presentation of such pictures posit self-determined agency in front of the camera through the implication that these men are responsible for their appearance. On the other hand, any reference to such individual agency behind the presented symbols is rendered obsolete by the supervening intention that ultimately motivated the presenters to select and present the clip to public eyes. At the same time, however, the significance of such pictures cannot securely be reduced to any communicative intention on the presentational side, if only for the obvious reason that the documentary's producers believed in the potential of their historical pictures to reflect reality-based significance.

Given the character of the compiled imagery, it can be assumed that one of the most prominent criteria for selecting the shots solely concerned their potential to attract the eye. In this reading, the presenters of the documentary selected their source material based on an evaluation of its potential as spectacle. If true, then the imagery's communicative significance resides not so much in the agency of those in front of the camera, as in that of the cameramen, that of the presenters not in reality or history, but in the dynamics of visual literacy. The established methodological framework of unified, controversial, and exotic visual symbols, icons, and spectacles would therefore specify a dynamic structure that guides pictorial significance by what compares to connotations in the realm of the verbal. Although those who select the shots based on their individual criteria are certainly in the position to communicate their own preferences, the connotations of visual literacy are ultimately managed collectively. As not only those who select pictures, but also those who watch them share in the process of collecting visual literacy, the typifying of their meanings is a dynamic, integrated part of their communicative structure. Against the background of the previously described logic of collecting, not only every new addition, but also every exhibition can change the relation between the collectibles, rendering some as "worn out," while a previously inconspicuous element all of a sudden requires special attention. In this up and down flow, the triadic criteria of the exotic, the controversial, and the unified appear to be an inherent part of the logic of typifying connotative significance. It is through inscribing the logic of collecting into the terms of visual literacy that these criteria can also provide a structure to interpret the documentary's imagery, in the absence of the classic standard of objectivity.

8 The Historicity of the Documentary's Imagery

The documentary's compilation of visual history parallels the rise of television to the nation's dominant medium by providing an image bank of around 2500 still pictures and clips that, broadly estimated, project some 10,000 generic visual symbols.[1] Of these, roughly 200 constitute icons when evaluated not by individual standards of visual literacy, but by the visual and verbal presentation of the documentary. Only twenty-three of them are cast on multiple occasions, reflecting the documentary's limited restaging of the historical iconization of these visual symbols, that is, how and on what occasions they became known to American audiences. By contrast, there are fewer emblems and their historical status is neither specifically introduced nor mentioned in any way. The implication is that all modern viewers of the documentary are familiar with the communicative history of the featured emblems, and that their semantic field has not been subject to any significant changes. The American flag is the most frequently depicted emblem, followed by army helicopters, the White House, the Capitol building, the UN building in New York, an array of emblematic references to Washington's Mall, and those standing for the national government, for example, the emblem decorating the presidential lectern. The latter symbol, as well as most castings of the flag, often relate with a series of symbols that have previously been defined as the insignia of the spectacle, such as shots of television and other cameras, the general audience and individual spectators, and camera flashes. When combined to forge an emblematic depiction of the broadcast spectacle, together with the icons whose stage they set, they represent almost 10% of all the featured visual symbols, meaning that much of the compiled historical imagery projects highly elaborated significance to those possessing the corresponding visual literacy.

Much more than reflecting on the history of America, the documentary's imagery thus provides a 1980s cross-section through thirty years' collecting of national visual literacy. The historical perspective thereby fuels the ongoing process needed to add novel shades of meaning and significance to visual terms in order to keep them active in modern visual literacy. Another effect of iconization that complicates the possibility of displaying visual history in the mode of the documentary concerns the collecting processes at the root of visual literacy in conjunction with the conventional tendency to see real people in two-dimensional visual symbols. This tendency is evoked during any reference to the neutral, unerring technical eye of the camera. Unified icons not only seem to be able to command deferential pictorial commentaries, their more extensive narrative contextualization, including their privileged presentation in the context of symbols of private life, also effects to render these symbols more vivid and certainly more powerful than controversial or exotic ones. By comparison, the latter appear much more disposable in the hands of broadcasters, and their semantic baggage and the narrative of their personality appear much more unfinished. It is thus as if the thinner semantic background of the controversial and the exotic icons also incorporates an element of passivity into their contours. This observation is also corroborated by the fact that the documentary almost exclusively accords a voice only to unified icons. It can thus be observed that the more familiar an icon and the more unified in scope, the more it can command a distinguished public lectern from which the portrayed personalities can be seen and heard directly according to their own intentions, as opposed to serving the communicative intentions of those who chose to present them.

Such observations qualify the presenters, in this case the historical documentary in combination with those responsible for the shots first broadcast, less as conveyors of information, than first of all as drivers of the typifying processes beneath visual literacy: Assuming that these presenters chose the selected pictures by anticipating their power to create spectacular sights for audiences, there is consequently a tendency to feature the established, tried-and-true spectacle and thus the unified symbols more often than the exotic ones, whose power to attract the eye rests more in the rarity of their sight. This process would thus favor symbols that are already initiated by repeated exposure, thereby further adding to their semantic richness, their future power to attract the eye, and their ability to anchor every picture as the most established narrative component. As a consequence, this form of accelerated iconization also betters the symbols' chances to achieve a unified status in visual literacy at large, and thus to become what could also be called fixed terms in the vernacular of American visual language.

If true, however, the particular logic of collecting and typifying not only concerns the narrative potential of distinguished icons and emblems, but also that of the many more generic visual symbols featured by the documentary's imagery. Visual symbols such as houses, trees, highways, clothes, but also those of unknown faces, of particular gestures, facial expressions, and so forth expound significance and meanings that are distinct to a society's culturing of visual language. Although less specific in content than those regulated by the iconic code, these types of visual symbols are nevertheless collected over time and classified according to their visual characteristics. Correspondingly, more typical symbols, for example that of a Victorian house, relay more refined meaning than those with more atypical characteristics, which are consequently less often encountered on screen. By the same standards as described for icons, a unique presentation of a rare piece of architecture renders the structure first of all as an exotic symbol of a house that is consequently also more susceptible to inviting controversial responses than more established, familiar symbols. The logic responsible for such a phenomenon appears to rest again in the collecting and ordering mechanisms that regulate the typifying of the symbols' visual characteristics in ways that can also be described as "thick" or "thin," much in the way that anthropologist Clifford Geertz used this differentiation for methodologically informed observation.[2] In conjunction with the proposed dynamic of visual literacy, the very existence of informed eyes problematizes the documentary's attempt to use pictures as a mirror of history, since pictures are made of symbols that themselves engage a historical dynamic in order to appeal to the visual literacy that is responsible for understanding the pictorial mirror in the first place.

When the documentary thus takes the viewers to ride the time machine back to the Vietnam War, showing, for example, the scenery of a Vietnamese street with Vietnamese houses, such pictorial documents necessarily project less detailed information and much thinner associations than would similar pictures of an American street. In American visual language, the featured houses in Vietnam can hardly communicate, for example, the distinctive symbol of the average farmer's home as opposed to that of a poor industrial worker. Western visual literacy can hardly trace their particular connotations, such as, for example, those of a particularly cozy, homey place, as opposed to any normal house. In the same way, because the icon of Ho Chi Minh—not to mention the iconization of the leader of the Vietnamese troops—is missing from the documentary's imagery, all the "little" Vietnamese symbols of facial expressions, of typical and atypical gestures, and so forth, tend to escape informed typifying. The communicative effect of these pictures in the presence of such a thin basis for typifying their potential significance is thus similar to that of the exotic or (possibly) controversial icons and emblems, without, however, these "little" symbols ever finding the attention necessary to develop their semantic field. One of the consequences of this logical mechanism of visual language would therefore be that in all pictures of Vietnam only American symbols, such as the chopper, the uniforms, the jeeps, the well-known faces of American journalists, and so forth, actually communicate informed significance to American-trained visual literacy—which communicative power also renders them "grammatically" more active than the signs and symbols of the exotic scenery. The historical background pictures brought home by journalists from Vietnam consequently lack the ability to address the visual literacy of general American audiences in ways that would allow the pictures to provide accurate information, for example, that combat was taking place in a typically middle-class Vietnamese location. When conveyed to distanced eyes, the exotic symbols in such pictures not only obstruct possible identification, but also limit the communicative potential of their content, thus conflicting with the purpose of conveying factual information.[3]

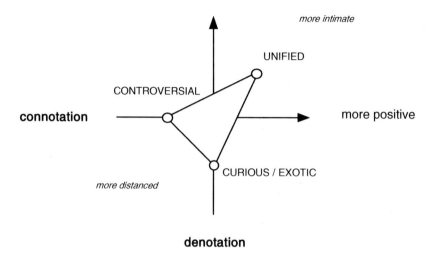

Figure 8.1. Aggregated denotations and connotations of visual symbols.[4]

In concluding these observations, it can be stated that the logic of collecting, including the triadic classifying scheme of the unified, the controversial, and the exotic, suggests a special connection between the semantic depth of the symbols' denotations and their connotations with regard to those symbols that are used the most regularly. Just because the terms of visual literacy depend on the dynamic aggregation of semantic contours in order to sustain meaningful use, it is this dynamic itself that needs to be a logical part of regulating both their basic denotation, i.e., "house," and their connotations, i.e., a "cozy" or "middle-class" house.

Pictures that appear the most sophisticated in their ability to refer to areas of visual literacy that carry the thickest tapestry of historically aggregated meanings have the strongest communicative potential. Therefore, the particular denotations and connotations of visual symbols have an impact on their use for communicative and, in particular, journalistic purposes. When a pictorial message is conveyed as impartial documentation of an event, its visual symbols need to make reference not only to the narrative's actual relation to an event, but also to the particular visual literacy of the addressed audience. Exclusively left to unspecified visual literacy, however, visual symbols assume significance in a somewhat haphazard fashion, that is, each receiver must "make do" by speculating about the symbols' reality reference or referring them to individually gathered expertise. For this reason, the increased use of the moving picture as an impartial source of public information tends to conflict with the symbolic logic of visual literacy. This conflict is also evident when trying to differentiate historical substance from the documentary's imagery.

But the conflict between viewing the documentary's imagery as a window into history and as an etymological ride through American visual literacy is most obvious in those instances in which icons still known today are (re)introduced as historical: The perception of all those pictures that gradually distinguish the contours of icons from other, more general visual symbols can simply not be reenacted by the historical documentary. Because of this insurmountable gap between an original, shade-by-shade process of acquiring and typifying iconic significance and the more or less consciously constructed (re)introduction of such icons as visual history, these terms of visual language develop intriguing properties: they start moving back and forth in history. We know the icon of John F. Kennedy, for example, before the documentary actually introduces his visual features, and we see the future president in them when they first appear, although that first appearance serves to introduce another man as the candidate of the Democratic Party. And this is only a fraction of all the conflicts that arise when trying to see (past) reality in symbols, of which the semantic baggage includes thousands of presentations in thousands of different pictorial contexts and narratives, some of them possibly also including pictures from different genres, such as family pictures or even fictional productions.

On the visual plane alone, the possibility of genre crossing, as in the example of the well-known Hollywood icon of James Stewart taking a stand against McCarthyism, further juxtaposes the historicity of visual language with the documentary's implied function of mirroring American history. The example highlights the particular status of icons that have accumulated significance from past fictional and nonfictional pictorial representations, and can indiscriminately access the accumulated significance when encountered anew. When an icon such as that of James Stewart has become characterized from many fictional angles, not only have its facial expressions, gestures, and so forth been familiarized by many "intimate" perspectives comparable to those accorded to the unified icons of the political world, but it has also relied all along on the participatory camera of the movie set. According to Robert Hanke, television "often blurs history and fiction" and "conflates historicity and contemporaneity."[5] This same principle needs also to be applied evaluatively to the documentary's more general visual symbols as in the discussed example of a Vietnamese street, since historical symbols can operate semantically through familiarity gained in contemporary, fictional movies.

Having so far focused predominantly on historical visual literacy as the logical heart of an American visual language in the making, part C, "Hyperrealism," elaborates not only on the power of visual symbols to move backward and forward in history, but also on their ability to step left and right over that ominous borderline between fiction and nonfiction.

Part C
Hyperrealism

9 Pictorial Supremacy

When commercial television was inaugurated in the late 1940s it immediately captured the attention of the nation. Unlike radio, which had to earn nationwide recognition, television's role in the American public sphere was anticipated from the beginning and was eagerly heralded until, by the 1960s, almost every citizen had access to a screen. Thus, with astonishing speed and virtually no resistance, the televised picture became the main carrier of cultural and political exchange in twentieth-century society. New uses of the photograph in scientific exploration, lithography, and the motion picture had laid the groundwork. But the broadcast picture exceeded all previous photographic media in its potential to bring all forms of social and cultural interaction into immediate proximity. Almost inevitably and without further reflection, the novel frame assumed the role of a national clearinghouse for virtually every previously used form of visual communication.

The uniquely powerful status of television, as a provider of both entertainment and information, built implicitly on the picture as the defining element. But since the televised picture often communicates through a presentation of other sign systems, such as written language, the effect of the logic of visual literacy and the principles of visual language upon these other systems must be taken into account. Setting aside for a moment audio systems, in the documentary, the on-screen picture easily subsumes written signs, such as the name of a restaurant or the lines describing an advertised product, the headlines of a newspaper or even a message on the news ticker at Times Square, as well as the graphical codes of traffic signs, an orchestra conductor's specialized gestures, or the commonly practiced gestures of body language in general. This subsuming of the written and almost all other practiced languages and sublanguage systems under the visual frame of the screen certainly demonstrates something other than a simple addition of different sign systems.

In about a dozen instances, the documentary *History of the 20th Century* features the signs of a newspaper's front page. With these shots, the documentary comments on the product of another medium, while incorporating its signifiers into the visual syntax of the screen. While these shots often only allow a glimpse of the newspaper's name and its main headlines, the filmed words seem often to convey information that would be difficult if not impossible to illustrate by visual language alone, as when, for example, they describe the slim margin of an election outcome, or reveal the mental problems of Thomas Eagelton, the running mate of George McGovern in 1972. To this extent, the documentary's presentation may actually reveal the inability of visual language to translate certain aspects of social and political life into pictorial expressions, at least in the nonfictional, informing mode of the photographic picture. In any case, the use of text to fill in for the invisible creates a quite complex communicative construct. Similar to the way the shots are contextualized as a direct window to historical reality, the filming of a newspaper's historical printed text suggests the unfolding of factual written content, but while the letters are still decoded based on the principles of written language, they also commence to signify according to the rules of visual language, which embeds the written signs in a mutual relationship with all other signs featured by the picture. (See also the section, "The Verbal, the Written, and the Visual" in the appendix.) The portrayed letters assume a double function, both as written signs and as visually specifying the outspread newspaper as a symbol. It might be a symbol of American newspapers in general, or, if the paper is the *New York Times,* it might be the emblem of a single, historically established institution with a more particular semantic profile and an enhanced communicative significance. The visual logic of the screen consequently provides the written word with a symbolic lectern designated to reference another authorship and, at the same time, to establish the factual status of what is conveyed in a quite anonymous (visual) mode. An intersecting layer laid down in the act of photographing thus begins to "overcode" the written with the logic of visual language, ultimately drawing the words into the realm of visual symbols and absorbing their authorship. In another manifestation of split transmittership, the act of presenting the newspaper's front page characterizes less the opinion of past journalists than of those who selected the shot and chose those journalists' words for communicating in a new context. What interferes with such a reading, however, is once again the technical notion of the camera's establishing of factual proof in combination with the conventional objectivity of the newspaper's written words, as if pictorial logic enforces the factuality of all communicated content. In another example taken from the documentary, six newspapers are thrown one on top of the other, barely allowing recognition of their names and/or some words of their main headlines, announcing the dismissal of General MacArthur by President Truman. The historical fact is illustrated through the written signs and, on top of these, a visual gesture. The gesture, of piling up, symbolizes rather than references a "mountain of evidence" or an "incontrovertible argument." Ultimately, these pictures simply imply the need of something to be proved, once symbolically in the form of the gesture, and once through implying the trustworthiness of the newspaper medium in conjunction with television's own authority for informing the public.

Such examples of the medium of television commenting on the medium of the newspaper seem not only to provide historical content but also to insinuate a certain superiority of television over the print medium. The very ability to choose and utilize newspapers and their written content for its own purposes indicates the privileged position of the television screen among the nation's main media. It also underlines television's, and with it the picture's, ascent to representing a central clearinghouse of societal communication. The semiotic point of view, however, needs to call into question the quite complex proposal of a harmonic, if not symbiotic coexistence of written, verbal, and other sign systems on the television screen.

THE VERBAL, THE WRITTEN, AND THE VISUAL

Pairing verbal with visual language was nothing new when television arrived, but in assuming the role as clearinghouse of public communication, the screen added to cinema and its newsreels the possibility of taking the viewer to all possible places at any given time. The continuous stream of daily programming was a novel situation for the screen, and thus demanded introducing pictures in novel ways. The cinema theater generally relied on the eventlike context of presenting newsreels in conjunction with a feature movie that had usually been advertised in advance. With the insertion of a break when changing reels and the ability to lower and raise the curtain again, together with titles and the other written signs of opening credits, any contextual difference between fictional movies and nonfictional newsreels could be securely marked. By contrast, television's ability to project a continuous flow of pictures demanded new ways of contextualizing the presented visual signs within the frame of the screen.[1] In what appears as a direct consequence of the missing external context, television imported the "master of ceremonies" into the two-dimensional world of the screen in the form of all types of announcers, such as anchormen, talk show moderators, and so forth. In addition to the role of contextualizing the pictures from within, these masters of ceremonies also perform the task of unifying visual and verbal signs through the presentation of a talking person on the hinge between fictional and nonfictional, artistic and nonartistic, and/or live or canned broadcasts.

Strictly speaking, broadcasters interconnect visual symbols and icons with corresponding audio in a comprehensive merging of two different techniques. The act of merging voice and image can only reflect theoretically on a context external to the visual world of the screen, such as a real person speaking, because, theoretically, the broadcasters themselves have furnished the person's lectern. The appearance of unity between verbal and visual signs on screen may appear commonsensical with regard to the mode of human perception, but it nevertheless emerges from the creative act of producing and presenting the broadcast, which incorporates a new transmittership, and likewise forges a new context for the communicated content. Against the background of such observations, it is interesting to note that theoretical conceptions of the combination of visual with written or verbal language often propose verbal and written language as the rational anchor of visual signs, as stated by, among others, Barthes.[2] This view, however, concerns only cases of speech or writing, such as a verbal commentary about a painting or a caption placed underneath it that projects itself from a presentational context external to the picture's frame. Within the confinements of television's contextually integrated communication, the rational potential of utterances tends to be confined by what Walter Ong describes as "secondary orality."[3] Due to the layer inserted by visual language, the screen reflects what Uta Quasthoff calls the "ambiguity" ("Doppelbödigkeit") resting in the projection of "physical presence" ("körperlicher Präsenz") to the perception of audiences through symbols such as eye contact or body language, while the consequences of such presence are excluded.[4] These complications, together with the split transmittership that drives a wedge between the utterance of a person and the mise en scène of her body, present a challenge to television's seemingly unpretentious merging of different communicative profiles onto its pictorial surface.

As also indicated in the theoretical outline in the appendix of this book, in a comparison of the relationship between still and moving pictures and that between written and verbal language, the visual signs in moving pictures tend to claim an autonomous semiotic profile that rests somewhere between verbal and written exchanges. If a painting allows a spectator to dedicate her own time to the act of contemplation, in the mode in which a reader can pause at free will, for example to reread a sentence, the moving picture determines a continuous pace of attention, as is necessary, for example, to follow a gesture executed with the hand, and this continuous pace of attention corresponds more with the act of listening to speech. As a listener can generally not return to "relisten" to an utterance, the viewer attends to the pictorial grammar of the screen at the pace of its movement, which is managed by the transmitter side. These "verbal" characteristics also apply when written words are projected onto the screen for a limited interval, creating a semiotic format that resembles that of a news ticker, like the one in Times Square quoted by the documentary. When there is a person speaking on screen, the rhythm and intonation of his utterance is controlled by the speaker, as is the rhythm of execution of his gestures. But on the other hand, the perspective on the person's appearance and the arrangement of all visual signs in general, as well as the rhythm of the cut, are controlled by the picture's creative and presentational transmittership. In an unmediated environment, the pace of attention is set by the speaker to (ideally) allow gradual, cumulative reception and thereby comprehension of his words by the listener. The invisible presentational transmittership interferes with the pace of reception intended by the speaker, while leaving no trace of its effect. The disorientation of reception of the elapsing sign systems subordinates these systems to the more fixed visual elements, the reception of which is not disoriented (or not in this way).

The resulting transmitter-receiver context is comparable to that of books and other written forms, since the overriding quality of the visual signs is their potential to communicate in the physical absence of their author. The absent transmitter can also characterize the exchange of verbal signs, for example, over the telephone, or in a context of macrocommunication, such as in radio broadcasting. However, even in these mediated forms of verbal communication, there remains an essential relation between the verbal signs and the individual arrangement and intonation of the utterance, whereas the screen's pictorial surface intercedes between the speaker and listener, and introduces a written element that distances the visual signs from everything that makes them comparable to verbal exchanges. In summary, visual signs may combine elements of both verbal and written exchanges, but the product of this combination appears closer to the logic of written words and thus stands in peculiar contrast to the lingering verbal aspect of television broadcasts.

When assessing the different semiotic time frames and communicative characteristics of the conveyed signs, it therefore becomes evident that the screen presents a highly complex communicative mélange, which curiously contradicts the ease with which it found audiences' response and acceptance. With a semiotic profile leaning toward the written aspect, the format of broadcasting may indeed resemble that of a news ticker, but one that speaks as well, and one that, furthermore, claims to create and project all its signs in real time, at least when broadcasting "live." Television's inauguration of the "live" picture may appear as a logical consequence of broadcasting's technological potential and may seem to set the television screen further apart from the format of the cinema screen, but the written characteristics of the visual signs conveyed in this format suggest the presence of something rather different from "live."

The claim of live status for a program must be made contextually. Conventionally, either a written line is inserted, as in one of the documentary's historical clips that still carries the words "OFF VIETNAM—BY SATELLITE," or a verbal announcement is made, for example, by a "master of ceremonies." However, once it is accepted that verbal and written signs are altered when merged with visual language, and that the television screen consequently knows no external context that would anchor its continuous flow of visual signs, there is nothing that could rationally differentiate a "live" from a "nonlive" picture, as both written words or those uttered by the visual symbol of an announcer are a part of the same picture upon the status of which they are supposed to comment. In other words, whether or not a "live broadcast" is indeed "live" depends exclusively on the trustworthiness of the acting, that is the presentational transmittership, which in turn is as absent and distanced from the screen's signs as is an author from the signs in a book. Yet unlike the merely absent figure of the author in written communication, the figure of the announcer stands in symbolically for the author, and even seems to be the author. This constellation may contribute to the seeming immediacy of an utterance. It also evokes the paradox of a speaker attempting to speak about a picture when she is an integrated part of that picture and when that picture has actually been made by somebody else. That "lectern," as previously used to denote the privileged position of those symbols the documentary's producers have accorded with a voice, is thus anything but a simple communicative construct, not least because the external rational anchor appears to be missing.

Furthermore, when there is nothing that could rationally clarify whether an announcer is speaking from within a "live" picture when introducing a "non-live" picture, or vice versa, what could possibly differentiate his speaking from a nonfictional picture when introducing a fictional one, or vice versa? The act of introducing a picture from within a picture or of speaking about a picture of which one is also an integrated part—thus simultaneously to have, to speak about, and to be a pictorial lectern—therefore emerges as itself a symbolic act. This symbolic act is based on the convergence of different sign systems under the seal of the visual and marks a communicative setting, the internal logic of which can no longer discriminate whether it refers, in de Saussure's conception, more to "langue" ("language" as an abstract system) or to "parole" ("speech" as a manifestation of that system), that is whether it is more of a written, cultural nature or a verbal, individual nature.[5]

ACTING, OR THE ART OF WRITING CHINESE CHARACTERS

If visual language hovers between the characteristics of the verbal and the written, the practice of assigning a communicative unity to people speaking on screen begins to seem questionable: utterances may still reflect the parole of a person in front of a camera, but the "visual parole," or the look and demeanor of a speaking person, is at least partially subsumed by the rules of pictorial "langue," the application of which rules by those not seen on the screen subsumes all the different sources of the communicated content. The placement of a person's symbol or icon within the frame, be it adjacent to the symbol of a couch, a rack of books, or other icons of particular semantic status, initiates the grammar of visual language in ways ultimately only controlled by broadcasters. Idiosyncratic characteristics of a person's appearance and demeanor on screen are furthermore mitigated by the dynamic of visual literacy, which passes over whatever is not comprehensible in its singular occurrence in favor of whatever resonates with previously accumulated meanings.[6] Yet if the picture of a person on screen represents a rather written type of sign created and presented by others, how then are we able to identify individually styled gestures, to recognize involuntary movements, such as a sneeze, and to develop a sense for a person's physical presence? The idiosyncratic visual characteristics of a person's appearance and demeanor obviously combine to breathe life into visual symbols and icons and to suggest the proximity and immediacy of a broadcast picture. The factors that combine to orchestrate such an impression are numerous, but should at least be broadly conceptualized. Pertaining to the question of individual agency in front of the camera, to the portrayed person's contribution to his or her sight on screen, and thus to the notion of "visual parole" within a somewhat written type of language, a first approach can hypothetically build on the metaphor of handwriting. As in a handwritten note that still carries an individual residue of its author in the contours of letters that simultaneously follow conventionalized forms, visual signs also carry such traces, albeit less directly since they are exchanged in convergence with a second transmitter-receiver context established by broadcasters. In order to come across and to carry more distinctive significance, such traces consequently need to be recognized based on a familiarity with their typical and/or atypical characteristics, which in turn refers them to the realm of the iconic code. Otherwise, the process of their interpretation might compare to graphology, a science in a constant clinch between qualifiable psychological indices and coincidental turns and twists.

It is at this point that the search for individual residue comes upon the boundary across which unconscious signals are transformed into conscious signs, and a person's own, idiosyncratic impulse is modified into gestures of formalized significance. The question of the degree to which a portrayed person can actively participate in the process of translating her agency in front of a camera into signs presented on screen essentially concerns the notion of acting, which separates involuntary, unconscious, and ultimately coincidental demeanor from a conscious act of "handwriting," which is able to achieve participation in the signs' transmitter-receiver network. At least in terms of "active handwriting," a number of parameters are responsible for preserving traces of the individual author, which parameters all involve the contribution of other people. In addition to cameramen, lighting experts, editors, publishers, make-up specialists, hair dressers, and so forth may also rightly claim a part in creating the individual contours of "visual letters" that specify a person's visual symbol, her gestures, her facial expressions, and her body language on screen. Although these considerations reveal the structural limits in locating individual intention behind such networked visual signs, it is nevertheless true that favorable looks, good comportment, and convincing acting in front of a camera impact the reception of content, at least when complemented by a well-meaning broadcast.

In this approach the possibility of individual residue in the contours of visual signs, visual symbols, and icons may be illuminated through a comparison to the art of writing Chinese characters. For centuries, the social status of people able to write the complex semiotic forms hinged on their facility to paint them according to prevalent aesthetic standards. The better a calligrapher observed these standards, the more recognition he or she received and the more likely he or she was to move up within the hierarchy of early Chinese bureaucracy.[7] However, in terms of painting the contours of one's own icon and one's own sign-based gestures and expressions, the reception of artistic talent may be based not only on aesthetic conventions, but also on standards of realism. Whether or not a gesture appears realistic, convincing, or even comprehensible thereby involves the very concept of individuality residing in these expressions, or rather a balance between idiosyncratically styled expressions and standardized, generally comprehensible sign forms. Moreover, the visual symbol of a portrayed person, which anchors all her gestures, already includes the aspect of individuality in its semantic field, meaning that those signs that can be actively painted already contain a formal reference to an individual personality (names also contain this formal reference). When considering the individual residue in visual signs and symbols on screen as "the art of painting one's own signature," another factor comes into play that also evokes Benjamin's notion of a lost artistic aura: similar to the technical reproduction of an artist's work, the technical reproduction of an actor's art appears logically to distance individual traces of her work.[8] Not only are the signs and symbols manipulated at the editing board, further reproduction and re-presentation of those signs and symbols contribute to rendering her icon and her gestures as "printed terms." Like those printed signatures meant to authenticate leaflets and advertising letters, the individual residue behind their contours is layered over by the anonymous, macrocommunicative context and the rules of general visual literacy take over: rather than *referencing* a real hand at the root of the visual terms, they *signify* such an individual hand. In other words, these signs communicate "this was created by a real person" in order to authenticate the record to which they have been appended.

ICONIC CONVERGENCE

In order to come across on screen, individual agency must forcefully demand an active part in the transmitter-receiver network, and it can only do so by engaging with the notion of acting. The viewer relies on the general human mode of visual perception to distinguish between true or faked expressions, and likewise between good or bad acting. However, broadcast pictures present sights manufactured by a number of different people, which makes it unlikely that we can understand them in the exact same mode that we use to evaluate expressions in everyday life. The attempt to differentiate good from bad acting and true from faked expressions nurtures prevailing conventions which presuppose the coexistence of the fictional and the nonfictional picture in broadcasting. The conventionally assumed potential of the broadcast picture to reflect unmediated reality requires the ability to differentiate between acting and nonacting and thus between staged and authentic individual agency on screen. Such differentiation in turn presupposes that individual agency acted out in front of a camera actually influences the resulting pictorial message in ways that would allow spectators to discern such original, individual intention, not only behind all the layers of collective authorship, but also behind the historical dynamic of visual literacy.

According to visual literacy's mechanisms of collecting and arranging significance, however, the idiosyncratic gestures of people we have never seen in real life project little meaning, because they cannot be compared and typified against the characteristics of other examples. It is indeed most likely that we first concern ourselves with better known and comparable visual structures, such as icons, before eventually moving on to speculate about other, more individual visual signs within a picture's frame, which we then decipher in direct relation to the better known symbols.[9] It is thus not the individual occurrence in pictures, but repetition that acts as the engine of visual literacy, which anchors not only pictorial significance, but also any attempt to authenticate it. From this perspective, "iconization" would consequently be a factor in evaluating good or bad acting and in discriminating between conscious and unconscious demeanor on screen, because only the accumulated visual literacy of a person's usual gestures can give enough grounds for typifying a more unique or atypical expression. Yet if repetition is required for differentiating "conscious, but good acting" from "unconscious, but authentic" demeanor, as well as for understanding the significance of expressions in either case, then visual literacy blends with the force of convention to further undermine the traces of true individual agency in pictures. In fact, it could be the difference between acting conventions and the equally conventional role of visual literacy in contouring the significance of a visual gesture or expression, which suggests unconventional and unmediated contribution to a picture's communicative potential. This quite surprising notion originates in Diderot's paradox of acting, which develops additional complexity when transferred to acting for the language of the screen.

As Richard Sennett interpreted the paradox, a theater actor's gesture of grief, for example, needs to convey a careful balance of individual contours and culturally established form to be both convincing and understandable for audiences.[10] The balancing of one's own, individual expressions with generally understandable gestures, facial expressions, and body language in front of theater audiences already involves the notion of signs since it implies an act of (repeated) coding of these gestures, and so forth, with significance according to prevailing conventions. But when transferred to the screen, the actor becomes part of a two-dimensional picture rendering established gestures and expressions indeed as the contoured material of signs. In this format, the actor is no longer required to reconcile his physical presence with his role in ways that can also persuade the back rows of a theater. The transformation of acting according to the parameters of the screen thus involves a different, more intimate perspective on an actor's body and face that not only renders any traditional repertoire of sweeping, dramatic expressions obsolete, but also requires that gestures be refined to the point where camera-conscious meets camera-unconscious acting in one two-dimensional visual term. The goal of acting, it appears, is no longer to change into another person, but first of all to create a comprehensive icon that stands as a realistic expression of an individual character. Thus an actor has to develop an iconic continuity and coherence for his expressions and gestures that is realistic, comprehensible, and able to withstand the scrutiny of front row audiences. Just as handwriting is based on the development of an individual style in correspondence with prevailing conventions, an actor's task would thus be to control the iconization of his visual term on screen, that is, through developing a coherent iconic style.[11] Such iconic style may then not only be reduced to one role, but can be developed over the course of various movies, broadcasts, and so forth. In this understanding, the convention of (realistic) acting thus merges with the equally conventional dynamic of visual literacy, which requires at least two appearances in a pictorial narrative in order to establish the necessary iconic grounds for making an individual contribution to a broadcast's collective authorship.

How then can people who appear for the first time on television, for example, a passer-by who is being interviewed for the local news, be understood in their individual visual characteristics? Who is speaking when their voice becomes combined with the close-up of a face that can only be rudimentarily typified because it has never developed an iconic familiarity and does not carry accumulated significance? And, finally, how can we know if the gestures and expressions of such a performance are acted or spontaneous, true or fake, and thus conscious of the camera or not? What is more, while the camera on the movie set is basically "friendly" to the collective task of creating pictorial art, television's self-designated task of presenting nonartistic and nonfictional representations necessarily suggests the possibility of an "unfriendly camera," one that could thus intentionally portray theatrical acting where none is actually intended. Yet should the possibility of such "manipulation" of peoples' individual agency in front of the camera be accepted, the possibility of maintaining any borderline between acting and nonacting becomes rather difficult.

For such reasons, an expression of grief captured by a news team appears to be less the reflection of the portrayed person's agency than a statement about it. In this mode, the translation of the captured gesture into visual language creates a general symbol of grief that anticipates audiences' visual literacy. Based on their literacy, the individual contours of the expression can ultimately be evaluated, in terms of whether the signs of grief correspond in a typical, unified or in a rather atypical, possibly controversial fashion to conventional standards of demeanor generally seen on screen. The conventionalizing force of visual literacy becomes especially apparent when reflecting on exotic, that is, by definition less semantically contoured, visual terms. Most Americans have never actually seen, for example, a traditional Arab woman grieving over a lost relative, but pictures have made that particular gesture familiar enough so that they can recognize the broad contours of the gesture and its general significance. Seeming curious, sweeping, dramatic, or maybe even dramatized by comparison to Western standards, such a set of symbolic gestures combines with the unfamiliar complexion of an exotic foreign face to denote grief, yet arguably without suggesting any information about that woman's individual personality. In fact, to the degree that the visual symbol of such a woman's face remains vague, the signs of her exotic gestures appear dominated by a very general, formal, and conventional association of grief. Those who lack the necessary visual literacy to detect and evaluate any individual variations in the gesture's display may even doubt its authenticity and receive it as an act.

In considering the difficulties involved in transcending Diderot's acting paradox with regard to the two-dimensional screen, and in considering the dubious possibility of discerning between good acting, bad acting, and nonacting when taking into account the rather written nature of visual symbols and icons, it appears suitable to begin analysis with a hypothesis that challenges just such differentiations: The mutual effect of the iconic principle and the convention of photographic realism is to present the joining of a person's real personality with his two-dimensional visual term. This "iconic convergence" is used to explicate not only the ability of icons to travel back and forth in history, as outlined in part B, "Kaleidoscopic Spectacles," but also their ability to jump sideways over that ominous borderline between fictional, acted pictorial representations and nonfictional, nonacted pictorial contexts. Rather than concerning any acting convention in particular, such as, for example, method acting, the concept first of all addresses the general convention of seeing "real persons" on the two-dimensional television screen.[12] In this context, Diderot's acting paradox extends to question also the role and agency of people who are either unaware of being filmed or who "stay themselves" in front of the camera. Without the chance to develop their own visual calligraphy or iconic style in symbiotic cooperation with well meaning broadcasters, the possibility of good, as in "realistic," acting (or the convincing portrayal of nonacting) appears limited, since it would not be recognizable as conscious acting. Because unconscious acting leaves all noncoincidental, communicative content to the domain of those who create and present the pictures, it too lacks the contribution of the person in front of the camera. What remains is the possibility of bad acting in order to signal individual presence and intention. In choosing to retain his agency by becoming a bad actor, would not the layperson like all bad actors then also strive to be a good actor, and thereby strive to conceal his own personality?

In summarizing this heightened paradox of acting for the screen, the hypothesis could thus be put forward: acting in front of the artistic camera needs to retain a sense of the actor's real personality in order to make the acting both visible and vivid, while being oneself in front of a journalistic camera needs a measure of artistic acting in order to make a visible contribution to the resulting visual message. In any case, the concept of "iconic convergence" will henceforth be used to analyze all those instances in which Diderot's paradox of acting, when translated into the rather written format of the screen, merges the convention of photographic realism with the iconic dimension of visual literacy.

FROM REALISM TO HYPERREALISM

The ability of an icon to move back and forth through pictorial history is enabled by the picture's cross-reference to its own fictional or nonfictional stages. The ability of an icon to move left and right across the boundary between fiction and nonfiction results, for example, in iconic careers that combine fictional with political aspects, such as in the case of Ronald Reagan or Arnold Schwarzenegger. As indicated, the crossing of the boundary first of all implies the connection between visual literacy's logic of iconization and modern conventions of acting for the screen, because only distinguished icons seem to be in the position to play with this borderline—or even to render it visible at all. Since the agency of unknown people in contouring their visual symbol can hardly provide enough grounds for securely distinguishing camera conscious and unconscious, good or bad acting, the borderline between the fictional and nonfictional is consequently also a matter of the spectacle, at least in so far as established icons attract the eye and mark a "mini-event" whenever they appear on screen. In this reading, both fictional and nonfictional pictures consequently evolve in conjunction with the spectacle's cornerstones of the unified, the controversial, and the exotic. "Good acting" would thus correspond with the unified icon, "bad acting" with the controversial icon, and nonacting or camera-unconscious demeanor would hold the distanced, less informed, and coincidental characteristics of the exotic icon. Yet, while Hollywood cultivated an artistic world of fictional spectacle, which started and ended with the opening and closing of real curtains, the broadcast screen catered to all types of spectacles, featuring vaudeville and theater plays, as well as events from the realms of sports and politics. Through broadcasting events orchestrated by others, television offered such spectacles a second stage, the way it also began to incorporate the productions of Hollywood and Disney, as well as the Oscar night in its continuous flow of pictures. [13] At the same time, television also developed its own distinctive style of production, which differed from the Hollywood genre not least because of different acting conventions. Cultural differences between the East and the West Coast were also a factor, as elucidated by Lary May. [14] Most importantly, there was a new attitude towards the photographic picture and the way icons could be positioned. Through claiming the ability of a "second stage," the broadcast screen allowed icons from all provenances, from Hollywood, vaudeville, theatre, sports, and politics, to mingle. What's more, through presenting the icons of the fictional cinema screen in a second pictorial frame, in which they appear in nonfictional reference to their individual agency, television also institutionalized the possibility for actors to act themselves, and therefore opened the door for icons to aggregate significance from both their fictional and nonfictional backgrounds. As a result, the iconic convergence of the art of acting and the dynamic of visual literacy became over-layered with a reference to reality, that is, to "real" personalities. In accentuating its reference to the nonfictional agency of people in front of the camera, television moved from the movies' type of realism to what can be called "hyperrealism."[15]

In Nicholas Abercrombie's words, television "seems to be describing the world as it is."[16] It is this quality of hyperrealism that enables television announcers to introduce both fictional and nonfictional programming as well as to define what is live and what is not, and that generally empowers masters of ceremonies to contextualize the very pictures from within which they are speaking. By the same standard that hyperrealism intensifies the phenomenon of "iconic convergence" on television and by the same standard that it cultivates the vividness of icons and thereby effaces the distinction between their fictional and nonfictional semantic background, it also appears as the driving force behind television's rise to the top of America's communicative landscape. Through successfully claiming for its pictures the supreme power to present its audience with a window to every possible place in the nation—including the backstage of television's own studios—and through broadcasting such sights in real time, and thus conferring upon itself the privilege of mirroring almost every traditional form of societal communication, while also introducing new ones, the television screen conquered and consolidated its supreme place in the nation's public sphere.

The following chapters apply the theoretical conflict between the semiotic logic of visual language and television's convention of hyperrealism to early broadcast shows, by discussing their role in generating a new brand of icon that gained nationwide recognition and significance. The central perspective is on television's own approach to iconic convergence and its corresponding conventions for screen acting. Looking at how the addition of the picture transformed the content of the successful radio play *Dragnet,* the analysis incorporates the difference between imaginative West Coast realism and the East Coast's drive to situate the novel broadcast screen more directly and more firmly in reality. A comparison of the semantic history of two prominent icons, *Dragnet's* Jack Webb and *I Love Lucy's* Lucille Ball, elucidates television's particular balance between the fictional and the real, together with its extraordinary potential to sustain audiences' visual literacy by running shows for many years. The effect of hyperrealism in a fictional mode is then contrasted with the rise of television journalism based on the iconic history of Edward R. Murrow and Walter Cronkite. Finally, the possibility of consciously managing the casting of one's visual symbol, and achieving for it a unified place on television's public tribune, is further considered in a case study of Muhammad Ali and his self-conscious iconic ascent through the world of the broadcast spectacle. These five cases, including some of the most well-known icons of television's established genres, are chosen for their capacity to reflect on the historical evolution of national television broadcasting, although they cannot do so completely.[17] These five examples also lend themselves to further pursuit of questions already encountered in the analysis of the pictorial historiography, and consequently to further study of the dance of icons on the hyperreal stage.

10 The Icon of Joe Friday
The Moral in the *Dragnet*

Like many other early television shows, *Dragnet* originated in another medium. Starting in mid-1949 on the radio, Jack Webb created the down-to-earth detective sergeant Joe Friday, who, week after week, undertook ordinary police work with a stern sense of factual logic that may not have pleased the criminal cornered at the end of each episode, but nevertheless delighted the series' numerous fans. After the show won several awards, NBC gave the green light to transfer it to the screen, setting the stage for one of early television's most popular and enduring police dramas. Based on actual cases of the Los Angeles Police Department (LAPD), the series aimed to profile the work of an ordinary police detective who solves the daily conflicts arising in the big city. The success of the show in both media had much to do with a realism dedicated to carrying the viewer into the world of everyday police work. The accuracy in detail reportedly even prompted police instructors to play recordings to trainees at the Los Angeles police academy.[1] At a time when the film noir fashioned by the cinema screen had undermined the image and credibility of the police, depicting them as bureaucratic and corrupt to the point of obstructing courageous private detectives in their search for justice, Joe Friday's pragmatic, down-to-earth manner was greeted as a welcome change. The new television hero was soon recognized by American audiences as one of the most celebrated detectives, alongside the likes of Sherlock Holmes and Hercule Poirot. In 1954, *Time* wrote that of all television shows only *I Love Lucy* was able to challenge *Dragnet's* popularity.[2] Although the show's top ratings may not have broken any records, the article's author was convinced that there was hardly a child above the age of four in the country "who does not know and constantly voice the brassy notes (dum du dum dum) of *Dragnet's* theme music."[3] When in 1967 the show returned for another three seasons, having been off the air since 1959, critics celebrated the return of the "hero of routine law enforcement ('My name is Friday, I'm a cop') and champion of terse dialogue ('Just give us the facts, Ma'am')."[4] Retiring in 1970 after three additional seasons, the icon may have aged but had not vanished from the popular culture dictionary of cherished terms. Lampooned on shows like *Saturday Night Live* during the 1980s, parodied by Dan Aykroyd in a motion picture

(*Dragnet (1987)*, directed by Tom Mankiewicz), the show was also revived in countless reruns, demonstrating the lasting impact of Jack Webb's creation on American popular culture and hence on the nation's visual literacy. The astonishing endurance of *Dragnet* and of America's familiarity with its star-icon may be best illustrated with a passing note in one of television's hit shows of the 1990s, *Ally McBeal*. In one episode its star, a thirty-year-old female lawyer, says of an attractive new colleague who is supposed to help the law firm in a murder case: "He looks like Jack Webb." Some thirty years after the second run of *Dragnet* in the late sixties—at about the time when the fictional Ally McBeal would have been born—American audiences were still expected to recall the visual characteristics of the historical persona and to enjoy the nostalgic humor of the reference.

In the face of such enduring popularity, any historical analysis of the fifties' show encounters problems similar to those described in the previous assessment of historical documentaries: how can the records of the show be interpreted as historical documents of their time when their artistic potential and their value as entertainment is still relevant? But, if early television is to be analyzed as a historical phenomenon, a show like *Dragnet,* that week after week displays the moral standards of society to millions of spectators, must have a place in history, if only as a historical document of a public act of popular mass communication. Furthermore, the historical significance of the show's communicative status appears heightened by its depiction of "true stories" taken from actual police cases. While the often-stated intention to portray real crimes and real police action is unlikely to have spectators confusing realism with reality, it at least makes the claim for a serious role in America's public sphere. The basically fictional style of reenacting several hundred cases of various crimes, superimposing one detective character over the many different policemen who worked on and closed the real cases, nevertheless contains a rational kernel of history with regard to the judiciary system of the late 1940s and early 1950s. The cases were only a few years old when serving as blueprints for *Dragnet's* stories and were therefore meant to include current overtones not only in terms of displaying "your police force at work," but also in shaping the contemporary boundary lines between socially acceptable and unacceptable behavior. If almost every four-year-old in 1954 could hum the show's theme music, the show's negotiation of moral boundary lines was apparently considered suitable for educating family audiences. Given that television audiences in the early fifties generally comprised middle and upper classes, the show's moral and ethical guidelines, as well as the absence of graphic violence—there were hardly ever any gun shots fired on the show—reflect on the professional channeling of middle-class values carried out by much of the successful mass communication at the time.[5] On both radio and television, the fictional figure of Joe Friday was thus staged as an incarnation of impeccable morals fashioned by middle-class audiences. The show's realism, which Jack Webb pursued in both media with great vigor and persuasion, may look monotonous to modern eyes, but it provided the basis for television's attempt to make entertainment accord with the civic status it was demanding during the 1950s. Combining the unquestionable facts and unequivocal moral decisions of closed police cases with fictionally enhanced story lines, *Dragnet* stood firm with one foot on the stage of society's public sphere, and one in the world of fiction.

THE RADIO PLAY: FACTUAL BACKBONE, FICTIONAL FLESH

On the radio, every episode starts with the characteristic line, "The story you are about to hear is true, only the names have been changed to protect the innocent."[6] Following the theme music and a commercial for the show's main sponsor, Fatima cigarettes, the announcer invites audiences to participate, telling them, "You are a detective sergeant," and giving them an outline of the "job" at hand. After another commercial for Fatima, the announcer completes the standardized introduction: "*Dragnet,* the documented drama of an actual crime: for the next thirty minutes in cooperation with the Los Angeles Police Department you will travel step by step on the side of the law through an actual case transcribed from police files. From beginning to end, from crime to punishment, *Dragnet* is the story of your police force in action." Jack Webb's voice then takes over to outline in a first narrative block the story's date, including the weekday, the time, the weather, and the place where he and his partner Ed Jacobs meet to discuss the assigned task, and so forth. Once the case is solved, the announcer is back to add the standardized conclusion. He first repeats the opening line in past tense, "The story you just heard is true [. . .]," then promises the "result" of the judiciary process "in a moment," and after a last commercial for Fatima cigarettes that almost always features "our star, Jack Webb," he discloses the trial's outcome as the last act of the show.

Between these narrative brackets, the story unfolds structured by a sequence of alternating narration and actual radio play. Usually between six and seven blocks of pure narration, done by Jack Webb, together averaging about six minutes (or one-fifth of the show's thirty-minute time slot) are followed by the same amount of actual play blocks that fill about another seventeen minutes of the show. The commercials, the standardized brackets, and the trailer complete the roughly thirty minutes of radio entertainment. Within the narrative blocks, Jack Webb guides listeners with a painstakingly detailed, protocol-like explanation of the story's context. The explanation follows original police records, making note of the hour and minute and the location, with street names, and referring to the exact procedures of police work with professional jargon (such as "R and I" standing for "records and identification") in order to shape a realistic backbone of the complete narrative and to give the effect of leading the listener step by step through a real case of police work. The transition from narration to the actual play is swift and seamless. The listener can often overhear background noises, for example, the footsteps of the detectives or the first lines of a conversation, before the narration ends. The actual play consists mostly of conversations between the two detectives and all kind of suspects, witnesses, and other police officers. With a total of only fifteen gunshots and only a few more physical scuffles in over 300 episodes, violent action scenes are rare and seldom the focal point of the narrative. Instead, most scripts head for a verbal confrontation between Joe Friday, Ed Jacobs, and their main suspect, which most often involves the detectives' presenting the suspect with facts with increasing intensity, the most irrefutable ones being tossed in at the end. Given that the outcome of the story is known from the beginning—if only because the cases are built from closed police files—the show's narrative line features a strong element of predetermination: there is no escape from the dragnet, as there is no escape from the controlled narrative flow. Yet within that monotony, the radio show nevertheless manages to keep listeners in suspense based on the relatively flat, but steadily and securely built tension. What emerges is a solid pattern that allows receivers to plunge into the everyday world of police detectives and indeed to follow them through the vagaries of life in the big city. The choice of cases fosters the kind of curiosity that arises from observing the outbreak of conflicts in everyday life. Certainly, there are a number of murder cases, but most concern smaller infractions, ranging from abandoned children to kleptomaniac warehouse theft, from distributing pornographic material to all types of juvenile delinquency. The choice of cases certainly reflects some of 1950s society's most debated topics, implying that the discursive content approximated audiences' own experiences and thus contributed to the realism fashioned by the show.

However, at the fringes of the play, the reenacted conversations appear to stray from the original police records, contrasting fictional flesh with the stern factual backbone of the narration. In one episode, a leader of a juvenile gang about to engage in a dangerous, armed gang war is referred to as "young Hitler," and as an overindulged, single child who complains about a soup served "too hot" by his mother. Another script dedicates more than six minutes to constructing the background of the villain, a fallen Hollywood producer who apparently indulged in nostalgic reviews of his past successes. Against this fictional ground, with little basis in the protocols of the police department, emerge the contours of Joe Friday's character. The well-balanced, very low-key impersonation of Friday is achieved through Webb's expression of Friday's moods and attitudes via barely perceptible changes in intonation, which become more momentous the more familiar listeners became with the police officer. In an episode about a baby abandoned at a bus station, Webb's modulated voice leaves no doubt about his empathy with the mother and her story of loneliness and moral dilemma. In this way, the realism of Webb's acting nevertheless allows for an accumulation of small characteristics that contour the fictional personality of Friday.

The factual, protocol-like style of the show's introduction and its narrative blocks thus finds a fictional counterweight in the scenes that shape the character portraits of those whose names have been changed to protect the innocent. Tuned to the world of the white suburban middle class, in which most cases are situated, there is rarely a black American accent, nor any other trace of the more complicated milieu of an inner city police station. While women appear most often in the role of housewives, and are most often interviewed in their homes, the show mainly reflects a white man's world of action and conflict, as well as typically male patterns of conflict resolution overseen and properly maintained by the notoriously tedious and effective Joe Friday. Standing for the ideal male deputy of "your police force in action," and for all those men who solved cases within the different LAPD departments, Friday was consciously ranked as a sergeant and not as a lieutenant—despite a temporary promotion. In this rank, he reflected the manliness of a lower-middle-class background, although having at his disposal enough "cultural capital," as Bourdieu would phrase it, to stand his ground in every conversation with those of higher-class background.[7] Such astute cultural behavior, paired with smart use of factual logic, gained Joe Friday the necessary popularity to enter the limelight on the stage of television.

THE TRANSITION TO THE SCREEN

When comparing the radio play with the television version, obvious differences are hard to detect. On screen the show retains the down-to-earth, humorless, somewhat monotonous style that it had established as its trademark on the radio. After some back-to-back comparisons it is obvious that the original radio scripts were taken over by and large unchanged: at first view, it is as if the audio version had simply been illustrated with pictures.

The television episodes feature exactly the same narrative structure, with an identical number of narrative and action blocks. However, after one or two comparisons some small differences emerge, the most obvious of which concerns the adaptation of the introduction. Instead of the line that the audience will travel step by step through a documented crime, (uttered by the anonymous announcer), Jack Webb narrates a text that routinely starts with the words, "This is the city [. . .]," accompanied by pictures of Los Angeles. Besides the slight change in the introduction, the same music and the same remark about the "true story" that one is about to "see" instead of "hear" prepare for the actual case. A consecutive analysis of four episodes broadcast on both radio and television revealed little differences in terms of the time allocated to the narrative blocks. In terms of the scripts, the radio and television versions are not identical, but very similar, and a number of cases in which single words were changed (for example, "rotten" instead of "filthy" when talking about the selling of pornographic material) do not offer much ground for interpretation. A little more interesting are the small changes necessary to adapt meticulous police descriptions of suspects with the visual symbols of the actors. Apparently, Jack Webb did not demand his make-up specialists to change the color of actors' hair, simply adjusting the script instead. In one episode called "Big Hands," which relates the case of a woman murdered in a hotel room, a necessary adjustment of the script was overlooked without, however, causing much more havoc than sending the viewer temporarily on the wrong trail. The selection of shooting locations sometimes also interferes with the original radio story. Again in "Big Hands," the detectives confront the now dark-haired villain in the generator room of an electrical company, while he was simply drilling for oil in the radio version. The impact on the story is a little more ambiguous than that of the other examples. The radio presentation of the case already leaves confusing indices for situating the social background of the protagonists. The murdered woman and her estranged husband are explicitly described as middle class, having been living in a "better than average neighborhood," but the husband worked at a hamburger stand on the beach that did not belong to him. Given that the villain rose from an oil-driller to an electrical engineer, it could thus be argued that television further elevated the milieu of the case in order to better adapt the narrative to the background of its own audiences.

Such occasional differences cannot be unambiguously interpreted as conscious acts, given also the time pressure to which the television show was subjected (Jack Webb prided himself on shooting an episode in little more than two days), but a couple of further indices confirm that the television version went further than the radio version in adapting the cases to a middle-class audience. The television show rarely allows glimpses into lower-class dwellings, and it usually even stops at the doors of simple motels. Kitchens appear taboo as well. A woman interviewed while cleaning the silver in the kitchen in the radio version is portrayed on television as doing the same in the living room. Although early television technique featured a relatively low picture quality, making it difficult to spot details, for example, of a painting hanging on the wall, the typical living room featured in most *Dragnet* stories also adds visual indices of financially well-situated households: fireplaces, antique furniture, impressive secretaries, and above all, very spacious rooms. While generous rooms are also a condition for unobstructed camera work, these visual details also anchor the characterization of the actors within the grammar of symbolic transfer.[8]

In many interviews, Jack Webb emphasized the effort he dedicated to accuracy in visual detail.[9] Readily taken up by the critics, the show was often lauded for successfully transferring its realist style from the audio to the visual medium. Often cited in this context are painstaking efforts in reconstructing the police offices. It is said that Jack Webb wanted every detail, from the doorknob to the telephones, to contribute to an accurate visual portrayal of the busy premises of police bureaus.[10] Except for illustrating a trend toward a more middle-class milieu, the back-to-back comparison of the audio with the visual versions of the same cases confirms the first subjective impression that the television version was a realistically illustrated version of the radio play. To search for more substantial communicative changes rising from the addition of visual language to an already popular series, a different, more basic perspective became necessary.

"UNDERPLAYING"

While the first results from the comparison of the audio with the visual version of the show identified a somewhat surprising similarity in the structural build of the narrative, this finding does little to explain the hype around the debut of *Dragnet* on screen in late 1951. It also neglects the effort Jack Webb put into filming the show in ways unusual for television productions of that time. Often filming outside the studio and using three cameras for a more dynamic capturing of conversations, Webb tried to implement actual Hollywood techniques of filming, which he considered more suitable for the purposes of "realistic documentary."[11] Looking at his first attempts with "growing horror," once he realized that the pictures would be seen on small ten-inch television screens, he resorted to telling the story with close-ups whenever possible.[12] The result is constructed scenes that most often combine a long shot of an encounter with two angles on the faces of those involved, alternating the close-ups according to the flow of the conversation. Although the first camera often sketches the scene, for example, the detectives standing opposite to a witness in the corner of an office or a living room, the effect does not completely compare with the technique of the establishing shot. The rooms are generally only partially revealed, the camera perspective appears very stiff to modern eyes and preceding shots of the vicinity are mostly lacking. For this reason, many clips convey a theaterlike aura. While spectators rarely see the outside of a suspect's or a witness's house, the mise en scène of the police department provides an exception. With what was once described by David Thorburn as "an arthritically pompous camera that's so worshipful toward buildings and representatives of official authority that it hardly moves," the department is often portrayed from street angles.[13] Thus, despite Jack Webb describing his camera technique as a "half an hour of motion pictures, not a half-hour of TV films," the general visual display of *Dragnet* still appears quite stiff and rudimentary.[14] Ultimately, the camera appears not only "arthritically pompous" toward the police building, but due to the strict regime of close-ups, also toward the icons of the actors.

While the radio version went to great lengths to add background noises to gain more immediacy for the play, the television's pictorial plane not only facilitated a better spatial orientation for receivers' imaginations, but also extended the aura of the figures' immediate presence through portraying their positioning even when they were not speaking. As on a theater stage, on television the actors can be in view when not directly participating in the action, but, unlike in theater, the decision of whether their visual symbols indeed make the frame belongs to others rather than to the audience or the actors themselves. The camera's mediation of presence or absence consequently shapes basic pictorial messages, such as "listening," when the camera switches back and forth between two characters in conversation, whether or not a facial expression discloses actual listening. The pictorially extended spatial orientation also enhances the on-screen presence of the actors, shaping the most "visible" structural difference between the radio and the television version of the plays.

This observation can be substantiated statistically by measuring the camera time allocated to Webb's icon, compared to his verbal presence in the radio play. On the radio, Webb speaks an average of roughly 5½ minutes, thereby taking up about ¼ of the show's actual audio time (on average 23 minutes, without ads and trailer). On television, his speaking time is more or less the same, but he can be seen for 10 minutes and 40 seconds, so his presence compared to the audio coverage is doubled. Although the average television version also lasts 5 minutes longer, Webb's figure is present in over 40% of the complete visual narrative, whereas on the radio he is responsible for 24% of all verbal statements. In fact, since the script of the television version is nearly identical to the radio script, the 5 extra minutes of show time can thus be solely explained by the substantially enhanced visual focus on Joe Friday. These 5 minutes are used to project his visual symbol, in the words of Jane and Michael Stern, like a—quite extensive—"Rorschach test."[15]

These 5 minutes also indicate a generally slower flow of the pictorial narrative. While the difference may be related to the visual addition of information about the whereabouts of the action, another explanation may reside in the particular demands of screen acting. With more than 10 minutes of on-screen time in each episode, Webb is challenged to match the subtle intonation of his sonorous voice with an equally subtle visual demeanor. With so much weekly exposure, audiences develop a familiarity with an actor, which theoretically renders even his most idiosyncratically contoured body gestures and facial expressions as comprehensible signs. As previously outlined, the effect of such continuity and such an intimate visual focus on the art of acting is thereby rather ambiguous. On the one hand, it enhances the proximity to the impersonated character and contributes to the aim of presenting a realistic figuration of life. On the other hand, the creation of Joe Friday's personality would need to be consciously controlled in all details and this over hundreds of episodes shot over many years under enormous time pressure. For that matter, frame-by-frame management of coherence and consistency in the vivid impersonation of another character would be a rather unrealistic demand for any actor.

After having been on air for more than five years, Jack Webb told *Newsweek* that the acting style he developed when moving the show to the screen reflected a conscious attempt to "underplay" his role.[16] This undramatic acting style was designed to enhance the show's realism and was complemented by what Webb specified as realistic make-up.[17] Intuitively, however, the concept also appears to match perfectly the task of acting for the novel pictorial format of the broadcast screen. Foregrounding the iconic convergence between the actor and his place within the picture, the acting serves to forge a new symbol, the semantic field of which needs to be nurtured with extraordinary continuity—a task that is certainly facilitated by a reduced set of gestures, or one that corresponds closely to the actor's demeanor in real life.

The more the viewer accompanies the character on screen, the more he becomes acquainted with his facial expressions, the more complete is the process of iconic convergence in detaching all visual meaning on screen from a rationally grounded reference to the acting or to the actor's physical presence in front of the camera. In this way, the television camera creates a hybrid life on screen, an icon of a detective that is both fictional Joe and real Jack at once. For similar reasons of iconic convergence, the television version of *Dragnet* altered one of the main characters of the play as early as the first season. When the actor Barton Yarborough, who played Friday's partner on the show, died after only three episodes had been filmed for the screen, Webb and his team did not simply replace him with a new actor, but also created a different fictional character that complemented the new face. What became a general standard for *Dragnet* as well as many other television productions, the switch from Barton Yarborough's "Ben Romero" to that of Barney Philipps's "Ed Jacobs" to that of Ben Alexander's "Frank Smith" indicates the particular phenomenon of iconic convergence against the setting of the extraordinary continuity of such television shows.

Finally, when the icon of Joe alias Jack appears again after the closing line of the drama, this time "literally" off stage, to promote cigarettes, after having done his work for *Dragnet,* television itself toys with its own inability to securely ground its fictional figurations in a context able to differentiate the continuous flow of pictures. Without the logical possibility of differentiating which reference to reality now underpins the icon, that to the actor as actor, or that of Webb playing himself, the commercial largely relies on the hyperreal aura of the actor's mise en scène. After all, any less known icon posing, for example, as a tobacco-loving Sherlock Holmes would arguably leave a much less compelling statement. In any case, the mise en scène of Jack Webb's underplayed personification of Joe Friday indicates a new type of realism, one that is no longer used as an artistic filter but, on the contrary, as a magnifier of the broadcast media's convention of referencing unmediated content.

TOWARD A FICTION WRITTEN BY REALITY

The television version of *Dragnet* succeeded in carrying over the popularity generated by the radio version, and established the icon of a newly figured champion in the fight against criminality soon after the show's start. The change to the new pictorial format certainly contributed to its popularity and, above all, secured lasting ratings. Its popularity remained undiminished when it returned to the air in the years between 1967 and 1970 and began a career of innumerable reruns by stations all over the country, which continues to this day. The addition of the picture to the broadcast of *Dragnet* thus impacted the show in substantial ways. The vastly extended focus on Webb's acting allowed audiences to develop an intimate familiarity with his icon, which grew over the years and with which they also grew older. The effect of such enhanced coherence between an actor, his role, and his audience thus tends to substitute visual language's iconic code with the experience of knowing a person in real life, rendering his icon as a lectern for his idiomatic way of speaking. In the way the words of an acquaintance gain more depth the better one knows the person's range of thoughts and emotions, the convergence of the iconic with the verbal idiom onscreen begins to resemble real-life interaction, although it is created and transmitted by different authors. The concept of the idiom thereby specifies a plane that is external to the immediate form of signs, since it depends on the diachronically (historically) informed, personal context of those involved in an interaction.[18] Recalling the notion of "secondary orality," the television icon of Webb can theoretically only simulate an interactive communicative plane, not only because of the physical absence of the transmitter and the impossibility of aspects like eye contact, as assessed by Quasthoff, but also because of the icon's double role as both author and content of what is conveyed.[19] Therefore, everything that would reference the idiomatic content typical of an exchange in real life becomes embedded in the symbolic contours of a visual term that is scripted and that, like the actor himself, develops over a certain period of time. In this light, it is interesting to note that Jack Webb actually painted the contours of his icon not only as the actor, but also as the director, as well as the author of the script. In terms of creating the impression of a consistent "iconic idiom," his individual agency as an author thus concerns both the general mise en scène of the imagery and the verbal lines of the icon's voice. Both the actor beneath the visual signs and the author beneath the verbal signs transmit coded content of which they are also an unmediated part when seen in direct reference to reality. But behind this seemingly homogenous composition of the icon and his words—one that would still equate with the structure of one transmitter, as in a book and its author—there still exist at least a couple of further, external authors, including the cameraman and those responsible for running the show over the NBC network, who printed the icon and presented it as the symbolic, idiomatic lectern for the spoken words.

The factor of iconic convergence in *Dragnet* may actually build on a quite stringent harmony between the actor and the author of the conveyed signs, but this harmony is not the sole cause for shifting the play beyond the boundary between fictional and nonfiction realism. After all, Webb's declared purpose was to create a hybrid between entertainment and documentary. Amplifying the show's realism with a reference to actual police cases may not have caused audiences to take the show's imagery too literally, but the insistence on a nonfictional kernel nevertheless succeeded in further concealing the artistic intention and agency of individuals responsible for its transmittership, in favor of accentuating television's particular realism as analyzed by Abercrombie.[20] Behind the show's verbal and visual transmittership is first of all a written record, a hidden text, which specifies the LAPD as its author, and a number of police detectives who worked in different departments of the institution. A representative of the police, in cooperation with NBC, chose records suitable for broadcasting from the LAPD archive. From this preselection, Webb chose his favorite cases for the radio play. With the switch to television, the element of selection resurfaces again, in Webb's decision only to move the "cream of all cases" from radio to screen—indicating among other things the high status anticipated for the screen from the beginning.[21] Thus, the agency of several individuals, the response of radio audiences, and two large institutions, the LAPD and the NBC radio and television network, assumed a part in the narratives' authorial context before Jack Webb started to direct and let his icon speak. All these steps reflect a complex of choices, selections, and decisions that distance the script from the original records, a distance typical of most forms of mass communication. The words ultimately spoken by Webb have therefore many origins, ranging from the political interests of the police department to the commercial considerations of the broadcast network and, by implication, of the show's sponsor, the cigarette manufacturer. These multiple influences on the script's authorship are further enhanced by the film crew's pictorial authorship, which adds a further round of selection, of the sights and symbols framed to visualize the chosen cases.

Against this background of various processes of selection, the realism of the show begins to resemble the kaleidoscopic output of the historical documentary, which also selected a limited number of pictures to generate a homogenous mirror of history, except that the main objective of *Dragnet* concerns the presentation of a historically anchored projection of society's morality. The final selection of *Dragnet* presents a collection of three hundred original police cases that typifies normal and extraordinary crimes and seeks to project, quite extensively, the everyday work of the city's police, as well as the moral standards of its judiciary system. But, although proposing more than just a pool of isolated examples, there is no basis in the presented imagery for determining whether or not the chosen cases are indeed typical of the city's moral conflicts, or rather have been chosen in anticipation of their potential to compel on screen, to generate a unified response, and therefore to meet the moral standards of its core audience. From this perspective, *Dragnet's* much emphasized claim that it presents "true stories" posits reality as the stories' author in the same way the documentary claims history is the author of its pictures: both productions override the various processes of selection in favor of letting the pictures and their narratives "speak for themselves." However, in contrast to the documentary's invisible voiceover, *Dragnet* offers the icon of Webb to guide viewers and serve as a common thread of the show's visual narrative. Incorporated into the show's realist setup, the icon speaks from a unified lectern that enables a fictional character to refer also to the voices of real policemen.

The previously assessed effect of the broadcast, of emulating a microcommunicative idiom as a stand-in for a macrocommunicative term of visual language, is complemented by a discursive context, which introduces general moral standards into the icon, as well as into the voice of Joe Friday. As with any discourse, as Foucault defined the communicative concept, what is conveyed builds on a common sense that can only be seriously critiqued when assuming a viewpoint at the margins of the social or cultural sphere governed by its particular arrangement of values. The center of such a discourse is usually occupied by one or more institutions that manage its historical inheritance, regulate the parameters of its logic, and nurture its widely accepted status.[22] In so far as the icon thus simulates a police sergeant or emulates an "iconic lectern" for Webb's articulation of moral standards, it also takes on the discourse inherent in the LAPD's approval of the cases for illustration on national television. Once this perspective is extended to the question of how far an icon can retain traces of individual agency or authorship, it would seem to conflict with the equally institutionalized discourse of television to project visual symbols in reference to individual personalities and thus to individual morality. Bridging the logical contradiction, according to the hypothesis, hyperrealism allows tying not only the actor, the director, and a fictional role, but also the moral standards of numerous police cases into a hybrid figuration of life. Only against such a background does it appear possible that *Dragnet* could have accumulated enough moral authority for the LAPD to screen Joe Friday's police work for police academy trainees and to engage Jack Webb to narrate its television recruiting propaganda.[23]

The hyperrealism of the show, manifest in its scripted approximation of the everyday work of a policeman and in the television series' particular setup of iconic convergence, thus hoisted the icon of Joe Friday alias Jack Webb onto a public tribune of ultimately unimpeachable status and authorship. Hovering between fiction and nonfiction, and between subjective and objective reflections of moral standards, the icon began to speak from a discursive lectern, rather than from the place of an individual transmitter. The addition of visual language to the play was therefore responsible for casting an intimate light on a person, thereby translating any of his individual agency or acting into a unified icon of visual literacy, while simultaneously claiming for him a hyperreal standing as an authentic figuration of life. However, since neither Joe Friday nor Jack Webb appeared in any symbolic conjunction with their private life alongside their professional roles as either policeman or actor, their particular convergence into a unified icon mainly developed by virtue of the show's continuity and, possibly, by the back-stage appearance of Webb smoking cigarettes, which proposed yet another anchor in reality. In any case, the setting of *Dragnet's* stage compares more to the nonfictional stage on which a politician accentuates his professional character based on his mere presence in front of a camera, than to an actor's artistic mode of letting his personality shine through his fictional role on screen. The iconic lectern of unified moral authority at Webb's disposal—both inside and outside the show, when he appeared "off-stage" in a commercial—supports the hypothesis that television used realism not so much as a fictional style, but rather as an integrated, discursive factor in its pictorially based frame of communication.

11 The Icon of Lucy
Queen of Television Comedy

Hyperrealism can be achieved in different ways. Early television's most popular show, *I Love Lucy*, employed a totally different approach from the stalwart realism of *Dragnet*.[1] From the start, the stage format of this pioneering sitcom leaves no doubt about the show's roots in the world of vaudeville and theater. At the same time, the show invests its histrionic portrayal of an unlikely marriage with an aura of hyperrealism. The core narrative builds on the everyday adventures of the red-haired Lucy and her Cuban husband Ricky Ricardo. Since comedienne Lucille Ball and entertainer Desi Arnaz were also real-life husband and wife, the narrative presumes to mirror the actors' own marriage. The narrative interplay with reality gives rise to an inspiring web of references that not only enriches the characters' profiles, but also serves as a source for many comic and ironic twists although, or just because, the verisimilitude to their real lives is not strictly carried through. Whereas Desi Arnaz acted the part of a very similar Cuban bandleader who frequented the world of show business, the well-known actress Lucille Ball portrayed a much different character. Lucille played a woman who, unsatisfied with her life at home, only dreams about a career in the public spotlight. The irony of a highly successful actress playing a hopelessly maladroit, albeit always hopeful, acting talent sustains the many plots that have Lucy scheming for her entrance ticket to the world of Hollywood or television. Her schemes usually disintegrate into small disasters, not least because Lucy never succeeds in shedding her clumsiness when managing to find the fictional limelight of a public stage within the actual spotlight.

Premiered in October 1951, the show proved so successful that it became the first television broadcast to reach 10 million homes.[2] Ball subsequently made the cover of *Time* magazine in May 1952, a reflection of her icon's national status. It is interesting to note that the iconic convergence of the actress with her fictional character on screen also serves as the central motif of the show. With Lucy and Lucille, as well as Ricky and Desi, shaping galvanized, twofold icons, the show began its second season with the heightened objective of approximating a real-life context. When the actress became pregnant with her second child, the couple at first saw the pursuit of their successful show as endangered. However, persuading the CBS network to accept the pregnancy as a new twist in the established narrative, the couple decided to simply integrate the "expecting"—as it was called in the censored language of early television—into an extended play with hyperrealism.

The integration of a pregnancy into a show would not have been possible in early television's usual format of live broadcast, but because *I Love Lucy* was created with movie cameras, the episodes on the progress of Lucy's pregnancy could simply be recorded on film and scheduled in advance. As a result, television allowed week-by-week glimpses at the advance of Lucy's pregnancy, which had actually unfolded in the past. From the perspective of the producers, the recording of these pictures required the two actors to jump ahead of their own life. But by coincidence and good luck, the episode dealing with the birth of Desi Arnaz IV was scheduled for 19 January 1953, which proved to be the day when the actress gave birth to her real son. The news consequently made nationwide headlines, reportedly even eclipsing President Eisenhower's inauguration.[3] By the end of the second season, it was Desi Arnaz, Jr. who graced the cover of the first issue of *TV Guide*.[4]

MADE FOR TELEVISION

Lucy's pregnancy made television history for several reasons. Against the background of the industry's notorious, largely self-imposed censorship, the public mise en scène of a subject generally considered personal, intimate, and taboo for the public eye certainly captured spectators' interest. The unprecedented intimacy of the topic itself brought the show closer to reality, while the show's fictional portrayal of the actor's motherhood found a coincidental anchor in reality that buttressed its hyperreal style. Over the following seasons, audiences could even enjoy appearances of a child that was born as a fictional character—or as an actor. If this inverted hyperrealism shaped the fictional narrative of the show, it also mirrored the show's stars in both an intimate and authentic light. In the typical mode of the spectacle, the show offered its audience a view into the private sphere of two nationally recognized icons, combining their potential to attract public attention with the complementary attraction of a private issue that traditionally evades the public eye.

The spectacular television event of Lucy's pregnancy also underlines the difference between the new medium and the world of cinema. While contemporaneous cinematography was less concerned with a direct reference to reality, the undertaking of such a parallel structure between fiction and reality in the form of an actual pregnancy is unlikely to have been feasible for the complex production of a feature film. But only because *I Love Lucy* was filmed with a cinematographic technique, was it possible to plan in advance the presentation of the fictional equivalent to the act of giving birth. In other words, the show paired cinematographic technique with television's potential to reach audiences at almost any given time in order to construct continuity and intimacy as the pillars of its own brand of realism.

Reality paralleling realism was not the only feature that made the show attractive. Apart from the situational humor drawn week after week from Lucy's condition, the topic of pregnancy also addressed the political arrangement of society's gender relations. In an era that circumscribed the social place of women within the boundaries of suburban households, the double reference beneath the icon of Lucy is both out of the ordinary and ahead of its time. Despite her pregnancy, the fictional Lucy is still looking for a job, and Lucille the actress is both carrying a child and pursuing a successful career in show business.[5] In fact, the show harmonizes two issues that for decades before and since have most often been presented as irreconcilable in public discourses. For these reasons, Lucy has been considered a female trickster in American culture. Lori Landay concluded that the role of the trickster often presented the only way for women to achieve success in male-dominated environments.[6] In the show, much of the humor is built on the contrasting characters of the red-haired American housewife and the black-haired Cuban bandleader, who acts as the patriarch of the family. With Lucy's various attempts to scheme her way out of the house and into the public sphere of show business, the traditional boundary between private and public as dividing the female from the male domain is constantly negotiated on the show. Because Ricky Ricardo symbolically incarnates a Latin-American man, the conflicts along that boundary are further heightened with regard to stereotypes specifying Latin machismo. The resulting plots usually assume the same course. While Lucy may temporarily succeed in getting a foot into the public sphere, the attempts are always bound to fail. As a result, Lucy's escapades often embarrass Ricky, who time and again is confronted with his inability to control the public appearance of his wife. The fictional characterization of Ricky's machismo is anchored both in contemporary stereotypes and in the actor's real life, as Arnaz was indeed Cuban-born and -acculturated. But like the shaping of the trickster icon, this double play with exotic machismo always remains transparent, since Ricky's inability to control Lucy adds to the comic display of fictional failure in the face of both actors' professional success on American television. Both the female trickster and the male macho always fall short of fulfilling that which determines the mise en scène of their fictional characters in the first place, that is the approximation to their real-life personalities.

SPINNING THE ICON CAROUSEL

Although *I Love Lucy* used the hyperreal format of the broadcast screen in quite ironic ways, the show nevertheless owed much of its vividness and situational humor to the pictures' conventionally implied reference to reality. Since Lucy's pregnancy dominated the headlines, the public sphere marked by the print media added another hue to the hyperreal aura of the screen and sustained television's principal convention of presenting its icons as figurations of life. However, after the tremendous success of their first seasons, Lucy and Desi Arnaz continued to develop the format of their show. Having established their own icons on the national stage, the show began to incorporate some of the most famous faces of that time. From William Holden to Harpo Marx, from Richard Widmark to John Wayne, from Superman to Bob Hope, "big names," and thus "big icons," appeared as guest stars in the Ricardos' home. The show's narrative was subsequently adapted to accommodate the new feature of guest star appearances: Ricky Ricardo had landed a part in a movie, which demanded the couple's move—and with them their next-door neighbors, the beloved Mertzes—to Hollywood. As a result, the show lost some of its previous intimacy through adding Hollywood's publicity-prone celebrities to the narrative. In the same way as the focus shifted to the staging of well-established icons, the hyperrealism serving as a pillar of the show's humor became ever more carnivalesque. Lucy's vain attempts to break out of her home and into the public realm of show business remained the same, but her many encounters with the cream of movie and television celebrities established a place among them that would usually only be reserved for those who are indeed "successful." In terms of visual language, the very appearance in a picture alongside a well-known icon caters to the process of symbolic transfer, which structurally interrelates the significance of both visual symbols. While common citizens rarely obtain the privilege of anchoring their visual appearance in conjunction with an icon, to say nothing of achieving the necessary exposure to establish icons of their own, Lucy's mostly ill-fated adventures in Hollywood nevertheless allow her to project a unified icon. The show's narrative placed Lucy on the same stage as the stars of television and cinema, despite her being merely the good-hearted but notoriously troublesome wife of a half successful entertainer. Between the visual literacy constructed by the narrative and general television literacy, the show's imagery specifies the ascent of Lucy's icon in both fiction and reality. More broadly, it is as if the show scripted its own success, both on and off the fictional stage.

The successive binding of superstars into the narrative ultimately changed the show's format at a fundamental level. The setup of the show still built on the tradition of vaudeville and theater: the Ricardos' living room formed the central stage with a door to the left leading to the inner area of their apartment and a door to the right leading to the corridor and the outside world. Everything in the living room was arranged to be seen from only one side, the side on which a small audience was placed to see the action from a similar perspective to the camera and thus, nationwide audiences. The studio audience reflects the immediacy of the acting performance by providing a response, and, in cultivation of this response, the style of Lucille Ball and her company still incorporated the sweeping gestures and the rolling eyes of actual on-stage performance. However, while the live audience may have influenced the performance of the actors and contributed to a sense of immediacy typical of a theater hall, it remained invisible to the spectators at home, providing only an audio background. In this mode, the inserted plane of the picture merges not only classic on-stage with for-the-screen acting but also a "live" audience with an audience at home in a symbolic gesture that emulates rather than recreates the physical immediacy of a traditional stage performance. The difference was certainly also manifest in the show's occasional excursions into the outside world, as when, for example, a filmed ride in the subway breaks the stage focus of the pictures. On these occasions, the concept of an actual stage appears juxtaposed with the concept of a fictional stage that claims an anchor in physical reality. But besides such occasional excursions onto the stage of public life, the increased featuring of guest star appearances altered the show's approximation of theater in a more lasting fashion: Through presenting cinema actors on a filmed theater stage, the show juxtaposed its own emulation of theater acting with Hollywood's brand of screen acting. As a result, it incorporated cinematographically iconized actors into its continuous television imagery, and by offering them a second public stage outside their original context, contrasted their fictionally modeled personalities with a presentation of them as theater actors. The icon of John Wayne, for example, thus appears first of all as the tough man whose strength and manliness is anchored in many Hollywood narratives, before such semantic history is referenced on the show by the symbolic gesture of a crushing handshake. Through such incorporating of an icon from another communicative context, the show combined its almost nostalgic emulation of a traditional theater stage with the fictional realism of cinema to thereby advance television's novel format of staging icons in double reference to a fictional and to an actor's real personality. Accordingly, the trailer of that particular show declares that John Wayne had been "playing himself."

Although not without humor, such a line nevertheless announces the mode in which early television unfolded its own style of entertainment. The circulation of icons between Hollywood and the television sitcom is only one aspect of the new hyperreal life on screen; genre crossing within the diverse television formats is another, and soon came to dominate the new medium. Ed Sullivan, for example, dedicated an entire evening of his show *Toast of the Town* to *I Love Lucy*. On this occasion, Sullivan and the Arnazes joined forces to shoot a portrayal of the couple onstage in their fictional living room. In an extraordinary twist, the filmed sequences presented on Sullivan's show narrate how he visits the Ricardos' house to invite them to his own pictorial stage, *Toast of the Town*, and how the fictional couple is elated by the opportunity (as were the Arnazes). Usually intending to introduce the real personalities behind well-known icons on screen, Sullivan bowed to the ironic star carousel of *I Love Lucy* and presented Lucy and Ricky as "playing themselves." But while variety shows, such as *Toast of the Town*, and talk shows, such as the *Tonight* show, broadcast since 1954, may have occasionally toyed with the reality reference of icons, they nevertheless maintained the objective of revealing actors' identities behind their icons. The icon carousel was therefore destined to enhance the icons' lifelike aura in symbolic conjunction with their fictionally created semantic field. Contextually defined as public stages, these variety and talk shows were manufactured to let icons speak for themselves without script and without being bound by a fictional narrative. Their spectacular parameters proposed a view of actors speaking about their professional work and thus speaking as the private person behind their public persona. In the convention of the early broadcast spectacle, the privilege of revealing a private side in public, however, would almost automatically suggest an icon's status as unified.[7]

In similar ways, advertising also climbed aboard television's spinning icon carousel in recognizing the benefits that spring from associating products with well-known figures in public life. Making use of symbolic transfer, their visual message concentrated on elevating a product to emblematic status in conjunction with the fame and popularity of icons already established as nationally unified terms. However transparent the intentions of advertisers, their works also contributed to the hyperreal status of icons, by prompting spectators to ask themselves, for example, if it was Lucy or Lucille who would actually like to drive a Chevrolet. This additional stage for icons developed their hyperreal aura, reflected their unified popularity, and finalized their semantic fields through presenting them in their key characteristics: Lucy's amiable character and Lucille's comedic talent, Joe Friday's moral integrity and Jack Webb's meticulous proficiency, or John Wayne's masculinity and John Wayne's celebrity as an actor would serve as oscillating bases for marketing cars and cigarettes, as well as themselves. By the end of the fifties, television had produced a pool of emblems and a community of icons that referenced objects and subjects between fiction and reality and that could be observed in their manufactured individual aura almost every night. Instead of spectators congregating in the ranks of a historical theater, the icons now populated the screen in one's own living room, offering a virtual stage from which society's most cherished personalities greeted the spectators at home. From the midst of this carousel of icons riding on emblems, Lucy emerged as the queen of television comedy, as the toast of a virtual town, and as one of the first "meta-icons" in the hyperreal public sphere of the broadcast screen.

It appears paradoxical that the accumulation of decades worth of information about Ball's icon, derived from television as well as from the many magazine and newspaper articles about her personality, could indeed shape such a reduced, clear-cut image of the red-haired queen of television comedy. If almost the entire nation came to know and to love Lucy, pragmatic logic would suggest that such an acceptance veils rather than permits an accurate and differentiated idea of the individual person behind it. However, hyperrealism involves not only the unification of real and fictional references on the visual plane, but also the balancing of the new medium's visual, verbal, and other communicative codes. Lucy's icon may have necessarily had to assume a reference to a real personality in order to spring to life on screen, while at the same time requiring sharply trimmed contours in order to sustain its vivid popularity over the years. The icon was therefore withdrawn from its original narrative context in *I Love Lucy* and presented as a streamlined hybrid, which, like the icon of Joe Friday, began to speak from a place beyond individual agency. While contemporary moral integrity became the voice of Friday, contemporary humor was the kernel of Lucy's iconic figuration of life.

Although Lucy's icon began to outshine the show in many respects, pre-suming among other things the symbolic authorship of the show's humor and irony, *I Love Lucy* nevertheless started out with a much more intel-ligent approach to hyperrealism than many of its peer productions. At least at the beginning, the onscreen narrative created by Ball and her com-panions was capable of ironic play with an intimate approximation of a couple's everyday life, with fictional and nonfictional references, and with cinematographic realism and broadcast hyperrealism. The show captured the core of its medium's novel communicative frame and parodied it on center stage.

AN ICONIC OBITUARY

The intelligent approach of *I Love Lucy* to the new and still developing medium, however, became watered down in the course of the fifties and could not set a standard against television's pervasive convention of hyper-realism. Once set in motion, the carousel of icons continued to spin for decades to come, and merged the actress's individual agency and intentions with her icon in irreversible fashion. In her later career, as for example in the *Lucy Show*, Ball certainly continued to cultivate her original iconic image, but once the symbol presented an established figuration of life within nation-wide networks of spectators, it also began to dictate the actress's range of expression. Ultimately a consequence of the historical codes of visual lan-guage, the symbol's semantic significance thus demands its part in every casting of the icon, a part governed by the history of the visual term and the assumptions and expectations with which it has been met by audiences. However, while such an interactive creation of meaning regulates the use of every language term, television's convention of hyperrealism began to over-power the ironic outline of the icon in *I Love Lucy*, forcing it into a corset tailored by the standardization of broadcasting.

When the actress died in 1989, ABC News aired an homage to the "leg-endary TV performer" on *Nightline*.[8] Advertising itself as bearing "witness to reality," the television magazine intended to pay tribute to "the pioneer of television sitcoms" whom "we have loved since we were young." In this setting, the host, Jeff Greenfield, intoned his eulogy with a restrained voice and a sincere attitude designed to signal appropriate respect for the departed. The tribute goes on to provide information about some of the actress's achievements, interspersed with clips of some of her most memorable scenes, such as Ball's quoting of Chaplin's *Modern Times* in the setting of a candy plant or her sketch of a live commercial gone awry, both taken from *I Love Lucy*. At this point, the verbal and the visual plane of information already begin to contradict each other or to assume the style of hyperrealism. The flashback to the actress's most memorable appearances solely focuses on the icon in unified, converged presentation, placing her one more time on stage as playing herself and consequently as sole author of her visual symbol, although this time without ironic overtones. In the setting of *Nightline's* presentation, the process of iconic convergence is thus reenacted through identifying the fictional character role with the personality of the departed actress, without there being any visual cue for the spectator to disconnect the hyperreal figuration of life from the actress beneath it.

The first part of the tribute ends with a quote from George Burns, who describes the actress as an "American icon" who employed a "universal language." It is, however, exactly the element of "langue," which, in the form of the icon's enduring popularity, has not ceased to exist with the death of the actress, and so the on-screen obituary moves to the brink of surrealism. Soon afterwards, the news show cuts to commercials, demonstrating that a television obituary cannot break with ingrained television standards. The second part of the tribute belongs to the icon carousel, with Greenfield interviewing Sid Caesar and Jerry Lewis on the career of their peer icon. In the typical mode of the spectacle, such multiple casting of widely recognized icons serves interactively to heighten the significance of all symbols presented on screen and to enhance the status of their presentation as worthy of the nation's eyes. Yet the guest starring of two meta-icons whose significance has been nourished by decades of mediated on-screen presence rather than by any reliable information on their private personalities, to say nothing of their actual relationship to the dead actress, also indicates the medium's tendency to draw the verbal under the visual rule of hyperrealism. Although host Jeff Greenfield dedicates one or two questions to the actress's part in proposing a new place for 1950s women, one that was not confined to the private sphere of suburban homes, the two icons refrain from joining a rational political discussion on the actress's feminist "trickster role," preferring instead to comment on her, that is her icon's, approach to acting for the early television screen. Sid Cesar thus asserts that television was so new when Lucille Ball arrived that "nobody knew how to act," adding the—quite interesting—notion that "being yourself" was the ticket to success on screen. Lewis, after rejecting any relation of Lucille Ball's work to feminism, goes on to diminish the actress's achievement with the conclusion that "she was a clown" who "instinctively" worked the new medium.

The irony behind these statements rests in their unconscious entanglement with a hyperreal approach to the screen and to screen acting, their reference to the two celebrities' own, decade-long presence on the television stage, as well as in their appearance within the obituary itself. While the notion of "being yourself" specifies how Caesar's own icon should be understood, Lewis further cements the essential unity between Ball's onstage clowning and her real character. In this context, it is interesting to add that the actress's children would later go to great lengths publicly to characterize their mother's private demeanor as anything but full of humor. Thus, Lewis's association of "instinct" with Ball's acting—or her "art of painting Chinese characters"—deserves a closer look. Like iconic convergence, it presupposes a unity between the actress and the character she plays, although in ways tainted by the parameters of hyperrealism, as well as those of another discourse, gender relations. The suggestion of instinct at the root of the actress's success fails to recognize the subtle balancing of vaudeville acts and theater histrionics with the broadcast screen's demand for continuity—nor does it recognize, of course, Ball and her husband's parody of television's reality convention.

Ultimately, Lewis, and to a lesser degree Caesar as well, contradict Greenfield's inquiry about the relation of Ball to feminism, through perpetuating the traditional mode of qualifying female success with passive notions of instinct or merely "being oneself." Later on, Lewis begins a second attempt to honor the dead woman and to comply with the protocol of an obituary. By asserting that "she was magic," so much so that "she made the people in Bangladesh forget that they were hungry," he vastly exaggerates the icon's recognition in countries outside North America and ignores not only the existence of different fields of visual literacy, but also the possibility of a poverty so extreme as to interfere with the ownership of a television set: at this point, not only the visual, but also the verbal plane of the show look set to move from hyperrealism to surrealism. In a news show that has supposedly invited them to speak "as people," Cesar and Lewis nevertheless act as prisoners of their own icons, which grant them a voice in public, but anchor their words' authorship in the symbolic no-man's-land between fiction and nonfiction. In the attempt to praise a real person and her professional achievement, the obituary creates a spectacle that culminates in lauding itself, television in general, and the icons it employs and continues to cast, whether dead or alive.

At the end of the episode, when the American emblems of the eagle and the American flag appear on the screen, Lucy's icon appears more alive, more significant, and more nationally unified than ever. Representing the symbol in various phases, from its first appearances on the stage of television to its "last public appearance" as an aging star on Oscar night in 1989, the tribute in its hyperreal style is nothing more than another cross-genre show, which diffuses rather than discusses the actress's achievements on and off the stage. Spun as an attempt to transfer to the screen the cultural rituals that mourn and accept the permanent loss of a person in death, the television memorial applies a meaningless reference of mortality to an icon of which at least one half of its converged reference continues to entertain, to live, and to flourish within the bounds of national visual literacy.

DISPUTING THE PICTORIAL INHERITANCE

In the early 1990s, Lucille Ball's children reacted to what they perceived as television's appropriation of their mother's icon and its treatment of her as the quintessential clown.[9] Some forty years after the original airing of the hit show, Lucie Arnaz together with her television-born brother, Desi Jr., felt compelled to bear witness that their real family life was not very happy or funny, that their mother was not particularly humorous, and that she was certainly not a clown at home. [10] Unfortunately, the result, *Lucy and Desi: A Home Movie*, only deepens the hyperreal effect of iconic convergence. The motivation of the piece is clearly to "tell the truth" about the private life of Lucille Ball, at least the truth that her daughter, who simultaneously acts as coproducer, costar, and witness, wanted to share with the American public. Although the daughter assembled the sources and provided the context of the (auto)biography, the authorship issue proves to be more complex, given the ongoing life of her mother's icon in collective visual literacy. Utilizing idiomatic family videos hardly meant to address national visual literacy, the new context nevertheless projects to modern American audiences a unified icon with a semantic field aggregated through its presence on public screens over several decades. Since the icon's history included its casting in fictional as well as nonfictional productions, which featured a multitude of different creative and presentational transmitters, the reappearance of the visual term on public screens encapsulates what could be called an unlimited chain of transmitter references. Whether or not the home videos thus reference the genre of microcommunicative family photography, the pictures' presentation on the national screen transforms them into yet another stage for Lucy's virtual figuration of life. As a result, the meta-icon's historically shaped claim to an iconic lectern that allows it to speak to audiences from within a picture comes to stand in opposition to her daughter, whose visual symbol is only at the beginning of iconization in the pictorial narrative in which she appears as author, as witness, and as part of the pictures she uses as historical records. The iconic juxtaposition engages the semantic exchange of symbolic transfer, according to which the historically more grounded symbol tends to assume the more active part (this effect is also discussed with regard to the historical documentary's staging of iconic marriages). It is thus as if the mother's iconic weight challenges the daughter's visual symbol and her authority to speak from within the pictures she is trying to use to prove her argument.

Like most home movies, these video pictures comment on the special occasions of the family's life, including the wedding of Lucille and Desi, their move into a new house, the celebration of their first baby, holidays, and the parties, accompanying all the major and minor highlights of the Arnaz's life. In this classical genre of family photography, the pictures depict rituals that contrast with everyday life and that motivated the use of a camera. Their main intent is to document the present for future viewing of the past. Whether this is done with a "scientific" approach to documentation or simply for the purpose of private entertainment, the pictures retain a reference to their original transmitter context, which extends into the content of the picture's signs and symbols. As long as people are aware of being filmed, they can add supplementary meaning; Lucille and Desi most often choose to demonstrate happiness and fun. Unfortunately, however, the shift from a micro- to a macrocommunicative context presents the visual expressions of the pictures' main icons not only as obstructing the verbal argumentation of the daughter, but also as visually contradicting what the pictures have been intended to prove, that is the lack of happiness and humor in the actress's family life. As a result, the verbal plane often contrasts with the visual, as when relating the "tragedy" that supposedly rattled Ball's own childhood, her own unhappy motherhood due to her and her husband's absorbing work, her problems with alcohol and depression, the ultimate breakdown of their marriage, and her final years spent in bitterness and isolation. To align such verbal messages with the typical genre of home video, the biography cuts and edits the pictures into a visual narrative that culminates with a couple of shots featuring close-ups of Ball and her former partner wearing sunglasses. In contrast to previously shown party scenes, the close-ups signify the isolation of the aging stars, whose sunglasses are taken to be a protective shield against each other and the world, although they could as easily have been intended to conceal traces of hangover. The two were obviously not sufficiently isolated to escape the company of a video camera.

In another example, the insoluble problem of harmonizing public with private references within a nationally unified icon surfaces very clearly. This example also demonstrates the difficulty of using pictorial symbols for the purpose of argument, and of creating a personal statement based on an established icon. At the end of that rather sad verbal résumé about a star who neglected her duties as a mother to the person who is acting post mortem as her director, Lucie Arnaz inserts what is meant as a positive note. Describing one of her favorite scenes from the home videos, a shot of her parents playing with herself and her baby brother in their pool, she nostalgically reflects about the intimacy of that past moment: "Just my father, my mother, my brother, and me." Yet that verbal expression of longing for a different family history, for the one of a more private, more intimate family, is directly contradicted by the nature of the pictures themselves: the statement neglects once more the presence of the person who shot the pictures. With the daughter's visual symbol being the least iconized of the four portrayed, these historical home video pictures simply refuse to sustain the first purpose of their publication: visually, the historical weight of the parents' public icons take center stage, once again pushing the daughter's narrative icon to the margins.

In a most peculiar twist, the biography about Lucy and Desi's "private family life" may rightly show that the clown was not simply playing herself on screen, and, consequently, that iconic convergence overrides any direct nonfictional reference of an icon to its actor. But in attempting to redraw the icon through pictures pertaining to the actress's private life, this production also engages the same hyperrealism that was responsible for shaping the star's image in the first place. Although, or precisely because, it appears rather doubtful that the publishing of a controversial perspective could substantially change the audience's view of their cherished icon, the biography, similar to the *Nightline* obituary, functions as a spectacle: it uses icon-loaded pictures to arouse curiosity and assert the significance of what is conveyed, without being able to refer either to the individual agency of the author of the "nonfictional" visual information, or to the individual agency of the conveyed icons. In the case of the biography, the hyperreal spectacle is even further enhanced through asserting the possibility of disclosing through hindsight a private pictorial angle on a public persona. In comparison to the historical documentary and its reflection, for example, of the Kennedys' private life, *A Home Movie* attempts to use the intimate, participatory video camera for staging a rather controversial mise en scène of an icon already unified in its status. Even if such an "intimate spectacle" is meant to critique the nonfictional referent beneath the fictional icon, and even if it had an impact on modern audiences' evaluation of the icon's semantic field, the spectacle inevitably seems to add to the icon's aura and to further ground the term as embodying a person of flesh and blood.

By the time of the actress's death at the latest, her icon had left the realm of hyperrealism to reach a heavenly place in virtual reality. Because the actress's death served as the ultimate chance to solicit audiences' identification with her nationally unified icon, the symbolic obituaries on screen carried the icon beyond any critique, from a professional or personal perspective, since all such pictorially anchored commentaries only redeem hyperrealism as the underlying discourse. Although Lucille Ball and her companions began with a fine, ironic play on television's still novel, hyperreal use of the broadcast picture, both the obituary and her daughter's futile attempt to set right her iconic inheritance ultimately commit themselves to casting the icon for their own purposes and in ways that rather distort her iconic heritage. Ball's subtle balancing of vaudeville comedy with theater histrionics innovated for the intimate broadcast screen what could be defined as "overacting"; her artistic approach to iconic convergence thus ended in a rather nonartistic hype about her nonfictional persona. By comparison, Jack Webb's rather nonartistic style of "underacting" appears to have evolved in directly the opposite direction, culminating in the many parodies of his fictional persona of Joe Friday. However, hyperrealism allowed both Joe Friday's incarnation of moral integrity and Lucy's embodiment of trickster humor to stand as virtual figurations of life on one and the same new, virtual stage.

12 The Icon of Edward R. Murrow
Master of "the Control Room of Studio 41"

On a Sunday afternoon in November 1951, the veteran radio journalist Edward R. Murrow aired the first of his news magazines *See It Now* on television. Termed "a public service of the CBS television network," the show originated on the radio where it had run as *Hear It Now*. As with *Dragnet*, the new weekly public affairs magazine attempted to transfer a successful radio concept to the pictorial world of the screen. In complementing hearing with seeing, Murrow and his producer, Fred W. Friendly, hoped to enhance their approach to journalism and consequently decided to refrain from newsreel and other file footage in favor of producing their own visual information. Setting out to prove that television could be used for thoughtful, professional journalism, their show indeed pioneered the genre of news magazines on the broadcast screen.

The first shot of *See It Now's* first broadcast presents a wall of monitors standing in what is introduced as "the control room of Studio 41."[1] The camera pans to the face of Murrow in front of these monitors, who starts with the words "this is an old team trying to learn a new trade." With the monitors in the background, the pictures convey a first sense of that new trade and the new technique of broadcasting. The stack of monitors in the control room symbolizes not only the possibility of "controlling" many sights at once, but also the journalist's new role in selecting and commenting on these sights for audiences. The presentation of Murrow as manager of many sights serves consequently as the first theme of the public affairs show. "Rather impressed by the new thing," Murrow introduces "monitor one" with a view of the Atlantic Ocean at New York, and "monitor two" with a view of the Pacific Ocean at San Francisco, and presents "the first time that man can sit at home and look at two oceans at the same time." Murrow continues his demonstration of the technological miracle by ordering the camera at the Atlantic to focus in on the Brooklyn Bridge and that at the Pacific to pan toward Alcatraz Island.

The live performance of this command on the public screen is programmatic in many ways. It first of all suggests the extraordinary, centralized power of "the control room" to monitor and survey at will every place in the nation. Furthermore, the demonstration asserts such power through insinuating unfiltered pictorial reality. The man at home, like the journalist in the studio, can "see" a moment in the reality of both coasts as if he were actually in two places at once. The content of the pictures themselves, however, is also programmatic, with respect to the possibilities of visual language. Presenting at first some poor quality, foggy scenes of breaking waves, the two sets of visual symbols, divided by a vertical white line on screen, could reference any waves breaking on any possible beach. Without external context, these very general symbols of waves offer little visual information and are ultimately only distinguishable because of the inserted contrast line, which adds a technically manufactured sign to the shots' hyperreal imagery. As the visual symbol of a boundary, the line offers content that actually has another origin, another author, and another logic than all the other signs and symbols on the screen, and thus poses inside the frame as the external context needed to identify the two sets of waves as being different in reality. Although impressive at first, the demonstration indicates the very limits of broadcasting's omnipotence, given that not even a marine biologist could have distinguished the geographical identity of the waves, nor analyzed the hyperreal visual signs behind the waves' symbols for any other, more specific information. The subsequent panning to the Brooklyn Bridge and the Alcatraz prison island moves from the very general visual symbols of the waves to the very specific and unique symbols of two well-known American sights. Hence, the common waves become contrasted with emblems of two American cities, which specify the geographical locus of the waves, as well as their own, historical status as emblems. Known to most Americans, whether or not they have seen the structures in person, the emblems are thus used as standardized terms of visual literacy: they have the potential to attract the gaze and to govern the meanings of all other signs and symbols on the screen. Similarly if not identically to iconic convergence, the many postcards and other pictures that audiences have seen of the structures thus merge with the sights on screen and anchor the significance of what is conveyed. In the mode of hyperrealism, the intention behind placing the camera on those beaches is consequently veiled through an external context that supposes reality, or the emblems themselves, speaks directly—or offers a direct bridge—to the audience. The symbolic and historic codes of visual language operate between the universality and particularity of the offered pictures, which project a metaphor that may attempt to qualify the broadcast picture as an immediate bridge to reality, but could as well reference the mediating force of collective visual literacy as it bridges the nation.

Nevertheless, within the complete context, including the panoptic aura of the control room, the presentation establishes a powerful message about the new possibility of the picture, if not so much for the eyes of audiences at home, then at least for the eyes of the show's own producers. On several occasions, Murrow states his awe of television's novel technical potential and subsequently calls for caution in handling the picture, especially with regard to the purpose of informing: "We shall have to learn how to use it and not to abuse it." Albeit not treating the picture as a vehicle of visual language, he nevertheless adds a critical remark on its transmitter context: a journalist trained always to question the source, he defines his new role as "leaning over the cameraman's shoulder and saying a word or two to illuminate or explain what is happening." While he does not go so far as to treat the cameraman as the author of a visual report, he recognizes the need to place the content of the conveyed pictures in a professional context. Although the first issue of *See It Now* starts with an expression of almost mythical awe for the technical potential of television journalism, it also includes a critical perspective on the new pictorial genre of "public service." While Edward R. Murrow subsequently became, in the words of Thomas Doherty, "the patron saint of broadcast journalism," it is the peculiar dichotomy between the awesome power of the pictures—manifest in the show's title *See It Now*—and the scrupulously rational mind of the journalist that would characterize Murrow's subsequent career on screen.[2]

THE VISUAL VERSUS THE VERBAL

Among the more memorable and often-quoted broadcasts from the early fifties are the *See It Now* reports from the Korean War. Again for the first time, American audiences were offered a view of their troops in action on television. Only a few years after World War II, images of which could only then be seen on newsreels in the movie theater, Murrow's tapes offered scenes of America at war on another continent to spectators in their own living rooms.[3] More importantly, Murrow's reports from Korea were specially formatted for television audiences, and were anchored by the continuity of his weekly magazine. Unlike the newsreels, all the pictures on *See It Now* were contextually tied to a single authorship, that of Murrow as both journalist and editor of their content. In this format, his icon appeared within the reports conducted by him in the field, as well as when "leaning over the cameraman's shoulder" in "the control room." In this double role, Murrow not only enabled television to live up to its much anticipated role of informing the nation's public sphere, but also invented a new type of journalist—the figure of the anchorman as the one responsible for selecting sights of public interest from monitors supposedly presenting reality as it unfolds, who thus represents at once the journalist responsible for creating the visual statement and the editor responsible for its publication. The result is a pictorially constructed journalist who can be seen at work, or while looking over "reality's shoulder."

Murrow departed for Korea with the classic journalistic assignment: to research and to convey the essence of what was happening by means of both verbal and visual information. Yet the reports he brought home reveal a similar predicament to the one inherent in his live presentation of two oceans at the same time. The pictures, shot in places unknown to most spectators, contain little substance that could possibly be scrutinized for relevant information. While his reports reveal some shots of American troops in action, mostly firing at invisible enemies in distant mountains, the actual content of the visual signs remains unspecific and spectacular only by their context. In one scene, the alignment of a firing canon possibly identifies some distant hills as the frontline without, however, providing any visible detail about that front, or indicating whether it is a central location of the war. Because the hills' reference to actual Korean geography remains arbitrary for any spectator without inside knowledge of the country, and because any relation of the portrayed skirmish to the real course of the war appears even more arbitrary, the pictures relate to reality in the way a breaking wave on a foggy day relates to the concept of the Atlantic ocean. As Murrow may have realized on his first field trip to Korea, the hope that the camera could instantly capture unfolding reality was proving to be illusory, and the combination of responsible journalism with television pictures was proving to be an impossible task.

In another part of the report, Murrow is seen interviewing American soldiers in the field. The clip illustrates the conflict between himself as journalist and the camera as visual reporter. To provide background information about the actual situation of the troops, Murrow finds himself forced to explain that the peacefulness conveyed by the pictures, that is the visual message in which he himself appears, does not correspond with reality since the danger of a skirmish is imminent. Telling viewers that the company had suffered casualties the day before, he reverts to the role of providing a context external to the pictures in order to assert immediate danger as part of the visual signs' hyperreal content, although such significance is neither within their semantic field, nor visible when seen in direct reference to reality. The episode indicates a conflict that the convention of hyperrealism is unable to resolve. In these pictures, Murrow himself is in the focus of the camera, speaking to it, and thus to his future audience, who would see the report some days later. In this setting, Murrow becomes a part of the very picture that he verbally denounces as misleading and not to be taken as a visual record of reality. If the visual commentary of the camera can be verbally declared as not corresponding with reality, how then can the visual signs denoting his own presence or individual agency be separated from those that do not reference reality? This calls to mind the case of the Cretan who declares that all Cretans are liars: either Murrow's own visual symbol, the other depicted symbols, or all of them have lost their anchor in reality.

The example pinpoints the conflicts arising from both the dialectic and the symbolic plane of pictures. The appearance of a journalist in front of the scene he wants to comment on relates him to the background, based on the principle of symbolic transfer and the dialectic and conceptual codes of visual language (see also the glossary in the appendix). Such a relation between visual signs essentially differs, for example, from the format of a radio report, the verbal signs of which do not grammatically connect with any background noise. But pictorial language not only reduces any sense of objective distance once it portrays the journalist as part of the unfolding action, it also recreates him as a visual symbol that mixes the symbolic status of journalism in general with the semantic field of an individual personality in order to construct the visual message "this is a journalist in action." In light of iconic convergence, the peaceful pictures of Murrow amid American troops establish a profound conflict between the pictures and reality, and they specify a general contradiction between the convention of hyperrealism and visual language's symbolic propensity: In the novel mode of broadcast journalism, the pictures of the journalist create a symbolic figuration of life on screen that can no longer stand in direct relation to his professional work in front of the camera. Comparable to the addition of the picture to the radio broadcast of *Dragnet,* the photographic illustration of the journalist at work heightens the focus on the mediator within the mediated and opposes his individual contribution to the art of painting his professional personality with visual language's mode of iconizing his appearance, thus shifting both his work and his appearance beyond the realm of subjectivity or objectivity.

In the way that Jack Webb looked with "growing horror" at his first attempts to transfer the realism of his show to the screen, Murrow appears to have recognized the futile undertaking of capturing the face of war directly. And much like Webb, he apparently resorted to telling his stories increasingly by means of close-ups. Instead of approaching the front and carrying the camera to where the war would supposedly be decided, his reports from Korea began to center increasingly on interviews and portrayals of American soldiers of various military ranks and functions. Yet in this changed approach to visual journalism, the awesome power of the picture to capture reality as it unfolds also began to fade. Most of the soldiers Murrow interviewed seized the opportunity to greet their folks at home, converting the program into an emotional vehicle of which the detailed idiomatic content could only interest a few friends and family members. While any objective assessment of the situation of the army was thus reduced to the quite general significance of conventionalized, symbolic gestures, the interviews created a more intimate tapestry of visual and verbal content, which ultimately may have bridged the geographic distance between Asia and America much more effectively than visual descriptions of guns firing in a strange landscape. In light of visual language's historical codes, the familiar symbols of American faces and uniforms, of American gestures and emotional expressions certainly provided these pictures with more discernable significance than any contextually isolated scenes in an unfamiliar and indistinguishable environment. By the same standard, Murrow's filmed interviews not only bridged space, but also time, bringing the soldiers closer to the historian's present understanding. In fact, the pictures' anchor in history appears loosened through the currentness of the emotions portrayed, which preserve their immediacy in service to convention, rather than to individual intention. It could even be said that the interviews contain a type of information that evades history, through constructing emotional messages according to the premise of the evolution of visual literacy. Nevertheless, whenever Edward Murrow's pioneering role in the genre of public affairs shows is at issue, his reporting from Korea is cited as a milestone in the history of journalism. In terms of television history, the reportage indeed provides a historical trajectory, but one that concerns less the war in Korea than the novel method of combining verbal with visual commentaries, and thus the medium's new, hyperreal take on nonfictional issues.

By taking on the role of delivering emotional greetings from Korea, Murrow gained national recognition and contoured his icon as referencing not only the journalist's proficiency, but also the popular role as symbolic mediator within families. Iconic convergence thus mixes his personal journalistic objectives with a symbolic image of his profession, and his intended endeavor of accurate reporting with the accidentally acquired privilege of serving as a harbinger of emotional news. However, the more familiar and the more intimate his impression on screen, the less factual the information and the more his icon shifts into the no-man's-land between fictional and nonfictional, artistic and nonartistic acting, or between subjective and objective parameters. Similar to *Dragnet*'s screen adaptation, Murrow's translation of his news magazine to the screen also proves the new medium's inclination to personalize all content through constituting its messages around central icons designated to contextualize the pictures as only a symbolic window into reality.

As a result, *See It Now* began, like any other show on screen, to manufacture a familiar figuration of life, which would gain more individual contours with every new story. Initially, Murrow still acted as the traditional journalist he had become before moving to television. His verbal reservations about the power of the picture, as well as his previously gained reputation as a thoughtful radio journalist, certainly indicate his laudable motives in utilizing television's potential for serving the nation's public sphere. But the need to stage one's own appearance in front of the camera, to act the journalist that one might also be, and to anchor the presentation of news with a personal credibility shaped from within one's own pictorial commentaries presented a challenge that had little to do with the traditional role of researching and presenting a story by means of verbal and written language. As a result, the omnipotence of the broadcast picture as symbolically referenced by "the control room of Studio 41" came to rest not so much in the sights presented by the many monitors, but in Murrow's own status as an icon shaped by them.

ICONIC SHOWDOWN IN CLOSE-UP

Because hyperrealism demands an authorless picture in order to accentuate the immediacy of those portrayed within it, there is a tendency to present a journalist in the self-referential, symbolic gesture of painting the contours that surround him as well as the rest of the picture. It is as if he stands not only as the author of his own symbol, but also of all other visual signs that contrast with his appearance. Murrow's transfer of his profession to the screen demanded that he act out his own image and, furthermore, that the presence of his visual symbol shape interactive semantic relations that impact both the general message of the picture, as well as the reception of his own symbol, in ways that he could not possibly control. The dynamics of visual language, however, conflict with the hype surrounding television's new broadcast technique, which Murrow himself had propagated when presenting the miracle of "the control room of Studio 41." In shifting the claim of directly picturing the war at the frontline toward drawing an image of the troops' state of mind, Murrow may have retreated from portraying reality as it unfolds, but not from that type of hyperrealism that claims pictures can objectively reference the individual agency of real people. In fact, by bringing the camera closer to the faces of the war's protagonists than ever before, the resulting pictures still suggest objectivity, albeit one that needs to be further differentiated according to the parameters of a deferential or distanced, participating or observing camera. In the end, however, the views of firing guns and the intimate angles on the war's protagonists both comprise typical characteristics of the spectacle, and as such contributed to Murrow's ascent to the status of a nationally unified icon: unified, because his symbol appears in participatory relation to those of American sons far from home and never in controversial conjunction with the war's motivating forces or the faces of the enemy. Visually, such imagery undermines any verbal objectivity of his war reportage, making the camera deferential to Murrow's icon in its symbolic role of bridging the war's emotional distance from America.

In the mid-fifties, Murrow's new status as a unified television icon was put to the test in a face-off with Senator McCarthy. Having broadcast a couple of critical reports about the excesses of the senator's witch hunt campaign, Murrow himself became the focus of McCarthy's endeavor to cleanse society of all subversive elements. The subsequent exchange of televised attacks on each other's motives, arguments, and personal integrity was soon drawn into the spiraling dynamics of propaganda. With the rational argument buried beneath the semantic weight of the two men's icons, the question was ultimately whether Murrow's visual representation of the traditional, objective journalist would prevail over McCarthy's image as the honest, homegrown politician out to save the nation from an invisible Communist disease. Murrow ultimately "slew the dragon" (according to Thomas Doherty) as a result of various historical factors, not the least of which being American audiences' capacity to cut through the general media hype generated around McCarthy's public tribunals.[4] But in terms of the transmitter side of television history, a broadcast of *See It Now* on March 9, 1954, presented the ultimate showdown between the two well-known icons, from which Murrow emerged victorious by putting the senator's quite unusual way of laughing on the hyperreal stage.[5] A mixture of grinning and laughing, in Thomas Rostek's assessment "eerie, even chilling," it went on for an unusual, almost painful length.[6] Bare of any other pictorial information, the clip proposed the sadistic, stumbling quality of the senator's laughter as a reflection of his authentic personality. As a piece of visual journalism designed to contribute to the portrayal of a nonfictional, political world, the selection and editing of these pictures clearly betray a predisposed, distanced, and anything but objective commentary. In terms of the symbolic code, the visual signs together with the audio present a very atypical symbol of laughter that contrasts with the culturally contoured understanding of "normal," "typical," or even "American" laughter. In terms of visual literacy acquired from moving pictures, the distorted grimace would arguably distinguish any actor's performance in the role of the villain. Although it is difficult if not impossible to judge how historical audiences reacted to the presentation of this close-up, the decision to broadcast it certainly displays a strong intent to denigrate not so much the senator's cause, but his personality. As a visual commentary aired by a news magazine committed to objective reporting, these pictures only make sense within the bounds of hyperrealism—that is, as a factual indication of the senator's real personality—since any other perspective on their content would seriously question the journalistic appropriateness of presenting such a lengthy clip of a politician laughing.

The close-up of McCarthy's icon was selected from files, contradicting *See It Now's* general policy of refraining from canned pictures. The camera shot Murrow's icon from above. With his head slightly bowed and his eyes looking upward, the veteran journalist is posed deferentially toward his audience; by contrast, McCarthy is made to seem imposing. However, the real contest seemed to play less on the symbolic, than on the iconic code of the broadcast pictures. Murrow's icon comprised the image of an American journalist who had demonstrated his patriotism in his reporting from Korea and who had established his icon over years of continuous public service on screen. McCarthy's image was still reaching for the status of a unified, national icon in the attempt to become associated with the fight against "un-American attitudes." Once pitched against each other, only one of these icons could possibly hold a unified status without controversial overtones. From this perspective, Murrow's lengthy portrayal of the senator's unusual laughter aimed at applying a visual sense of "un-Americanness" to the politician's icon, and to the cause that propelled McCarthy to nationwide iconic recognition. If this is true, it seems as if Murrow beat McCarthy with his own weapons, although in their visual rather than verbal embodiment.

Whatever the actual impact of the show on audiences' judgment of McCarthy, much of the famous political controversy demonstrates the hyperreal characteristics of the television spectacle, which builds on a symbiotic relation with reality while simultaneously loosening all ties to it. For this reason it is difficult to establish Murrow's actual role in the subsequent downfall of the senator. What can be observed, however, is that McCarthy's icon began to disappear from public screens, from then on being cast as a controversial symbol in American history or American visual language. With hindsight, the confrontation between Murrow and McCarthy may be seen as having actually put an end to the more politically dangerous and excessive uses of the new medium of television, but the fight itself also sustained the pervasive convention of approaching visual symbols and icons the way one would an unmediated, interactive encounter in everyday life. In other words, hyperrealism not only made the iconic showdown on the public screen possible, but it also strengthened television's role in the American public sphere. From this perspective, *See It Now* created a spectacular clash between the discourse of traditional American journalism and the discourse of anti-Communism, and carried out the clash by means of two championing icons in the intimate arena of television's hyperreal public sphere.

JOINING THE ICON CAROUSEL: *PERSON TO PERSON*

By attempting to use for political ends an intimate close-up of McCarthy as a hyperreal mirror of his character, Murrow abandoned his pledge of journalistic caution toward the omnipotent broadcast picture. If nothing else, the episode indicates that his attempt to bring enlightened journalism to television had been compromised by the task of harmonizing rational workmanship with the symbolic and iconic dynamic of visual communication. Like the report from Korea, the McCarthy coverage had also begun with a more rational critique, in the form of a rather objective assessment of the Milo Radulovitch case broadcast on October 20, 1953, before ending on the "personal" and "intimate" plane of the described iconic showdown. This trend in the development of Murrow's work on screen can be further observed when relating the role of his icon in the public affairs show to that in a second show called *Person to Person*, launched in 1953. In ways curiously comparable to the career of Lucille Ball's icon—and for that matter to the careers of many other television personalities—with *Person to Person* Murrow entered the central platform of early television's icon carousel. The show aimed at introducing the stars of its time in their private homes: Frank Sinatra, Marilyn Monroe, the Marx brothers, Humphrey Bogart and Lauren Bacall, Elizabeth Taylor and John Todd, Paul Newman and Joanne Woodward, Marlon Brando, Kirk Douglas, Benny Goodman, Milton Berle, Bette Davis, Jesse Owens, Arthur Rubinstein, John and Jackie Kennedy, and many more celebrity icons appeared on one of the monitors in Edward Murrow's studio, from which he conducted most of the interviews. Again thanks to the wonder of television technology, coast-to-coast coaxial cables transmitted from the celebrity's home to Murrow, who in turn acted as mediator of the pictures for spectators in their living rooms. Networking the homes of the entire country, the show was designed to allow spectators a hyperreal glimpse into the private homes and lives of screen personalities, as if they were next-door neighbors. Although resembling the format of "the control room of Studio 41," *Person to Person* was designed to entertain rather than inform its spectators. In setting the icon carousel in motion, the private views of public stars featured much of the hyperreal play executed so extraordinarily on *I Love Lucy* without, however, adding one-liners such as "John Wayne playing himself." On Murrow's monitor, Marilyn Monroe is seen as a shy blonde in the protective company of a befriended couple, Harpo Marx in his usual costume is seen running crisscross through his home, introducing his family with his trademark whistling, and Frank Sinatra is seen marveling at his Oscar statue, displayed on a bookcase, before he exists his own home-stage because of an "important appointment." These glimpses into the private homes of celebrities were certainly at least partially scripted, and irony likewise occasionally played a role. Sinatra's appearance, for example, toyed with the spectator by juxtaposing the significance of a nationwide live audience with that of an individual "important appointment." Harpo Marx obviously enacted his on-screen persona when playing the whistling host to American audiences and guiding them through his private home, adding to the show a touch of *I Love Lucy's* double hyperrealism. But visits to the homes of many other celebrities, such as Arthur Rubinstein or Marlon Brando, left the reference between the iconic and the real untouched by any distinguishable irony. Using the promise of portraying the "private" side of a "public" persona to stimulate curiosity, the show provided a spectacle for the voyeur and thereby celebrated the iconic convergence of professional actors with their icons. But as entertaining as this formula proved to be, it also further hobbled Murrow's attempt to bring traditional journalism to the screen. By virtue of symbolic transfer, every appearance of Murrow's icon alongside another icon builds visual content through interrelating their semantic fields. If the icons in focus developed in the world of movies, advertisement, and television shows, their fictional contours radiate onto the journalist, just as his nonfictional icon sponsors an actor-icon's authenticity. In terms of visual language, each episode of *Person to Person* thus celebrated the ritual of "iconic marriage," which joined Murrow's icon with a bit of celebrity fame often nurtured in the fictional rather than the nonfictional stage. When shuttling back and forth between the parallel stages of *Person to Person* and *See It Now,* Murrow's icon carried all the newly acquired semantic shades with it.[7] Such genre transgression further impacted Murrow's early career on screen by elevating his icon step by step to a novel, quite individual type of "celebrity journalist," comprising both fictional and nonfictional shades of significance.

ICONIC ENLIGHTENMENT

When analyzing Murrow's icon as subjected to a process of "symbolification," if not fictionalization, the idea is less to question the journalist's life-long search for transparency, than to reconceive his struggle with hyperreal pictures and the power of the broadcast spectacle. With only hindsight, it is very difficult, if not impossible, to evaluate accurately whether or not he developed a consciousness of the problems of iconic convergence when taking his profession on screen. In part a consequence of the failure of the new medium to disclose the authorship of its content, it can only be established circumstantially that his work on screen reflected a development toward a more "savvy," as opposed to "objective," use of the picture's power. As manifest already in his showdown with McCarthy, he and his editor, Friendly, certainly developed an acute sense for the picture's symbolic power and for the significance of the journalist's icon in anchoring any verbal arguments brought to the screen.

In one of Murrow's last big appearances on national television, the broadcast of *Harvest of Shame* on November 25, 1960—the night after Thanksgiving—the journalist intended once again to enlighten his audiences by visual means, this time about a bitter reality within the nation's borders.[8] Focusing on the plight of black migrant workers, whom he portrays as modern slaves in a time of economic progress and prosperity, Murrow offered the nation an unusually critical perspective of its backyard in the format of what at the time appeared as the equally unusual, still novel genre of television documentary.[9] When separately analyzing the verbal and visual planes of this television broadcast at the beginning of what Michael Curtin called the "heyday for the network documentary," the dichotomy between the intention to report objectively and the propensity of visual symbols to overshadow rational facts is again in evidence.[10] The documentary opens with a shot of Murrow standing in a cornfield, in an almost biblical pose that brings with it as much association with the external context of Thanksgiving as with the icon's decade-old on-screen history. As familiar as audiences might have felt with the icon, it seems to be acting on a rather fictional stage. It is not possible to conclude from the pictures whether Murrow was acting the celebrity journalist, or merely himself, but there is an unbridgeable distance between his icon and the visual symbols of migrant workers' unknown faces. Following some families on their journey through America's produce fields, a series of interviews detail their lives, marked by child labor, less than minimum wages, inadequate health care, nonexistent education, and so forth. The exposure of the "sweatshops of the soil" that bring in "the harvest for the best-fed people in the world" is thereby contoured by a personal angle on some of the migrants' faces and their individual fates. However, as close as the camera zooms in to describe the fate of these unknown faces, it seems to be only Murrow's iconic characteristics that speak.

On closer investigation, the documentary features what can be described as two different cameras. One is the deferential, participatory camera that allows Murrow to choose his position and to enact his gestures in ways almost comparable to a movie set. The other is the distanced, observing camera that comments on rather strange and exotic persons, who are unlikely to have influenced their mise en scène in any way that would allow retracing their individual agency from the resulting pictures. The presentation of Murrow's icon in participatory, loyal, even "fictional" mode projects an active role in front of the camera, whereas the distanced format of a documentary displays the individual migrant workers in "nonfictional," and thus nonartistic, rather passive roles. In terms of visual language alone, the documentary does not give these black men a much needed stage from which to speak on national television, but rather lends them by means of symbolic transfer the face of a white American icon, and the limelight generally reserved for those appearing routinely on national screens. However, the intention of the critical perspective applied here is less to characterize Murrow's motives and intentions when producing the piece, than to expose the ambiguous genre of nonfictional television documentary, which *Harvest of Shame* would popularize. Seen by many as "one of the shining moments when the medium matched up to its potential to inform and enlighten the American public," the documentary, like many others around that time, owed much to what Curtin described as the "dramatic realism of Hollywood cinema" that its producer, David Lowe, brought to the "journalistic pretensions of objectivity."[11] As one of the first documentaries on social issues that made the screen at that time, its pictorial narrative not only built on the discursive basis of the medium's hyperrealism, but also featured an artistic treatment, thus mirroring the convergence of the distanced, observing and the deferential, participatory camera. As "one of the most famous television documentaries of all time," *Harvest of Shame* can therefore serve as an example of the symbolic propensity of visual language to render the authorship of pictorial content similarly to an artist's handling of symbols.[12] As a result of this symbolic propensity, the discussion of a political issue in television's public sphere assumes the character of an event. Thus, while serving as the attention-demanding mise en scène of Murrow's icon, the very unusual showcasing of poverty, deliberately presented on a date in the vicinity of Thanksgiving, resulted in a much-talked-about sensation. For a political documentary, the power of the presentational transmittership also lies in its institutionalized potential to count on nationwide audiences, whose response in turn inevitably enhances the significance of the presented pictures. In the era of the three networks, the primetime broadcast of *Harvest of Shame* under the symbolic authority of Murrow's icon could still rely on the institutionalized privilege of attracting millions of eyes that would otherwise be reserved for well-established social and cultural events.

The question of the ability of visual language to transcend the symbolic no-man's-land between fiction and nonfiction is thus bound up with the ability of the medium to fulfill its self-declared objective of informing or even enlightening. The factor of iconization may well present another problem for journalism on screen, since it tends to obstruct pluralism by marginalizing the expressions of all those who have not yet established their icon. From another angle, if aspects of spectacle are necessary to reach nationwide audiences no matter what the nature of the conveyed content, then the possibility of the medium of television to mirror every possible place and every possible topic on its public tribune is drastically reduced. As a consequence, *Harvest of Shame*, while being one of early television's most laudable efforts to shed light on people and topics invisible to the "general" public, also implies the medium's shortcomings in terms of what other issues remain hidden from the spotlight. Therefore, the panopticum that Murrow introduced in the form of "the control room of Studio 41" in his first episode of *See It Now* was indirectly debunked on the occasion of his last big role on the public screen. When reviewing his iconic career, it is indeed as if his wariness of the pictures' power came to resonate less with regard to their hyperreal assumption of panoptic omnipotence, than with regard to the spectacular status the pictures generated for his own icon. In the end, Murrow's on-screen history reveals the several aspects of his struggle: between his enlightened approach to journalism and the pictorial laws usurping his presence in his own reports; between fair and thoughtful reporting and symbolic pictorial messages that negate the categories of subjectivity and objectivity; and between the initial intention to look over the shoulder of a cameraman in "the control room" and the gravitational draw that brought him to the center of that camera's focus.

13 Walter Cronkite
Court Reporter of the Spectacle

Walter Cronkite's first "big story" concerned a gas explosion in a Texas school in 1937, which he covered for the United Press service. Cronkite was the first at the scene of an accident that claimed the death of 400 children in what he called the "most appalling disaster in American history."[1] His second "big story," during World War II, set up his future career as a television reporter. Paramount had asked him to participate in a newsreel story on "the occupation of North Africa by American troops." The feature starts with a picture of a text board, reminiscent of the era of silent movies, announcing: "An eye-witness report by Walter Cronkite . . . first American newspaperman back from Africa."[2] The following clip displays Cronkite sitting in front of a typewriter—his own by implication of the dialectic code (see also the glossary in the appendix). He turns to the camera and declares, "I am just back from the biggest assignment that any American reporter can have." The third "big story" of his early career, according to his own assessment in his (auto)biography, *Cronkite Remembers*, covered the coronation of the queen of England.[3] Having made the transition from newsreel to television journalism, he celebrated the new technical possibilities of the medium because they enabled him to convey reports to his audience more quickly. While transatlantic broadcasting was not yet possible, the taped report of the coronation was carried by plane, received in a "live broadcast" by another CBS reporter standing on the field of Boston's Logan Airport, and subsequently introduced on national screens as "the first film from Walter Cronkite from London."[4] After he took over the role of anchoring CBS's *Evening News* in the early 1960s, Cronkite's "big stories" not only became too numerous to count, but also prompted the expansion of the show from fifteen to thirty minutes in 1963. Sitting under a huge board that read "Walter Cronkite" and, below in smaller letters, "with the CBS News," Cronkite dedicated the first episode of the expanded public affairs show to an interview with John F. Kennedy, conducted in the president's private residence.[5] Between the 1950s and the early 1990s, there is not one president with whom Cronkite would not appear in an intimate setting. In 1963 his "live" announcement of Kennedy's death in Dallas made media history. Cronkite just happened to be the person closest to the news ticker in the CBS News studio and therefore gained the privilege of informing the nation about the tragic news.[6] He was also the first to present the Beatles to American audiences on national television, and remembers having received a phone call from an eagerly interested Ed Sullivan after the show. From the Beatles to the Chicago Convention, from most of the space program's rocket launches to Vietnam, from sports car races to the impeachment of President Nixon, this era of television history belongs to the "eyewitness reports" of Walter Cronkite, whose icon became an integral part of whatever he was presenting as pictorial news.

A declared patriot, a liberal, but at best in the "nonpolitical sense of not holding deep-seated positions on issues," as Epstein notes, and the incarnation of the quick and successful news reporter, Cronkite cut a different figure from Murrow, a politically committed liberal who set out to enlighten his audiences with thoughtfully researched information.[7] The two also maintained contrasting attitudes toward the picture. While Murrow never stopped grappling with the tricky nature of visual commentaries, Cronkite welcomed visual information as an enhancement of his work. While both were dedicated to the idea of objectivity, they tackled it from contrasting angles. More in the tradition of the newspaper reporter, Cronkite aimed from the beginning of his career at being in the right place at the right time to mediate a still unfolding "story" as instantaneously as possible. Describing his own approach to his profession (and referring specifically to the example of the explosion at the Texas school), he believed that the later a reporter arrived on the scene, the less likely he was to gain an objective view, because in a delayed or repeated interview, an eyewitness would alter the character of his statement. In other words, the more time passed, the more removed the interviewed person would be from the reality he is trying to describe. Cronkite thus located objectivity as much in the emotional response of a witness, as in the actual facts of a story. For this reason, he embraced the camera as allowing him to portray an event as instantaneously, as immediately, and as intimately as possible. Murrow, in contrast, tried to research his stories deliberately, to acquire information carefully, and to produce his own pictures in order to present objective reportage. Although eventually adjusting to the iconic dynamic behind his appearance on screen, he always remained committed to objective distance, even though the pictorial plane of his commentaries may not support this attitude.

Despite their differences, for both newsmen the relationship between their icons and other visual symbols on screen comprises a grammatical relation that operates independently of journalistic demeanor. When creating the war report from the African front for newsreel, a much younger Cronkite had already experienced the peculiar effect of being hoisted on stage by his visual reportage. The first shot constructs his visual symbol in relation to that of a typewriter, and introduces him as "the first newspaperman back

from the American landing in Africa." He then proceeds to report not for
a newspaper, but for a camera, and he comments not with typewritten
letters, but by means of verbal and visual signs. Seizing the opportunity
of large audiences watching at home, he emphasizes the importance of
both his message and his professional status, declaring: "I am just back
from the biggest assignment that an American reporter can have. . . ." Part
youthful enthusiasm, part professional ambition, this presentation also
marked the beginning of the Cronkite iconic career on screen, which made
him a symbol of the quintessential reporter, always present at "big events."
Moving to television, Cronkite soon appeared alongside "big icons," such
as the queen, all contemporary American presidents, and many other
celebrities of public life. By the early 1960s, his icon's status had grown to
symbolize his individual authorship of the *Evening News* in ways that left
the reference to CBS as a mere footnote on a background board bearing
his name.[8] By the 1970s, his icon "no longer talk[ed] of the principals,
but to them," as Dayan and Katz note, and by the 1980s, his arrival at
an America's Cup represented an event in its own right, symbolizing the
appearance of the "world's media," as John Hartley observes.[9]

Like Murrow's *Person to Person*, that first broadcast of the expanded
Evening News took Cronkite and his audience into the home of a celebrity. The intention of the report was to characterize President Kennedy's
personality and to test his presidential demeanor in front of the camera.
Cronkite would later criticize Kennedy for another interview given during
the election campaign, in which the latter allegedly insisted on redoing an
answer, which he had "flubbed" the first time around. Recalling that episode decades later, Cronkite still fumed at Kennedy, claiming that they had
agreed to air the interview unrehearsed.[10] The conflict not only reveals both
men's awareness of the power of television, but also indicates Cronkite's
general approach to on-screen journalism. Aiming at a "live" type of broadcasting, Cronkite was very unwilling to break the emotional immediacy of
his interview: believing in the truth of the moment, Cronkite strove for that
first answer and that first impression, and relied on the broadcast camera
as a technical means to enable unmediated communication.

Once Cronkite had reached the grail of television journalism through
achieving his own news show in 1962, his icon became the successor to
that of Edward Murrow, who was in the process of leaving the screen for
health reasons. Assuming the status of a nationally unified icon, Cronkite
took up Murrow's tradition in employing a personal line to end his show.
While the veteran journalist said goodbye to his audience with a personal,
almost emotional "Good night and good luck," his successor chose the
more rational words, "And this is how it is." With both lines achieving
trademark recognition with national audiences, they specify the truly privileged place both newsmen had achieved on screen. They furthermore indicate the differences, as well as the similarities, in the approach of the two
men to visual journalism and the handling of their iconic image. While the

more cautious, circumspect Murrow chose to end with a personal touch, the more affectionate Cronkite ended with an assertion of objective truthfulness, as if staking his reputation on the parity between his show and "how it is."

THE FIRST EYEWITNESS OF THE SPECTACLE

Aiming for "firsthand" pictures via unflagging punctuality, Cronkite unsuspectingly faced the core problem of visual journalism. As the first reporter on the scene, he was also the first well-known symbol of the news on screen, which in turn meant not only that his icon would inevitably mark a focal point, but that it also would reflect on the way he was doing his job for a substantial part of the complete, visual report. His quest for the first witness statement was depicted via visual information about his own demeanor, which had to be as emotionally authentic as the words of the interviewed witness. In other words, for the emotional aura of the moment to be preserved, he had to participate in what he wanted to comment about: he had to act as if he were a witness, too.

When positioning him to address the nation with the news of John F. Kennedy's death, CBS could not yet support the reporter's words with actual pictures and focused instead on the reporter himself. At the end of his message, read with a tight voice, Cronkite removed his glasses and took a moment for himself. The visual symbol of the gesture marked the immediacy of the news, presenting the icon as both a firsthand reporter and a firsthand receiver, responding so that national audiences could respond. In this instance, the visual gesture of removing his glasses blended with his verbal statement to signify the emotional truthfulness of Cronkite as author, presenter, and receiver of the broadcast's signs. When later asked whether the solemn commemoration of the President's assassination was indeed truthful, since he had personally disliked Kennedy, Cronkite appeared rattled, even shocked.[11] Rejecting all such doubts in his (auto)biography, Cronkite not only affirmed his deep, almost deferential respect for the presidential office, but also asserted the emotional immediacy of the moment in the national spotlight.[12] However, while chance had allowed him to be the first to receive the news at CBS's internal news ticker, the situation surely provided him enough time to prepare for his presentation in front of the broadcast camera. In this setting, he visually acted as the first receiver of the message for a nationwide audience, while verbally representing himself as its first transmitter.

In most of his other memorable reports on television, however, Cronkite did not need the aspect of chance or a reporter's good luck in order to get a story. Instead of having to beat other reporters to the scene, he was required by the television version of his guild to take each assignment according to the hierarchical parameters of the CBS network, at least with regard to preannounced "big events," such as the queen's coronation. In live-commentary events, in which the course of action is known in advance, the status as a broadcast spectacle appears guaranteed, and the significance as a "big story" is historical rather than immediate, the reporter's role begins to resemble that of a historian, researching the historical background of an event in attempt to comprehend its rules, albeit with the motive of anticipating its course of action in the future. In this outline, the live broadcast of a spectacle presents itself as the perfect opportunity for Cronkite's kind of "live" reporting, since the general predictability of a preannounced event facilitates the mise en scène of its most noteworthy moments. In his (auto)biography, Cronkite recalls his time as a radio reporter of football games in a small local studio. Since the means for a live broadcast was not yet available, he used the scarce bits of information wired to him by a colleague in the stadium to create quite inspired verbal images of running quarterbacks and imposing blocks. The possibility for such ingenious commenting, or "narrating of news," rests exactly in the spectacle's format, which almost entirely comprises historically prestructured information. Any variations in the structured course of action only emphasize the reality of the moment and shape its value as entertainment without threatening the reporter's ability to relate it to statistical and other historical background information. And when indeed something surprising or unexpected happens, it is the reporter's designated role to react with emotional spontaneity. In this setting, the spectacle inoculates itself with a measure of unpredictability that establishes proof of its instantaneous nature and allows the reporter to merge witnessing with reporting.[13] Once transferred to the screen, that double role of witness and reporter corresponds smoothly with the iconic convergence of professional image and private persona: the visual symbol thus mediates between the reporter as professional conveyer of information and the reporter as the avant-garde of the response of his audience.

Besides anchoring *CBS Evening News*, Cronkite is probably best remembered for his role in leading American audiences through the space program. Having been fascinated by the technical progress of flight since early childhood, Cronkite was as intrinsically attracted to the space program as he was to reporting. In his autobiographical records, his account of the progress of space flight carries a sense of predetermined vocation: "This was my story." Cronkite took over mediation of the space program from the first, still very failure-prone rocket tests to the successful launching of the first manned space flight and the landing of men on the moon. For over a decade, he had accumulated the experience and knowledge that made him not only an expert on the space program, but also an icon of its visual display on screen. Because he knew how to convey his knowledge in understandable terms and how to combine his technical know-how with personal enthusiasm—"Look at this baby . . . that huge beast of a thing," he declared when introducing the model of a Saturn rocket—Cronkite attained the first broadcast desk at Cape Canaveral.[14]

When CBS prepared the ultimate broadcast spectacle of the moon landing in 1969, Cronkite's icon had achieved a status that made its appearance behind the desk as predictable as the spectacle's general protocol of action. To enhance his role as first host of the spectacle even further, and presumably to augment the significance of the live broadcast, the astronaut Walter ("Wally") Schirra was summoned to relay "firsthand" expertise. Thus, two icons of the space program were deployed to narrate its much-anticipated climax and to manage any possible vagaries in the course of the broadcast. But should all evolve as planned (as it did), how would Cronkite comment on the historical moment of the Eagle's landing? A telling anecdote has it that Schirra asked Cronkite before the broadcast whether he had prepared a line in advance for that moment. Reportedly, Cronkite just shrugged his shoulders but nevertheless let the astronaut know that he would have something "important to say" when it was time. When the Eagle landed, however, all the "world class journalist" (Schirra's designation) could manage was "Oh jeez! . . . Oh boy!" But while the anecdote gives a personal perspective on Cronkite's work, it also demonstrates his perfect handling of the spectacle's predetermined areas of emotional immediacy. If Cronkite had indeed shied from preparing a comment in favor of letting his professional instinct and personal emotions find the right words, then it was the decades-long build-up of the spectacle's background that prepared the place for those emotional moments on the public screen. And if Cronkite had not already demonstrated his proficiency in commenting on technical wonders, he would arguably not have gained the privilege of hosting the event and expressing the first response for millions of other spectators around the world.

But the live broadcast of the moon landing not only reveals the ambiguous role of the reporter icon, who is called upon to project individual emotion onto the spectacle he is covering, it also relates paradoxically to history, at least to the reporter's part in it. As much as the broadcast spectacle's value as a source of information lies in its roots in the past, it also tends to assert its significance for the future, offering the reporter a virtual tribune in history. Cronkite, of course, did not fail to consider his broadcast—with his own icon in the middle of it—as "history in the making." And while the emotional comportment of his icon may carry a measure of subjective truthfulness, Cronkite had definitely also prepared a statement for his moment on the historical stage, which he delivered after he gathered his composure: "People have the audacity to say nothing new is going on these days."[15] And further, allowing the spectacle to engulf all societal reality, "I'd like to know what these kids are saying who pooh-poohed this. How can one turn off from a world like this?" In this view, the broadcast of the moon landing shaped the quintessence of the unified television spectacle: it was so powerful that one could not avert one's eyes without thereby banishing oneself from the family. The iconic master of ceremonies once more equated the actual event with its display on screen. He stood on the shoulders of all those who actually made the landing possible, and used their authority to continue to speak about all aspects of public life, as long as the hyperreal picture was on the air.

THE SIGNIFICANCE OF THE FIRST PICTURE

When preparing for the most spectacular live broadcast in early television history, CBS had one major concern: that the transmission of audio and video from outer space could be jeopardized by technical transmission problems, and that the garbled content would be unfit for worldwide broadcasting.[16] Pushing a new technological frontier, the key ingredient of the broadcast spectacle, that is the camera as both the subject and the object of its display, threatened to fail. While the broadcast would be able to incorporate any failure of the mission itself into the spectacle's narrative, it would require successful transmission of pictures in order to do so. In extensive cooperation, NASA and all three American television networks had therefore concentrated their efforts on the one camera designated to create that first shot. Mounted on the leg of the lunar capsule, the camera indeed operated as planned and transmitted the desired picture. When Cronkite received that "live" picture, he became the first eyewitness of the landing. With the camera positioned even closer to the moon's surface than the astronauts were themselves, Cronkite seized the moment for the history books, possibly before history had actually happened.

When installing the camera on the Eagle's leg, experts had realistic expectations. In light of the capability of the camera and the technical limitations of a "live" transmission from space, the visual content of that first picture was all but unknown. Indeed, the resulting jagged black shapes and foggy white patches conveyed visual signs that only initiated eyes could possibly conceptualize as symbols of the lunar capsule's leg resting on the surface of the moon. In anticipating that shot as the first highlight of its broadcast spectacle, CBS thus faced a twofold challenge. They had to ensure that worldwide audiences would be able first to read the visual signs of the picture, and second to understand their symbolic significance. For this reason, Cronkite and his coauthor used much of the lengthy "pregame show," during which they had no actual pictures from the mission, to explain how the camera had been mounted and what spectators-to-be should expect from its pictures.[17] In other words, they prepared the visual literacy of spectators to assimilate the first picture's code, before that picture was even taken. CBS had also constructed a model of the Eagle, allowing the hosts to explain the process of the flight to the moon, as well as the reciprocal flight of its image onto the broadcast screen. In terms of visual language's iconic code, this preparation of the first shot ensured the spectator's ability to recognize the structure of the Eagle on the moon, by creating an emblem of the lunar capsule before most spectators had actually seen the visual symbol of the "real one" in action.

The historical significance of that first shot can also be assessed by reflecting on what Steven Stark named "Space Television," which he ranked as one of television's most popular shows of the 1960s.[18] In terms of the visual plane, the seemingly unmediated significance of the first picture was culturally established a decade before its transmission, not least by many shows that had visualized fictional space flights. Its status thus hinged predominantly on whether or not audiences would apply a nonfictional reference to the pictures' visual signs. Such a reference, in turn, cannot be provided by the picture alone, but needs contextual build-up, which is exactly what all the earlier nonfictional television broadcasts had contributed when placing the space program on the public stage. Over a decade of broadcasting decked the space program with all the accessories of the broadcast spectacle as already described, such as symbols of cameras, photographers' flashes, audiences, individual, mostly female spectators, and celebrity spectators (in one "historical shot" the icon of President Johnson watches a rocket launch on his own television set). For the particular genre of space television, CBS had added yet another element to the classic mise en scène of the broadcast spectacle. On the occasion of Alan Shepard's sixteen-minute space walk, the broadcast was not only transmitted "live" to television audiences at home, but was also displayed on a huge screen mounted at New York's Grand Central Station. In utilizing a public space as a theaterlike stadium, television not only set out to incorporate the format of cinema into its own mode of communication, but also to prove its "physical presence" in the public sphere. As a result, television itself was put on a public stage, and curious passers-by at Grand Central Station were portrayed for the viewer at home, as evidence of the significance of both the launch and television's part in it. Although Cape Canaveral also featured some tribunes of its own, television had constructed its own stadium to emulate audiences' response as a visual symbol for the significance, the reality, and the credibility of the conveyed pictures.[19] Thus, when Walter Cronkite declared "the tension is mounting," these "live" audiences of the "'live" broadcast would react to what they saw and heard from him, and when their response was subsequently cut in, it would confirm the reporter's mastery of ceremonies.

When the moon landing was on the agenda, CBS repeated the format, this time mounting public screens at John F. Kennedy Airport and, maybe even more appropriately, Disneyland.[20] To emphasize the international status of the broadcast spectacle, further live cameras were installed around the world in places familiar to American audiences, such as Trafalgar Square in London, where the echo of the broadcast spectacle was authenticated by Mike Wallace's well-known reporter icon.[21] In truly circular fashion, the broadcast spectacle of the moon landing incorporated symbols of audiences' response into its imagery to illustrate for the spectator at home how others were responding to the pictures they were watching. And in truly circular fashion, television used the genre of the sports spectacle to sponsor the visual literacy necessary to understand the significance of the first shot, as well as the other codes, rules, and protocols governing the event's course of action. In the course of such manifold symbolic build-up, a virtual transmitter-receiver network replaced all individual authors of the broadcast, by putting visual literacy on center stage, and by constructing spectator ranks to gaze at the very television screen that portrays them in the act of witnessing reality. In the middle of it all, the icon of Cronkite projected a symbolic individual, with the emotional sensitivity and the political integrity of the first receiver of the first picture.

FROM THE PERFECT TO THE IMPERFECT SPECTACLE

In many ways, Cronkite's profession on screen culminated with the role of commenting on the perfectly executed spectacle of the moon landing. The positive reception of his expressions of emotion on screen augmented his privilege of being the first reporter on the scene with the right to state the first response for national audiences. As reporter and witness in one person, he nevertheless believed in the objective and even historical dimension of his work; he believed he was broadcasting "history in the making." In his (auto)biography *Cronkite Remembers,* aired in 1996, he assesses the 1960s Space Program and his own role in annotating it as follows: "I think that our conquest of space will probably be the most important story of the whole twentieth century." A quarter of a century after the fact, the same icon that visually anchored the spectacle of the moon landing once again predicts its future place in history. But acting as a "historian of the future" within pictures that project the semantic field of his sixties icon onto his appearance in the nineties, with words that simply perpetuate his past assessment of the spectacle's significance, any lines between the past, the present, and the future dissolve. And what, after all, is Cronkite's (auto)biography: is it a private man in the act of subjectively remembering his own life, or is it a well-known reporter icon commenting with historical distance about American broadcast history, one icon assessing itself?

While any "remembering" without thoughtful distance also contributes to a hyperreal approach to visual history by asserting that what can be remembered equates with reality, the title of the (auto)biography also pertains to his role as commentator on the Vietnam War, and the possible part he played in changing public opinion. When evaluating the historical footage Cronkite brought home from two field trips to Vietnam, one detects the same problems that had hampered Murrow's reports from Korea. Faithful to his modus operandi, Cronkite had also set out to find the places where the war was being decided and to be the first to inform the nation about its progress. On his first trip to Vietnam in 1965, Cronkite managed to come as close as feasible to where the war was raging and American bombs were being detonated. As an established reporter for CBS news, he was permitted to accompany a B57 mission and to film a bomb raid for his audiences at home. When the jet delivers its load, Cronkite cannot hide his passion for jet flight and shouts, "A tremendous G-load as we pull out of the dive" and "Ah, I know something about what these astronauts might be going through, wow!"[22] Back on the ground he approaches the pilot, microphone in hand: "Well, colonel, this is a great way to go to war!" Later, Cronkite frankly admitted the clip to be "slightly embarrassing," since it obviously neglected all concern for "what the bombs did on the ground."

The footage contains little visual information of any historical significance, besides this revealing demonstration of Cronkite's style of reporting for the screen. Not only do the pictures fall short of objectively assessing the war's course or, for that matter, the real effects of the bombs, Cronkite's search for truth in terms of emotional immediacy also appears thwarted by his retrospective embarrassment. Demonstrating a capacity for self-critique, he diffuses the immediacy of the historical pictures by adding what appears to be a more distanced perspective. He nevertheless remains faithful to his workmanship in framing his critique in terms of an emotion, embarrassment. In his view, the emotions conveyed by the pictures are still a true reflection of his past agency. However, in so far as his emotions are an expression of his hyperreal existence within the pictures, his recollection of them on screen and for the screen can hardly convey useful historical information. A historically relevant question would, after all, concern first of all the intention of those who created the shot and those who edited it for national audiences. The iconic convergence at the root of this clip, that is the unification of the double reference to Cronkite as professional reporter and as private man with personal emotions, would specify the CBS network as responsible for legitimating the broadcast. But the creation of the pictures was never meant to document the havoc caused by American bombs on the ground, and their presentation was likely never aimed at narrating anything but a spectacular image of the war underlined by a hyperreal commentary *about* Cronkite's emotional immediacy and truthfulness.

Regretting the particular choice of words, but not the choice of pictures, since they were documenting history, Cronkite came into conflict with the convention of war reporting that dominated the screens of the past. Meant to bring the home spectator closer to the front than ever before, television created a one-sided broadcast spectacle that only focused on the American side of the conflict, and began to concentrate on the reporters themselves. Like Murrow before him, Cronkite also turned to interviewing individual soldiers. Seeming grotesquely to reiterate the *See It Now* report from Korea, he comments at one point: "It's hard to realize that the Vietcong was right here this morning. They will be coming out of this area perhaps tonight, maybe tomorrow, if they dare challenge this airborne outfit."[23] More than a decade after *See It Now*, Cronkite, and with him most American war reporters, had made a virtue of Murrow's confusion about his own appearance in a picture that he simultaneously declared as containing a false reference to reality. In Vietnam, the invisibility of the foe alleged by the camera became a motif of many broadcasts. Verbal reference to the "elusive Vietcong" enhanced the significance and the immediacy of pictures that visually referenced American troops with the reporter's courageous icon among them. The epithet constructs the invisible as present, as the icon also conjures the hyperreal presence of an individual among unknown faces.

Cronkite's first visual broadcasts from Vietnam contained the eye-catching characteristics of a spectacle, albeit an imperfect one in so far as he had failed to portray visually a "real" skirmish or the "real" course of a battle conducted by two present foes. Without the moon landing's preannounced protocol of action, Cronkite was not able to realize an equivalent to that "first shot" of the event, and thus remained unable to comment on both sides of the conflict. But what is more, he also never intended to prepare audiences for such balanced visual information. As with most other reports about Vietnam in the American news, there was never a concern for the necessity of acquainting American audiences with the visual symbols of that foreign culture. But without having first been incorporated into the historical code of visual language, the faces of Vietnamese people remain as opaque as the visual signs of their homes, the historical characteristics and cultural significance of which cannot be distinguished without acquired expertise. In the visual mode of the television news, symbols of Vietnamese provenance could not escape their distant, exotic shapes, which also marked the visual symbols of Vietnamese who served as American allies. On the other hand, the many shots of symbols, icons, and emblems of American provenance bridged the distance to the war through their basis in homegrown visual literacy. Cronkite returned home with only one significant insight, which consequently only pertained to the American context of the war: he had recognized a large build-up of American facilities and arrived at the conclusion that the administration was lying about the size of its engagement in Vietnam.[24]

After his second mission in Vietnam, during the Tet offensive in 1968, Cronkite returned home with a similar, one-sided conclusion. Without saying a word about the enemy, he states in essence that the war is a "quagmire" and that "the only rational way out then will be to negotiate not as victims but as an honorable people who lived up to their pledge to defend democracy and did the best they could."[25] The words hardly complement the pictures, meant to illustrate the insight he gathered from witnessing the military offensive of an invisible foe. These clips reveal the "fatherly trusted dean of television news" standing in the middle of a devastated street in Saigon and "wearing a steel helmet and flak jacket" in what Tom Wells describes as an act.[26] Although the pictures portray dead or injured American soldiers being transported by helicopters, flashes of exploding shells in the background, soldiers firing their guns in panic, and so forth, Wells raises doubts that the reporter was ever in danger.[27] As opposed to his verbal statement, the coincidental, even controversial pictures of a violent war may give grounds for considering the American people as the victim;

apart from this tendency, the news special merely repeats the motif of an invisible enemy by employing the metaphor of the quagmire and so denying the agency of the Vietcong. From this perspective, his much-discussed news special may have helped to shift public opinion, but certainly not by means of concrete visual evidence. The 1968 report is significantly different from the 1965 report in that Cronkite's emotional perspective is declared openly at the beginning. The news special introduced the report as a "first-person story," meaning that the assessment of the condition of Vietnam rested solely on the individual opinion of the reporter.[28] When speaking in retrospect, Cronkite comments rather defensively on the much-discussed effect his broadcast had on President Johnson and thus on the nation's history, explaining the disclaimer "first-person story" as indeed signifying a "personal opinion." In his own words, he had simply conveyed what he had "felt" at the time, and his feelings were meant to contextualize the pictures in terms of "emotional objectivity." The symbol of the quagmire can be taken as emotionally objective.

Because quagmires, like most symbolic concepts, carry little in the way of historical contours on their own, Cronkite's famous commentary can serve as a further example of the way he adjusted the verbal to the visual plane of symbolic communication. Confronted with the impact his reportage had on the administration, Cronkite admits that he may have overstepped his bounds as a television reporter. At the same time, he also suggests that President Johnson's famous exclamation that losing Cronkite's support meant losing the war, might nevertheless have been exaggerated.[29] Although Cronkite manifests a certain humility in his (auto)biography, such an attitude stands in contrast to the national significance he had achieved for his icon. Already in 1966, *Time* had placed his icon on the cover and hailed it as "the single most convincing and authoritative figure in TV news."[30] But while implicitly hinting at the discrepancy between the icon's reference to his personality, including the way he felt about Vietnam, and his public persona, which was arguably on the same stage as the icon of the president, Cronkite offers no explanation as to what could possibly harmonize the public and the personal character of one and the same hyperreal personality.

In retrospect, Cronkite's long chain of pictorial narratives always positions him in a basically deferential attitude to the events he portrayed. Pictorially, his icon participated in most of the events without challenging their general protocol of action. His reporter-icon always radiated a respectful attitude toward unified, national icons and institutions, even when he verbally critiqued one or another aspect of them. At the same time, however, the dynamics of visual language's symbolic and iconic codes loaded his icon with larger-than-life significance. When CBS decided to call one of its programs *Walter Cronkite's Universe*, it knew, as Neil Postman notes, "that Walter Cronkite plays better on television as the Milky Way."[31] His deferential, participatory attitude towards the broadcast spectacle had thus yielded an equally deferential, participatory camera angle on himself. Ultimately, he was provided with the same unified, iconic lectern that belonged to a selective few at the top of the nation's pictorial public sphere, who normally served as the subjects of his commentary. Not only as the "most trusted man," but possibly also as the "most powerful" in broadcast history, his iconic lectern in the CBS broadcasts of the 1960s was acknowledged by more than twenty million Americans each night.[32] In this virtual arena, he became court historian for the nation's most recognized icons.

14 Muhammad Ali
Champion of the Screen

Like most sports, and arguably even more so, boxing offers the classic spectacle. Man is pitched against man in a fight for survival that traces itself back to the gladiator contests of ancient Rome. The British Empire reinvented the circus games under the seal of fairness and promoted boxing all over the world, whereby the sport also reached American culture. While the first American champions were still of British descent, the spectacle in the ring soon entered the national spotlight. By the 1950s, television joined in and elevated the sport to a broadcast spectacle, with its own parameters and its own ritualized place in the weekly program. As with any spectacular event, and as with sports in particular, boxing began to develop its own history, supported by a wealth of statistical data and many sets of visual symbols, emblems, and icons, which conveyed their specific meanings to the initiated, fueled every new fight with accumulated significance, and established the status of every fight before it even took place. Boxing names and icons, such as those of Joe Louis, Rocky Marciano, or Sugar Ray Robinson, made the history of the spectacle and obtained a central place in the American public sphere. By the 1960s, the popularity and ritualistic status of American professional boxing even outshone Olympic boxing, which was not considered relevant to the "real" arena. When Muhammad Ali won the light heavyweight title in Rome as the young Cassius Clay, the gold medal was hardly worth the entrance ticket to a professional career, let alone able to guarantee competition with the real gladiators, Sonny Liston and Floyd Patterson.[1] Since the gold medal was not enough for him to join the national spectacle, Ali started from early on to craft his image, using among other things poetry to attract the nation's attention: "To make America the greatest is my goal—So I beat the Russian and the Pole—And for USA won the medal of Gold—Italians said 'You're greater than the Cassius of old.'"

In preparing himself for the "big fights" and beating his way through the lower ranks of professional boxing, he used—and arguably improved—his poetry to prophesy victory in prefight announcements, even predicting the specific round in which he would overwhelm his opponent.[2] Facing the veteran Archie Moore, for example, he declaimed: "When you come to the fight, don't block the aisle, and don't block the door. You will all go home after round four." Inspired by the (in)famous wrestler Gorgeous George, whom he had met on several occasions, according to David Remnick, he added narcissistic one-liners to his prefight show, such as "If I lose, I'm going to crawl across the ring and kiss your feet."[3] But although beginning to arouse the interest of the media, Ali was still years away from being accepted for the national arena among the established icons of boxing at the time, such as those of Patterson and Liston. Touring the rings of the country in his "Cassius Clay Enterprises" bus, Ali revealed yet a new facet of his marketing strategy that soon became part of the boxing spectacle itself: the prefight confrontation. Using the bus as a mobile camp, as well as a vehicle for advertising, with its huge sign declaring, "World's Most Colorful Fighter: Sonny Liston Must Go in Eight," his team decided to visit the reigning champion at his private Denver home. Having tipped off the media in advance, Ali rang out an unsuspecting Liston, reportedly dressed in pajamas and silk robe, and mocked and challenged him in front of the reporters' cameras: "If you don't come out of that door, I'm gonna break it down!"[4] Calculating that Liston would not engage, whether because he would be too surprised, because Ali was still a disregarded outsider, or because he would not wish to play into his already "bad image" as a former prison inmate, the quite controlled set-up was determined to be successful: it made the idea of a fight between the two men feasible by indicating its potential as a spectacle and by setting up press pictures with Liston's icon in symbolic transfer with Ali's. In short, it asserted that the two symbols were in the same spectacular league.

The confrontation on a Denver sidewalk not only helped to set up Ali as a challenger, it also broke with the tradition of the classic sports spectacle. Unlike the Roman games and the British sports tradition, it extended the showdown into areas previously defined as separated from the act of the contest, thus challenging the boundary between the private and the public realm of the sports event. The hedging of violent encounters by the rules and rituals of fair play inside the ropes enabled private aggression to be watered down almost in the fashion of wrestling, albeit here called "psychological warfare." However, when traditional fair play demanded handshakes, whether enacted or not, as symbolic expressions of the boxers' rational ability to separate their sportive from their private personae, the incorporation of "psychological warfare" indicates hyperrealism in yet another light. By extending the psychology of a violent encounter into areas outside the ring, the traditional boundary between public and private behavior appears to erode in favor of a subconscious reflection of the boxer's personality. The concept thus unifies the boxer's character as a fighter with that of his personality outside the ring—much like the way iconic convergence melds on-screen with off-screen references. The collaboration of television thus appears to have significantly contributed to this new type of pregame spectacle that enhanced the showdown of fists with the boxers' character image outside the ring. Announced and unannounced visits to the opponent's camp, depictions of training in front of the camera, as well as skirmishes on the occasion of "weigh-ins" would soon be part of a new boxing spectacle inspired by Muhammad Ali's grotesque showmanship. The new sports spectacle prenarrated the stories before they unfolded, loaded the symbolic images of the "actors" before they acted, and effectively established their icons before the actual face off.

When Ali arrived in Miami to fight Liston, he had already established himself as worthy for the spectacle, despite the fact that newspapers had evaluated his boxing skills as immature, a judgment reflected by the bookkeepers' odds of 7:1 in favor of Liston. Unaffected by his lack of credentials as a boxer, Ali continued to initiate his iconic status, and as the nobody that he still was on the national stage, he managed to get his picture taken with the Beatles, who happened to be in town.[5] Further playing on the symbolic function of the visual, although by verbal reference, he also began to lecture the media that "a champ should be pretty" and that Liston was simply too "ugly" to be the king of the spectacle. On every possible and impossible occasion, he continued his trademark act and prophesied not only the specific round in which his victory would come, but also the style and tactics he was going to use to defeat the "ugly bear."

What Ali was doing in effect was constructing his sports icon before it had taken shape in the ring, and establishing the spectacle before it had actually taken place. In front of the camera, he simply performed himself as the serious challenger, prenarrated his future icon as that of a heavyweight champion, and seized the role of the spectacle's master of ceremonies. In contrast to Cronkite's combined role as the first transmitter and the first receiver on screen, Ali acted out the very story that he also commented on. Such commenting inevitably conflicted with the reporters guild, which saw its monopoly on mediating reality and its traditional power of publicly evaluating events and protagonists challenged. Yet, all the lines subsequently written about the "big mouth" from Kentucky, who would certainly take a heavy beating at the hands of the "real" champion, only reflected their ineptness in the face of Ali's mastery of the spectacle. After all, if Ali was really that inferior to Liston, the spectacle itself—and with it the reporters' presence in Miami—was unjustified. But since the spectacle was already in the works and the expert reporters had all been deployed to comment on it, every one of their words was fated to grant Ali more public recognition, and in consequence, to participate in their demotion from mediators to mere front-row spectators who can only wait for what's to come.

The antipathy most commentators developed toward the usurping icon of Ali reflects the general shift of the sports spectacle from print to television. When an event was "big" enough, newspapers would traditionally only send their most established columnists, "big" names such as Jimmy Cannon from the *New York Post,* Arthur Daley from the *New York Times,* or *Esquire*'s Norman Mailer, a member of the literati. The trend to celebrity coverage was taken up by radio and then television, which, however, altered the principle by using icons such as former champions for cohosting the broadcast and for backing up the visual rather than the verbal significance of commentary. When the fight was live-broadcast on closed circuit by TNT (the Theater Network Television) to connected sets all over the country, the television presence had already established its place within the spectacle and altered the ritual protocol of the event. After taking some seconds to introduce the main actors of the evening, the ring announcer directed the audience's attention to celebrity spectators, such as Sugar Ray Robinson, whose presence enhanced the significance of the occasion.[6] However, he spent a good part of his introduction articulating a connection between some of the honored guests and television itself, presenting coanchor for ABC radio Rocky Marciano, and then, "doing the commentary for Theater Network Television, probably the most beloved boxer of all time, defending his title twenty-five times in his nine years as heavyweight champion, the brown bomber . . ." Joe Lewis.[7] The icon of the TNT cocommentator can then be seen on screen, as he stands up and waves to the applauding spectators. Soon afterwards he would assume the role as "iconic historian" of the spectacle by evaluating the beginning of the fight as the "greatest first round in a very long time." Yet even in the face of so much history, ritual, and celebrity aura, Ali retained control of both the spectacle and the ring. Pausing only to make the symbolic expression of a "big mouth" to the camera and to all who would understand its contextual significance, he proceeded to win in seven rounds, and immediately afterward offered up the line that would go down in sports history: "I shook up the world!"

AN UN(FOR)SEEABLE KNOCKOUT PUNCH

The fight was not memorable for any spectacular scenes or for any outstanding displays of boxing skills. Certainly, Ali demonstrated what appeared as a new brand of intelligent, fast-moving boxing paired with an impressive athleticism that first surprised and later wore down the "ugly bear." Yet a real highlight, such as a knockout or at least any visually outstanding punch that could be recognized as a turning point of the encounter, was missing from the broadcast. In the conclusion, Liston simply did not rise from his corner to face another round. If the fight nevertheless made boxing history, it was because Ali had announced himself as "king of the world," because he had prenarrated the script of his coronation, and because he had then accomplished "his-story" in unparalleled fashion. In appropriating the grotesque showmanship of the wrestling business, he preempted the core mechanism of the sports spectacle, which selects and crowns icons on the nation's most observed stage. In replacing the television spectacle's hyperrealism with what Mikhail Bakhtin would have identified as "grotesque realism," Ali not only pioneered modern sports rituals, he also brought commentators and audiences to sense for the first time the surrealism of the spectacle.[8] The court reporters of the spectacle had to "eat their words" as Ali would later gleefully detail, and the only way for them to preserve their belief in the truthfulness of the spectacle's visual display was to muse about the possibility of a "fixed" fight, which many did, albeit not yet publicly.

A year later, the expert commentators gathered again to witness the rematch between the two fighters, hoping for what Ali himself had once declared as the main attraction: the chance to see his "big black mouth polished." The second pregame show featured, as previously, Ali working the punching ball, Ali working the heavy bag: a reconstruction of his visual symbol as an extraordinarily talented boxer. It was a symbolic mise en scène, and an artistic enactment of his professional persona, which he complemented with the equally symbolic words, "Float like a butterfly, sting like a bee." Like the first fight, the second also came to an abrupt and surprising end. Although this time Ali knocked Liston to the floor, subsequent confusion caused by the official in the ring, a former boxer and so-called "celebrity-referee," prevented the orderly execution of the ritual count to ten. While the officials conferred in one corner, the two athletes resumed fighting, until they were separated again and the fight was ended on the assumption that Liston must have been down for more than ten seconds during the confusion. Boxing matches are not supposed to end like this. Champions should not resign while sitting in their corner, nor should referees lose track of how long a contender has been down. What's more, none of the commentators had actually seen the knockout punch, and this time they alleged a "fix." In the subsequent days and weeks, the television pictures of the fight were analyzed by all possible experts, who went over the details of the visual records time and again. Even today, the pictures invite us to join the discussion.[9]

The issue compares with the famous Zapruder film of President John F. Kennedy's assassination in Dallas: the decisive moments are actually captured by the camera, just not at an ideal angle. The very idea of an ideal angle of a picture could only be possible in the context of a spectacle, which designates its main areas of interest in advance. In other sports spectacles, for example hockey, the surveillance of the goal line by specially arranged cameras is meant to substitute for a referee's eyes; the surveillance only works because it can anticipate the exact location of the possible conflict due to the scripted format of the game. The resulting pictures further profit from the "artificial" goal line painted into the ice to separate scoring from not scoring. The painted goal line therefore reflects the code of the game in the form of a boundary, which when transferred to visual language is complemented by the logic of the dialectic code, which builds equally on the twofold nature of boundary lines.[10] Unlike the line between Murrow's two oceans that specifies content added by the presenters, the photography of a painted goal line merges the rules of the game with the precise contrast line of a pictorial symbol on screen. In the boxing arena, however, there are no painted lines and the two moving athletes make it difficult to control their mise en scène on the screen. The pictures documenting the Ali-Liston fight prove there was a punch to Liston's face, but not much more. There were efforts to reconstruct the action, to translate the visual signs into the realm of natural science by measuring the physical power that could possibly have been transferred. But all attempts to make a summation of the possible kinetic energy of a forward-moving Liston and the estimated power of Ali's shot from the hip proved inconclusive. The mystery of the two-dimensional clash in pictures resisted all attempts at scientifically deduced certitude.[11]

Ultimately, the search for truth in those pictures remained as symbolic as the pictures' content. The dialectic and conceptual principles (see also the glossary in the appendix) first of all propose the reading of a fist making contact. For this to be understood, the spectator needs to construct the verblike significance based on the visual contours of the fist and chin. The boundary between them, however, is a purely two-dimensional contour line that first of all initiates an interpretation based on cultural principles (or the symbolic and the iconic codes of visual language, see the glossary in the appendix). As a result, the verblike gesture of the punch itself becomes a symbol that is qualified as either typical or atypical of all other knockout punches the observer has seen. This sorting against the background of the collected visual literacy of the sport is further enhanced by the iconic code, which then adds the semantic weight of Liston's and Ali's icons to the equation. If previous encounters with Ali's icon on-screen had forged the visual narrative of an imposing man able to execute extraordinarily powerful punches, arguably nobody would have doubted the knockout. There are many examples in the world of cinema in which the iconic code not only constructed an actor's image as a strong man, but also the gesture of his punch as extraordinarily powerful, without the corresponding visual signs being analyzable in their reference to reality. In cinema's brand of realism, however, there is no doubt about punches being faked; the iconic code merely demands that a punch be believable against the background of the icon's fictional history, as well as that comprising other, comparable cinematographic representations of punches. By contrast, the hyperrealism of the sports spectacle insinuates its pictures as different, even though it proves equally inept in assessing the punch's actual impact. In its setting, the on-screen punch had to refer to reality, and experts were on hand to authenticate that reference. But while insiders can certainly acquire an informed sense for the significance of a fight's details, such knowledge emerges from the experience of seeing many fights in person. Transferred to the realm of the picture, the view and its angle is altered, and as similar as the picture might appear to what is perceived in the arena, additional experience specific to reading pictures is demanded. In any case, all pictures of knockdowns ever seen on screen, whether real or faked, contribute to visual literacy, which converges all pictorial gestures with all those witnessed in unmediated reality. By the same measure, the icon on screen merges its own history with that of the boxer's, which in Ali's case did not yet denote a heavy hitter, as it would in later years.[12] The very public questioning of the second fight's authenticity thus hinged as well on the missing knockout in the first fight. As a consequence, it was less the power of the punch than the authority of the icon that was questioned, in a contest between Ali's still rather controversial and unfinished iconic contours and Liston's icon's superior semantic weight in referencing a hard-nosed, prison-trained, very experienced professional.

Without the possibility of determining with certitude whether or not the fight was fixed, the media found itself again tied up in the spiraling logic of the broadcast spectacle. Not ready to accept the pictures as a predominantly symbolic reflection of the event, the media may have temporarily questioned the status of the boxer's icon, but because the possibility of proof was missing from the pictures, Ali triumphed once again as king of the spectacle. Years later Ali would still mock the media for hanging on to the concept of the camera's supreme ability to record reality. With extraordinary wit and irony, Ali offered the argument that his famous punch had simply been too fast: too fast not only for Liston, but also for the audience's eyes, as well as for the camera's shutter.[13] First joking that his fist was faster than the blink of an eye, and that all the ringside spectators must have blinked at the same time, he then added a technical argument for those who had witnessed the fight on screen: the picture per second rate of the average television camera would actually leave gaps lengthy enough to fit in a quick knockout punch.[14] What he offered as an ironic commentary on his own agency would have filled the Greek philosopher Zeno of Elea with great satisfaction (See the theoretical sections in the appendix.) In effect, Ali questioned the empirical capacity of human perception, as well as of human logic, to recognize and define movement within elapsing time and extended space. Like Zeno's arrow, Ali's fist theoretically remained in repose in any given instant of its flight, as it was in practice immobile in every single frame on the celluloid. According to the dialectic logic of visual language, its impact on Liston's chin can therefore only be reflected by one arbitrary, motionless contrast line that separates two sets of visual shapes via a symbolic interpretation— thus resembling rather Murrow's boundary between the two oceans than that of a goal line. Once again, Ali transcended the spectacle that nurtured his icon, this time through challenging the camera as the technical arbiter of reality in the on-screen spectacle.

The episode from Ali's second big fight can serve as a further example of the inability of the picture to inform experts—as well as historians— about what it pretends to convey, in this case the actual agency and the actual boxing skill of the men behind visual symbols. Ironically, however, the demonstrated ineptness of hyperrealism did not harm the authenticity of the television spectacle and that of its iconic experts, but rather rang the bell that signaled the final round for ring-based newspaper reporters in the national spotlight. Those who translated their unmediated perception into written letters were replaced by those who "painted" their own visual symbols within their commentary, and thus wrote their own ritualized role into the pictorial narrative of the broadcast spectacle.

GROTESQUE REALISM MEETS CARNIVELESQUE POLITICS

Soon after his first triumph over Sonny Liston, Ali employed the big stage for reasons traditionally seen as outside the bounds of sports spectacle. Having become acquainted with Elijah Muhammad's Nation of Islam and having befriended one of his main lieutenants, Malcolm X, he publicly changed his name from Cassius Clay to Muhammad Ali.[15] Again pressing the bounds of the spectacle's traditional parameters, the change was a symbolic play with political connotations. Ali, whose given name referred to the history of the Roman empire, and his surname to a benign white slave owner in the nineteenth century, objected to the fact that his own and most other black Americans' names did not reference their autarchic historical, genealogic, or geographic roots. With the adoption of the Islamic name, he not only established a reference to the African roots of his people but also publicly disclosed his relationship to the Nation of Islam, an organization known for its radical rhetoric and aggressive attitude toward white culture and politics. While the adoption of pen and stage names was nothing new in the public arena, a politically motivated change of name after having established iconic status was highly unusual, and moreover was threatening to the continuity and consistency of the icon's reference to its history in the public limelight. For years to come, the media would struggle with the implications of the name change, often using both names with one of them framed by brackets, while some papers, like the *New York Times*, refused to print the Islamic name altogether. In historiographic dimensions, the change of name apparently posed a problem for many authors, who established the convention of referring to Ali as Cassius Clay until the first Liston fight and only afterwards switching to Muhammad Ali. Compared to the convention applied to women at this time, who lost their original name when marrying, it appears odd that Ali's change of name could not be accepted as extending backwards in his chronology. The problem at hand bears witness to the discourse associated with publicly established identity: once a person is publicly recognized, a change of name appears to threaten the diachronic—rather than historical—consistency of the public image associated with the name. From this semiotic angle, the verbal name resembles the visual term of an icon whose reference also grew diachronically and bundles many facets within one symbolic identity. The reluctance to grant Ali the individual right to rename his icon thus appears also to concern the hyperreal status of his "visual name," which although created and presented on screen by many other people was still meant to reflect an essential reference to his personality in reality. Without their consent, Ali was redirecting the work of these many creators and presenters towards something beyond their ken.

While the public had to get used to the new name, the spectacle had to cope with the political content injected by the one chosen to reign upon its stage. In terms of the previously established categories of the spectacle, Ali had gained his iconic place in the unified spectacle of heavyweight boxing through consciously attracting curiosity with his poetry, his wrestling-inspired banter, and his carnivalesque bus tours (to say nothing of the boxing itself), only to push his icon back to the realm of the controversial when he reached the top. Apart from its reference to contemporary politics and its ironic critique of the spectacle's media, the name with its foreign roots also deviated from the pattern of the nationally accepted icon. When he publicly rejected the draft in 1968, a very sober-talking Ali further distanced his icon from the American citizenry and thereby provoked once again the unconventional constellation of a controversial, exotic icon on the throne of a nationally unified spectacle. Unlike other celebrities, such as Elvis Presley, whose stint in the army enhanced his icon's American aura, Ali began publicly to take issue with the American government. The press conference featured not the usual witty, big-mouthed showman, but a mild-mannered, almost deferential man, attempting rationally to justify his decision to put a foreign religion before his country's war. The attempt to project his religious belief by means of logical argumentation and a deferential attitude, however, suggests a second, quite different personality beside his iconic reference to the big-mouthed heavyweight champion. Projecting an unusually wide gap between artistic and nonartistic acting on the public stage, the dichotomy conflicts with iconic convergence in so far as it challenges the "hyperreal bandwidth" of a person's character and behavior on screen. In other words, his appearance at the press conference was not easily classifiable in terms of conventional discrimination between acting and not-acting, as the spectacular aura of his icon was not easy to harmonize with the rational critique carried out in his verbal statement.

Ali's increasing incorporation of political issues into the realm of the broadcast spectacle also reflects the spectacle's general development within the 1960s, when political movements were trying different means for gaining the attention of the media and the nation.[16] The Civil Rights Movement in particular concerned the conquering of the public sphere in social life; the pictorial aspect of this agenda aimed to have black faces in a position to be iconized on national screens, a task it achieved in different ways. Martin Luther King, Jr.'s March on Washington and the strategic mises en scène of other huge demonstrations were able to generate political spectacles that not only attracted the media, but also achieved the deferential camera that eventually rendered King's icon in unified status. On the other hand, the more intellectual and also more militant movement popularly called Black Power had difficulty attracting the camera in the first place, to say nothing of controlling the resulting visual commentaries.[17] This side of the black uprising found in Ali the chance to seize national attention via a well-established national sports spectacle, a tactical move that the organization would later repeat with the famous Black Power salute on the occasion of the sprinters' award ceremony at the 1968 Olympic games in Mexico. The organization furthermore began to adapt to television's visual predisposition through gradually developing a recognizable imagery based on a set of distinct symbols meant to serve as its political trademark. Staging all kinds of objects of African provenance, from mythical masks to colorful robes, when anticipating the presence of cameras, the movement began to have more influence on its representation by the media. When celebrating the medal winners of the 200-meter dash at the Olympic games in Mexico, John Carlos and Johnny Lee Smith, Stokely Carmichael awarded the athletes elephant tusks before offering a verbal explanation of the visual gesture: "We want to let the United States of America, the whole world, know that we are going to pick our heroes from today on. And brother Tommy Smith, brother John Carlos, and brother Harry Edwards join the ranks of brother Muhammad Ali because we want black people who concern with us first and with sports second."[18]

Not only did such words challenge the supreme status of the sports spectacle, the carnivalesque display of the press conference also presented a new and unique form of expressing political content. The exotic visual symbols inspired curiosity and attracted the camera. They also conveyed a message constructed in part through their peculiar context-relation to the nationally unified sports spectacle, in part through their contrasting, exotic symbolic content, which tested the margins of audiences' visual literacy. The African symbols hardly enabled the average white American spectator to differentiate their semantic fields in other than very basic categories, such as their general provenance as "African" and their significance as vaguely situated in obscure rituals and religious practices. Within the modern media spectacle, these symbols communicated solely based on their contrast to those visual symbols at the center of national visual literacy. The alignment of these exotic symbols with icons of American sports and politics was thus designed to influence the resulting picture so as to underscore the controversial message of black difference from unified American culture.

However, a message of cultural difference hardly suits a convention of hyperrealism that posits one globally shared visual literacy striving to authenticate the staged symbols as referencing unmediated reality. The exotic sights placed in a national, political context thus evoked the sense of a constructed scene, a "false" spectacle that was different from the "real one" because its imagery could not be taken for granted. In any case, these pictures nevertheless reflect the attempt to "make do" with the general mechanisms of the media spectacle, in so far as the cameras were invited, their angles anticipated, and the protagonists' motives were arranged to have at least some impact on the translation of the event's course of action into a pictorial message on screen. To that extent, the political symbolism of Black Power ideology on the public stage of national television thus appropriated the unified broadcast spectacle by using icons fabricated in the mills of the nationally endorsed sports spectacle for attracting the media's attention to a politically controversial argument. By replacing the traditional imagery with foreign symbols of mystical significance, the movement furthermore added a curious, exotic connotation to its representation that brought into play the grotesque realism of the carnival. Together, the appropriation of the broadcast spectacle and the incorporation of elements from carnival gave rise to a unique brand of controversial spectacle, the purpose of which seemed to include the mocking of the spectacle itself, as well as the media's engagement with it. In this way, the media politics of the Black Power movement parallels what Charles Lemert describes as Ali's "trickster" role in a "culture of irony."[19] When pioneering the curious and the grotesque as his ticket to the stage of the unified spectacle, Ali was managing the career of his icon, whose power he then harnessed as a public lectern for expressing messages of often controversial, political character.

FROM EXOTIC TO CONTROVERSIAL TO NATIONALLY UNIFIED ICON

When Ali began to voice his opinion on the Vietnam War on television and other public tribunes in 1966, his old critics seized their chance finally to dethrone the usurper: "Cassius makes himself as sorry a spectacle, as those unwashed punks who picket and demonstrate against the war."[20] The quote by columnist Red Smith could not be more telling. Referring to the icon by his old name, it maligns the controversial symbol at the margin of society as a "sorry spectacle." Just when he is trying to place verbal argument above visual show, the critic cites the spectacle itself as the template for Ali's behavior. Symbolically, the statement gives the sense that the national soul would mourn Ali's lack of patriotism and that the implied hinge between national icon and national idol had gone awry. In the same year, the American government confiscated Ali's passport. In 1967, Ali was sentenced to five years in prison for refusing the draft. Shortly afterwards his boxing license was revoked. All within a few months, Ali was officially declared unfit for the national spectacle, stripped of his passport, of his liberty, and of his right to work as a boxer. After Ali's pardoning three and a half years later, however, the power of the icon to raise curiosity and with it his mastery of the carnivalesque spectacle and grotesque politics triumphed once again. Having won the first big fight against Joe Frazier after his comeback, he was ready to regain his boxing throne from George Foreman. For the location, he preferred Kinshasa to an American city. Thus the spectacle of American heavyweight boxing was exported to the middle of the African continent, far from modern media culture, but closer to the symbolic roots of the masks that dominated the imagery of the press conferences.

The choice of location was grotesque in many ways. Under the eyes of a worldwide audience, two Americans took the ring in a stadium that had served as a prison and a torture and execution chamber for the regime of Congo's corrupt dictator Mobutu, this peculiar stadium's chief financier. Yet, the attraction of the event overpowered local politics and ultimately also justified the export of the national spectacle. The "Rumble in the Jungle" came to mark the height of the black American counter spectacle, and symbolized American race relations rather than African reality. But perhaps comparable to the moon landing as the culmination of early television's traditional spectacle, Kinshasa also marked a turning point in Black Power's counter-spectacle.

The more the political contours of the controversial sports spectacle began to fade, the more its most exotic, most grotesque, but also most widely recognized icon became renaturalized. The process was initiated, according to Mike Marqusee, by a portrait session with Andy Wahrhol that allowed the previously "divisive" figure to join "Marilyn and Elvis among the artist's gallery of American 'icons.'"[21] By the time it became publicly recognizable that Ali was suffering from Parkinson's disease, his icon was already in the process of being established as a truly unified symbol of American culture and history. Presented with the honorary task of opening the Olympic games in Atlanta in front of three billion television spectators and selected for diplomatic missions in the name of the American government, Ali's icon was finally fit for the unified national spotlight.

Before he disappeared from public sight for more than three years in the late 1960s, the media had chosen to illustrate Ali's defense of his rejection of the draft with close-ups of him in the act of scratching his nose (see also the section "Controversial and Exotic Icons" in chapter 7). Although Ali had just established himself as heavyweight champion on a national stage, the nationwide broadcast of these pictures inscribed on his icon a reference to a childish personality that undermined the rational significance of his words. The intimate portrayal of his face and his gestures followed the convention of hyperrealism by presenting the pictures as an unmediated window into the mind of the person behind the icon. Three decades later, the intimate angle on his trembling body enhanced the icon's visual semantics by once again disconnecting his image from his critical tongue. Paradoxically, the disease not only allowed the camera to neglect his slowed speech for the sake of the unified spectacle, it also reconstructed the icon's reference to the "real" Ali who had lived for so long by the carnivalesque grotesquerie of his own big-mouthed showmanship. In its representation of what might be termed iconic martyrdom, the new staging suggested his trembling as a symbol of personal suffering, which in hyperreal fashion invoked sympathy with the fate of the individual beneath a visual symbol once again contoured in characteristics that imply lack of self-control. With its emotional reference to a very real, vulnerable, and above all nonacting individual, the icon was finally freed to enter the nation's cherished selection of standard bearers, although—or just because—his heroic individuality had ultimately been curtailed. Likewise, his controversial tongue was put to rest within his visual symbol on screen.

15 Premodernism

The renaissance of the picture as a means of macrocommunication in 20th-century Western societies marks a historical development that appears somewhat at odds with the typical association of modernity with extraordinary advances in science and technology. Before eventually losing its central communicative status in the face of the Gutenberg revolution and the Enlightenment, the picture had allowed the Catholic churches of medieval Europe to foster the hegemony of religious thought in all areas of public life, including politics. Based upon its own set of religious symbols, emblems, and icons together with a number of symbols of secular potentates, a rudimentary visual language was established, with regional variations. Up to the time when German humanists began to use "emblemata" for a popular, symbolic critique of the interlaced aristocratic and ecclesiastic reign, these painted icons and emblems were generally crafted by a deferential, participatory brush that strived for an effect of supernatural reality. Painting was seen as a religious privilege, and there was little leeway for individual expression. Italian artists of the Renaissance sought to legitimate their creativity with the concept of "furor divinus," meaning that their artistic expressions and messages were of transcendental origin.[1]

With the rise of the printed word and humanism, the religious corset that restrained all macrocommunicative exchanges was also loosened for pictures. Realism became free to place common life on the tribune of the canvas, as exemplified, for example, in the transition from Rubens's to Rembrandt's motifs. Although in the era of the Enlightenment the printed word was generally favored, at this time the picture was considered a useful tool for scientific research and documentation. But while the discovery of photography at first contributed to the endeavor to enlighten by means of visual facts, further technological innovations in the form of color lithography, motion pictures, and finally broadcasting altered the picture's role in modernity: although it retained its secularism, the picture once again combined political information, entertainment, and science within one discursive stratum. Under the seal of what has here been called hyperrealism, the new pictorial frame encompasses written, verbal, graphic, and gestural language, as well as many more sublanguage systems. It makes an accented reference to reality that proposes an unmediated reception of significance with the individual eye, in the place of locating the individual intentions of the pictures' invisible transmitters with the collective logic of visual literacy.

When television brought to fruition at midcentury what had already been seeded in the cinema theaters, that is the projection of fictional movies and nonfictional newsreels under the same roof and within the same frame, it added a further element to visual communication, namely the continuity of the stream of daily broadcasts. Further accentuating the overall pictorial basis of the conveyed mélange of signs and symbols, the television screen fully developed the potential of the iconic principle at the root of visual language. Rapidly encompassing all pictorial genres, television seized the opportunity to nurture and cultivate a national, visual language, not least because it succeeded in establishing the broadcast picture as the nation's supreme communicative carrier. This pictorial clearinghouse allowed many visual symbols to gain the exposure necessary to accumulate semantic content, to establish their iconic contours, and to aggregate their significance. Commanding pictorial lecterns that can also be used to disseminate verbal messages, such icons no longer communicate a transcendental mystery, but instead convey the myth of individual authorship of what is actually "painted" by a complex network of authors. In the place of "divine ferment," it is now the hyperreal aura of the photographic picture that allows artists (and all others) to appear as "real human beings" within the same frame that had previously been reserved for their brushwork.

In the kaleidoscopic order of visual literacy (rather than any more logically consistent grammar), the novel pictorial stage commenced to serve, if not to implement, the rituals of society's spectacles: Transferring the carefully contained pyramidal structures of coincidence, emotion, and significance to the language of the screen, broadcasting created pictorial lecterns for a limited number of icons of both secular and religious provenance and purported to represent the elite of society's actual, public life. As in ancient China, where the art of painting characters allowed an individual to join the ranks of the reigning bureaucracy, proficient handling of one's icon in conjunction with the rules of the spectacle enabled advancement into the court of television's aristocracy. This virtual court is not governed by primogeniture, democratic transparency, or religious doctrine; instead, it is ruled by the parameters of the symbolic and by the management of those who create, select, and present icons and emblems, according to these parameters, in the national spotlight. The broadcast picture's pervasive claim that it can mirror not only cultural but also political life with "objective realism" is certainly indebted to the allure of the extraordinary invention of camera technology, but the consequent reinvention of transcendental transmittership and presentation of reality as the engine of pictorial significance resonates with Bruno Latour's declaration: "We have never been modern!" [2]

The possibility that a two-dimensional icon, such as that of Walter Cronkite, can become so powerful as to be assessed as a factor in changing the course of the Vietnam War should ultimately draw more attention than should speculations about the private person to which the icon refers. The power of this icon, as well of those standing for the decision makers in the White House and on Capitol Hill, reflects on its source in a language that uses the dynamic of collecting, rather than of rational differentiation, to allocate privilege to semantically charged symbols within every picture projected to the public. Sooner or later, every language begins to incorporate the social practices of its use into its logical structure, and also commences to incorporate what Bourdieu called societies' "small distinctions."[3] Whenever broadcast hyperrealism lifts personalities of American society on its public stage, however, it not only accords a privilege to these people but also to their icons through pictorially ascribing status to them, such as with the described typology of the unified, exotic, and controversial spectacles. In addition, the status of visual symbols differs according to the depth of their semantic profiles, which among other things affects their ability to attract the eye, and this relative difference constructs the grammatical outline of pictorial messages, the understanding of which always begins with the best-known elements of the picture. According to semiotic logic, repeatedly staged symbols have a privileged status by comparison to all other visual symbols, which appear new, uninformed, and thus exotic to the collective eye. It follows that only a select few visual symbols can possibly command the privilege of an iconic lectern and capture the attention of the public. By the same standard, only well-iconized symbols of actors appear to be in the position to project conscious individual contribution to the art of screen acting. It is for this reason that icons of well-known actors easily find the pictorial history books, while symbols of little-known actors, no matter how talented or proficient, hardly ever make it from one channel to the next, to say nothing of being given the privilege to address generations to come. In the historical practice of television, only icons with sophisticated semantic contours are in the position to speak with an informed voice.

When assessing the pictorial history of icons, such as those of Ali, Webb, Ball, Murrow, and Cronkite, on public screens, the purpose can obviously not be to evaluate their real personalities. Instead, the pictorial history of these icons is proposed as a kind of etymology, albeit one that is political in character because it encompasses the nation's central framework of symbolic power. The possibility of critiquing such an etymology is not derived from these icons' established semantic fields in national visual literacy, which continues to allow for their grammatical use and historically solidified denotation, but from the central logical conflict that arises when their historical mise en scène makes an accentuated reference to a reality, and thereby to society's collective public sphere. In consequence, all five case studies are arranged to highlight the many contradictions, discrepancies, and communicative conflicts that rest in the details of their subjects' mediation as "hyperreal" human beings of public stature, whose public faces are formed by somewhat written, even printed visual contours. In order to analyze these symbolic stand-ins within broadcast history, semiotic concepts, such as differentiating the transmitter-network behind the creation and the presentation of visual content, such as iconic convergence, or such as the art of painting Chinese characters, have enabled these conflicts to be envisioned in concepts and figures. Some of these include "underacting," "overacting," "instinctive acting," "iconic inheritance," "iconic carousel," "the control room of Studio 41," "leaning over reality's shoulder and saying a word or two," "the first transmitter as the first receiver," "historians of the future," "I shook up the world," or the "un(fore)seeable knockout punch." These figures all illustrate the fundamentally marred attempt to communicate content with visual signs of which one is also constructed as the author. Murrow grew wary of a picture that focused on himself in the role of the journalist—as in the Cretan's statement that all Cretans are liars.

In the chiefly artistic, realist realm of the cinema, most of the discovered inconsistencies would vanish without trace, except in those productions that play with iconic convergence when cutting in a televised press conference with the (hyper)real president. When applied to the cinema's fictional screens, an assessment of icons as unified, controversial, or exotic would equally lose some of its immediate political relevance. But while removing the need to differentiate between the deferential, participatory and the distanced, predisposed camera in favor of an artistic authorship, the cinematographic stage also cultivates iconic convergence by making pictorial reference to actors of flesh and blood. The double nature of this reference is readily taken up by magazines, newspapers, advertising, and, above all, by television itself.

In comparison to the movies, the main difference of the television picture certainly rests in the continual stream of its images. In order to sustain the stream, television asserted its supreme ability both to entertain and to inform the public within one and the same electronic frame. The broadcast screen would go on to subsume all established means of communication, including Hollywood's movies, and would simply copy the performances in theaters, concert halls, and sports arenas onto a second stage faithful to the original.

The discourse of hyperrealism suggested this ability to "mirror" all public interaction with technologically based objectivity—and thereby opened up a myriad of discussions concerning the possibility of "manipulating" such "hyperreality"—but hyperrealism may itself be rooted in television's novel continuous stream of pictorial communication, rather than in any technological advance. At least, the factor of continuity in addressing the audiences of the nation appears much more significant in its impact on the core mechanism of visual language, that is the shaping and networking of the significance of a pool of visual terms for large audiences. While the iconic principle was already a factor before the arrival of television, both the continuity and the spectacular attraction of that second, versatile public stage fueled the process of condensing pictorial content to the point of generating a visual literacy shared by a large part of American people. In responding to them, these audiences further worked generic visual symbols, icons, and emblems into sophisticated terms that dominate both the grammar and the content of pictorial messages. Thus television added to the pictorial world of movies and magazines the continuity necessary to collect, sort, and arrange visual literacy with unprecedented thoroughness.

Yet although more intelligent and sophisticated than ever, the new visual language appears marred by the same discourse that contributed to its genesis. The convention of ignoring those who select, produce, und present the broadcast messages in favor of highlighting those who are part of the messages' content has thus been able to simulate a public sphere populated by a selective number of icons and emblems. The power of this hyperreal arena rests in the hands of those who manage the process of shaping the terms of collective visual literacy, who manage the terms' access to the public stage, who buy this stage, as in the case of advertising, and/or who conquer it, as done, for example, by Muhammad Ali. As an iconic simulation of life, the broadcast picture harnessed the entertainment potential of visual language in extraordinary ways, but as a mirror of reality it also integrated a contradictory political dynamic into its communicative potential. In this historical approach to broadcasting, the screen created a pool of hyperreal figurations of life that commenced to network American society as if it were a small community. Free to move back and forth in time, as well as left and right from the fictional to the political frame, the new icons rose to the fore, forging a new framework of symbolic power. As much as television thus enhanced visual language's intriguing potential for symbolic communication, and as much as it contributed to generating a densely interwoven visual literacy of national scope, it ultimately also opposed the individual artistry of the pictures' creation, the agency and intention of their presentation, and the collective nature of their symbolic language through clinging to the discourse of hyperrealism.

Appendix

16 Four Codes of Visual Language

Throughout history pictures have displayed an intriguing communicative potential. Common sense values a picture at a thousand words. If a picture were considered a document of language, it would consequently provide some one thousand visual signs, except that the fluid shapes and contours of pictorial entities make these signs impossible to tally. The boundless wealth of visual signs not only defies any traditional classification, as by a dictionary, but also challenges the potentially historical nature of visual communication in general: if visual signs change their form each time they represent a two-dimensional sight, they are a reminder of the philosophy of Heraclitus, who found that it is impossible to throw a stone twice into the same river. If the same river also cannot be looked at twice, or photographed twice, how then can the river or its photograph be seen with the eyes of a historian?

When trying to access the legacy of the twentieth century, historians find themselves confronted with the rise of a visual culture, which in one way or another proposes to document the past. Yet, how can these documents be analyzed for historical traces, if they provide no logical hold on the nature and characteristics of their historical content, beyond the individual, visual intelligence of the researcher? In the face of such inadequacy, a number of historians, such as Alex Bolvig, Jean-Claude Schmitt, Robert Hanke, and Philip Rosen, to name only a few, have called for new methodological approaches to the visual past.[1] All of them recognize the need to introduce theory into historical study in order to handle the particular temporal relation of photographic pictures to history. What requires challenging, first of all, is the all too pervasive claim that the photographic picture records a moment in reality and preserves it as a historical fact for future viewing. The problem, however, is not only that "we do not look at the same pictures as did our forefathers," as Bolvig notes; there is also the widespread confusion of fictional and factual aspects of pictures.[2] In a critical answer to a *New York Times* op-ed by Charles Colson, "When History is Up for Grabs," the historian David Walkowitz reflects on an "objectivity crisis created by the postmodern linguistic turn" when observing how movies, such as Oliver Stone's *Nixon,* merge fact with fiction.[3] Seeing the boundaries between history and memory, between nostalgia and heritage dissolve on public screens,

Walkowitz asks how historians will be able to influence public discourse on the nation's history and what role they will have in the production of future, visual historiography of all sorts.[4] However, as long as it remains unclear how pictures actually relate to reality, how they mediate content, and how this content can actually be analyzed for historical purposes, it is also unclear how they can be worked into professional historiography. In any case, whatever the impact of postmodernism on the possibility of distinguishing fictional from nonfictional pictures, it is unclear whether it is the academic approach to the historicity of the picture or the pictorial reflection of history in the practice of visual communication that is at the root of the problem. In his "*Quantum Leap:* The Postmodern Challenge of Television as History" Robert Hanke argues it is "ordinary, everyday television" that "often blurs history and fiction" and "conflates historicity and contemporaneity."[5] And Kathleen Higgins adds that the breakdown of the "art/reality distinction" in the case of television is not "just the result of the failure to keep television from collapsing into reality," but may also be the reverse, "the failure of the habitual viewer to keep reality from collapsing into the world of TV."[6]

While the symptoms are described, the question still stands as outlined: how do we look at history in pictures, when reality tends so easily to collapse into the pictorial world of the television screen? There have been many attempts to describe the figurations of life suggested so persuasively by the screen; most of them, however, tend to involve an indistinct rationality at the heart of visual communication. Encapsulated by the proverb "seeing is believing," the conventional conclusion is that viewing pictures in their unlimited wealth of pictorial shapes compares or even equates with perceiving reality in all its individual variations. Like perception in everyday life, perception of pictorial shapes thus caters to subjective belief, but never to rational certitude. For this reason, psychological approaches, such as, for example, those of the Gestalt school are prominent in the project of mapping out the underpinnings of visual communication.[7] Modern scholars such as Ann Marie Barry interrelate the theory of gestalts with neurological research in order to prove scientifically the human mind's tendency to respond emotionally to visual impulses. In her definition, all images are neurological gestalts "made up of fragments of visual experience processed modularly and then coordinated through perceptual process."[8] Giving rise to what Walter Lippmann calls the "pictures in our heads," these gestalts become the psychological fabric of social interaction. To integrate the social dimension of psychological gestalts, Barry proposes the concept of a collectively shared "visual intelligence" at the root of visual communication. Through modern neurological research, Barry emphasizes the particular property of pictures to stimulate an emotional response in the brain more quickly than words. What remains once again indistinct, however, is the character of such gestalts and the logic that, for example, enables the media to manage these psychological figurations in such economically determinate fashion. Like Barry, scholars such as Robert Hanke and Marita Sturken, among many others, have gone on to establish concepts such as "collective" or "cultural memory" that would at least indicate the possibility for gestalts to transit into the past.[9] Recognizing that memory always involves an act of remembering and forgetting, Marita Sturken uses her concept of "cultural memory" for a thorough examination of the interplay between nostalgia and heritage, history and memory.[10] However, as "memory" once again is associated with reality, a kind of theoretical hybrid is effected when the word is used to describe significance that springs from mediated pictures. By comparison, the concept of "visual literacy," as taken up and developed in the 1990s by scholars such as Paul Messaris, Günther Kress, and Theo van Leeuwen, places more emphasis on the mediated nature of pictures.[11] But although going one step further, they too refrain from defining the pictorial figurations as communicative entities. While Messaris ultimately rejects the notion of a visual language altogether, Kress and van Leeuwen seek to describe visual literacy through single characteristics—for example, shot selection can be intelligibly differentiated into close-ups, medium-range shots, and so forth. Ultimately, however, Bolvig's quest for a "new iconology" implies "that traditional approaches to images are becoming inadequate," because they fail to provide the logical grounds that would allow for understanding photographic pictures as two-dimensional artifacts and consequently for distancing their reference to reality, at least in historical retrospective.[12]

Rendering the mediation of pictures as a communicative act and evaluating it as such for historical purposes can only succeed when pictorial content can be localized outside a photograph's possible relation to reality, and thus outside the confinements of individual experience and memory. For a true historical perspective, the new iconology would have to account for what Schmitt describes as "iconographical series" with potentially infinite possibilities of "constructing and above all of cross-referencing them," and would have to extend beyond the realm of pure art history.[13] In taking the notion of such iconographical series into the realm of television, the new iconology would furthermore provide the possibility of a visual etymology, according to which the on-screen appearance of a public persona, such as John F. Kennedy, could be treated as an icon, the historical dimension of which as a term of visual language is fundamentally distinguished from the history of the real man. Such a semiotic iconology could thus account for the "etymological problems" that arise, for example, when publishing "historical pictures" of John F. Kennedy taken before he assumed a prominent role in the visual media, since such instances conflate the pictures' original place in history through addressing a visual literacy that was developed at a later time. Furthermore, only a true etymological perspective appears suitable to characterize the historicity of gestalts as icons and to analyze their communicative careers in public pictures including pictorial narratives of both fictional and artistic origin.

It may seem surprising that such an etymological perspective has not yet been tried on the modern, pictorial world, especially given the increased interest in the value of pictures as source material for historical analysis, but there are a number of serious, theoretical problems that obstruct the equation of visual literacy with a historical, dynamic pool of expressions. Most of these problems arise in the attempt to define visual communication as a self-contained, logical language system, which demands some sort of sign structure. Already in the early 1970s, Donis Dondis introduced a type of sign structure meant to account for a picture's pictorial qualities that can be shared by all viewers. She proposed a set of ten visual elements, such as dot, line, color, and so forth, which she described as the raw material of visual literacy. Recognizing that these elements can serve to produce "compositional wholes" able to shape a "vocabulary of expressions that correspond to the structural arrangements of words in verbal literacy," she asked for further research on how visual literacy can be understood as a language system.[14] But her attempt, as well as others,' to define "compositional wholes" has never been refined and collective visual literacy has not been provided with anything comparable to a dictionary.

While the search for "compositional wholes" that might serve as a visual communicative basis has been further developed by a few scholars, among them Umberto Eco and Gerhard Braun, semiotic research has turned to a different approach that exclusively builds on Charles Sanders Peirce's concept of icons.[15] Rather than exploring the communicative logic of the picture based on small structural components, as might be associated with the semiotic philosophy of Ferdinand De Saussure, this body of work approaches large pictorial entities within the frame of a picture.[16] Studies, such as those of Jostein Gipsrud, Richard Howells, Ellen Seiter, Tilo Prase, Keyan Tomaselli, and many others, that use Peirce's concepts of indexical signs and icons for their analytical framework, generally imply that an icon comprises its entire figuration, so that the depiction of a person includes all facial and other details, as well as clothes and so forth.[17] Equally, indexical signs are taken to describe broader narrative fragments that contain several components, such as, for example, smoke rising from a wrecked car. Although such a semiotic perspective serves well for the particular analyses of the studies mentioned, it is nevertheless important to note that none of these works attempt to specify more detailed, semiotic components, or to describe grammatical rules that apply to the interaction of significance within a frame. Given that any pictorial detail, for example, a prominent nose, a special hairdo, a particular design of glasses, or thick, black, fast-moving smoke and so forth, could very well be seen as an adjective-noun complex, a more detailed approach to the sign structure of pictures would appear very promising. Yet, such a search for a sign structure that could in some ways compare to verbal or written structures of significance has essentially dried up over the past few decades. The German scholar Tilo Prase even concludes that all attempts to define structural elements, as proposed among others by

Dondis and Braun, have failed to work out pictorial patterns comparable to the logical components of words, phonemes, and morphemes.[18] For this reason, modern semiotic approaches to pictures stop short of analyzing any detailed grammatical interactions of visual characteristics such as, for example, describing Gerard Depardieu's impersonation of Cyrano de Bergerac as a constructed expression based on the interplay between the actor's iconic appearance and the masking effect of the big nose. In contrast to such open questions concerning detailed syntactical patterns of visual significance, however, Christian Metz's conclusion, which reduces any grammatical operations in film exclusively to the handling of the cut, still influences many modern approaches to pictorial narratives.[19]

The reluctance to examine pictures for more detailed semiotic structure highlights a deep-seated set of problems rooted in the very notion of equating the realm of pictures with language. What distinguishes "representational from linguistic systems," in the words of Nelson Goodman, still appears as an open question in the semiotic approach to the picture.[20] Although most scholars who build on Peirce's concept of icons and indexical signs, as well Goodman, Metz, and Barry, use the term "language," they do not define this term according to the semiotic principle that requires specified formal contours able to relate conventionalized significance between partners in communication. In the absence of a description either of the grammatical relations between pictorial entities, or of the author-spectator context, which Barbara Zelizer identifies as "collective authorship" with regard to television news, there remains in these studies the somewhat awkward question as to which gestalt is communicating on screen and how such a gestalt differs from a mediated icon.[21] In other words, once again it is the reference to reality that enables an icon on screen to speak in the place of the picture's author and thus to project the contradiction in terms that is the sign and its author within one and the same contour. Faced with similar problems, Eco proposed early on to exclude the factor of reality reference altogether from the communicative logic of pictures.[22] Recalling the basically arbitrary character of signs, he went on to critique Peirce's model of icons, according to which significance is constructed by means of resemblance to the represented model in reality.[23] He argued that due to the two-dimensional character of pictures, any resemblance, or "iconicity," between an icon and its three-dimensional model can never be complete. Logic indeed demands that even if a depiction succeeded in creating an almost identical visual impression, the difference, however minimal, would necessitate accepting the icon as being a little bit other than the empirical reality and, consequently, a different identity than that which constitutes its referent.[24] In other words, if A does not equal B, B must be evaluated in its own right. B's content should not constantly be muddled with that of A, and B should be appreciated as a two-dimensional composition manufactured with a purpose. Like a sign, B attains significance not in any absent reality, but in semantic processes, which construct a sign as "everything, which can be taken as significantly substituting for something else."[25] Thus, the sign constitutes its own, self-contained reality and the "something else" to which it refers "does not necessarily have to exist," or at least, does not necessarily have to have the exact same significance.[26] Hence, Eco concludes that icons can be best described in the logic of signs: their significance is constructed and their interpretation is predominantly a matter of convention. This position, however, has never achieved consensus among scholars. The German semiotician Günther Bentele points out that Peirce had already recognized the conventional aspects of icons.[27] Although to some degree correct in the conclusion that Eco ultimately attempts to pass through a door already open, Bentele himself cannot avoid opening a backdoor for the reality issue again, when accepting in icons an indistinct coexistence of conventional and nonconventional aspects.[28] Ultimately, the modern conception of Peirce's icons cannot overcome a hybrid status; the figurations of life on screen continue to be seen as being half motivated by reality, and half by convention.

What crystallizes from the discussion of the Peircean icon is a theoretical dichotomy that either emphasizes the arbitrary, conventional aspect of icons, or their unruly reference to a referent in reality that is absent from the picture. This dichotomy appears as the root of the academic divide in assessing the semiotic character of pictures, and the point of resistance in many related questions, such as of the possibility of producing a pictorial etymology based in the modern realm of photographic pictures. If Eco's radical approach to the arbitrary character of signs failed to meet secure consent among semioticians, it also left a theoretical gap in terms of the reality issue, as well as the quest for advancing and refining Peirce's definition of the icon. The blurred definition of icons as relatively broad gestalts, the significance of which is simultaneously anchored in convention and in empirical reality, is thus likely also the main reason why no attempt has been made to connect systematically the concept of visual signs with that of visual literacy.

The advantage of Eco's approach is that it builds on a concept of visual language which may not yet define the detailed contours of icons, but which establishes them as conventionalized "compositional wholes" in some ways comparable to the vocabulary of verbal and written language. Only such a view, it appears, can then be further used to account for the effect in visual communication whereby picture after picture adds layers of meaning to the icons of persons, whom only the tiniest number of spectators know in person. The aggregation over time of such semantic layers, following the logic of collecting as described in the part "Icons in the Museum," therefore prioritizes icons chronologically; following an early hint of Thomas Sebeok, this chronological prioritization can give rise to a revision of the traditional, semiotic definitions of visual signs and of visual literacy.[29] The central argument of the new approach to icons thus shifts the emphasis: in place of anchoring the reference of icons mainly in their resemblance or likeness to real things, or "iconicity" as proposed by Charles Sanders Peirce, the definition of icons will be built on their iconic reference to the same or to a similar visual symbol as introduced in the semantic context of previous pictures.[30]

However, such a synthesis of the different definitions of icons and the different approaches to the language of pictures necessitates another step in order to reconcile smaller elements of visual content with larger ones, such as icons—if only for the sake of Depardieu's nose: If theory were unable to differentiate between a nose, which when taken on its own has little recognizable "etymological" history, and the complete icon of the actor, which contains a distinct semantic history, a movie such as *Cyrano de Bergerac* would be unable to provide a conclusive pictorial narrative.

To close the gap between elementary components and larger complexes of significance, such as the icon, this study proposes a four-layered model that is built on the dialectic principle of boundary lines. What contours visual signs, and for that matter gestalts, are boundaries reflected by technically produced contrast lines, which according to the modern neurological research outlined by Barry connect with the mind before their content produces emotional stimulation.[31] The contrasts that contour pictorial significance always feature a two-way, dialectical interaction, for example, as in figure-ground differentiation when contrasting a person's head with a rack of books in the background, but also when differentiating the head from the body, and then the arms, hands, fingers, fingertips, and so forth. The dialectic principle can thus be worked into a conceptual understanding of pictorial significance that builds on sign chains rather than on single signs. Once all the signs have been ordered in conceptual chains, "compositional wholes" are established, which relate to each other according to the grammatical rule of contrast-lines. In a third step, these compositional unities are assessed as general "visual symbols," the content of which is part of a visual literacy cultured on the level of family and community, as well as on the level of society. The fourth step finally addresses icons, individually recognizable sign-structures or visual symbols that have been made familiar over a period of time through multiple exposures in the same or similar arrangements of visual characteristics. In this model, the first two steps engage the fundamental dialectics of visual perception, which still correspond to a certain degree with the general, empirical mode of seeing in the realm of reality, while the final two steps account for the possibility of visual expressions to accumulate diachronic, that is culturally and historically colored, significance in the realm of pictures.

The proposed sign structure may not attain the degree of abstraction present in verbal and written language, but it nevertheless pinpoints an element of "double articulation" comparable to the structure of words. Although grounded in the notion that significance in pictures does not spring from any absent reality, the approach does not exclude the potential of photography to aid scientific research. But in light of all those instances in which the external context of the picture is inaccessible to scientific analysis, it concentrates on the communicative nature of pictures, their transmitter-receiver context, and the semantic dynamic of a sign structure. It is such a sign structure which, however dynamic, allows for a methodological approach to the picture on the basis of pictorial etymology. Etymological comprehension of collectively shared visual literacy then frees the modern picture from the absent reality of the gestalts or the temptations of a time-traveling ride through history, by setting logical boundaries within the constant flow of television's unlimited variations of pictorial shapes.

FROM EMPIRICAL TO ARBITRARY BOUNDARY LINES

As theory always follows practice, the application of an arbitrary sign structure to visual communication encounters an interesting problem when compared to the genesis of verbal and written language. Given that the first utterances preceded written language, the evolution of visual communication appears more complex. On the one hand, visual signs such as cave art could possibly have paralleled or even preceded the genesis of verbal language. On the other hand, visual language is more comparable to written than to verbal language, not least because it also needs the help of technical tools. While hieroglyphs followed verbal concepts and letters followed sounds, the signs on the cave walls thus had no comparable predecessor, except possibly for object language. But even if handmade objects contributed to ritual communication and served as inspiration for drawing the first contours of visual signs, one can nevertheless observe that visual communication resembles a written type of language without requiring a conscious act of code-making as in the genesis of the letter. A subsequent question, therefore, concerns the root of the intelligence that entered the signs on the cave wall and added the pragmatic code able to propel their basic communicative significance throughout history.

Umberto Eco once noted that the simple drawing of a horse on a sheet of paper presents one "continuous black line," which reflects "precisely the property that a real horse does not possess."[32] While he used the argument to support the case for the arbitrary resemblance of visual signs to any model in reality, the observation also contains a key for assessing the profound logical principle residing in visual perception. Responding to Eco, the philosopher and semiotician Gerhard Braun noted that although the contouring of a horse is indeed far removed from its model in reality, it is not so distant from the general model of human perception ("visuelles Wahrnehmungsmodell").[33] Braun went on to point out that the human model of visual perception tends artificially to reinforce contours in order to improve the possibility of figure-ground differentiation in both the three-dimensional and the two-dimensional world. But although a natural phenomenon of visual perception, the contours on a two-dimensional surface originate in painterly or photographic techniques that present a humanmade translation and thus a conscious emphasizing of the phenomenon of "feigned contours" ("Scheinkanten") or "overstated contrasts" ("Kontrastüberhöhungen") common to general human perception. In fact, when contemplating photographs or watching television, one can observe the phenomenon of various types of contrast lines, ranging from black to sometimes even white lines of variable thickness, that demarcate individual shapes depending on the arrangement of spotlights and the photographic techniques used. In some cases, the characteristics of such a contrast carry significance on their own, as when, for example, the particular contours of a Hollywood monster have been constructed from scratch and edited into the picture. Convention then determines whether the special effect looks "natural," although this determination hinges on the one property that does not exist outside our system of visual perception, the ultimately always manmade contrast lines.

The phenomenon of contrast lines indicates a logical arbitrariness at the root of the human mode of perception that implies more than a simple biological mechanism of seeing. Taking up Hegel's concept of dialectic reflection, the philosopher Racek observed that the existential boundary separating a meadow from a forest might appear as a continuous contrast line when seen from a certain distance, but this line dissolves the closer an observer approaches.[34] While Hegel used the demarcation between meadow and forest to describe the general process of dialectic thought, it can also be taken to demonstrate a central empirical faculty of visual perception.[35] The empirical processing of a sight can be described as the dialectic transformation of extensions perceived by the eye into immaterial contours of the mind. In order to recognize contrast lines, the mind marks out boundaries that override a mass of potential information, which reaches the eye with conceptualized, abstract significance. Such dialectic boundaries may sometimes correspond more or less with actually touchable edges, as in the example of a wall, and sometimes not, as in the case of the line between a meadow's last stems and the first roots of a forest's trees; they always add an "artificial" or "arbitrary" element to the process of seeing. In some cases, constructed and refined boundary lines have historically functioned as autonomous concepts of significance, as in the case of the "horizon," which for centuries signified not only the demarcation line between the sky and the sea, but also the conceptual notion of a new, third entity of meaning: that which lies beyond the end of the world.

The arbitrariness or the theoretical nature of boundary lines was already a subject of dispute among the first philosophers of ancient Greece. Zeno of Elea centered his famous paradoxes of movement on a conclusion he drew from an attempt to map out space with exact lines: when crossing a hall with the intention of first reaching the half mark, then half of the second section, and so forth, an unlimited number of boundaries will theoretically prevent a person from ever reaching the other side.[36] The paradox also works the other way around: when halving the first section, and again the first part of that first section, and so forth, a person cannot even begin to cross the first boundary, hence the theoretical impossibility of movement and a remarkable opposition to Heraclitus's position that everything is in flux. While Diogenes reportedly countered Zeno in a literally pragmatic way, that is by standing up and walking a couple of steps up and down before returning to his famous barrel home, Aristotle's answer has enduring currency: embedding the paradox in his dialectic philosophy, Aristotle concluded that every point and consequently every line reflects a twofold mark, containing the end point of one extension and the starting point of the next.[37]

When this conclusion is applied to the human mode of visual perception, seeing with the help of contrast lines becomes intrinsically interwoven with the dialectic properties of an empirically acquired logic that enables rational thought. Not only are boundaries immaterial, referenced rather than reflected by contrast lines, they also relate indirectly or arbitrarily to the objects they demarcate. In mathematics, separate but adjacent points can be considered in a state of unlimited approach, a continuum that identifies geometrical lines and marks with the objects they are designated to define. This continuum reflects a logical process similar to a dialectic synthesis, which establishes a new realization removed from the opposing elements on which it was built.

In this philosophical outline, the rational transformation of contrast lines into dialectic boundaries can be used to infer, at the root of visual perception, a type of empirical intelligence that codes visual shapes within intelligible contours. When the materiality of an actual contrast converges with the immaterial nature of a dialectic thought, both the transmitter, by means of brush or photographic technique, and the receiver, by means of dialectically modeled perception, share in a process of applying dialectic boundary lines. In terms of Hegel's boundary between a meadow and forest, any picture of such a sight marks an arbitrary framing of the ephemeral contrast line, which transfers the empirical condition of its visibility into a communicative one that regulates, among other things, the angle and perspective of the portrayed sight. As a result, the depicted meadow and forest juxtapose each other not because they do so in reality, but as a dialectic condition necessary to render the picture's basic significance comprehensible. Based on such a dialectic model of visual perception, the classic concept of figure-ground differentiation can also be re-evaluated as an empirically anchored logical method of contouring significance. Although arbitrary, the method is generally shared by all humans, and it unfolds a communicative potential already recognized by our cave-dwelling ancestors.

THE FIRST CODE OF VISUAL LANGUAGE

It has been argued that visual communication does not provide an equivalent to the logical property of "double articulation" that can be attributed to verbal language in the form of phonemes and morphemes.[38] Phonemes are defined as the theoretical structural elements of verbal language that allow for demarcating consonants from vowels. As the smallest audible units of language, these arbitrary elements cannot generally carry distinguishable significance on their own. Morphemes are the smallest signifying units of language. An exception is, for example, the genitive "s" that is both a phoneme and a morpheme, because it carries significance on its own. In any case, double articulation refers to the logical combination of meaningless phonemes and meaningful morphemes. Upon analysis, a picture's simultaneous projection of adjacent shapes and the dialectic boundary that separates them can be considered as resembling the principle of double articulation.

In two- as well as three-dimensional perception, contrast lines are not only often enhanced or carried across where they do not exist as continuous lines, they can also emerge from the contrast in color and light between adjacent shapes. This phenomenon projects to the eye a fine, dark, sometimes even white line, which neither originates from a delineating brush nor stands in any essential relation to the objects it contours. Contrast lines thus derive from and at the same time serve to demarcate different color and light patterns, which they additionally establish in their basic extension and shape. In their demarcating function they can be considered similar to phonemes. Patterns of color and lightness interact with contrast lines and combine to forge twofold shapes. The shapes created by the interplay of boundaries offer further relations of size and spatial arrangement, as well as movement in the case of film, which together with the characteristics of color, lightness, and pattern (or texture) comprise a set of visual variables that structurally compare to morphemes. In building on the function of the contrast line as a central, dialectic hinge, the comparable catalogue of basic visual elements proposed among others by Dondis and Braun can be gradually modified and placed in a dynamic scheme according to how they structure perception on different levels.[39]

The graphic representation illustrates the interplay of visual phonemes and morphemes in characterizing a twofold percept that can be tentatively considered as the basic structure of visual signs. However, the "molecular" illustration of that structure indicates a more dynamic, flowing, and variable interplay of visual phonemes and morphemes than the one specified by double articulation. Unlike verbal and written signs, visual signs are obviously not coded in precise form and consequently need a more pragmatic assessment of their logical framework. Visual signs further involve what Eco described as "a certain mode of acting [or gesticulation] of lines" ("un certo modo di atteggiarsi delle linee").[40] Generally containing more significance than verbal phonemes, contours can make "elegant" or "bulky" shapes, contrast lines can be "disarranged" or "interrupted," as in Picasso's work, and photographic contours can be endowed with more than basic significance using technical effects. Likewise, the visual equivalents to morphemes generally assume more significance than their verbal

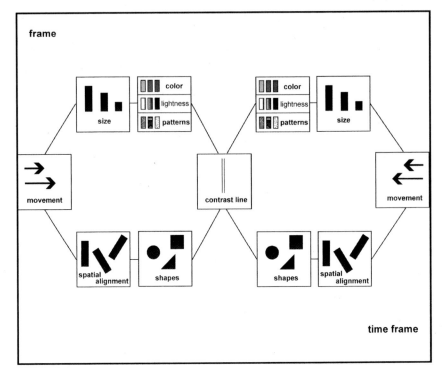

Figure 16.1. Visual variables.

counterparts: for example, colors carry more content if only that one hue always contrasts a second one, and size serves together with spatial alignment as the central tool in adding perspective to a two-dimensional depiction.[41]

Those visual characteristics added by the frame and by movement present a special category of visual variable. The frame anchors the perspective by completing the characteristics of size and spatial alignment, and provides a stable background to contrast with movement, which in turn interacts with the time frame of the shot, as well as the rhythm of film. The three variables, frame, time frame, and movement, thus relate with each other in ways that complete the dialectic interplay of visual phonemes and morphemes. In film, the moving frame of the transmitter's camera is conjugated with the motionless frame of the receiver's television set. The receiver's frame is thus responsible for anchoring all spatial and temporal movement within the conveyed pictures. The interplay of the spatial and the temporal frame extends to regulate a film's rhythm through controlling the time available for perceiving each frame, while also establishing the significance of movement through marking any difference between faster- and slower-moving shapes as additional, morphemelike characteristics. The visual variable of movement therefore interrelates with those contrast lines made to move within the picture and ascribes to them significance that is partially comparable to adjectives, such as "fast" or "faster." The process of creating and perceiving movement therefore confirms the outlined logic of dialectic perception and is a reminder once again of Zeno's paradoxes. His third paradox specifies that a moving arrow is in stasis in every moment of its flight, at least within the boundaries that mark its own extension. This paradox can be applied to the technology of film reels: all the visual variables of each frame are at rest, not only within their respective extensions, but also in any moment (or time frame) short enough to equate with the inverse of the picture per second rate of their projection. When applied to the modern, digital production of movement, however, the paradox retreats to its theoretical dimensions, since the computed picture involves a myriad of dots informed by asynchronous sequences. In any case, however, the characteristics of movement add a temporal dimension to the so far spatially accentuated outline of visual sign structure. Rather than demarcating visual percepts solely with regard to their spatial alignment (which also requires a particular moment in time), the portrayal of movement demands a temporal syntax, or a time frame that adds significance in ways partially comparable to the rhythm of spoken language. The rhythm of movement regulated by the time frame together with the perspective set by the spatial frame comprise variables of particular structural scope, which together with those described as visual phonemes and morphemes provide the logical basis for coding visual significance into an abstract sign structure.

It can then be said that a visual sign is a twofold percept regulated by one central contrast line. It follows that one visual sign cannot exist on its own, but necessitates the search for adjacent entities of significance. In fact, when constructed by one boundary line at the center, the shapes divided by it create new boundaries above and below, as well as to the left and right. In the example of the meadow and the forest, the realization of the boundary between them already involves the idea of at least two further boundaries marking further significance, the sky and the arbitrary square of the frame. A frame always stands at the end of such a dialectic grid of boundaries, regulating the interplay of contrast lines and visual signs as their most formal boundary. Within the frame, each visual sign may be looked at as an independent entity, but only after its contours have been interrelated with the complete dialectic grid of all signs. The consequence is that not only the signifier, but also the potential signified of a visual sign depends on the interplay of all visual variables and their particular arrangement of visual characteristics. To conclude this outline of the theoretical structure of visual signs, ten visual variables can be identified in three different categories:

- Contrast lines* that divide basic visual shapes in the mode of phonemes;
- Basic twofold shapes,* the characteristics of which include color,* lightness,* patterns* (or texture), size,* and spatial alignment* in combinations that can be considered the visual equivalent to morphemes;
- The frame* and, with regard to film, the time frame,* which synthesize the previous two categories for the additional variable of movement* and which provide the basis for arranging the perspective, syntax, and rhythm of pictorial expressions.

The interplay of this set of ten visual variables can serve as the first empirical principle of visual language, but describes only one aspect of visual perception's dialectic mode. In addition to a mode of deciphering pictures that commences with the details of visual percepts in their contrast relations, the practice of visual recognition also moves in the opposite direction, from the whole to its parts.

THE SECOND CODE OF VISUAL LANGUAGE

If contrast lines provide the first key in the process of deriving meaning from a picture, and if they set up what has been called a picture's dialectic grid, they serve to limit a picture's wealth of detail by transforming into abstract contours of significance. This transformation accompanies the phenomenon of the arbitrary creation or emphasis of contrast lines where there may be none in reality. At the same time, the eye does not need to follow each contrast line in all its turns in order to demarcate entities of significance. This perceptual phenomenon is related to the mind's ability to "fill in" where nothing actually is, which occasionally causes our perception to invent things.[42] Perception consequently transforms the detailed characteristics of actual pictorial contrast lines into immaterial, abstract boundaries. In other words, the formal contours of visual signs and the dialectic grid that perception applies to a picture exist only in the rational mind, although they are inferred from contrast lines that actually exist on a picture's surface. However, to transform unlimited detail into formal lines that can serve as an immaterial signifier of visual signs, a concept is needed that justifies the demarcating of shapes with a signified of equally formal outline. In perception, the theoretical dichotomy of signs, the splitting into a signifier and a signified, is therefore associated with the question of what comes first, the demarcation of formal contours or the recognition of conceptual significance carried by the shapes divided by them, such as "person," "head," or "eyes." Similarly, the realization of a conceptual signified needs a starting and an end point in what can be large compounds of visual signs. Between a city and the chimney of a house, between a forest and the branch of a tree, or between a mass of people and a person's head, the conceptualizing of a picture's contrast lines certainly offers much leeway for the unfolding of significance. While the dialectic grid of contrast lines demands perceiving adjacent shapes as belonging together, the beholder nevertheless needs to finalize such chains of proximity, to order and to group them into separated entities of significance. The boundaries set for this purpose are neither material nor visible but spring from what can be called generic concepts. A few branches in the foreground of a picture, for example, can be associated with the generic concept of a tree, even if much of that tree remains outside the depiction.

Referencing a knowledge that rests outside the picture reflects a necessary step in recognizing the immaterial significance of visual signs within their dialectic grid of contrast lines. This second process enforces a fundamental rule of visual communication, which demands that knowledge and experience flow to the picture before any rational information can be conveyed by visual communication. Possibly with the exceptions of scientific exploration, of children at the beginning of their cognitive development, or of experimental art, the recognition of visual signs therefore stands and falls with a basic knowledge and experience that counters the individual variation of visual sign forms with the ability to conceptualize them in abstract contours of significance. This ability appears largely to correspond to the understanding of concepts allocated to words. The conclusion, however, that we can basically only see those visual shapes that we can also name, would nevertheless be misleading, because we dialectically map out our environment with generic concepts, and possibly pictures as well, long before acquiring speech. The acquisition of a pool of generic concepts consequently appears to relate first of all to the empirical development of the rational mind, before sponsoring the understanding of both visual and verbal sign concepts.

Even if visual signs seem to demand verbal articulations, and verbal signs seem to be associated with mental images, the generic concepts at the root of their ability to signify have an abstract framework and require a pragmatic logic. What actually belongs, for example, to the generic concept of a "house" may range from walls and windows to roof, doors, and stairs to central heating, doorbell, and much further detail, which can hardly be contained in any precise, formal code in terms of either verbal or visual signs. However, any detailed account of such generic concepts suggests not only differing social and cultural backgrounds, but also individually differing knowledge. If the allocation of generic concepts to signs comprises a conceptual code, such a code characterizes only the association of a very formal idea of a house, a broad notion that is usually further specified by the syntactical context of the sign. In written or verbal language, such specification, such as by adjectives, may then shape a particular angle on the content of the generic concept, such as characterizing a "house" in terms of its architectural style ("split-level") or the level of comfort it provides for inhabitants ("ramshackle"). At this point, however, the logic with which visual signs build on generic concepts departs from that of verbal and written signs. While the generic concepts of verbal and written signs usually add much more formal significance to their content than do syntax and context, the dialectic matrix of visual signs unique to every picture is what generates the visual signs' formal contours in the first place. At the same time as visual signs combine to project the formal concept of a house, they already add details, such as color, shape, size, and other visual characteristics that render its depiction as a particular, individual example of a house. Even in the most abstract graphical representations of a house styled, for example, with a triangle on top of a cube, the visual signs carry individual characteristics that detail the denotation of the generic concept "house," for example, as a little one with a large roof. Yet at the same time that the visual signs add detailed flesh to the rational bone of their generic concept, they also hide characteristics that would specify its abstract framework: an undistorted photograph of a house always leaves at least two of its walls invisible. Thus the process of applying generic concepts to visual signs resembles the mode of recognizing contrast lines: just as the outlining of contrast lines hardly follows actual details, the conceptualizing of shapes both adds, as well as omits, detail from the depiction. All those shapes that cannot be fitted into chains of significance or related with a generic concept need first of all to be dropped in order to understand a picture's basic outline of significance. Once comprehension of the picture is conceptually finalized, all visual signs are furthermore interrelated in ways much more essential than the grammatical sequencing of words. What appears as a simple black dot on a person's face, for instance, is not only connected to other adjacent percepts, but also to a larger concept, including, for example, the gender of the person, which allows finalizing the sign's denotation, such as "a mole on a woman's face." In addition, further concepts that may characterize the woman's clothing or objects in her environment signify in interdependent ways, reflecting back to each individual visual sign within the frame. When conceptualizing visual signs, a compromise must be made between recognizing detailed visual characteristics and applying formal significance symbolically, as in the case of the mole. Neither visible in all its qualities, nor seeable in pure formal contours, every visual sign ultimately arrives at its concept less in deductive than in inductive fashion: in this outline, the visual sign of the woman's mole creates first of all one actual example of all possible moles, while the equivalent sign in verbal and written language codes its signified as the more abstract and formal concept of all possible moles in general.

A further difference between visual and verbal or written language resides in the possibility of conceptualizing visual shapes at differing levels of detail, possibly also beyond the original intention of the sign's transmitter, depending on the empirical experience of a beholder. A dermatologist, for example, may be able to decipher more information from the depiction of a mole than the average beholder and to conceptualize it based on medical knowledge. Such analytical scanning for information, however, would generally be reserved for a second glance, which, much like rereading a text, can break the interactive plane at the core of communication in favor of an individual perspective. But despite comparable issues when discussing the cultural and historical praxis of visual language, the outlined mode of conceptualizing basic significance provides enough common ground among viewers to allow for structuring basic, conceptual significance in a quite precise fashion.

The conceptual principle of visual communication relies on an empirical perceptual intelligence that assigns shared significance to demarcated contours. While the human mode of perception adds the formal logic of boundary lines to actual contrast lines, rational concepts specify the shapes divided by them in an equally abstract mode. The arbitrariness of the conceptual principle thereby resides in the way details are negotiated: they are not equated with a strict code or, for that matter, identified in any direct relation to a hypothetical sight. But while words basically address single concepts in more direct fashion, visual signs demand a more pragmatic process of negotiating unique detail and accessing generic concepts. The result is a very particular type of synthesis. It gives rise to visual sign forms, neither flesh nor bone, that are unique to their dialectic context, but that nevertheless signify based on a code, albeit one that characterizes their significance in dynamic, symbolic logic.

FROM THE EMPIRICAL TO THE CONVENTIONAL DIMENSION OF VISUAL SIGNS

When defining the empirical code of visual language as drawing on the logic residing in the human mode of perception, such codes are necessarily less functional than any A = B equations of, for example, the Morse code. More flexible and more dynamic than the application of a one-to-one correspondence, the recognition of contoured significance resembles rather what Eco characterized as "modes of sign producing."[43] From this angle, such a mode interrelates the creation of sufficient grounds for two-dimensional contrast with the ability to recognize manmade boundaries as the central helpers in structuring significance. However accurate or iconic the technically produced visual variables may appear in comparison to sights in reality, their visual characteristics always betray the mediated nature of the sight and enact a shift of general perception into a pictorial mode. The subtle difference between the two equally dialectic modes of seeing may seem of little importance, but it carries significant consequences, especially with regard to the properties of visual variables. As the most arbitrary of all visual variables, the structure of the frame mediates a picture by carving out a set of percepts, and extends to impact the outline of all its selected contours in substantial fashion. While the frame suggests a direct transfer of three-dimensional into two-dimensional percepts in "window perspective," it simultaneously engages a dialectic grid of signifiers that would not be engaged in any actual sight framed by a window, a telescope, or by the lens of the camera itself.

The art historian Wölfflin described two methods of framing, "open" or "closed," the latter pertaining to pictures that keep the gaze centered on the significance mediated within the frame, and the former to pictures that encourage the beholder mentally to extend his dialectic chains of significance beyond the frame.[44] Such a differentiation only highlights one particular aspect of the frame's role as dialectic boundary, but it nevertheless indicates its crucial ability to arrange visual signs in ways that influence the conceptual code. While the dialectic grid of signifiers concatenates the significance of all visual signs, any arbitrary capping of the signifying chain also impacts the signified of each sign. The frame not only regulates the general syntax of a picture's message by either proposing or not proposing that a receiver venture beyond its boundary, but also extends to impact the significance of each demarcated signifier, and the allocation thereto of a context-dependent signified. A photograph displaying pieces of garbage on a street, for instance, forges dialectic significance based on a framed contrast relation between the visual signs "pieces of garbage," "asphalt," and a "meridian strip," which dialectically interrelate to denote "a dirty street." By contrast, when presented with the sight of the street in reality, a person might recognize "garbage on the street." The subtle difference between unmediated contrast relations and mediated contrast relations is engaged by the intention behind the handling of visual variables and their concepts. In setting the frame, a transmitter arranges the dialectic context of all visual characteristics and proposes to conceptualize them accordingly. In the case of an open frame, the contrast relations of the visual signs ask for inferring further garbage beyond what is visible, accentuating the conclusion, a dirty street. In the case of a closed frame, the contrast relation between garbage and street does not extend beyond the boundary of the frame, placing the focus on the nature of the garbage itself. Either way, an arbitrary, inductive logic enables the visual variables to signify within a dialectic context that is not only independent of any original sight, but also always differentiated by the handling of each of its visual characteristics. The visual variables can thus be defined as a set of grammatical tools used not only to create and emphasize contrast lines in artificial ways, but also to enable a contextual grid, the contours of which are unique to the picture. The notion of this contextual or conceptual grid thus maintains that every single visual variable has the potential to cause a chain reaction; altering the significance of one sign, and thereby the nature of its dialectic interrelation, can change the complete pictorial message. Both a special emphasis on a particular detail in the foreground, such as the color or shape of one piece of garbage, as well as whether or not a particular detail of the background is included in the picture's frame, can thus alter the significance of all the featured signs and consequently also whatever significance could possibly spring from the signs' direct relation to their model in reality.

The structural kernel of the outlined principles of pictorial communication is nevertheless a dialectic rationality that enables most beholders to decipher pictures based on the quite rational, formal logic of allocating basic significance to spatially outlined contrast relations. So far, the rationality of visual perception corresponds with an empirical intelligence that also enables the scientific use of pictures. However, with the recognition of the arbitrariness behind the arrangement of visual variables, it can be seen that every picture caters intentionally to the human mode of perception, which transfers the rationality of the boundaries outlined by the dialectic and conceptual code into a symbolic mode of comprehending the signs' significance. The particular juxtaposition of invisible generic concepts with basically unlimited variations of visual detail enables meaning to be received from contours which are at the same time very formal and abstract, and unique to every picture. The interplay of the dialectic and the conceptual code not only mitigates the question of whether perception begins with larger entities of significance or with individual contours, but also blends the significance of immaterial generic concepts with that of the details unique to every visual sign. If visual signs vary from picture to picture, their measure of uniqueness is thus balanced by the formal tendency of visual variables to interrelate their characteristics within larger sign compounds. In order to comprehend some of the uniqueness offered by each new picture, a viewer bundles its visual variables into compounds that comprise at least two visual signs and then compares these with compounds conceptualized and memorized in the past.[45] In this outline, the larger visual entities of significance, as defined by Gestalt theory or by Peirce's concept of icons, are built of visual variables, which structure sets of visual signs, the abstract forms of which necessarily translate into interwoven, symbolic contours of significance, before any secondary, analytical gaze may trace the signs' individual shape, the implication of their uniqueness, or, for that matter, the relation of their unique features with their model in reality.

The dialectic and conceptual mechanisms of visual perception suggest an emphasis on symbolic significance, because visual signs—with the partial exception of more abstract graphical signs—always embellish their generic concept with detail.[46] In the place of a pictorial "dove" that could stand as an abstract blueprint for all birds of this species, the visual variables always add at least some particular such as, for example, white color, spread wings, and so forth. In consequence, each dove painted or photographed simultaneously individualizes its abstract generic concept and generalizes its particular, visual characteristics, blending different entities of significance into one, specific subcategory of doves. It thus signifies neither as a unique specimen, nor as a generic concept, but as an example of, say, "all white, flying doves." As such the visual symbol references a culturally volatile semantic field that stands in accordance with some of the visual characteristics of the depicted visual signs and that outlines one or more vectors of symbolic significance. Because the visual signs that comprise the dove are further constituted in relation to other sign compounds within the frame, for example, with the horizon of the sea as background, these other visual characteristics also combine and contribute to the projection of particular vectors of symbolic significance to the visual literacy of a beholder.

At first sight, neither any single visual variable, nor any individual, visual sign standing for a dove's wing, head, or bill can support the unique aspects of their display with any correspondingly detailed rational significance, although a second glance can go back in order to analyze some of the details and possibly even to correct the first impression. These observations on the particular tension between visual detail and generic entities of significance suggest a process of balancing novel with memorized shapes, which process incorporates visual literacy on top of the ability simply to allocate formal significance in terms of generic concepts. This type of visual literacy would tend to invoke larger compounds of visual variables and signs, as these are easier to recollect, and to designate rather symbolic figurations of significance. An assessment of what kind of garbage is being portrayed on what kind of street thus emerges through a process of perception that suppresses empirical detail in favor of symbols. Any reference to a real existing street is thus made secondary to the purpose of communication, as is the notion of any real bird behind the historically cultured symbol of a dove. For these reasons, it can be concluded that the empirical logic of visual perception provides a rational base for defining visual signs, but also projects their communicative significance to a receiver's visual literacy in the inductive mode of a symbolic logic. In contrast to verbal signs, which first of all convey abstract concepts that are then detailed by the context, the dialectically interrelated nature of visual signs always forges a typified example of the respective generic concept. As entities of significance in between the abstract and the individual, visual signs receive contributing significance through their dialectic interrelation with one another, which all refer to culturally contoured semantic fields conditioned by collective visual literacy.

THE THIRD CODE OF VISUAL LANGUAGE

The two empirical codes describe the fragile mitigation of a potentially unlimited variety of visual shapes delineated by contrast relations with a more manageable set of basic rational concepts, thus accounting for the rather ephemeral character of visual signs. Different pairs of eyes build different chains of signifiers, although less so with regard to a picture's main generic concepts, than in terms of the details noticed and memorized. Most people may generally recognize the depiction of a man in its conceptual outline, but single visual components of the compounded sign concept, such as the color of his hair and eyes, his articles of clothing, his posture, his age, and so forth, may prompt different understandings depending on individual interpretation. While the creator of such a depiction can encourage a particular focus, for example, through spotlighting a watch on the wrist as a symbolic characteristic of the man, the empirical process of recognition still engages an individual perspective that appears to compare with unmediated perception in reality. For this reason, the term "iconicity," referring to the similarity or resemblance between perception from pictures and in reality, resurfaces in most discussions of visual signs. As outlined so far, the empirical mode of perception indeed provides the basic grounds for understanding pictures, yet less through making an assessment of any more or less detailed resemblance of visual sign compounds to sights in reality, than through finding or creating sufficient contrast relations to set up the dialectic logic of perception.

The extent to which visual variables may actually compare to or resemble a sight in reality can thus be seen as secondary to the way each visual shape can be interrelated with the others and conceptualized accordingly. In consequence, it becomes possible axiomatically to detach the aspect of reality behind the notion of iconicity in favor of a communicative function of perception that is able to convey contoured significance independently of a picture's resemblance to a sight in reality. Furthermore, while the first code specifies the a process of demarcating significance from contrast lines, the second code specifies a process of categorizing or classifying abstract concepts with the help of a visual literacy collected in the past, thus paving the way for integrating the historical (diachronic) dimension into the perception of pictures. As the empirically grounded act of perception integrates spatial with conceptual aspects, the next level of perception integrates temporal with symbolic aspects in the form of diachronically shaped cultural significance, for example, in order to assess the social status of the inhabitants of a depicted house. Against this background, photography's reference to a moment in time cannot possibly govern a picture's semantic significance. First of all, the framed shapes relate more directly to the moment of their present contemplation, than to the moment in time captured by the camera. Secondly, the duration of the act of contemplating can be controlled by the presenters of pictures, as in the case of film. And thirdly, the two-dimensional shapes that enable pictorial perception are referred to experience gathered both from similar depictions, as well as from comparable sights in reality, which referral in each case adds a historical dimension that obstructs a direct link between a picture's semantic significance and its generic reference to a moment in time. Organized by visual literacy, such gathered experience enables a diachronic, historical type of iconicity, whereby details of a picture are compared with shapes that have been memorized in the past, rather than with any model in an absent reality.

Because single visual signs, such as the individual contours of a person's ear, vary in their form from picture to picture in ways that can barely be memorized, visual literacy needs to be made up of larger pictorial entities comprising several visual signs that feature recognizable patterns of variables. For this reason, it is important to emphasize the particular character of visual signs as signifying interdependently, only completing the signifier-signified relation when their unique patterns can be symbolically typified according to generally memorized patterns. It is reasonable to assume that the patterns and shapes of objects encountered most often in both everyday life and in visual communication also provide the most detailed tapestry of symbolic significance. For an American viewer, any depiction of an American suburban house certainly holds more symbolic content than, for example, a depiction of a South-Asian house (see also chapter 8, "The Historicity of the Documentary's Imagery"), the individual visual signs of which can be conceptualized as a generic term, but the details of which cannot be enriched with significance drawn from visual literacy: whether the depiction presents a particularly luxurious or an especially cozy house thus evades the signs' communicative potential in this particular receiver context. Yet, for such reasons, visual literacy is less a passive register of visual terms, than an active process of comparing, categorizing, and typifying visual signs as symbols. Transmitters and receivers may not perform this processing of significance in the exact same way, but it can nevertheless be anticipated and taken into account. The faculty of visual literacy thus enables a third level of assigning meaning to two-dimensional shapes that will here be defined as the symbolic code of visual language.

Once the empirical codes have comprehended the "basic grammar" of a depiction and have established the basic condition for pictorial perception, the symbolic code develops the signs' full communicative potential under the condition that the visual literacy of transmitter and of receiver are pragmatically adjusted in the process of communication. If the symbolic potential of the signs is disregarded, for example, through depicting the unfamiliar faces, gestures, or clothing of people participating in a political demonstration in another country, audiences are limited in evaluating whether the pictures present a typical or an atypical scene. By contrast, if the symbolic code addresses the specific visual literacy of viewers, the visual message of the demonstration builds a symbolic statement in less coincidental and more communicative fashion. Through selecting faces and gestures for close-up that appear typical to a protest, the transmitter has the possibility of rendering the visual signs with distinctive symbolic significance, but only when recognizing the symbolic code as a means to directly address the visual literacy of spectators. The possibility of "manipulating" significance by means of the symbolic code therefore rests in a direct reference of the picture—not to any actual demonstration, but rather to the way similar protests have been portrayed in the past and thus to the way these pictures have been nurturing the collective visual literacy of audiences.

In this outline, the symbolic code specifies a third dynamic principle of visual communication, which not only enables visual signs set up by the empirical codes to be interpreted symbolically, but also introduces a historical dimension to the way semantic fields of meaning become connected to visual sign structures. In addressing these fields of meaning, a transmitter can not control individual comprehension of the signs provided, but he can anticipate a general knowledge about their content based on how they have been circulating within visual culture. The result is that the symbolic code, and with it visual communication as a language form, hinges on the extent to which pictures are traded within the culture of a particular society or community. In general, the more pictures circulate as carriers of visual communication, the more solidified the cultural aspect of visual literacy becomes, and the more precise visual signs become in their ability to reflect a transmitter's intention. Enabling a process of classifying or typifying visual signs as symbols that hover between abstract concepts and individual contours, the symbolic code thus accesses a kind of cultural memory in order to project socially comprehensive significance. Such significance consequently transcends individual "making do" with visual signs in cases where a spectator disagrees with the intention behind the presented visual characteristics of a visual symbol.[47] For example, a depiction of a young, blonde, blue-eyed man dressed in contemporary fashion presents an array of different visual signs, which once conceptualized all stand in symbolic relation to the figure's main significance. While each sign may potentially be evaluated differently by receivers, their symbolic interplay can nevertheless forge the attributes of "male attractiveness" based on visual literacy: whether or not everybody agrees with the actual arrangement of each single visual characteristic, with the transmitter's intention to use such a symbol, or with the culturally forged standards of esthetics in general, the denotation of the symbol is nevertheless present and informs the symbolic code for any future typifying of "male attractiveness."

THE FOURTH CODE OF VISUAL LANGUAGE

As the last principle of visual language, the iconic code builds on the previous ones and further emphasizes the diachronic (or historical) orientation of visual symbols. In the process of accumulating visual literacy, visual signs are ordered in groups specified by similar characteristics, as well as by a common field of symbolic significance. Every new symbol received from a picture is classified according to established categories, based on the semantic structure of difference and similarity. Each appearance of a sign usually features new detail, and moreover each appearance of a sign usually brings new significance through its dialectic interconnection with a new configuration of other signs and symbols, adding new vectors of significance to the collection of all instances of the sign. Hence, in the mode of the logic of collecting that orders each new acquisition according to the pattern outlined by those previously collected, visual literacy manages the semantic fields of visual symbols by adjusting their individual characteristics to diachronically developed standards. In other words, every new tree, every new mountain, or every new face unfolds its significance according to symbolic patterns memorized in the past. In general it can be said that the more typically the symbol of a model or an actor (for example) relates to an established category of significance, the more exchangeable it is within the picture. By contrast, the more novel and atypical the offered symbol, the more dynamic the process of typifying becomes, perhaps even resulting in the generation of a new category of significance. However, while such processes underlying the symbolic code apply to typifying novel, still rather unspecific and ultimately replaceable visual symbols, the diachronic factor of visual literacy also takes up all those situations in which the same symbol finds multiple exposures, be it within the narrative of a movie, or across different types of still pictures. Such symbols begin to develop iconic patterns of visual signs that can be memorized, which development adds to their symbolic comprehensibility within larger groups of visual terms the possibility of being comprehended as individual entities of meaning. These particular symbols can be called icons, such as Marilyn Monroe, or emblems, such as the White House. But besides such overarching "meta-symbols," those visual symbols that become memorable and identifiable in their individual visual sign structure, if only for the duration of a single movie, an advertising campaign, or a political event, are also imbued with iconic recognition.[48] When such icons and emblems are part of a picture's context, they influence its message differently than those visual symbols containing less historically specified contours. They are also not replaceable without significantly changing both the denotational and the connotational significance of a picture's message. As long as the familiar iconic pattern is basically preserved, every new angle also presents an emblem or an icon within a new dialectic interrelation to other symbols, adding each time a new shade of meaning to the symbol's semantic field. Visual symbols based on an iconic pattern reference less their actual model in reality, than all those pictures that in a diachronic fashion have established the possibility of recognizing them in the first place.

At this point, the issue of "iconicity" or resemblance between visual signs and sights in reality resurfaces for a last time, albeit in a new perspective. Instead of impacting the understanding of visual signs by comparing them to objects in reality, this form of iconicity impacts understanding by comparing visual signs to their counterparts within visual literacy, which are drawn both from past individual life experience and from socially traded visual signs. Like the symbolic code, the iconic code of visual communication builds more on the social and cultural side of visual literacy than on individual experience. That a person may have once encountered the president of the United States or actually seen the White House certainly adds to the individual understanding of the symbols in a picture, but it hardly changes their basic pictorial significance; nor would it impact their verbal significance, if the person should read the name of the president or the words "White House" in a newspaper article.

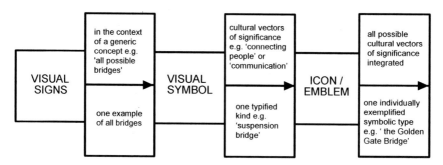

Figure 16.2. Sign–Symbol–Icon.

In summarizing the difference between the symbolic and the iconic code, it can be stated that the latter builds on the former in terms of carving out recognizable, individually memorable sign patterns that add a type of definite article and a type of visual name to a symbol. As such, the iconic code develops an individual field of meaning that still relates to comparable symbolic groups, the way the emblem of the White House relates to similar architecture, or the icon of the president connects with the visual symbols of politicians in general, but it also develops new vectors of meaning with regard to the icon's or emblem's particular semantic history.

The figure illustrates the way a depiction of, for example, a suspension bridge builds on uniquely shaped signs that allow for conceptualization of its properties. Although the visual signs potentially identify one individual bridge in one particular moment of time, the communicative nature of the depiction transfers the individual contours into a culturally shaped field of significance. The bridge's unique signs are thus negotiated in a process that typifies them with regard to all similar symbols of suspension bridges. Within this process, the symbol assumes cultural vectors of meaning, such as that of "connecting people" or "communication," which are arbitrary in relation to the uniqueness of its visual signs, as well as possibly to its basic generic concept, that is the properties of all suspension bridges, but not to its picture's pictorial context. Once its contours have become familiar enough to be identifiable based on characteristic sign patterns, as the "Golden Gate Bridge" may for example be recognizable even when removed from its original place in a picture, the bridge assumes a third, emblematic status as a (re) individualized symbol. On this level, additional vectors of significance, such as a reference to San Francisco, or more generally, to the historically evolved status of California within the U.S.A., specify its range of meanings. As an outstanding term of visual language, such an emblem communicates neither in reference to any individual bridge, nor to all bridges in general, but first of all in reference to its particular history in pictorial communication.

To finalize this attempt to define an iconic code of visual language, the suggested difference between emblems and icons needs further consideration. The definition of icons as standing for humans, and emblems for all other things, springs from an observation that concerns the general mode of visual perception. It can generally be argued that the characteristics of human faces are most familiar to us and, consequently, relate to the most sophisticated part of our visual literacy. More importantly, however, we are also culturally preconditioned to allocate individual identity to each human face that we encounter, which allocation does not occur during the perception of objects. Generally, all other life forms are also seen differently, both in the way we allocate identity to them, and in the way we notice and conceptualize individual details of their appearance. For this reason, movies portraying wildlife can cast different animals as one and the same character without most viewers noticing. If the iconic code still regulates an animal's pictorial narrative, it is thus with the intention to endow the emblem with a human character. Apart from such exceptions, emblems specify everything that is nonhuman and consequently cannot possibly have any conscious influence on the creation of a picture. The symbolic code also presupposes a limitation in evaluating any portrayal of an unknown face: it appears that such depictions can hardly disclose whether or not the projected significance is rooted in the conscious agency of the person portrayed or in that of the shot's creator, editor, or publisher. As a consequence, the outlined distinction in the iconic code between emblems and icons takes into account the nature of the familiarity with a frequently depicted person, not only with regard to her characteristic pattern of visual variables, but also with her symbol's semantic field. This familiarity can lead viewers to sense that they "know" the portrayed person, although the author of that person's demeanor is completely obscure. (The question of the possibility of influencing the outcome of a pictorial message from a place in front of the camera is further discussed in the section "Acting, or the Art of Writing Chinese characters" in part C, "Hyperrealism.") In any case, the proposed model of an iconic code not only challenges the traditional perspective on people portrayed in pictures, but also excludes many symbols commonly termed "icons," for example, those on a computer screen. The reason for this exclusion resides in the difference between visual language in general, and graphical subsystems of visual communication, the codes of which are based on a limited number of signs and symbols with relatively fixed characteristics and significance, such as the subsystem of traffic signs or that of computer "icons." Such signs are also much more independent of a transmitter's individual influence, which renders their communicative status more as visual signals than as interactive visual signs.

While a portrayed iconic character might to some degree override a transmitter's intention and contribute individual agency to pictorial communication, icons function first of all as a semiotic type of visual name, before referencing any actual personalities. As terms of a language, they are always subject to a historical dynamic that alters their significance for as long as they circulate in visual culture. The iconic code is thus the collective product of all those who create their own version of the symbols and contribute to their pictorial dissemination, and of all those who respond to their semiotic significance. In this very dynamic semiotic structure, icons and emblems appear as visual language's most precisely contoured forms, and simultaneously as the visual terms of which the content appears arguably the most detached from the subjects and objects that posed as their model in reality. In this light, icons and emblems develop significance that is particular to their history as terms of visual language, but not necessarily to the history of the subjects and objects they name pictorially.

The four outlined codes thus build on each other, starting with the empirical process of demarcating contrast lines and allocating abstract, generic concepts to visual signifiers and ending with typifying general, visual symbols, as well as icons and emblems. Like Baudrillard's simulacrum, these gradually lose their anchor in immediate reality when developing significance specific to a society's cultured visual literacy. [49]

17 Notes on the Syntactic Function of the Four Codes

In verbal and written language, a message is built in simple, but effective logic, which underlies every sentence with a first syntax through incorporating the basic concept of explaining something to another person. Communication always involves the mediation of novel significance with signs that have been coded in the past, and syntactical arrangement is what enables a new expression to be formed with old signs. The syntactic logic compels certain signs to be chosen in the place of others and gives these signs meaning that is different from their general use. In principle, any utterance begins with a "theme" specified by signs referring to a known context.[1] The theme is usually followed by a verb that sets up the "rheme," which orders all other signs in a sequence that in principle gradually adds novel significance to the theme. In general, the signs comprising the rheme of a sentence are arranged layer by layer with the last one reflecting the most important or most novel piece of information. Variations are of course possible, as are exceptions that often develop meaning in indirect reference to the rule—and so are misunderstandings. The simple, but effective logic of this one-dimensional syntax compares at first oddly to visual perception. Not only do pictures provide various syntactic vectors, but they also project meaning in a fraction of the time it takes to utter a sentence and, apart from film, lack the temporal structure of sequencing either signs or groups of signs. With respect to the four codes, however, the basic logic of the theme-rheme principle can nevertheless be compared with the pictorial syntax of pictures. The key to structuring visual signs' syntactic order rests in setting a focal point, for example, by placing the main symbol in the foreground or by emphasizing particular signs by means of other visual variables, such as color and lightness. Exploiting the potential of the visual variables, the setting of a focal point marks the theme to which all other signs and symbols relate in the fashion of the rheme: they add layers of meaning, which help to develop the theme and thus to enable a new expression. In contrast to sentences, pictorial syntax follows a rather circular path, usually beginning and ending with the focal signs and symbols, and in doing so it synthesizes a verblike concept. Due to the dialectic principle that vivifies all contrast relations, the theme-rheme hinge imbues verblike significance in the contrast line between adjacent signs—such as, for example, "belongs to"—which complements the grammatical structure of a visual message. When analyzing the logic of advertising, the German linguist and sociologist Wolfgang Fritz Haug called such "grammatical" interrelation of visual significance "symbolic transfer."[2] This dialectic relationship works in both directions, since a product in the center may not only profit from the semantic content and status of (for example) a nearby icon, but may also add to that icon's semantic field in return. Whatever the person is doing with the product, holding, eating, throwing, or walking towards it, may not construct a visual shape on its own, but reflects in its verb concept an invisible dialectic relation between the main visual symbols. At minimum, the symbolic transfer of the picture's theme-rheme hinge thus proposes that two things "belong together," as for example when an advertisement introduces a car in front of a house, or a news spot depicts a politician in front of a bookcase. Symbolic transfer thus proposes a grammatical arrangement of significance as opposed to a coincidental context, meaning that a picture's statement can be assessed as either true or false, which assessment reflects upon those who present the picture to others.

The guiding of a receiver's gaze in pragmatic fashion and the structuring of visual signs and symbols in verblike relations can be assimilated with the specific characteristics of the four codes, as follows.

THE SYNTACTIC PRINCIPLE OF THE DIALECTIC CODE

A yellow leaf among the generally green leaves of a tree, or the contour of a mountain highlighted by special light conditions, is able to focus the gaze through a single visual variable. A single variable within a system of dialectically ordered signs and contrast relations can accentuate some signs over others, which then determine the first generic concept and, consequently, the first visual symbol of a picture. The gaze may then wander over the picture to conceptualize other signs and symbols, but in doing so, it also attempts to verify those shapes and contours first conceptualized as its theme. The symbolic classification of all other signs thus serves as a rheme that endows the particular characteristics of the main symbol with additional significance, in a circular fashion. With regard to one yellow-colored leaf in the otherwise green foliage, for example, such a circular theme-rheme hinge may complete an expression such as "fall is around the corner." Once such a theme-rheme hinge is established, all other details in a picture, as long as they do not contradict the main expression, are usually either neglected or else subsequently subjected to the syntactical theme of the first symbol in focus.

THE SYNTACTIC PRINCIPLE OF THE CONCEPTUAL CODE

Through structuring the dialectically interwoven visual variables in chains or compounds of visual signs that can be matched with generic concepts, the conceptual code can also contribute to specifying a focal point: for example, through offering the most detailed, sign-rich entity of significance as the main theme of a picture. This possibility also allows for some leeway in the spatial arrangement of a picture's syntax, since such a sign-rich entity need not necessarily be placed in the center or the foreground. However, in building on the dialectic code, the conceptual code requires the identification of at least one other conceptual entity, and projects a relationship between the two that enhances their contrast relation with verblike significance. A picture of a person standing in an empty room projects at its most basic level a third concept: the person "is in," "belongs in," or "pertains to" that room. The arrangement of the visual signs marking the actual contrast between the body of the person and, for example, a window, further specifies that synthesized concept as a type of "visual verb" or visual gesture: the person "is standing by" the window or "is looking out" of it.

THE SYNTACTIC PRINCIPLE OF THE SYMBOLIC CODE

Adding a symbolic layer of meaning to the concepts of visual signs and sign chains, the symbolic code enables dynamic categorization of visual symbols in relation to culturally established fields of significance. While standard sets of visual symbols, such as suburban houses or a certain style of make-up, hairdo, and so forth, typical to a society, may help to anchor a picture's message, more atypical symbols can serve to attract the gaze and spark curiosity about their particular visual characteristics. Influenced by the dialectic code, any symbolic transfer relation between typical and atypical symbols, for example, a beggar as opposed to a politician in front of a bookcase, may furthermore pinpoint the main theme-rheme hinge of a picture. In the same mode, verblike concepts are rendered through symbolic expressions of gestures and movement, which add to a picture's syntax and can accentuate its main message, for example, when projecting a quick movement or characterizing a rather peculiar, unfamiliar gesture that relates oddly to visual literacy. In each case it can be noted that the choice of symbols presented in a picture anticipates the symbolic categorizing and typifying of their semantic fields, a type of anticipation that assumes syntactical functions of its own. Calling on both culturally and individually gathered visual literacy, a picture of a beggar contrasted with rows of books obviously relates the two symbolic fields of meaning differently than would a well-dressed person in the same pictorial context, and this difference in relation can be anticipated by the pictures' presenters. Furthermore, culturally attuned symbolic figurations, such as a silver-haired scientist wearing glasses and a white coat, renders the process of symbolic transfer with regard to books almost as a cliché. In summary, conventionalized presentations of symbols typical to a culture's visual literacy tend to anchor a picture's expression, while symbols of more unfamiliar, atypical, or exotic figurations send the gaze to inquire more about them.

THE SYNTACTIC PRINCIPLE OF THE ICONIC CODE

Establishing the most specified terms of visual language, the iconic code is essential in constructing visual narratives. Either through the choice of familiar faces already iconized in the past, or through the active familiarization of spectators with a person's visual appearance within the narrative context, a visual symbol is rendered with what can be called a definite article, which usually specifies it as part of the main symbolic transfer relation. Although the other codes may favor other symbols as the main topic of a picture, icons and emblems have a superordinate power to attract the gaze and thus to pinpoint the theme-rheme syntax of a picture. This hierarchy is further refined, since it generally appears that the more specified the semantic significance of icons and emblems, the more they cast meanings onto all surrounding visual signs and symbols: the icon of Albert Einstein in front of a bookcase, for example, categorizes the symbolic significance of the books as complementing in one or the other way its semantic background. By comparison, the iconically contoured image of a well-known action hero, such as Arnold Schwarzenegger, may render the same symbolic juxtaposition as an exotic figuration, or even cut off the dialectic syntax based on the icon's power to monopolize the gaze on the strength of its own visual characteristics and significance. The latter possibility indicates that an icon's semantic history may even outweigh the dialectic code, and has the power to signify without being influenced by adjacent signs, thereby rendering other symbols, such as a row of books, as insignificant in context. Nevertheless, a shot of an emblem like the White House that reveals, for example, a certain amount of garbage on the lawn, forges a different message than that of an untidy lawn in the foreground of an unknown house. In the latter case, the visual symbols relate to signify a property as generally neglected; in the former, they relate as a rather atypical and exceptional combination, at least in association with the experience acquired from previously viewed pictures of the emblem. However, while icons and emblems carry basic significance that is partially independent of the actual pictorial context, they are nevertheless generally subject to the dialectic grid and to the picture's theme-rheme syntax. In terms of a picture's verb structure, icons and iconic figurations further enhance, for example, the process of synthesizing main contrast lines, resulting in a type of iconic verb: although the verb "to punch," either in still or moving pictures, can only be seen in terms of the contrasting two-dimensional symbols "fist" and "face," a fist associated with a well-known icon such as Schwarzenegger is understood as punching powerfully. As a condition for presenting such an iconic verb, however, the gesture of the punch should correspond in its visual characteristics with a figuration of the actor's typical punching style.

In summary, pictorial syntax is structured comparably to the theme-rheme compound of verbal and written language, although it sequences signs and symbols differently. Unlike the one-dimensional alignment of a theme followed by a rheme that generally reserves the most important information for the end of the sentence, the two-dimensional picture balances theme with rheme and completes the understanding of mutual symbolic transfer with a verb concept. Once such a verb concept is dialectically constructed in between symbols and/or by the visual variable of movement, other grammatical attributes further regulate the pictorial syntax with answers to a set of more or less mandatory questions, such as who, where, with what, why, and so forth.[3]

The described aspects of pictorial syntax move in a circular fashion back to the initial focus and feature a number of logical tools, ranging from accentuation of visual variables to choice of extraordinary visual symbols, and from proposal of verblike concepts to structure of action and movement with attributes. Together, the four codes thus govern a particular, dialectic syntax, which qualifies the transmitter's ability to guide a receiver's perception by pragmatic means and to influence his basic mode of comprehending the outlined message. When applying these observations on the syntactic patterns of visual language to the analysis of the historical documentary, some parallels to the broadcast spectacle emerge. The attention-seeking character of the spectacle finds an equivalent in pictorial syntax, which chooses a focal starting point able to attract the eye. By the same standard, the use of icons—or the narrative iconization of visual symbols—relates directly to the grammatical function of providing an anchor for understanding all other sign chains. The arrangement of unified icons amid the attention-directing attributes of broadcast spectacle thus refers to the grammatical structure of visual language before it refers to the possible structure of attention-seeking events in reality.

18 Notes on the Pragmatics of Visual Language

The particular nature of visual language certainly rests in its proximity to the empirical mechanisms of human perception. While this proximity fuels the conventional association of a picture with "in front of the camera" reality, the dialectic mode of seeing also can be artificially stimulated through a picture's manufacture. From this perspective, creating and arranging a grid of visual variables by photographic techniques is analogous to an act of producing language, at least as long as enough of a basis is established for a receiver to conceptualize significance. In so far as the picture is indeed intended to relate significance to a receiver, it profits from an element of double articulation that is part of the cognitive capacity of humans and can thus be manipulated for purposes of communication. But if the communicative structure of pictures contains elements similar to those at the root of verbal and written language, the question is how visual signs compare with these linguistic units. On the one hand, visual signs share with written signs a deferral in time between the moment of their production and that of their presentation. On the other hand, modern broadcast techniques allow for "live" broadcasting, which reduces such deferral to the realm of seconds, thus approximating the immediacy of speech with its transmitter-receiver context. Furthermore, the ability of the clip to structure the time frame of visual syntax resembles more the pacing of words in speech than the independently determined following of lines of a text. Yet despite sharing some elements with verbal communication, the production of pictures always excludes the transmitter from the spatial context, which exclusion ultimately also requires a temporal break, however minimal.

Against this background, Derrida's notion of "différance" can be useful.[1] With the aberrant spelling of "différence" (difference), Derrida implied the verb "différer" in the gerund, which besides "differing" can also mean "defering." Building on the Saussurean idea of language as a system of differences, Derrida used différance to indicate the radical consequence of an infinite chain of signifying traces. Because every trace leads to all others, and because every trace only exists by virtue of another trace, the concept of différance precludes any exact code at the origin of signs, rendering every exchange a form of "arche-writing." According to Derrida, arche-writing "can never be recognized as the object of a science," because "it is that very thing which cannot let itself be reduced to the form of presence." [2] From this perspective, verbal signs also contain an element of "writing" in the sense that they too draw on a differential network of significance, the historical dimension of which equals that of written signs. Thus reducing the communicative difference between verbal and written language, Derrida's postmodern approach relates both very smoothly, and the same time very awkwardly, to the presented model of visual language. In contrast to written signs, it is not so much the signified as the signifier of visual signs that first of all suggests a theoretical continuum in the form of unlimited possible shapes. The mass of visual signs, symbols, and icons already equate with the notion of arche-writing, as even icons never really appear twice in the exact same contours. Moreover, the generating of a signified for a set of visual contours ultimately involves itself a type of arche-writing. While Derrida ultimately proposed the concept of arche-writing to deconstruct the concept of coded signs, since the notion of unlimited deferral also disqualifies their potential to relay formal significance between transmitters and receivers, it actually contributes to the pragmatic definition of visual literacy and its terms in the logic of the four codes.

Although the concept of visual language is built out of a diachronically dynamic visual literacy characterized by the lifelong collecting and ordering of visual symbols into differential networks of signification, it is also obvious that such signs, symbols, and emblems can never be understood by two persons in their exact same signified. Yet, while postmodern thinkers such as Derrida deconstructed (sign-)structure in communication and thereby concluded that words necessarily fail to relate a dictionary type of content, visual communication was never associated with a stringent logical structure in the first place. For such reasons, Baudrillard was led to associate photographic (hyper)realism with "the evil demon of images." [3] Arguing that the production of a picture influences the very reality that it displays, his take on visual communication may rightly deconstruct the pictorial sign's reference to a moment in reality, but it also debases its context within a transmitter-receiver relation. Baudrillard's evil demon only takes the floor when visual signs disappear behind the construction of a direct reference to the continuum of reality. However, once pictures are contextualized as an act of communication, the moment of their contemplation and comprehension counters whatever moment in reality the pictorial content may reference. In light of Heraclitus's axiom of a reality that is always in flux, any act of communication could be described as setting an arbitrary mark, which much in the way of a contrast line forges an abstract boundary that specifies the before and after within what is otherwise an indistinct flow of historically limitless scope. Against this background, it is as if the continuum of arche-writing needs the evil demon of communication in order to be able at all to mark a "before" and an "after" and thus to secure each others' existence. What is thus needed is an outline of what Peirce already described as the pragmatic part of communication: the part that complements the semantics of signs and their syntactic arrangement with an approximation of how such signs' understanding can be founded on shared content coded in the past and at the same time can convey content in the present that is novel and unique to the context of the exchange.

THE PRESENT PERFECT CONTINUOUS
OF THE SIGN EXCHANGE

Although coded in the past, every sign always asks for an at least slightly novel interpretation that is adjusted to the equally novel context of every new exchange.[4] Without such novel shades created by the syntactic arrangement and the semantic understanding particular to the moment of their exchange, as well as to the relation between the involved personalities, the signs could not even begin to accumulate the distinctive traces needed to forge a semantic arch. As the aim of communication is always to relate new content in known forms, there is constant negotiation of what is new for the partner in communication and what understanding can be presupposed. On the level of syntactics, this process of necessarily pragmatic scope relates to the previously described logic of theme-rheme handling. The theme-rheme sequence, however, concerns first of all the "synchronic context" of an utterance, the spatial side of the arrangement of signs in the present. The "diachronic context," by contrast,

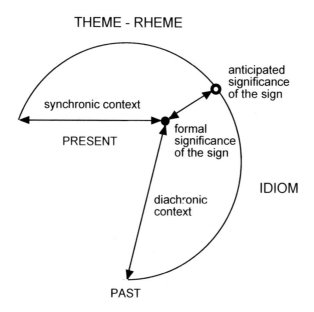

Figure 18.1. Diachronic-synchronic context.

or the historically rooted information that influences the exchange, concerns how the partners in communication know each other, or, in other words, how they anticipate each other's understanding based on the experience gathered from previous exchanges.[5] In the pragmatics of sign-exchange, the diachronic context, previously termed "idiom," interconnects with the handling of the synchronic context as illustrated in Figure 18.1.

In this graphic outline, the synchronic context would, for example, specify the restaurant two people are talking about as the one they mentioned earlier in the conversation or the one in front of which they are standing. The diachronic context in turn involves whatever these two people know about each other, how they have talked about such and other restaurants in the past, and how they accordingly anticipate each other's understanding. Depending on experience from past interactions, the idiomatic understanding can, for example, also allow for grammatical omissions or unusual sign-definitions without provoking misunderstandings.

Differentiation of the synchronic and the diachronic sign context allows for the possibility of integrating the pragmatics of communication into the definition of a sign's semantic form. In the model, idiom thereby enables the "translation" of significance defined in the past by an impersonal, dictionary-type code into novel significance proper to each new exchange of signs.

Comprising the influence of the synchronic and the diachronic context upon the significance of the signs being used, the idiom does not simply feature the characteristics of a continuum, but specifies a "present perfect continuous" that keeps old and new shades of meanings present for future exchanges between the same partners in communication. In accordance

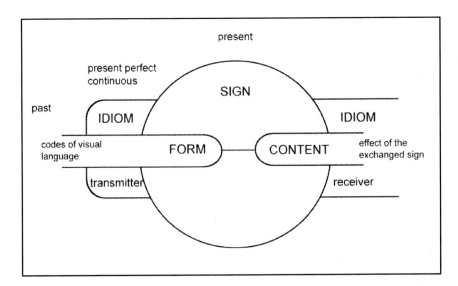

Figure 18.2. Form-content idiom.

with the Greek root of the term, the idiom thereby defines everything that is "proper" to the current transmitter-receiver context of an exchange, and thus to the (micro)language that develops between people whose use it. [6]

In this interpretation, idiom specifies a third temporal vector for signs in the form of the present perfect continuous of the transmitter-receiver context, which bridges the continuum of a sign's content established in the past with its novel, ephemeral content particular to each single act of communication. In Figure 18.2, the term "form" designates the signifier-signified dichotomy and specifies the dictionary definition of its significance, including the sign's concept and all those facets of meaning coded by general visual literacy in ways potentially comprehensible everywhere. The sign's "content" side, in turn, designates the sign's subjective interpretation by the individual mind in the synchronic context of its exchange. Between those extremes, idiom first defines the theoretical potential of the sign to interrelate significance at all and, second, characterizes the interactive plane as pragmatically accessible in scope. Referencing an "arch" connecting transmitter and receiver based on their gathered knowledge and their expectations as to each other's intentions and agency, the present perfect continuous of the idiom not only enables the anticipation of a sign's particular content, but also its future use between the partners in communication. Such an idiomatic effect on the sign's use might not be material or measurable, but it highlights the sign's place in a reality proper to communication that mitigates not only Derrida's "arche-writing," but also Baudrillard's "evil demon." In their place, idiom offers an interface between the timeline of individual thought and the factual presence of a coded sign, which differentiates an act of communication from the otherwise indistinct flow of reality.

IDIOMATIC NETWORKS OF SIGNIFICATION

As a pragmatic concept of communication, idiom characterizes, for example, everything that a teenager means when surprising his parents with the information that he has acquired a new jacket. The sign form "jacket" may stand as an arbitrarily coded concept for all possible types of garments worn as a second layer of clothing. Its sign content usually depends on the way the abstract concept is rendered by the synchronic context in terms of the theme-rheme syntax, which specifies the ability of the context to innovate a sign's significance in any new instance of its use. In this arrangement, the content features the most ephemeral vector of the sign's significance, one that, furthermore, only exists in an individual perspective. Taken as the third structural part of the sign, idiom thus contributes to mediating not only old with new significance, but also individually with collectively contoured significance. In the example, the teenager and his parents represent what Stanley Fish would call the "interpretative community," which attempts to understand the sign's idiom based on various, historically informed speculations and evaluations ranging, for example, from the teenager's fashion sense to his current financial assets.[7] What emerges reflects a pragmatically adjusted concept of the sign, for example, a diffuse mental image of a black, worn-out leather jacket bought second hand. While every family member certainly develops a different notion of the sign's content, this tendency is pragmatically countered based on the shared knowledge about the transmitter's side of the idiom that "arche-writes" the sign within a limited diachronic dimension that contrasts with its general history as a term of visual literacy. Furthermore, the present perfect continuous behind the idiom provides the grounds on which the ephemeral content in the present and the unlimited specter of the sign's reference to the past contribute to the ability of signs to change over time even in their most basic contours of significance. As the conversation about the jacket proceeds, the idiomatic part of its significance becomes adjusted with each new piece of information. To finalize the teenager's idea of his jacket, any added information needs not only to follow the synchronic logic of the theme-rheme syntax, but also to harmonize the sign's significance with regard to the idiomatic background of all family members. As a result, every member of the family may still retain an idiosyncratic idea of the jacket, but only to an extent that allows for the sign's future use in slightly novel idiomatic contours of significance.

To describe such a dynamic idiomatic process of signification, the modern theory of networks as developed, among others, by Bruno Latour offers a useful angle.[8] Comprising many "actors" and at least one institution serving as a "clearinghouse," a network of people constantly negotiates who is a part of it and how its members interact. Within the network, each interaction, including between those at its margins, influences its social dynamics. In the example of a family, the dinner table could stand for the institution that regulates its core membership and serves as the central place for managing the communicative network of idiomatic signification. Any conversations held between members in other rooms, for example, between the younger sister and her teenage brother, are part of the network's dynamic and add to the idiom particular to the siblings as well as to that of the family, even though the parents may ignore the further details disclosed by their son about his newest acquisition. Depending on the arrangement of power within the family network, any important detail will sooner or later be shared with all members of the network.[9] If this were not the case, it would indicate a conflict or even a rupture within the idiomatic network. De Certeau's notion of linguistic "poaching" or Fiske's semiotic guerrilla warfare can be incorporated into the idea of such idiomatic networks, at least to the extent that these concepts describe the element of anticipation transmitters and receivers project into each other's intention when communicating.[10] Without the transmitter's and receiver's mutual intention to understand the other side, to accept a minimum of shared idiomatic plane, and to participate in what Habermas specified as the ethical ideal beneath communication, signs are generally stripped of their interactive potential to the extent that they can no longer be differentiated from signals.[11] In contrast to signs, signals access significance coded in the past without making any personal reference to the identity of the transmitter. Lacking the idiomatic dynamic that would add to the characterization of their context, a signal like an SOS projects significance in much more formal and enduring contours than a sign. Because they reference a transmitter's intention only in indirect, abstract form, signals are much less subject to the diachronic processes that can transform their signified over a period of time. A broken idiomatic plane could be associated with either a conscious or unconscious "misunderstanding" of signs as signals, which almost by definition implies a one-sided or vertically structured power relation between transmitter and receiver, but never a horizontally balanced interaction.[12] In the same, one-sided mode that a signal can overpower a receiver, be it emotionally, psychologically, or with the support of the law, as in the case of an SOS call, it can also stimulate the receiver's power to ignore or pretend to ignore it, to misinterpret it consciously or unconsciously, and so forth. The moment in which a signal becomes a sign therefore hinges on the recognition of a partner in communication, on a minimal anticipation of the intentions behind both transmitting and receiving, and thus on their acceptance as interactive carriers of significance. In this outline, the initiation of communication between two strangers on the street is first of all accomplished with signals conveying significance based on a code less specified by language than by the cultural conventions of politeness. If the exchange is accepted, a rudimentary idiom is built that supports the interactive plane of signs, but if it is refused, the initial words remain signals that leave their transmitters in a mutually isolated position.

As an integrated part of communicative pragmatics, the negotiation of idiomatic relations amounts to the handling of power in sign exchanges, rooted in what Foucault terms the "will to knowledge." This quest for the new matches the communicative power of signs to arbitrate between old forms and new content within established or refused idiomatic relations.[13] On the microcommunicative level, the idiomatic relation between transmitters and receivers can therefore be seen as negotiating not only a shared understanding, but also mutually acknowledged power relations, which again from Foucault's perspective appear the most effective when news and information are shared on equal terms. Because the idiomatic plane as defined here presupposes that the transmitter has a certain knowledge of the receiver's style and personality and vice versa, it first of all describes more intimate exchanges on the level of communities. The opposite, society's more distanced and anonymous style of communication, could be characterized as the discursive part in the communicative context of signs. Characterizing, for example, acceptable standards of hygiene or current conventions of politeness, Foucault's concept of discourse comprises socially established knowledge with common-sense certitude. Like idiomatic networks, discourses feature recognized institutions, such as universities or the media itself, as clearinghouses in which significance is created and regulated, albeit in much more anonymous fashion. Recalling the community-society continuum described by the German sociologist Ferdinand Tönnies, the two concepts of idiom and discourse delineate the tension field between micro- and macro-communicative signifying praxes, as the two sides of one coin. [14]

To return to the example of the family, societal discourse would thus determine what style of jacket is acceptable for which situation. While exchanges in the family may involve less societal discourse and while a governmental statement may provide little idiomatic content, both forms of communication are necessary to balance one's own language with that of society.

In summarizing the concept of idiom, any type of (historically based) social structure that contextually contributes to the production, trading, and comprehension of signs can be analyzed as a network with a circulation of significance particular to its members. In its most basic and most pure form, idiom requires only two partners in communication, such as a couple or two friends. In this form, it can also be used to reference the particular idiom of one person, although always in interrelation to at least one specific partner in communication. Matching the different social roles a person assumes in everyday life, that person's idiom alters according to the different circles he travels in, which may extend to include the entire community of a village, or, in the case of a nationally known politician, the general public of a nation. However, particular attention must be paid when the diachronic concept of idiomatic and discursive networks of signification is brought into contact with the equally historically dynamic realm of visual literacy.

ICONS AS DISCOURSE

As discussed throughout the analysis of historical television, visual signs combine to form symbols, which can become iconized as individually contoured terms of visual literacy with distinct semantic histories. For extended periods of time, such icons can seemingly develop parallel to the people behind them, and thus they seem to "grow old" together. The condition for such parallel development is that "iconicity" be maintained, meaning that there is enough exposure, as well as enough resemblance between the icon of the young and that of the older person (which, incidentally, usually excludes infancy from a person's arc of iconization). More importantly, however, such parallel structure is also challenged: the semantic significance of an icon can further develop long after a person's death, different spectators can encounter an icon in different contexts and chronology, and the dynamics of visual literacy can produce their own shades of significance by means of collective typifying and arranging in relation to other visual symbols. Given these forces of symbolic signification at work, it would be highly improbable to assume that an individual could fully control "his" icon, let alone that the icon would stand one to one for his personality. But if an icon is beyond the control of the person it represents, then icons cannot be easily incorporated into the communicative framework of idiom.

Besides the collective mills of visual literacy, which determine the significance of an icon as much as those who cast it or those who enact it in a mode comparable to calligraphy, an icon's staging on a broadcast screen also involves what has been called a "collective authorship" in many idiomatic planes. In the example of an anchorman such as Murrow interviewing an Army officer in the field, the communicative strata of the broadcast would include the different calligraphy of the two symbols of these men; symbolic attributes such as uniform, possibly including medals, which refer to an institutional discourse; plus the idiom of the camera crew, those on the editing board in the studio and those who make the general decision to run the news show, and so forth. This amounts to a wide variety of potentially influential traces of individual idiom and collective discourse on the pictorial plane alone. The verbal plane further includes the work of additional technicians plus two voices, those of the journalist and the Army man, which are to different degrees influenced, or possibly even scripted, by others—that is, by Murrow's producer when preparing the show or by Army rules, instructions, or even training in dealing with the media. The proposed concept of split transmittership must be applied not only to the pictorial part of the broadcast, but also to the verbal part, since the words can also be selected and edited in the studio.

With so many different individual and institutional contributions to a single clip, it appears very difficult for spectators to differentiate them in order to recognize traces of individual style and idiomatically contoured content. What is more, by comparison to fictional productions that may presuppose a common goal for all involved—such as producing a stylistically consistent artistic work—the nonfictional broadcast presupposes by definition the possibility of dissent. But when an interviewee with a basically unknown visual symbol differs with an established anchorman whose icon is unified by collective visual literacy, how then does one such idiomatic dissenting trace stand up against the combined communicative influence of all the other persons involved in creating and presenting the broadcast? And what if the camera crew captures one of the symbols from a better angle, in a better position, and with better lighting than the other, placing one in front of a garbage can and the other in front of a Jeep, or instead of cutting away maintains a close-up when one of the persons is awkwardly scratching his nose? If visible dissent should be the defining difference between the journalistic, nonfictional and the fictional, artistic picture, then there are apparently also pictures that can include side-by-side symbols portrayed with an objective intent and those portrayed with a friendly intent, as when including an anchorman in the frame.

In a final analysis of the conditions governing the production of fiction and its generally intended balance between artistic accomplishment and commercial success, it can be observed that although dissent is certainly a reality whenever teams work together, it hardly ever shows in the presentation of the final cut, at least not in any specific expression. Even should a disgruntled actor turn in a lackluster performance, an audience is hardly able to ascribe this performance to dissent (as also indicated in the section "Acting, or the Art of Writing Chinese Characters" in chapter 9). And even should such an evaluation be possible in general terms, it would be difficult to evaluate the performance as originating in the actor's work and intention, given the influence of the presentational authorship, for example, on the editing board, which ultimately decides which version of the actor's gestures in which positioning vis à vis other symbols should appear in the final cut of the pictorial narrative. So, while convention in the world of movies fosters individual style and artistic contribution, and thus aims to keep certain idiomatic traces present, not least in the form of the credits in the trailer, it also tends to homogenize its authorship for the sake of a coherent narrative and/or artistic style. Yet if it is almost impossible to comprehend a movie's multitude of idiomatic traces groomed for a collective artistic style, is it then any easier to understand the significance of a nonfictional production that declares itself as ungroomed, and thus as a communicative multitude of individual contributions that may intersect or even conflict in countless ways and forms? Or is it not academic to search for further differences that would legitimate keeping fictional and nonfictional pictures with their visual symbols and icons apart, given that icons appear to take most of the credit in both the realism of film and the hyperrealism of broadcasting?

Yet in addition to the difficulty of recognizing individual contribution in both fictional and nonfictional productions, and to the complexity, if not impossibility, of differentiating between acting and nonacting, and correspondingly of characterizing "good" and "bad" acting in any concise way for both film and journalistic formats, there is also the issue for both formats of visual literacy. Before any individual contribution to the mediation of content can be assessed, it is not only crucial to differentiate that part of an icon or visual symbol controlled by the person in front of the camera and that part controlled by other transmitters, but also that part regulated by the status of these visual terms in collective visual literacy. The more impossible these multiple requests for differentiation appear, the more unlikely is the existence of a separate fictional and nonfictional world of pictorial symbols.

When the collective nature of authorship in broadcasting in particular has been accepted, the logical consequence is thus to resist the temptation to homogenize all communicative strata into the two-dimensional figurations of life that speak on screen, as recommended by the discourse of hyperrealism. But once the two signifying planes of an icon have been distinguished as the one generated in the mills of collective visual literacy and the one added by the idiomatic network, an alternative mode of broadcast communication could come into being with a more sophisticated fashion of relating information. This more sophisticated fashion would emulate painting, drawing, or graphic representation rather than photography. Graphic symbols of men and houses do not fall prey to the hyperrealistic urge to find significance in the reference to an absent reality, because they propose instead a search for the intent of those who produced and presented them. Graphic symbols also feature a closer resemblance to words, as their contours are generally more polished, more formal, and more abstract than the unique shapes of faces and houses in photographs.

In concluding these observations on the logic of visual language and the character of broadcast communication, it can be noted that the technological evolution from photography to film and to broadcasting has produced new forms of communication, the complexity of which has been underestimated for a long time. Although much attention has been paid to the "virtual reality" of the digital era, broadcast technology in particular has apparently been seen as a quite "natural" form of communication, a form of radio with the addition of the picture, rather than the other way around. When broadcasting asserted its pictorial supremacy as a hyperreal reflection of both fictional and nonfictional American life, it became a powerful generator for symbols, emblems, and icons and an accelerator of the networking of a national visual literacy, while at the same time it belied its collectively shared influence on the semantic significance of its terms.

When the realm of broadcast communication is considered as a network, following Latour's concept, it consequently is found to comprise the idiomatic agency of many "actors" in combination with "actants," such as cameras, computers, and editing facilities, plus the current discourses of the involved institutions, such as the big networks, the cable companies, and so forth, as well as the collective visual literacy cultivated by all networked members, including the audience.[15] When, furthermore, such a network is broken down to component ones built around specific shows with their distinctive icons, single idiomatic traces of individual agency or artistry can become visible, particularly in the contours of icons, but even in such cases the visual symbols still signify rather as a signet than in reference to a "real person." Like a printer's mark, a seal, the emblem of an organization, or also a quality stamp, an icon would then stand first of all as a symbol for a collective authorship, whose political purpose, artistic style, and organizational character it expresses. Only in such a role can the symbolic character of these pictorial terms, as well as the greater communicative potential of visual language, be fully assessed. And only in such a role can icons and their participation in the collective historical character of visual literacy be accounted for.

19 Glossary
Four Codes of Visual Language

THE EMPIRICAL CODES BEHIND VISUAL PERCEPTION

A. The Dialectic Code

OUTLINE	PROPERTIES	SYNTACTIC FUNCTION
Visual perception operates empirically through the demarcation of visual shapes within contrast lines. The human eye emphasizes contrast in order to simplify the great amount of visual detail potentially perceivable. This gives rise to a dialectic logic of seeing that constructs immaterial boundaries, polishes the contours of shapes, and selectively concentrates on accentuated visual characteristics. Visual communication caters to this logic by technically reproducing contrast lines and adding a definable number of further visual characteristics, including the frame as the most arbitrary boundary of a picture. On this basis, the dialectic logic of visual communication is comparable to the "double articulation" of verbal language, and similarly allows for deriving a sign-based structure of pictorial significance.	In the mode of phonemes, contrast lines* juxtapose basic, visual shapes,* the characteristics of which, including size,* spatial alignment,* color,* lightness,* and pattern* (or texture) are comparable to morphemes. The frame* and with regard to film, movement* in conjunction with the time-frame,* present a third category of visual variables. This set of ten variables structures the signifier of visual signs. Between the frame and the first demarcated contrast, the eye synthesizes a grid of signifiers unique to each picture. Each signifier connects over a boundary line with its neighbors, forging bivalent signs that interrelate their visual characteristics with one another.	• The signifiers of all visual signs within a picture are interconnected to forge a bivalent sign structure that projects a dialectic syntax. Finalized by the frame, the arrangement of signs constitutes a grid of boundaries, which projects significance between adjacent shapes. Each exterior contrast involves the next sign, e.g., "mole-skin-cheek-hair-curtain-frame." • Accentuated visual variables, such as contrast lines, colors, size relations, movement, and so forth, attract the gaze and syntactically structure perception, the way a yellow leaf in the otherwise green foliage of a tree marks either the theme or the most significant part of a depiction's rheme (information specifying the theme).

(continued)

A. The Dialectic Code (continued)

INTERPRETATION
As a construct of the mind, contrast lines belong neither to the objects they contour, nor to their background. Perception furthermore polishes their twists and turns to allow swift recognition of significance within immaterial boundaries. When technically reproduced on a picture, this element of arbitrariness is emphasized and enhanced by the frame. The agency and intention behind setting the frame reflects back on the dialectic arrangement of all visual variables within the picture. Turning percepts into visual signs, the modeling of the ten visual variables transforms the process of recognizing visual significance in a subtle but fundamental way. The grid of boundaries interrelates visual characteristics not so much in the essential fashion of perception in reality, but rather in a technically emphasized, "grammatically" structured logic of signs. Disconnected from any exterior, these signs assume an interrelated signified unique to their contiguous relationships within the frame.

B. The Conceptual Code

OUTLINE	PROPERTIES	SYNTACTIC FUNCTION
The conceptual code stands for the general fact that one can only visually perceive what one basically knows. To assign significance, perception orders the dialectic grid of signifiers according to generic concepts, such as house, man, tree, or village, crowd, forest, and so forth. These concepts bind the signified of each visual sign within larger compounds. Each picture that carries a communicative sign structure features a minimum of two generic concepts, due to figure-ground differentiation. Between generic concepts, as well as within them, significance is derived from dialectic contiguity.	The code navigates the grid of signifiers through chaining visual signs according to their respective generic concept. Conceptualized chains of signifiers endow single visual signs with an interrelated signified, e.g., "that yellow-oak-tree-leaf." The relationship between conceptualized signs, e.g., a tree and a house, takes the dialectic mode of perception to the next level by activating a third concept, such as "belongs to" or "is standing in front of."	• Generic concepts dialectically interrelate with each other, activating a third concept in between them that assumes the function of "visual verb": two adjacent concepts, e.g., a person in front of a house, project basic significance, such as "belongs to" "pertains to" and so forth. The verb can furthermore explain a gesture or intuit movement with a concept such as "is walking toward the entrance." • The arrangement of generic concepts impacts the theme-rheme syntax, often with the most centrally placed or the most detail-rich sign concept taking a leading role in guiding the gaze. • With regard to film, the time frame furthermore not only anchors "visual verbs," but also regulates the receiver's capacity to perceive details.

(continued)

B. The Conceptual Code (continued)

INTERPRETATION
While the dialectic code builds on somewhat visible contrast lines and refines these mentally, the conceptual code adds an abstract framework of significance to the demarcated visual shapes. That framework stipulates, for example, the importance of one leaf of a tree over all others, and proposes the idea of an oak tree even if many of its further features, such as trunk, roots, and so forth, are not readily visible. In both still and moving pictures, movement, e.g., in the form of a gesture, is furthermore not visible within its own contours, but first appears as a contrast relation between adjacent signs. Also in this regard, the dialectic principle of immaterial boundary lines serves as the basis for demarcating the basic concepts of "visual verbs," because the eye cannot detect all visual characteristics that combine to project a gesture. The conceptual knowledge needed to ascribe visual signs with basic significance therefore adds abstract meaning to a picture, where none is necessarily visible.
Together, the dialectic and the conceptual code transform the potentially unlimited variations of visual signs into mentally coded entities of significance: once through interrelating the signifiers of visual signs, and once through bundling their signifieds with generic concepts. The codes demonstrate that signs signify neither solely with regard to their individual visual characteristics, nor solely with regard to their abstract concepts. It follows that perception selectively emphasizes some visual characteristics over others and conceptualizes significance with rather inductive logic. The technical accentuation of visual variables allows that inductive logic to be addressed through conveying visual signs that can be decoded based on the formal principles of the dialectic and the conceptual code. However, this is only the first step toward assigning meaning to pictures. Conceptualized significance is necessarily finalized with symbolic characteristics. A picture of a house compares itself structurally with all houses ever seen, presenting itself as another such specific model, but interwoven with the picture's sign context, it signifies something that is in between these individual instances, as a refined but still general symbol, e.g., of an example of all "cozy, suburban houses."

THE HISTORICAL CODES BEHIND VISUAL LITERACY
C. The Symbolic Code

OUTLINE	PROPERTIES	SYNTACTIC FUNCTION
The symbolic code combines the formal structure of visual signs with the cultural and historical plane of visual literacy. While the dialectic and conceptual codes simplify a picture's abundant details in light of a picture's communicative intention, they manage visual signs, the signifiers of which are still unique to the dialectic context	Providing the necessary condition for networking significance based on difference and similarity, visual literacy involves an active process of collecting and classifying visual symbols. The underlying logic compares with the exhibition of a collection in which different groups of objects endow each other with	1. Visual symbols can only be designated with indefinite articles or demonstrative or possessive pronouns, but not with definite articles (see iconic code). 2. By means of the dialectic and the conceptual code, all symbols in a picture are interconnected with contiguous symbols activating differentiated, symbolic verb concepts. For example, an airplane is

(continued)

C. The Symbolic Code (continued)

OUTLINE	PROPERTIES	SYNTACTIC FUNCTION
known to fly fast; any of each picture. In this form, the detailed visual characteristics of visual signs cannot be memorized. Their generic concept in turn only reflects abstract, basically invisible, logical properties used to decode the signs in the first place. That which can be memorized amounts to selective patterns of visual variables with which a picture constructs the signs of a particular hand, a face, a house, and so forth. These entities of significance, or visual symbols, can be collected, classified, and typified according to their particular characteristics. Over time, a pictorial symbol is incorporated into individual visual literacy as a pool of terms with socially and culturally nurtured fields of significance.	significance, as well as transferring significance to outstanding objects within the groups. To communicate with visual symbols, a transmitter needs to create a tapestry of visual signs which enables its symbolic vectors of significance to anticipate the historical dimension of a spectator's collective visual literacy. In general, the better the symbolic code is observed, the more sophisticated the picture's communicative potential. For example, a chosen symbol can be structured to denote a typical example of a cozy suburban home in the American South or a more atypical example of the Victorian architecture common in the North.	depiction presents itself as either typical or atypical with regards to that knowledge. 3. The relationship between adjacent symbols further sets up a process of "symbolic transfer" that hinges their significance in syntactic fashion. For example, a woman contrasted with a row of books forges a symbolic, but nevertheless grammatically logical statement about her: she is "literate" or "well read." 4. The more familiar or "thick" the semantic field of a visual symbol in terms of collective visual literacy, the more it anchors the significance of all other signs and symbols. The more atypical, unfamiliar, or exotic its semantic field, the more a symbol serves to attract the gaze, to set a theme, and to draw clues from all other signs and symbols.

INTERPRETATION
The semantic fields of visual symbols are sponsored both by individual experience gathered from perception in reality, and by knowledge solely acquired from pictures. The resulting visual literacy nevertheless reflects a culturally homogenized basis of visual language. Individual perception in reality is not based on signs that mediate visual symbols in dialectic contexts framed by the intention behind presenting pictures. The trading of visual symbols furthermore sponsors a communicative history for each type of symbol that is particular to the pictorial culture of a community or society. While the boundary between individual and collective visual literacy may be only of a theoretical nature, the symbolic code only applies to the mode of typifying significance from conveyed signs (and not from real percepts). In a picture, the attractiveness of a person is supported by the context relation of many signs, as well as by historically developed symbolic standards, in ways that render the symbol's reception a culturally coded statement, rather than an exclusively subjective interpretation. Seeing the same real person on the street, by contrast, engages not only individual perception, but also individual evaluation.   In this outline, the significance of visual signs is further removed from the actually visible contours of their depiction. Their visual characteristics are selectively enhanced to compare with the socially and culturally relevant terms of collective visual literacy. The historical dimension of this literacy, to which any act of visual communication contributes new shades of significance, is proper to the depicted symbols, but not to the objects to which they might refer.

D. The Iconic Code

OUTLINE	PROPERTIES	SYNTACTIC FUNCTION
The iconic code enhances the diachronic (or historical) plane of visual language through differentiating icons and emblems from general categories or types of visual symbol. An icon, such as that of Marilyn Monroe, or an emblem, such as that of the White House, features an individually recognizable pattern of visual characteristics. The more pictorial representations they find, the more vectors of significance they accumulate from the unique dialectic context of visual signs within each picture.	The most active use of the iconic code rests in the construction of a continuous visual narrative, e.g. by a television show or a movie. Once introduced as main characters or central objects, icons and emblems commence to accumulate new shades of significance with each further appearance. This process of familiarizing their significance can extend beyond the context of a narrative, if the particular symbols continue to be cast in all types of further pictures. According to the degree of exposure, these 'meta' icons and emblems fuel collective visual literacy as a limited, albeit historically volatile, number of very specific visual terms. As the jewels of the collection, they still draw on the significance of related types of symbols, but present an individualized category of their own, a symbolic type that in the pictorial grammar is always given a definite article.	1. In movies, the iconic code provides a central narrative structure through specifying some symbols with the equivalent of a definite article, which marks their central role in the theme-rheme syntax of a picture. 2. In general, those icons and emblems that have accrued the most extensive narrative exposure or generally the richest pictorial history assume the focal point of every picture. 3. Based on the dialectic code and the grammar of "symbolic transfer," icons and emblems endow all the other signs of a picture with meaning particular to their respective vectors of significance. 4. In contiguous relation to other symbols, icons and emblems activate the most differentiated visual verb concepts. The punch of an action film star, such as Arnold Schwarzenegger, denotes a quite powerful hit, even though such significance is not visible in any actual contours.

INTERPRETATION
Icons and emblems present the most precisely contoured, but also the most arbitrary terms of visual language. A "meta" icon such as that of the movie star Arnold Schwarzenegger combines multiple symbolic vectors standing for general categories, such as Hollywood acting, physical strength, bodybuilding, male attractiveness, and so forth. The diachronic dimension of the symbol further details its symbolic references with memorable scenes in- and outside of fictional narratives. Without necessarily giving preference to any particular aspect of its pictorial history, the icon thereby merges the statements made by multiple pictorial contexts and completes the logical disconnection of its contours from any direct reference to reality. The icon thus signifies not only in the physical absence of the actor himself,

(continued)

D. The Iconic Code (continued)

INTERPRETATION (continued)
but also independently of his intentions. It first of all unfolds significance with respect to the agency of those who created and presented its contours in relation to other signs and symbols within the frame, and secondly with regard to a historical dimension that is proper to the visual term itself, but not to the actor. In a similar way, the contours of the emblem of the Concorde jet project the visual verb "is flying faster than the speed of sound" in terms of the dialectic as well as the iconic code. The visual variable of movement is assumed through dialectic contrast relations with signs and symbols in the background, e.g., clouds, and again from the symbolic history of the emblem, even if such diachronic significance fails to reference any particular flight of a real airplane.

Notes

NOTES TO THE INTRODUCTION

1. Made in a well-known memorandum dating from 1963, Reuven Frank's reflection on the use of pictures on NBC's *Evening News* already recognizes the general tension field of "symbolic truth" and "supposed reality." When quoting him, Edward Epstein makes reference to Walter Lippmann's notion of a "repertory of stereotypes," observing that these stereotypes appear "self-perpetuating" so that "cameramen, film editors, correspondents and producers take their cues for selecting symbols for future stories." At this point, Epstein comes close to the hypothesis of this study, which places television's continuous flow of pictures at the root of a modern, historically dynamic visual language based predominantly on visual symbols. See Edward Jay Epstein's doctoral thesis dating from 1973, *News from Nowhere: Television and the News* (New York: Random House, 2000), pp. 5–6.

2. Although he assigns a "symbol system" to pictures—and names his study "Languages of Art"—Goodman stops short of differentiating it as a representational or as a linguistic system. In a similar way, Ernst Gombrich's important study on the force of convention in the expressions of art ultimately leaves open the question of how pictures can "represent" a sight in reality and simultaneously convey conventionalized significance that is detached from such representational reference—or even sponsored by the very endeavor to represent as realistically as possible. Nelson Goodman, *Languages of Art: An Approach to the Theory of Symbols* (Indianapolis: Hackett Publishing Company, 1976) p. xi and pp. 41–42 and Ernst H. Gombrich, *Art and Illusion: A Study in the Psychology of Pictorial Representation* (New York: Bollingen Series, 1960), pp. 33–62.

3. In bringing visual and verbal literacy to a generally comparable level, Donis Dondis already recognized in 1973 the need to transcend the notion of a "natural" understanding of pictures and critiqued the "monolithic slowness" of the educational system in accounting for the media's increasing emphasis on pictorially structured messages. However, the concept of visual literacy has not yet been used to denote a pool of visual terms, but rather to characterize the general ability to comprehend the construction of visual information and narratives. For more on the concept and on the many different approaches to its definition, see chapter 16 in the appendix. Donis A. Dondis, *A Primer of Visual Literacy* (Cambridge: MIT Press, 1993), p. 10.

4. The integrative role of audiences in shaping collective visual literacy is recognized by the study, but only theoretically explored (see, for example, chapter 18, "Notes on the Pragmatics of Visual Language," in the appendix). An empirical examination of collective visual literacy as defined throughout this

study would, of course, be desirable but could not be afforded here. In any case, the concepts of reader-response theory applied when discussing audiences and their participation in the trading of significance builds on the works of Henry Jenkins and Stanley Fish. Henry Jenkins, *Textual Poachers: Television Fans and Participatory Culture* (New York: Routledge, 1992), and Stanley Fish, *Is There a Text in This Class? The Authority of Interpretative Communities* (Cambridge: Harvard University Press, 1980).

5. The breakdown between fiction and nonfiction on the television screen has been generally observed and discussed from different angles by a number of scholars, whose conclusions are outlined in chapter 16, "Four Codes of Visual Language," in the appendix.

6. The terms "discourse" and "discursive" follow Foucault's definition of a macrocommunicative topic that is regulated by one or more institutions; its objects, expressions, and arguments have converged with common sense to the extent that their logical basis remains unquestioned over a period of time. In the appendix, the concept is juxtaposed with that of "idiom," which specifies its counterpart in the realm of microcommunication. Foucault continued to develop the term "discourse" throughout his work; see, for example, "Orders of Discourse," in *Social Science Information* 10 (April 1971), pp. 7–31, *The Archeology of Knowledge; and the Discourse on Language* (New York: Dorset Press, 1972), or *Discipline and Punish: The Birth of the Prison* (New York: Pantheon, 1977).

7. For more on the self-referential character of broadcasting and the many logical contradictions that arise from its format of communication, see the previously mentioned works of Marshall McLuhan and Mary Ann Doane, as well as chapter 16 in the appendix. Marshall McLuhan, *Understanding Media: The Extensions of Man* (New York: Signet, 1964), p. 7 and 18, and Mary Ann Doane, "Information, Crisis, Catastrophe," in Patricia Mellencamp, ed., *Logics of Television: Essays in Cultural Criticism* (Bloomington: Indiana University Press, 1990), pp. 222–39.

8. Abraham Zapruder recorded the assassination of John F. Kennedy on November 22nd, 1963, in Dallas on 8 mm film. The pictures provide what is generally considered the best angle on the crime and have repeatedly been used for analyzing its course. To this day, the film and single shots have also been published on numerous occasions, making its pictures a part of national visual literacy.

9. See Jean Baudrillard's study, which is further discussed in chapter 18, "Notes on the Pragmatics of Visual Language," in the appendix. Jean Baudrillard, *The Evil Demon of Images* (Sydney: Power Institute of Fine Arts, 1987).

10. The following distinction is inspired by Barbara Zelizer, who focused her analysis of the author in American TV news on the "*presentation* (not formation) of news." Barbara Zelizer, "Where is the Author in American TV News? On the Construction and Presentation of Proximity, Authorship, and Journalistic Authority" in *Semiotica* 80–1/2 (1990), p. 46.

11. The photograph *Raising the Flag on Iwo Jima*, by Joe Rosenthal of the Associated Press, was taken in the World War II battle on the Japanese island in 1945, won the Pulitzer Prize in the same year, and became one of the most reproduced pictures in American history and as such a symbol of the war and even of history itself.

12. In his first comprehensive work on semiotics, *La strutura assente*, published in 1968, Umberto Eco began the search for a pure sign structure in pictures, which in contrast to the model of icons developed by Charles Sanders Peirce builds on a purely arbitrary and conventional status of visual significance. In *A Theory of Semiotics*, he published a modified approach that further develops

the concept of visual signs or sign production as a semiotic system able to convey significance independently of any reference to a picture's model in reality. Umberto Eco, *La struttura assente* (Milano: Tascabili Bompiani, 1987), pp. 105–88, and *A Theory of Semiotics* (Bloomington: Indiana University Press, 1979), pp. 178–241.

13. In recent years a number of scholars, such as Alex Bolvig, Philip Rosen, and Richard Howells, have recognized the need to develop new tools suitable for analyzing the dynamic temporality of pictures. The call for a new pictorial etymology presupposes a consensus as to how compositional fragments within a picture can be defined, although the early semiotic work of scholars such as Eco and Dondis on a visual sign structure has not been developed into a consensus. While scholars such as Prase come to the conclusion that the search for a detailed language structure has failed altogether, others, such as Fernande Saint-Martin, still hold that the problems haunting the semiotic analysis of pictures reside in the inability to determine meaningful visual units from pictures. Without the ability to define such visual units in pictures and to pinpoint logical principles at the source of their signifying power, it also appears futile to determine tangible traces of historical value within their frame. See Philip Rosen, *Change Mummified: Cinema, Historicity, Theory* (Minneapolis: University of Minnesota Press, 2001), Richard Howells, *Visual Culture* (Cambridge: Polity Press, 2003), Alex Bolvig's introduction to *History and Images: Towards a New Iconology,* Alex Bolvig and Philip Lindley, eds., (Turnhout, Belgium: Brepols Publishers, 2003), pp. xxiii–xxx, Tilo Prase, *Das gebrauchte Bild: Bausteine einer Semiotik des Fernsehbildes* (Berlin: Vistas, 1997), and Fernande Saint-Martin, *Semiotics of Visual Language* (Bloomington: Indiana University Press, 1990).

14. In Charles Sanders Peirce's groundbreaking approach to the logic of signs and to semiotics in general, "icon" specifies "a sign which stands for something merely because it resembles it." For more on the concept of "iconicity" and the definition of icons in the tradition of Charles Sanders Peirce, as well as on Eco's critique, see the theoretical exposition in chapter 16, "Four Codes of Visual Language," in the appendix. Charles Sanders Peirce, *Collected Papers* (Cambridge: Harvard University Press, 1931–58), vols. 2 and 3, §§ 2.274–2.308 and § 3.362, and Umberto Eco, *A Theory of Semiotics* (Bloomington: Indiana University Press, 1979), pp. 191–218.

15. See Benedict Anderson's study of the role of language in generating the impression of a homogeneous society. The term "imagined community" appears to match perfectly the purpose of establishing the theoretical framework of visual language and of studying its genesis on national television, as long as the "imagined community of the nation" is not "used to invent and explain another: the television audience," in John Hartley's words. But while Hartley emphasizes that nations are, like audiences and signs, constructs of discourses, rather than "of any external, referential world," he also critiques the "essential nation-ality" of television, which is "as imagined, or fictional, as the idea of the nation itself." Yet, once television is analyzed as conveying content based on signs, the assessment of its language necessarily develops on—and caters to—the basis of constructed significance, which when carried through entails an immaterial "vocabulary" shared by transmitters and receivers. Although such a vocabulary, like any other, is certainly not confined to the members of a national community, visual literacy, which is here characterized as a historically dynamic pool of visual terms, functions best among initiated viewers who developed a deep familiarity with the visual symbols, icons, and emblems depicted by the programs they watch most. For this reason, Hartley's critique of, for example, Ellis's statement that television is "the private life of the nation state," denies the semiotic angle on visual

language, which like any other language—and due to its similarity to collecting, possibly even more so—tends to develop national and local "dialects." For such reasons, Hartley's observation that television could be envisioned as "a more vivid metaphorical figure" for Anderson's "imagined communities" appears both right and wrong at the same time. Wrong, because Hartley assumes that television, like a nation, represents institutions "with no essence but only difference from other television, other forms, other institutions" and thus ignores the constitutive dynamic of visual literacy at the core of visual language. But also right, because visual literacy—however intertwined it may be with experience collected in the real world—can also only reflect an imagined cultural citizenship. Benedict Anderson, *Imagined Communities: Reflection on the Origin and Spread of Nationalism* (London: Verso, 1983), John Hartley, *Tele-ology: Studies in Television* (New York: Routledge, 1992), pp. 103–104, John Ellis, *Visible Fictions*, (New York: Routledge, 1993), p. 5.

NOTES TO CHAPTER 1

1. See, for example, Fred J. MacDonald, *One Nation Under Television: The Rise and Decline of Network TV* (Chicago: Nelson Hall Publishers, 1990).
2. Walter Benjamin, "The Work of Art in the Age of Mechanical Reproduction," in Hannah Arendt, ed., *Illuminations* (New York: Schocken Books, 1969), pp. 222–23.
3. For more on the definition of visual literacy, see the theoretical exposition "Four Codes of Visual Language" in the appendix.
4. Krzysztof Pomian describes the collection as rooted in the cultural sphere between the invisible and the visible and emphasizes the aspect of language as its constituting force. Krzysztof Pomian, *Collectors and Curiosities: Paris and Vienna 1500–1800* (Cambridge: Polity, 1990), pp. 26–27.
5. See the chapter "The Collection: Between the Visible and the Invisible." Ibid., pp. 7–41.
6. In taking up Michel Foucault, Tony Bennett compares the role of the museum with that of the penitentiary, describing their respective relations to discipline and knowledge as the "Janus face of power." Tony Bennett, *The Birth of the Museum: History, Theory, Politics* (London: Routledge, 1995), pp. 87–88 and 98.
7. Quote in Bennett (1995), p. 76: cf. Germaine Bazin, *The Museum Age* (New York: Universal Press, 1967), p. 167.
8. Pomian (1990), pp. 43–44.
9. On the significance of the central positioning of museums in cities, see Bennett (1985), p. 87 and 98.
10. The most significant donor for the Museum of Television and Radio in New York was William S. Paley, founder and former chairman of CBS. See, for example, the article by Glenn Collins in the *New York Times*, July 22, 1991, p 13.
11. In the tradition of medieval and Renaissance carnivals, people shared for limited periods of time a world of equality without political, hierarchical boundaries or moral, ecclesiastic regulations. According to Bakhtin, the grotesque realism of the carnivalesque, however rough it may have been, enabled fraternization between the ridiculed and those who were mocking through the shared acceptance of parody, satire, and pleasure. Bakhtin conceptualized this historical background to describe an artistic form of humor that expresses less an angry, serious satire of social and cultural realities than a self-ironical portrait of life. This humor embraces the whole world, for those who laughed, laughed at themselves too. See Mikhail M. Bakhtin, *Rabelais and His World* (Bloomington: Indiana University Press, 1984), pp. 11–25.

12. In this particular design, the Museum of Television and Radio provides an atypical example that evades to some degree the classic opposition between fairgrounds and museums, as characterized by Foucault. In a different context and from a different perspective the Museum of Television and Radio could be considered to occupy a place in between those opposites, where Tony Bennett has also positioned fixed-site amusement parks. Foucault (1986), p. 26; cf. Bennett (1995), pp. 3–4.

NOTES TO CHAPTER 2

1. See the article by Leslie Bennetts in the *New York Times*, December 22, 1985, p. 29.
2. Marita Sturkey, Tangled Memories: The Vietnam War, The AIDS Epidemic, and the Policies of Remembering (Berkeley, University of California Press, 1997), pp. 9–12.
3. See "The Precession of Simulacra" in Baudrillard (2000).
4. Umberto Eco, *Travels in Hyperreality: Essays* (San Diego: Harvest, 1986), p. 8.

NOTES TO CHAPTER 3

1. As indicated, for example, on the videotape covers of *Yesteryear* and *History of the 20th Century.*
2. The historical documentaries surveyed for this analysis are *History of the 20th Century,* produced 1980–1985; *Yesteryear,* 1982; *The Fabulous Sixties,* 1970; *The Sensational 70s,* 1979; *The Class of the Twentieth Century,* 1991. For bibliographical references see "Film and Television Sources" in the appendix.
3. In addition to the archives of the ABC network, the documentary lists, among others, the National Archive, the Library of Congress, the Sherman Grinberg Film Libraries, Thaxton Associates, Inc., and also a number of private archives for its film and still picture resources.
4. The simple statistical analysis is meant to provide the reader with a general impression of the documentary's structure, much in the way I used it to acquaint myself with the diversity of its rich imagery. The quantitative analysis cannot and will not be used for deriving any scientific findings.
5. To check the legitimacy of this first characterization of the documentary's structure, I went on to count the total number of cuts in each segment and divided the result by the 250 topics I had allocated. ("Cut" defines a clip of footage comprising one picture or one continuous camera movement.) The result of the analysis prompted a surprisingly coherent average of ten cuts per topic for all segments. I counted 9.2 cuts per topic for the segment on the 1950s, 11 for that between 1960 and 1964, 8.3 for that between 1965 and 1969, and 11.5 for that on the 1970s. The general average between 1950 and 1980 is 9.8, based on a total count of 2456 cuts for 250 topics.
6. The numbers only reflect a rough count of icons that were repeated in the documentary. Due to the limitations of my own visual literacy it is possible that I missed certain icons. As far as the number of emblems is concerned, I only list those appearing on more than five occasions.
7. This count of all icons is also rather rough and even more influenced by the limitations of my own individual visual literacy than the number that were repeated (see also the previous note). As any other person would most likely arrive at a different result when counting the compilation's icons (or emblems), the only way to attain greater accuracy would have been to subject several people possessing a more or less typical American visual literacy to the diligent work of such a count. In any case, I counted a total of 352 icons, of which 23 were repeated 186 times, prompting the total of 189 different icons that I found in the compilation.

8. Kurt Tucholsky, brilliant journalist, essayist, poet, and critic, who was stripped of his German citizenship by the Nazi government in 1933, loved to suggest that life always evolved among the same two hundred people. See, for example, his poem "Deine Welt," in Kurt Tucholsky, *Gesammelte Werke* (Reinbek bei Hamburg: Rowohlt, 1985), vol. 6, p. 107.

9. Guy Debord, *Society of the Spectacle* (Detroit: Black and Red Books, 1977); Daniel Dayan and Elihu Katz, "Performing Media Events," in James Curran, Anthony Smith, and Pauline Wingate, eds., *Impacts and Influences: Essays on Media Power in the Twentieth Century* (London: Methuen, 1987), pp. 174–97; Douglas Kellner, *Media Spectacle* (New York: Routledge, 2003); Richard C. Rollins, "Victoria at Sea: Cold War Epic," in Gary R. Edgerton and Peter C. Rollins, eds., *Television Histories: Shaping Collective Memory in the Media Age* (Lexington: University Press of Kentucky, 2001), pp. 103–22; Christoph Türcke, *Erregte Gesellschaft: Philosophie der Sensation* (München: C. H. Beck, 2002).

10. Erik Barnouw, *Documentary: A History of the Non-Fiction Film* (New York: Oxford University Press, 1974), p. 287.

NOTES TO CHAPTER 4

1. See the listing in the section "The Spectator as Witness."

2. See the discussion in chapter 16, "Four Codes of Visual Language," in the appendix, pp. 190–191.

3. In this interpretation of a characteristic hinge in the broadcast history of television, it could even be said that the documentary's pictures anticipate McLuhan's conclusion in the typically symbolic fashion of visual language. For more on the media as the extension of man and the self-referential character of broadcasting, see Marshall McLuhan, *Understanding Media: The Extensions of Man* (New York: Signet, 1964), pp. 7 and 18.

4. For more on Wolfgang Fritz Haug's concept of "symbolic transfer" see the section "The Fourth Code of Visual Language" in the appendix, and his research of the mechanism of advertising in general and of pictorial advertising in particular in *Warenästhetik und kapitalistische Massenkultur—"Werbung" und "Konsum"* (Berlin: Argument-Verlag, 1980), p. 45.

5. On the concept of hailing the individual, see Louis Althusser, *Essays on Ideology* (London: Verso, 1984).

NOTES TO CHAPTER 5

1. For more on the use of "we" that always also implies a "them" see also Dayan and Katz (1987), p.180.

2. Barbara Zelizer, "Where is the Author in American TV News? On the Construction and Presentation of Proximity, Authorship, and Journalistic Authority," in *Semiotica* 80 (1990), p. 46.

3. Dayan and Katz (1987), p. 174.

4. The percentage at the root of this differentiation is based on an initial categorization of the different topics in relation to the interpretive distinction between the presentational and the creative or idiomatic account of cameramen. In this rough, interpretative approximation, 141 themes involve the camera of the spectacle, while 105 involve either the idiomatic camera, such as that behind family pictures, or the creative camera, such as that behind both fictional and journalistic accounts, with the four remaining pictorial narratives devoted to scientific accounts that come without the insignia of the spectacle.

5. Barnouw, p. 287. While Barnouw already questioned the usefulness of the categories of objectivity and subjectivity in pictures based on the notion of "endless choices"—an argument here pursued by expanding on the logic of collecting at the root of visual language—the analysis of authorship in these historical pictures further sustains this suggestion.

6. For more on the concept of idiom developed here see chapter 18, "Notes on the Pragmatics of Visual Language," in the appendix.

7. The question thereby concerns whether it is at all possible to create a journalistic message by means of visual language if those portrayed are not in the position to participate in the outcome. On the one hand, an intact idiomatic plane requires that all involved in the production of pictorial significance have a part in addressing audiences, as is more or less the case in fictional productions. On the other hand, journalism subsists on the ability to make statements about others, which, however, introduces an element of coincidence to a pictorial portrayal, especially when pictorial content is understood as referencing reality in some significant way. If a journalistic portrayal of a person turns out as a negative commentary that runs, for example, against the possible interest and intentions of the portrayed, the origin of the pictures' content appears ultimately inconclusive: either it would be a coincidence that allowed the journalist to capture a potentially negative reflection of the portrayed—a reflection that could furthermore only correspond coincidentally with any objective statement—or else the production of the shot mirrors the journalist's intention, but in either case what reality can contribute to the visual content of such a message? Hence, the notion of a journalistic statement competes with the reality reference of pictures, tending to blur the distinction between a coincidental, "objective" or an intentional, "subjective" character of the message. In order to resolve this dilemma, the suggestion is here to read pictorial signs as symbolic expressions constructed according to a camera journalist's general opinion or judgment. Such a reading, in turn, implies a communicative act based on symbolic expression, rather than on rational arguments, thus comparing first of all with the work of artists. It is therefore appropriate to place the journalistic type of pictures in the same category (of creative pictures) as those of artists, who are used to working with symbols and to claiming authorship for the conveyed content.

8. Ludwik Fleck was the first to describe the phenomenon of popularizing scientific knowledge. In his outline, the findings of the scientific community sooner or later find their way into popular magazines, thereby changing their form and commencing to influence the conception of a new generation of scientists. This cycle involves the process of rendering "scientific facts" more "vivid," which necessitates what can be called a translation from formal into symbolic logic, often via the use of graphical and visual signs. See Ludwik Fleck, *Genesis and Development of a Scientific Fact* (Chicago: University of Chicago Press, 1979) and Thomas S. Kuhn, *The Structure of Scientific Revolutions* (Chicago: University of Chicago Press, 1962).

NOTES TO CHAPTER 6

1. See note 4 in Notes to chapter 5.

2. The use of the term "public sphere" follows Habermas's concept as outlined in *The Structural Transformation of the Public Sphere: An Inquiry into a Category of Bourgeois Society* (Cambridge: MIT Press, 1981).

3. The following analysis only characterizes a general style of editing short narratives of spectacles, which may not correspond in every detail with their original cut. However, although the main focus remains on the analysis of the

documentary as a pictorial historiography of the 1980s, some of its compiled footage reveals such a strong coherence and continuity in its narrative account that it suggests the general matrix of the original format. Furthermore, many other sources, those viewed, for example, in the archives of the Museum of Television and Radio in New York, in Fred MacDonald's private archive, and in the Museum of Broadcast Communication in Chicago, as well as the material presented by other popular documentaries of that time, corroborate the assumption that the documentary is generally congruent with the narrative matrix that dominated the presentation of news in the 1950s and 1960s.

4. This assumption is also likely given the extensive work that is needed to separate and rearrange the visual and audio of original footage. However, this is only a speculation that could not be further validated in detail, because the possibilities of a frame-by-frame comparison of the documentary's footage with any material from other archives that could be identified as original sources are very limited. See also the previous note.

5. Given the complexity of disentangling and rearranging the original cutting matrix of the visual and the audio, the shortening of some of the clips' time frame and/or the removal of an entire clip appears to be the most economical way of handling the reediting of historical footage. However, such instances of reediting do not directly impact interpretation, because the general assessment corroborates the projection of a historically conventionalized style of narrative news matrix, and also because the main focus remains on history as it is presented by documentary itself.

6. Debord (1977), no. 3.

7. Dayan and Katz (1987), p. 184.

8. Epstein (2000), p. 16.

9. Mrs. Nhu, also referred to as the "Dragon Lady," was married to Ngo Dinh Nhu, the closest adviser of his brother, the South Vietnamese president, Ngo Dinh Diem. She often served as first lady for her bachelor brother-in-law.

10. For more on the students' political protest, the SNCC (Student Nonviolent Coordinating Committee), and the Black Power movement, see, for example, Todd Gitlin, *The Sixties: Years of Hope, Days of Rage* (New York: Bantam Books, 1987) and W. L. Van Deburg, *New Day in Babylon: The Black Power Movement and American Culture, 1965–1975* (Chicago: University of Chicago Press, 1992).

11. The controversial status of Carmichael reflects also in the fact that NBC had banned him and H. Rap Brown from its news coverage. See Epstein (2000), p. 192.

NOTES TO CHAPTER 7

1. The 1939 drama by Frank Capra narrates how a naive leader of the Boy Rangers stands up against political corruption in Washington. It made James Stewart a major movie star.

2. Radio audiences of the first debate apparently had a more favorable impression of Nixon, while those of the television broadcast leaned toward Kennedy. John Hellmann observed that although the two men were more or less the same age, Kennedy, who had always tried to cultivate a "star image," much in the way of a film actor, succeeded in projecting a youthful, even "erotic," vision of his political personality. John Hellmann, *The Kennedy Obsession: The American Myth of JFK* (New York: Columbia University Press, 1997), p. xii and pp. 126–29; see also Michael Schudson, *The Power of News* (Cambridge: Harvard University Press, 1995), p. 117.

3. The question of whether either the presenter of the clip or Nixon himself attempted an ironic statement cannot be answered here. In general, the possibility of shaping an ironic message solely by means of visual language appears very limited, given that the proposed categories, the unified, the controversial, and the exotic, provide small grounds for securely anchoring irony.

4. John Berger, *Ways of Seeing* (London: BBC and Penguin Books, 1972), pp. 45–47.

5. Ibid., p. 46.

6. Joan Scott characterizes these limitations of female activities in the public sphere also with regard to symbolic representation. In alignment with her findings, it can be observed that the category of the unified icon can probably only be applied to women who retreat to role patterns of motherhood in general, or of the Virgin Mary in particular. See Joan W. Scott, "Gender: A Useful Category of Historical Analysis," in *American Historical Review* vol. 91, no. 5 (December 1986).

7. Although Jacqueline Kennedy's icon may appear almost as removed as that of Mona Lisa, it still contains an exotic element that, enhanced by her second marriage to the Greek icon, Aristotle Onassis, counters her pure image as mother of John F. Kennedy's children. See also the previous note.

8. At the time, the camera belonged almost exclusively to the male domain. While rendering any reference to camerawomen unnecessary, the historical fact may, however, explain some of the gender-biased mises en scène of the broadcast spectacle.

9. On the other hand, however, it is also quite possible that too much exposure in conjunction with controversial or exotic icons and emblems can compromise the status of a nationally unified icon.

10. Scott (1986).

11. Edward W. Said, *Orientalism* (New York: Vintage Books, 1994).

12. The only two black icons among those twenty-three who found multiple exposure in the documentary are featured on nine (Martin Luther King) and three (Muhammad Ali) occasions, as opposed to the average of over eight times accorded to all other "meta"-icons, or to the average of over ten times accorded to those of white American provenance.

NOTES TO CHAPTER 8

1. The estimation is based on the assumption that each clip concentrates on roughly four distinct visual symbols, which when multiplied by the total of 2500 clips and still pictures used to document the years between 1950 and 1980, produce the total of 10,000 different visual symbols. In terms of generic concepts, such as "tree," "house," and so forth, the number would be smaller due to the factor of repetition. In any case, the notion that the documentary reflects a pool of 10,000 general visual symbols, together with those featuring specific iconic or emblematic characteristics, is only meant to provide a general impression of the visual "vocabulary" of the documentary.

2. Clifford Geertz, *The Interpretation of Culture: Selected Essays* (New York: Basic Books, 1973).

3. For such reasons, any useful finding on television's role in reporting the Vietnam War needs to have it taken into consideration that understanding of the visual messages depended on visual literacy generated largely by the same medium. As factual as television's impact on the American consciousness may have been, it depended on the general symbolic tapestry of meanings woven by the main icons, emblems, and visual symbols projected during the course of the

war, rather than on any rational assessment of the war's background. It is thus not only that the first documentary on Vietnam broadcast to larger American audiences (*Why Vietnam?* 1965) conveyed "distorted" facts, but that its visual plane was hardly adequate to adjust American visual literacy to the significance of Vietnamese symbols. See also Barnouw (1974), pp. 271–273.

4. The illustration attempts to capture the partially overlapping vectors of a visual symbol's connotations with regard to the categories of the unified, the controversial, and the exotic and of its denotations with regard to the amount of detail with which its semantic field is informed by national visual literacy. It describes the observed trend that those symbols reflecting the most historically detailed semantic contours are also those that generally develop the most positive connotations. Generally, symbols presented as unified appear more likely to find intimate portrayals and are often bound to assume the status of national celebrities. The historically dynamic collecting and typifying of visual symbols implies not only a particular bundling of denotations and connotations, but also a specific propensity for integrating or segregating visual terms according to national characteristics.

5. Hanke (2001), p. 61, see also chapter 16, "Four Codes of Visual Language," in the appendix.

NOTES TO CHAPTER 9

1. Compare Doane's statement that the "only context for television is itself." Doane (1990), p. 225.

2. Barthes rightly describes how verbal or written signs are often used for anchorage, relay, or control of the "symbolic message," as for example in advertising. Because visual language does not allow for rationally analyzing visual signs, as discussed in the theoretical sections of the appendix, the notion of a semiotic dominance of the verbal and written over the visual appears plausible. With regard to television's particular transmitter context, however, the issue can also be seen from the opposite angle: utterances and texts in their anchoring function refer to an invisible transmittership or to a transmittership represented by an inanimate object (the camera), which reference is insupportable by rational logic. In the following, it will be argued that television provides many examples that indicate a dominance of visual language's symbolic propensity over the rational potential of verbal and written signs, especially with regard to the prevailing conventions of presenting the author of what is conveyed within the conveyed picture. See Roland Barthes, "Rhetoric of the Image" in *Image-Music-Text* (New York: Hill and Wang, 1977), pp. 37–41.

3. For more on the notion of "secondary orality" and the projection of communicative interaction in the realm of macrocommunication, see Walter J. Ong, *Rhetoric, Romance, and Technology: Studies in the Interaction of Expression and Culture* (Ithaca: Cornell University Press, 1971), pp. 284–303, and Bernd Ulrich Biere and Rudolf Hoberg (eds.), *Mündlichkeit und Schriftlichkeit im Fernsehen* (Tübingen: Gunter Narr, 1996), pp. 7–8.

4. See Uta M. Quasthoff, "Mündliche Kommunikation als Körperliche Kommunikation: Beobachtungen zur Direkten Interaktion und zum Fernsehen" in Biere (1996), p 24.

5. On the differentiation between "langue" and "parole" see Ferdinand de Saussure, *Course in General Linguistics* (London: Duckworth, 1983).

6. See also the discussion of the term "idiom" in chapter 18, "Notes on the Pragmatics of Visual Language," in the appendix.

7. The "three perfections," poetry, calligraphy, and painting, combine to reflect both China's traditional understanding of art, and its cultivation of written communication. Because of this extraordinary semiotic constellation, Wen Fong assumes that no other civilization accorded art "as vital and as central a role in culture and society." Since the Chinese Empire never developed a supporting middle-class, art and aristocracy combined to rule society, making it possible for a talented poet and painter such as Wang Meng (the youngest of the Four Great Masters, ca. 1308–1385) to serve as provincial prosecutor. When calligraphy became ever more important in the bureaucracy of the empire, a civil examination system acted as a "clearing house" for social advancement. For more on the extraordinary social and cultural role of Chinese calligraphy see Weng Fong, *Beyond Representation: Chinese Painting and Calligraphy 8th–14th Century* (New York: The Metropolitan Museum of Art, 1992), pp. 3–5, p. 302, and p. 455; cf. also Albertine Gaur, *A History of Calligraphy* (London: British Library, 1994), p. 113 and p. 127.
8. Although the technical production of movies and shows necessarily conflicts with Benjamin's notion of an artistic aura, especially with regard to how the unique object connotes the lingering presence of its individual creator, the aura nevertheless appears to be at the root of the semiotic dynamic that magnifies an actor's icon the more it becomes reproduced or restaged. See Walter Benjamin (1969).
9. See also the discussion in chapter 17, "Notes on the Syntactical Function of the Four Codes," in the appendix.
10. Diderot asked how the same emotion can be expressed twice, thus recognizing the dilemma between an actor's search for a "conventional sign" that epitomizes an emotion and his artistic endeavor to provide a compelling impersonation of a character's individual and unique range of spontaneous expressions. While Sennett uses the paradox to describe the trend of enacting private in public life, it appears especially useful for specifying the crumbling boundaries between the public and the private woman on the television screen, at least when the two-dimensional reflection of acting is indeed seen as a sign-based, pictorial statement, one that follows more the rules of visual language than those of the theater stage. Sennett (1974), p. 112.
11. Because it takes a lot of on-screen time to develop iconic contours and thus an "iconic style" that audiences can discriminate, such iconic acting reflects a privilege that is reserved for only a few actor-icons.
12. In this context, method acting directly relates to the conventional force of "iconization" in so far as it concerns the selection and methodical repetition of a set of symbolic characteristics with the goal of merging them within an individually established icon. In terms of "iconic convergence," the acting style appears helpful in establishing a certain depth for the actor's icon, which allows it, as in the case of Marlon Brando, to unite a greater set of different roles within the reference to one and the same person. As a result, the conventionally applied reference to the real personality of the actor has the tendency to render his real personality even more "deep," "unfathomable," or "mythical" than that of his enacted character. In any case, the play between the real and the acted personality reflects what is here called the "iconic convergence" and only concerns the written terms of visual language.
13. For more on the medium's process of consolidation during the 1950s and the many dramatic changes in primetime programming, as well as significantly growing audiences, see, for example, William Boddy, *Fifties Television: The Industry and Its Critics* (Urbana: University of Illinois Press, 1990).
14. For more on the historical factors that pushed the early motion picture industry westward, including economic incentives as well as the search for a more

liberal, and less Victorian, cultural and political environment, see Lary May, *Screening Out the Past: The Birth of Mass Culture and the Motion Picture Industry* (New York: Oxford University Press, 1980), pp. 168–69.

15. The term "hyperrealism" presents a variation or modification of Umberto Eco's approach to the "hyperreality" of American popular culture in its emphasis on the reality reference of pictures—or "the reference to a reference to reality"—as a general style element of television broadcasting. Cf. Umberto Eco (1986).

16. Abercrombie describes the realism particular to television as based on the "concealment of the production process" that allows for mediating "rationally ordered connections between events and characters" in narrative form, while generally claiming to present a "window on the world." See Nicholas Abercrombie, *Television and Society* (Cambridge: Polity Press, 1996), pp. 26–27.

17. Because the five case studies concentrate on two of the most popular icons of early primetime entertainment (Jack Webb and Lucille Ball), on two of the most well-known icons of news shows (Edward Murrow and Walter Cronkite), and on one of sports' most lasting icons (Muhammad Ali), they reflect rather on the extraordinary, than on the general imagery of historical television. The extraordinary status of these icons, however, also guarantees their established place in national visual literacy, thus rendering them suitable for the semiotic study of their careers on screen. A second criterion for the selection of these case studies concerns their relationship with genres that were typical for early television. In building on the medium's possibility of continuous programming, the chosen icons and shows all appear typically to reflect on the essence of the new medium's semiotic format.

NOTES TO CHAPTER 10

1. See the article "Detective Story" in *Newsweek*, January 14, 1952. For further sources and information on Jack Webb and *Dragnet*, see also Michael J. Hayde, *My Name is Friday: The Unauthorized but True Story of Dragnet and the Films of Jack Webb* (Nashville: Cumberland House, 2001).

2. In 1954, Jack Webb also made the cover of the famous magazine, see *Time*, March 15, 1954.

3. Ibid.

4. See the article by Richard C. Neuweiler, "Dum-Du-Dum-Dum Revisited," in the *New York Times*, January 8, 1967.

5. What Lawrence Levine described as the endeavor of educated upper-class Victorians to appropriate cultural forms of all kinds, such as popular Shakespeare dramas, and to sanctify them as "American culture," coincided with the commercial interest in making them accessible to the middle class, as was also the case with vaudeville. However, unlike jazz, for example, which in Neil Leonard's assessment first had to be tamed before it could achieve commercial success, some early television addressed at first rather high-brow values before the medium shifted to more commercial programming, for example, by incorporating Hollywood movies or Disney productions. According to Boddy's assessment this shift occurred in the middle of the 1950s. Lawrence W. Levine, *Highbrow / Lowbrow: The Emergence of Cultural Hierarchy in America* (Cambridge: Harvard University Press, 1988), Neil Leonard, *Jazz and the White Americans: The Acceptance of a New Art Form* (Chicago: University of Chicago Press, 1962), and William Boddy (1990).

6. The chapter on *Dragnet* is based on the following four episodes, which were aired on both television (NBC 1951–1959/1967–1970) and radio (NBC 1949–1957): "The Big Secret" 1/22/1953 (radio: "The Big Show" 4/10/1952);"The

Big Ante" 5/21/1953 (radio: "The Big Hands" 11/22/1951); "The Big Producer" 8/26/1954 (radio: 2/21/1951); "The Big Juvenile Gang War" 4/10/1958 (radio: "The Big Juvenile Division" 1/17/1952). For bibliographic reference see "Film and Television Sources."

7. For more on the concept of cultural capital and distinctions of taste as marking class, see Pierre Bourdieu, *Distinction: A Social Critique of the Judgment of Taste* (Cambridge: Harvard University Press, 1984), and Bourdieu with Jean-Claude Passeron, *Reproduction in Education, Society, and Culture* (London: Sage Publications, 1977).
8. See the discussion of the concept of "symbolic transfer" in the section "The Fourth Code of Visual Language" in chapter 16.
9. See, for example, *Time*, March 15, 1954.
10. Ibid.
11. *Newsweek*, January 14, 1952.
12. *Time*, March 15, 1954.
13. Quoted by Steven Stark in *Glued to the Set: The 60 Television Shows and Events That Made Us Who We Are Today* (New York: Delta, 1998).
14. *Newsweek*, January 14, 1952.
15. Jane Stern, *Jane and Michael Stern's Encyclopedia of Pop Culture: An A to Z Guide of Who's Who and What's What, from Aerobics and Bubble Gum to Valley of the Dolls and Moon Unit Zappa* (New York: HarperPerennial, 1992), p. 153.
16. What Jack Webb himself characterized as "underplaying" was also described as "low key naturalism." See Richard G. Hubler, "Jack Webb: The Man Who Makes Dragnet" in *Coronet*, September 1953.
17. Reportedly, Webb also refused to let his male actors use make-up, and asked women to apply their own. *Newsweek*, January 14, 1952.
18. See also the discussion of the concepts "idiom" and "discourse" in chapter 18, "Notes on the Pragmatics of Visual Language," in the appendix.
19. See the discussion of "secondary orality" in the section "The Verbal, the Written, and the Visual" in chapter 9, and Uta Quasthoff (1996), p. 24.
20. Abercrombie, (1996), pp. 26–27.
21. *Time*, March 15, 1954.
22. For such reasons, Foucault's concept of discourse that needs a central stronghold for authentication ties in with the modern theory on networks that also need a central institution, for example, in the role of a clearinghouse. From this angle, *Dragnet's* communicative network initiates viewers to moral standards reflected by Friday's demeanor and by the selected cases, which in turn incorporate judicial standards as regulated by an institutionalized discourse that is basically external to the show. The icon of Jack Webb alias Joe Friday thus comes to stand simultaneously as an idiomatic reflection of individual agency and as an epitome of a social discourse, continuously converging personal characteristics with impersonal significance. See also the section "Idiomatic Networks of Signification" in chapter 18.
23. See the article by Richard Warren Lewis "Happiness Is a Return to the Good Old Days: At 48, Jack Webb Has Turned the Trick," in *TV Guide*, October 19, 1968.

NOTES TO CHAPTER 11

1. Sources used for the chapter on *I Love Lucy* (CBS 1951–1957): "Lucy is Enceinte," 1952; "Lucy Goes to the Hospital," 1953; "Lucy and John Wayne," 1955; "Lucy Visits Grauman's," 1955; *The Ed Sullivan Show (Toast of the Town—*

1948–1971), CBS 1954; *Lucy and Desi: A Home Movie*, 1994; "Lucille Ball Dies—Wednesday, April 26, 1989," *Nightline* ABC News 1989; *Vintage Commercials II and IV: Sixty More Minutes of Classic Television Commercials from the 1950s and 1960s*, Shokus 1989. For bibliographical references see Film and Television Sources.

2. After six month on the air, the show was the first to reach 10 million out of 15 million possible homes, according to Susan Horowitz, attracting 30 million spectators or nearly one-fifth of the nation's population. Susan Horowitz, *Queens of Comedy: Lucille Ball, Phyllis Diller, Carol Burnett, Joan Rivers, and the New Generation of Funny Women* (Amsterdam: Gordon and Breach Publishers, 1997), pp. 29–30.

3. Alex McNeil, *Total Television: The Comprehensive Guide to Programming from 1948 to the Present* (New York: Penguin Books, 1996), pp. 401–402.

4. Ibid., p. 401.

5. Ball's career included the managing of her and her husband's own company, Desilu, which she managed on her own after 1962.

6. Lori Landay, *Madcaps, Screwballs, and Con Women: The Female Trickster in American Culture* (Philadelphia: University of Pennsylvania Press, 1998).

7. See chapter 7, "Iconic Lecterns."

8. The *Nightline* special was aired on ABC News on April 26, 1989; for bibliographical references, see Film and Television Sources.

9. Reportedly they were reacting to the broadcast of *Lucy and Desi Before the Laughter*, see McNeil (1996), p. 403.

10. *Lucy and Desi: A Home Movie*, Lucie Arnaz (1994).

NOTES TO CHAPTER 12

1. The footage analyzed for this chapter was taken from *Good Night and Good Luck: The Edward R. Murrow Television Collection*, CBS News 1991. Additional *See It Now* footage comes from the Museum of Television and Radio, New York, and from the private archive of J. Fred MacDonald, Chicago. For bibliographical references see Film and Television Sources.

2. Thomas Doherty, *Cold War, Cool Medium: Television, McCarthyism, and American Culture* (New York: Columbia University Press, 2003), p. 161.

3. Murrow had to tape the pictures and send them home by aircraft, where they would be edited and broadcast some days later. As a result of the taping, these pictures also became preserved for future viewing.

4. See Doherty's chapter "Edward R. Murrow Slays the Dragon of Joseph McCarthy," in which he argues that although television was by no means the only forum for anti-McCarthyism, it nevertheless marked a "seismic shift in Zeitgeist," if only because Murrow's critique contrasted with the media's general devotion to "100% acceptance." Doherty (2003), pp. 161–88 and p. 162.

5. The report opened with the—hyperreal—disclaimer that it would be "told mainly in [McCarthy's] own words and pictures," although the clips were, of course, edited and paced by Murrow and Friendly in the biased fashion of a presentation that anticipates controversy. See Thomas Doherty (2003), p. 173.

6. Thomas Rostek concludes that the "Report on Senator McCarthy" is "far from mere 'objective report' and equally far from 'biased attack,'"—an assessment that suggests the problems typically encountered when analyzing the verbal and visual plane of journalistic reports that claim to present objective records of reality. Thomas Rostek, *See It Now Confronts McCarthyism:*

Television Documentary and the Politics of Representation (Tuscaloosa: The University of Alabama Press, 1994), p. 114 and 123.

7. Steve Barkin concludes that "if Edward R. Murrow was one of the pioneers of broadcast journalism, he was also one of the pioneers of celebrity journalism." While this conclusion is supported by the semiotic analysis of his icon's career, it should also be noted that, according to Joseph Persico, Murrow was never really at ease with his primetime show, although it made him a "moderately rich man." Steve Barkin, *American Television News: The Media Marketplace and the Public Interest* (Armonk, New York: M. E. Sharpe, 2003), pp. 121–25 and Joseph E. Persico, *Edward R. Murrow: An American Original* (New York: McGraw-Hill, 1988), p. 353.

8. According to Steven Stark the scheduling reflects the networks' ambivalence towards "tough documentaries," because the night after Thanksgiving would usually be "one of the worst television viewing nights of the year." See Steven Stark (1997), p. 59.

9. In the wake of the quiz-show scandal, the big networks rearranged their approach to entertainment and news, creating among other things large, permanent news divisions, the first product of which was a set of documentaries that included CBS's "Harvest of Shame." Stark (1997), p. 108.

10. The golden age of television documentary in the early 1960s began to fade almost right away, mainly because the documentaries' modest ratings in comparison to entertainment suggested lost revenues in the minds of network officials. Even the attempt to introduce "quality ratings" designed to characterize the documentaries' appeal to affluent audiences failed to convince sponsors. Michael Curtin, *Redeeming the Wasteland: Television Documentary and Cold War Politics* (New Brunswick: Rutgers University Press, 1995), pp. 246–48.

11. According to Curtin, the marriage of cinema and television conventions was typical for the documentary work from this period. Among other things it probably also reflects the networks' need to import strategies for out-of-the-studio productions. Ibid., p. 1 and pp. 191–92.

12. Ibid., p. 1.

NOTES TO CHAPTER 13

1. The sources for this chapter are Cronkite's pictorial autobiography *Cronkite Remembers* (CBS 1996); CBS *Evening News*, September 2, 1963; *Vietnam: Chronicle of a War—Narrated by Walter Cronkite* (CBS News 1981); *Man on the Moon: With Walter Cronkite* (CBS News 1989); and footage of the CBS live broadcast of the moon landing, 1969, from the Museum of Broadcast Communications in Chicago and the Museum of Television and Radio in New York. See Film and Television Sources.

2. *Cronkite Remembers* (CBS 1996).

3. Ibid.

4. Ibid.

5. The first expanded *Evening News* aired on September 2, 1963.

6. *Cronkite Remembers* (CBS 1996).

7. In an interview with *Variety,* Cronkite defined himself as "liberal," describing his political viewpoints as "not bound by doctrines." See Epstein (2000), p. 214.

8. *Cronkite Remembers* (CBS 1996).

9. Dayan and Katz (1992), p. 116, and Hartley (1992), pp. 189–90.

10. *Cronkite Remembers* (CBS 1996).

11. So much so that he would still try to counter such allegations decades later in his nationwide-aired autobiography *Cronkite Remembers* (CBS

1996). The doubt concerning his emotional truthfulness when reading the message of Kennedy's death apparently challenged his fundamental belief in his professional role as a servant of truth and the nation. His reaction indirectly underscores his deferential attitude to the spectacle, even though he occasionally also critiqued the demeanor of a politician carrying a unified icon.

12. Epstein observed in 1973 that almost all newsmen eventually came to hold public officials in low esteem, but not the office itself. Mirroring Cronkite's opinion of Kennedy as evidenced in their dispute about the original version of the interview discussed earlier, Epstein quotes an NBC correspondent who asked, "How can we respect people who change their answers with every retake?" Epstein (2000; originally published in 1973), pp. 215–16.

13. The idea to use inoculation as a semiotic concept was introduced by Roland Barthes in the essay "Operation Magarine." Roland Barthes, *Mythologies* (New York: Hill and Wang, 1994), pp. 41–42.

14. *Cronkite Remembers* (CBS 1996).

15. *Man on the Moon: With Walter Cronkite* (CBS News 1989).

16. Ibid.

17. Ibid.

18. Stark (1998), p. 139.

19. *Cronkite Remembers* (CBS 1996).

20. *Man on the Moon: With Walter Cronkite* (CBS News 1989).

21. Ibid.

22. *Cronkite Remembers* (CBS 1996).

23. Ibid.

24. *Vietnam: Chronicle of a War—Narrated by Walter Cronkite* (CBS News 1981).

25. *Cronkite Remembers* (CBS 1996).

26. Tom Wells, *The War Within: America's Battle Over Vietnam* (Berkeley: University of California Press, 1994), p. 242.

27. Ibid.

28. Cronkite's first-person story reached nine million Americans, see Wells (1994), p. 242 and also *Cronkite Remembers* (CBS 1996).

29. In this context, it should be noted, with Schudson, that "by the time Walter Cronkite declared (on February 27, 1968) that the war was a stalemate, he was only coming around to the views of middle America." See Michael Schudson (1995), p. 23. For more on the issue see also Hallin (1986) and Baughman (1997).

30. Stark (1998), p. 189.

31. In this context, Postman further concludes that "television's strongest point is that it brings personalities into our hearts, not abstractions into our heads." Neil Postman, *Amusing Ourselves to Death: Public Discourse in the Age of Show Business* (New York: Penguin Books, 1985), p. 123.

32. By that time, most Americans had also turned from print to television for receiving their information. Stark (1998), p. 189.

NOTES TO CHAPTER 14

1. David Remnick provides an excellent account of Muhammad Ali's political persona in *King of the World: Muhammad Ali and the Rise of an American Hero* (New York: Vintage Books, 1998).

2. The footage used for this chapter is taken from *I Shook Up the World: Clay vs. Liston 1964* (TNT 1964); *When We Were Kings*, Leon Gast, 1996; *Champions Forever*, Dimitri Logothetis, 1996; excerpts from *Muhammad Ali*, Gemstone

Entertainment, 1998; and clips from the Museum of Television and Radio in New York. See Film and Television Sources.

3. Remnick (1998), pp. 119–20 and p. 120.
4. Ibid., p. 142.
5. Ibid., pp. 157–58.
6. *I Shook Up the World: Clay vs. Liston 1964* (TNT 1964).
7. Ibid.
8. On Bakhtin's notion of grotesque realism, see the section "The Dark Room" in chapter 1, and Bakhtin *(*1984), pp. 11–25.
9. See Remnick (1998), pp. 256–66.
10. For a discussion of the dialectic concept of boundaries see the sections "From Empirical to Arbitrary Boundary Lines" and "The First Code of Visual Language" in chapter 16.
11. Remnick's own account appears inconclusive. The twisting of Liston's neck and the lifting of his left foot visible in slow-motion amount to gestures that can only symbolically be typified, as they occur numerous times in every fight. In general, the notion of scientific fact appears rather ambiguous in the context of the broadcast sports spectacle. The invocation of science in this context refers less to any factual significance outside the pictures' frame, than to the style element of its hyperreal mise en scène. Ibid., p. 257.
12. The reconstruction of the diachronic quality of visual language thus demonstrates that Ali's boxing talent cannot be evaluated in hindsight, at least not by means of historical pictures.
13. *When We Were Kings* by Leon Gast, 1996.
14. Ibid.
15. For more on the issue, see, for example, the chapter "Victory for Allah" in David K. Wiggins, *Glory Bound: Black Athletes in a White America* (New York: Syracuse University Press, 1997), pp. 152–74.
16. For more on the issue see Gitlin (1987).
17. For more on the Black Power movement see, for example, W. L. Van Deburg (1992).
18. *History of the 20th Century* (ABC, 1980–1985), vol. 8, 1965–1969.
19. In contrast to Lori Landay's characterization of Lucille Ball as a trickster, Lemert sees Ali's status as more controversial, reflecting a more aggressive expression of irony. Charles Lemert, *Muhammad Ali: Trickster in the Culture of Irony* (Cambridge: Polity Press, 2003) and Lori Landay (1998).
20. Quote in Remnick (1998), p. 288. According to Van Deburg, Ali's public stand against the Vietnam War had initially caused outrage among black soldiers serving in Vietnam, but by 1968 their acceptance of him was being restored. Van Deburg, pp. 129–44.
21. Mike Marqusee, *Redemption Song: Muhammad Ali and the Spirit of the Sixties* (London: Verso, 1999), p. 286.

NOTES TO CHAPTER 15

1. For more on the concept of "furor divinus" or "furor poeticus," see Mathias Feldges, "Ein Beispiel für das Weiterbestehen Mittelalterlicher Denkstrukturen in der Barockzeit" in *Wirkendes Wort*, vol. 20, 1970.
2. See Bruno Latour, *We Have Never Been Modern: Essays in Symmetrical Anthropology*, trans. Catherine Porter. (New York: Harvest Wheatsheaf, 1993).
3. For more on the concept of cultural capital and distinctions of taste as marking class, see Pierre Bourdieu, *Distinction: A Social Critique of the Judgment*

of Taste (Cambridge: Harvard University Press, 1984), and Bourdieu with Jean-Claude Passeron, *Reproduction in Education, Society, and Culture* (London: Sage Publications, 1977).

NOTES TO CHAPTER 16

1. Alex Bolvig calls for a "new iconology" better able to capture the historicity of modern pictures. In this context, Jean-Claude Schmitt outlines the potential resting in the collaboration of art history and history and asks for a new methodology for the analysis of images that would benefit both disciplines. In response to this charge, Philip Rosen assesses the particular relation between history, historiography, and historicity in order to characterize the particular temporality of pictures in his "Change Mummified"; Robert Hanke characterizes the postmodern challenge of television as history. All of these works recognize the particular problems involved in locating and analyzing pictorial content from a historical perspective and ask for new approaches that evade the traditional boundaries between art and history, history and reality, or reality and art. Robert Hanke, "*Quantum Leap:* The Postmodern Challenge of Television as History," in Gary R. Edgerton and Peter C. Rollins, eds., *Television Histories: Shaping Collective Memory in the Media Age* (Lexington: University Press of Kentucky, 2001), pp. 59–78; see also Jean-Claude Schmitt's article "Images and the Historian" and Alex Bolvig's introduction in Bolvig and Lindley (2003), or Philip Rosen (2001).
2. Bolvig (2003), p. xxviii.
3. Cf. Charles W. Colson, "When History Is Up for Grabs," *The New York Times*, Dec. 28, 1995, p. A21, with Daniel J. Walkowitz, "Rescreening the Past: Subversion Narratives and the Politics of History," in Tony Barta, ed., *Screening the Past: Film and the Representation of History* (Westport: Praeger, 1998), pp. 45 and 47.
4. Walkowitz (1998), p. 55.
5. Hanke (2001), p. 61.
6. In this study, I will try to link such and similar questions with the semiotic conception of a visual language, arguing that the particular sign and symbol system of pictures, as well as their particular transmitter-receiver context, limits the ability of audiences to discriminate logically between fictional and nonfictional significance, at least as long as no further verbal or written information is available. Thus, Higgins's conclusion that audiences share responsibility for the breakdown between fictional and nonfictional significance on the television screen is here analyzed as the historical discourse of "hyperrealism." Kathleen Marie Higgins, "Television, Realism, and the Distortion of Time," in Ruth Lorand, ed., *Television: Aesthetic Reflections* (New York: Peter Lang, 2002), p. 112. Cf. also John Ellis (1993).
7. Developed by Max Wertheimer, Wolfgang Köhler, and Kurt Koffka in the early 20th century, the Gestalt school approached visual perception as a group of psychological processes whereby wholes are constructed that are more than the sum of their parts. While the definition of visual signs and their construction of visual symbols outlined later in this study involves a similar dynamic, the semiotic approach to the language of pictures necessarily assumes that pictures address the human mode of visual perception as manmade vessels of significance. In consequence, constructing and conveying pictorial content may address the individual mode of perception, but in ways that anticipate an understanding that can at least to some degree be

collectively shared. However, although questioning the premise of the Gestalt school that ultimately equates the reception of visual content with the mode of individual perception of reality, the semiotic premise does not mean to exclude psychological aspects from the analysis of visual communication. For more on the theory of gestalts, see for example, Ann Marie Seward Barry, *Visual Intelligence: Perception, Image, and Manipulation in Visual Communication* (Albany: State University of New York Press), pp. 40–47.

8. Ibid., p. 69.
9. See, for example, Marita Sturken, *Tangled Memories: The Vietnam War, the AIDS Epidemic, and the Politics of Remembering* (Berkeley, University of California Press, 1997), pp. 1–17 or Robert Hanke (2001), p. 74.
10. Sturken (1997), p. 3.
11. Compare Paul Messaris's "reluctant" use of the term visual literacy, as he excludes the notion of language from the mode of perceiving pictures, with the approach of Günther Kress and Theo van Leeuwen, who admit a transmitter-receiver frame and a grammar, but not a sign-structure, into the analysis of visual communication. See Paul Messaris, *Visual Literacy* (Boulder: Westview Press, 1994), pp. 2–4 and p. 165, as well as Günther R. Kress, (1996) and Theo van Leeuwen, *Reading Images: The Grammar of Visual Design.* (London: Routledge, 1996), pp. 15–21 and pp. 119–58.
12. Bolvig (2003), p. xxiii and Schmitt (2003), p. 34.
13. Schmitt argues that the potential of a new iconographical methodology can only be fully developed when the disciplines of history and art history cooperate better. His inspiring perspective on the cross-referential nature of iconographical series, however, also suggests the potential of semiotic methodology in this cooperative work of developing new approaches to the analysis of pictures. See Schmitt (2003), pp. 21 and 34.
14. Dondis (1993), pp. 15 and 183.
15. See the work of Gerhard Braun, *Grundlagen der visuellen Kommunikation* (München: Bruckmann, 1987) and cf. also Jacques Bertin, *Semiology of Graphics: Diagrams, Networks, Maps* (Madison: University of Wisconsin Press, 1983).
16. Ferdinand de Saussure developed the philosophical conception of the sign divided between "signifier" (sound-image) and "signified" (concept). This dialectic structure at the root of communication is further underscored by other bipolar distinctions, such as "langue-parole" or "synchrony-diachrony." Ferdinand de Saussure, *Course in General Linguistics*, Roy Harris, ed., Wade Baskin, trans., (London: Duckworth, 1983).
17. In general, these scholars (such as Jostein Gipsrud) follow Charles Sanders Peirce's model, which differentiates between those signs that have an arbitrary, conventional relation to what they stand for, icons or iconic signs that resemble what they stand for, and indexical signs that reference meaning based on a cause-effect relation, such as smoke indexes fire. In the perspective of Jostein Gipsrud, for example, the "photograph of the US President is consequently an iconic sign for the US President." In the approach outlined in this study, the element of resemblance is not disputed. It is argued, however, that the issue of resemblance tends to be overrated, that it does not necessarily contradict the arbitrary or conventional character of iconic significance, and most importantly, that it obstructs the possibility of detaching the history of an icon on screen from that of, for example, a real US president. For this reason, I try to work de Saussure's structural linguistic concept of the sign into the definition of Peirce's iconic sign in order to define visual signs as classic signs, which, based on arbitrary, structural elements (such as technically reproduced contrast lines), combine to shape icons as larger entities of significance. Cf. Jostein

Gipsrud, *Understanding Media Culture* (London: Arnold, 2002) pp. 106–10, and for more on Charles Sanders Peirce's approach to the logic of icons, see Peirce (1931–58), vols. 2 and 3, §§ 2.274–2.308 and § 3.362. Other scholars who build on Peirce's model of the icon include, for example, Richard Howells (2003), Tilo Prase (1997), Keyan Tomaselli, *Appropriating Images: The Semiotics of Visual Representation* (Hojbjerg: Intervention Press, 1996), and Ellen Seiter, "Semiotics, Structuralism, and Television," in Robert C. Allen, ed., *Channels of Discourse, Reassembled: Television and Contemporary Criticism* (Chapel Hill: University of North Carolina Press, 1992), pp. 31–66.

18. Prase (1997), pp. 51–52.
19. Christian Metz claims that the "text of film" does not feature structural entities comparable to words and emphasizes the range between conventional cuts and the "shock" provoked when pictures are sequenced in an unconventional fashion. See Christian Metz's influential work on *Film Language: A Semiotics of the Cinema* (New York: Oxford University Press, 1974), p. 32 and *Der Imaginäre Signifikant: Psychoanalyse und Kino* (Münster: Nodus Publikationen, 2000), pp. 165–69.
20. Nelson Goodman (1976), p 41.
21. Zelizer (1990), p. 46.
22. See especially Eco's chapter "Critique of Iconism" and compare his approach with that of Charles Morris. Winfried Nöth provides an excellent survey of the theoretical debates surrounding the concept of iconicity. See Eco (1979), pp. 191–218, Charles Morris, *Signs, Language, and Behavior* (New York: Prentice-Hall, 1947), and Winfried Nöth, *Handbook of Semiotics* (Bloomington: Indiana University Press, 1990), pp. 121–27.
23. See Peirce (1931–58), vols. 2 and 3, §§ 2.274–2.308 and § 3.362.
24. The main argument against the concept of iconicity concerns the formal logic that demands that if a picture is not the exact same thing as a sight in reality, the relation cannot be A = A, but something like A = A-1 (or A+1). As a result, there are two autonomous entities, say A and B, which differ in at least one element. As long as this fundamental difference in identity is not fully observed, the concept of iconicity tends to obscure, rather than to illuminate, the relation between visual signs and their referents. In any case, the difference between a photograph and its model in reality is also constituted by an element of arbitrariness, which however it may be defined in detail, characterizes the human part in producing a picture. The semiotic definition of (visual) signs is designed to capture this element of arbitrariness and to account for the difference in identity between a picture and its model in reality.
25. See Eco (1979), p. 7, and also Winfried Nöth's article, "Can Pictures Lie?" in Winfried Nöth, ed., *Semiotics of the Media: State of the Art, Projects, and Perspectives* (Berlin: Mouton de Gruyter, 1997), pp. 133–46.
26. Eco (1979), p. 7.
27. Günther Bentele, *Zeichen und Entwicklung. Vorüberlegungen zu einer genetischen Semiotik* (Tübingen: Gunter Narr, 1984), pp. 23–24.
28. Ibid., p. 243.
29. Such revision based on the temporal aspect of icons is tried here. See Thomas A. Sebeok's chapter on the "icon" in *Contributions to a Doctrine of Signs* (Bloomington: Indiana University, 1976), p. 106.
30. In this approach to the historicity of icons, the aspect of convention is twofold, concerning on the one hand the production of visual signs and, on the other, their reception. The production of visual signs builds, especially with regard to photographic techniques, on a certain likeness between visual signs or icons and their object in front of the camera. While convention certainly also has its role in the creation of pictorial narratives, it appears even more

important with regard to the reception of visual signs and icons by audiences. Given that the presentation of pictures in a communicative context necessarily implies the absence of the reality referenced by the two-dimensional contours, it appears logical to assume a conventional dynamic at the root of the possibility of understanding the conveyed contours: a process of perception that is, at least partially, removed from the mode of experiencing unmediated sights in reality—however similar the two ways of seeing may ultimately appear. In this view, Peirce's definition of icons places too much emphasis on the actual act of producing the signs' form. It should be noted, however, that Peirce defined icons not so much for the purpose of analyzing the logic of visual perception, but instead based on his interest in the philosophical concept of likeness. For this reason, he also defined geometrical diagrams as icons and, most likely for this reason too, he did not develop a specifically diachronic perspective on their significance. While he does recognize that some symbols "grow" in meaning, and while he also sees them as developing out of "other signs, particularly from icons," his philosophical approach to the logic of icons places these rather complex vessels of meaning on the same plane as ordinary signs. By contrast, the attempt is made here to define the logical concept of visual signs as the basis on which symbolic significance can unfold. In this perspective, icons are very specific symbols, which have grown to reflect a unity between their individual contours and their historically charged significance. Thus, the likeness between an icon's contours and the person it represents may still have a part in its unique sign form, but at the same time, an icon's conventionally developed content suggests a mode of reception that is as distanced from any external reality—and possibly even more so—as from the content of any other sign. Cf. Peirce (1931–58), vol. 2, § 2.302.

31. "Boundary contours" represent, according to Barry, "the first data that the brain receives," thus also preceding the triggering of emotional response. See Barry (1997), p. 26.
32. Eco (1979), pp. 193–94.
33. Braun (1987), p. 120.
34. Alfred Racek, *Philosophie der Grenze. Ein Entwurf* (Wien: Herder, 1983), p. 28.
35. Georg W. F. Hegel, *System der Philosophie. Die Wissenschaft der Logik* in H. Glockner, ed., *Sämtliche Werke in 20 Bänden* (Stuttgart: Frommann, 1940), vol. 8, p. 220.
36. Aristotle, *Physik; Vorlesung über die Natur* (Hamburg: Felix Meiner, 1987), vol. 8, 263b, pp. 13–20.
37. Ibid.
38. Prase (1997), pp. 51–52.
39. The graphic figure builds on a "catalog of visual variables" proposed by Gerhard Braun, who was inspired by Jacques Bertin and Gyorgy Kepes. The proposed set of variables is further informed by Dondis's outline of ten basic visual elements. However, the new approach to these visual variables features several variations, which, in accordance with the different perspective on visual signs, concern the implementation of the dialectic principle in the form of the contour line, the frame, and the time frame. Cf. Gerhard Braun (1987), p. 10, and Donis Dondis (1972), p. 15. Cf. also Jacques Bertin (1983) and Gyorgy Kepes, *Language of Vision* (Chicago: P. Theobald, 1944).
40. Eco (1987), p. 126.
41. Compare also Max Bense's approach, which differentiates form and color as the constitutive elements ("chromemes" and "formemes") of visual sign perception, in *Zeichen und Design: Semiotische Ästhetik* (Baden-Baden: Agis, 1971).
42. On perceptual filling in, see Barry (1997), p. 26.

43. Eco (1979), p. 217.
44. See Heinrich Wölfflin's *Kunstgeschichtliche Grundbegriffe: Das Problem der Stilentwicklung in der neueren Kunst* (München: Bruckmann, 1915), in particular, the chapter "Geschlossene Form und Offene Form."
45. Theoretically, an emblem such as the Japanese flag can suggest two generic concepts, "sun" and "sky," based on only one visual sign and its contrast relation with the background. Without the highly conventionalized context of the flag in place, the simple depiction of a circle against a plain background would need at least one further characteristic such as, for example, lines standing for rays, to secure the understanding of the figure as representing the sun.
46. The exception of graphically styled visual signs concerns, for example, traffic signs or airport signs that guide travelers to a meeting point and so forth. These signs are generally stripped of all unnecessary pictorial detail and thus equate their formal contours with equally formal significance. However, such signs nevertheless provide a minimum of unique visual characteristics and generally serve as symbols. Although they are sometimes formalized to the degree of functioning within an established code, these graphical signs therefore reflect a structural similarity to the proposed definition of visual signs.
47. On "making do" as a semiotic concept, see Michel de Certeau, *The Practice of Everyday Life* (Berkeley: University of California Press, 1984), pp. 29–42.
48. On the cultural dynamics of icons, see also the works of Paul Rutherford, *The New Icons? The Art of Television Advertising* (Toronto: University of Toronto Press, 1994) or Stuart Ewen, *All Consuming Images: The Politics of Style in Contemporary Culture* (New York: Basic Books, 1988).
49. In some ways, the model of the four codes resembles Baudrillard's description of the process that turns visual representation into a "simulacrum" in four "successive phases." First a visual representation "is the reflection of a profound reality"—that of visual perception. Second, "it masks and denatures a profound reality"—through binding it with abstract, generic concepts. Third, "it masks the absence of a profound reality"—through presenting the symbol as a reflection of reality. And fourth, "it has no relation to any reality whatsoever: it is its own pure simulacrum." This pure simulacrum is the icon, the identity of which comprises the semantic history of all its previous representations. See Jean Baudrillard, *Simulacra and Simulation* (Ann Arbor: University of Michigan Press, 2000), p. 6.

NOTES TO CHAPTER 17

1. The theme-rheme concept was introduced by the Prague school of semiotics. María Ángeles Gómes-Gonzáles provides an extensive discussion in *The Theme-Topic Interface: Evidence from English* (Philadelphia: John Benjamins Publishing Co., 2001).
2. See Wolfgang Fritz Haug's approach to the mechanism of advertising in general, and to pictorial advertising in particular, in *Warenästhetik und kapitalistische Massenkultur—"Werbung" und "Konsum"* (Berlin: Argument-Verlag, 1980), p. 45.
3. In addition, the editing in moving pictures or the sequencing of still pictures also adds to the dialectic syntax of the picture and to its particular verb structure. There are many different ways to illustrate action without actually showing it, e.g., focusing on a hand grasping a car key and then cutting to a car driving on the street to mean "he is driving away." In any case, it seems possible logically to describe all such possibilities with the dialectic interplay of the visual variables in the proposed model of the four codes. The latter two, the symbolic and the

iconic codes, would then also explain all those instances in which car tires squeal on dirt roads, i.e., instances in which convention has begun to relieve empirical verisimilitude as the main generator of syntactic logic.

NOTES TO CHAPTER 18

1. For more on Derrida's fine conceptual distinctions behind "différance," see Jacques Derrida (1978), pp. 23–24 and p. 65.
2. For more on the notion of "arche-writing," see Derrida (1978), pp. 56–57.
3. Jean Baudrillard, *The Evil Demon of Images* (Sydney: Power Institute of Fine Arts, 1987).
4. This semantic dynamic relates with Claude Lévi-Strauss's notion that every form holds content that sets up another form. See Claude Lévi-Strauss, *Structural Anthropology*, vol. 2, (London: Jonathan Cape, 1976), p. 131.
5. In order to improve the readability of the text, the term "diachronic" has so far been used synonymously with "historical." However, there is a difference between the two terms, which, similar to the difference between the "synchronic" and the "external context," concerns the relation between signs and their model in reality or historical reality. The relation of a visual sign, icon, or emblem to its referent can be described as a one-dimensional bond with both a present and a past context, as opposed to the plurality of bonds that characterize the perception of objects and subjects in the flow of everyday life. The diachronic significance of an icon thereby specifies its particular, semiotic historicity, as opposed to the history of its referent. Iconic significance is further influenced by the additional diachronic aspects of the transmitter-receiver context, which, however, is external to the icon's semantic field of meaning.
6. The concept of the idiom as referring to the diachronic context of partners in communication attempts to synthesize diverse semiotic and linguistic approaches, such as, for example, Peirce's "interpretant," Searle's "speech act theory," Foucault's "discourse," or Todorov's "registers of discourse," which address the issues of reference and significance with regard to the presence or absence of anterior discourses. However, in predominantly qualifying a microcommunicative setting, the pragmatic definition of an idiomatic plane is designed to complement the more macrocommunicative concept of discourse, as discursive significance also infiltrates exchanges in everyday life. Basically external to the semiotic form of single signs and symbols, idiomatic content influences their significance by way of their grammar, thus influencing the logic of a message's theme-rheme arrangement as well. See, for example, Peirce (1931–58), vols. 2 and 3, §§ 2.250–2.253 and §2.274, Tzvetan Todorov, *Introduction to Poetics* (Minneapolis: University of Minneapolis Press, 1981), pp. 13–58, or John R. Searle, *Speech Acts. An Essay in the Philosophy of Language* (Cambridge: Cambridge University Press, 1970), pp. 16–21.
7. To some extent, the concept of the idiom is also designed to bridge the transmitter-receiver divide in communication. However, the idea is not to exclude the possibility that receivers can understand and discuss what is conveyed in an independent fashion, but to characterize such an approach to signs as a different communicative context that reduces the interactive potential of signs in favor of another, more discursive interpretation of their significance. Stanley Fish, *Is There a Text in This Class? The Authority of Interpretative Communities* (Cambridge: Harvard University Press, 1980), pp. 303–21; cf. also Henry Jenkins, *Textual Poachers: Television Fans and Participatory Culture* (New York: Routledge, 1992), pp. 88–89 and 277–87.

8. Actor-Network Theory (ANT) is generally ascribed to Bruno Latour and his research on the social dynamic behind managing information and (scientific) knowledge in conjunction with technology. ANT itself has become subject to such dynamics, as its interpretation by the academic community evolved predominantly on the Internet. To start with, see, for example, Bruno Latour, "On Actor-Network Theory: A Few Clarifications" (Center for Social Theory and Technology, Keele University, 1997) and *We Have Never Been Modern: Essays in Symmetrical Anthropology* (New York: Harvest Wheatsheaf, 1983) as well as Geoffrey Walsham, "Actor-Network Theory and IS Research: Current Status and Future Prospects," in *Information Systems and Qualitative Research* (London: Weinheim, 1997), pp. 466–80, and Barry Wellman, "Network Analysis: Some Basic Principles," in *Sociological Theory* (San Francisco: Jossey-Bass Inc., 1983), pp. 155–200.

9. The concept of power used here builds on Michel Foucault's assessment of an omnipresent will to knowledge. The resulting dystopia is mitigated by Foucault's implication that power can also be productive and creative, especially when it meets opposition of comparable weight and when it is thus channeled into more horizontal structures—see, for example, his outline of the interactive power relations between a priest and a confessor. Applied to sign-based communication and the semiotic concept of the idiom, the model of a horizontal power balance relates to interactivity as the foundation of sign-based communication: without an intact idiomatic plane, that is, without a mutual interest in each other's intentions, signs lose their potential to relate information. If a disrupted idiomatic plane admits misunderstandings, in doing so it demonstrates the complex balance of power relations behind each act of communication. In assessing the possibility of vertical semiotic power relations, Hannah Arendt's conclusion that real power does not emanate from the barrel of a gun comes to mind. Her definition that "power and violence are opposites; where the one rules absolutely, the other is absent" can also be applied to the realm of communication: signs turn into instruments of violence when they can no longer be challenged in communication, or when, for example, their transmitter is consciously misunderstood, ridiculed, or simply ignored. By contrast, the possibility for different individual understanding, interpretation, and even dispute of the conveyed signs implies a dynamic, rather horizontal power-relation present during creative communication. Cf. Hannah Arendt, *On Violence* (New York: Harvest Book, 1970), p. 11, p. 37, and pp. 43–56, with Michel Foucault, *The History of Sexuality* (New York: Vintage Books, 1990), pp. 59–73—the original title, *La volonté de savoir* ("The Will to Knowledge") appears more accurately to outline his account on truth and power in discourses on sexuality.

10. See John Fiske, *Reading the Popular* (Boston: Unwin Hyman, 1989) and *Understanding Popular Culture* (Boston: Unwin Hyman, 1989), as well as de Certeau (1984). See also the previous notes.

11. With his ethical conception of the ideal speech act, Habermas outlines a different approach to the relation between power and significance than that debated in the previous notes. Jürgen Habermas, *The Theory of Communicative Action* (Boston: Beacon Press, 1984).

12. See the discussion in the previous notes.

13. See note 2 in chapter 17, "Notes on the Syntactical Function of the Four Codes."

14. For more on Ferdinand Tönnies's famous distinction between social interaction in communal and societal networks see *Community and Society* (East Lansing: Michigan State University Press, 1957).

15. Latour (1997) and also *La Clef de Berlin, et autres Leçons d'un Amateur de Sciences* (Paris: La Découverte, 1993).

Film and Television Sources

HISTORICAL DOCUMENTARIES

- *History of the 20th Century* 1980–1985
  Also published as *Focus on the Last One Hundred Years:* Videotapes, volumes 1—9, Video Collectibles Corporation/ABC Wide World of Learning; executive producer Jack Healy; producer, Richard A. Klein; directors, David Thaxton and Richard Klein; assistant director, Kevin Green; editors, David Howard and Thomas D'Onofrio; writers: Richard A. Klein, David Thaxton, Kevin Green, and Chuck Neff; film research, Richard A. Klein and Frank Gaffney; still picture research, Shirley L. Green; historical research, Ann Fusz, Ellen Fusz, and Nancy Sachs (only named for the chapter on the 1950s); narrators, Larry Lewman and Tom Lewis; ABC production liason, Sharon Silha; copyright, American Broadcasting Company, Inc., and ABC Video Enterprise, Inc., 1980–1985; packaging and design, copyright, MPI Home Video, 1990.

- *Yesteryear* 1982
  Yesteryear 1969 with Dick Cavett, producer and director, Bruce Cohn; written by Mitchell Barry; editor, Ron Brody; senior researcher, Nathan Rosen; cameramen, Hank Gevings and Tom Doak (for the scenes with Dick Cavett); Copyright, Bruce Cohn Production, Inc., 1982; distribution, United American Video/HBO.

- *The Fabulous Sixties* 1970
  Narrated by Peter Jennings; executive producers Philip S. Hobel and Douglas Leiterman; producer John Smith; executive editor, Don Haig; written by James Eayrs and Alexander Ross; associated producers, Mary Brown and Mark Blandford; edited by Don Haig, Tom Berner, and Bill Fruet; research, Gene Ferraro, Geoff Eger, and Lachlan Leiterman; copyright, Document Associates, Inc./Hobel Leiterman Productions, Inc., 1970; packaging and design, copyright MPI Home Video, 1990.

- *The Sensational 70s* 1979
  Producers, Philip S. Hobel and Douglas Leiterman; director, James Orr; narrator, Harvey Kirck; written by, Robert Emmet Hoyt with Sue Acourt;

editor Stephen Withrow; director of research, Henry Ehrlich; copyright, Hobel Leiterman Productions Ltd./Document Associates, Inc., 1979; packaging and design, copyright MPI Home Video, 1990.

- *The Class of the 20th Century* 1991
  Vols. 5 and 6, executive producers, Charles Grinker and Martin L. Waldman; produced and directed by Merrill M. Mazuer; producer and writer, Pamela Blafer Lack; supervising editor, David Pentecost; director of photography Shaun Harkins; A&E program executive, Michael Cascio; copyright, CEL Communications, Inc. and Arts and Entertainment Network, 1991.

JACK WEBB

Dragnet, television (NBC 1951–1959 / 1967–1970)

- "The Big Secret" ("The Big Show") 1/22/1953
- "The Big Ante" ("The Big Hands") 5/21/1953
- "The Big Producer" 8/26/1954
- "The Big Juvenile Gang War" ("The Big Juvenile Division") 4/10/1958

  MRK VII LIMITED, executive producer, Stanley Meyer; produced by Jack Webb and Michael Meshekoff; directed by Jack Webb; screenplay, James E. Moser; actors, Jack Webb (as Joe Friday), Barton Yarborough (as Ben Romero), Barney Philipps (as Ed Jacobs), and Ben Alexander (as Frank Smith), among others; director of photography, Edward Colman; art director, Feild Gray and Gibson Holley; supervising editor, Robert M. Leeds; film editor, Lynn Harrison and Irving Schoenberg; camera operator, Bud Mautino; announcer, Hal Gibney and George Fenneman; music, Walter Schumann; technical advice for the filming of *Dragnet* came from the office of Chief W.H. Parker, Los Angeles Police Department; based on a radio play by James Moser; distribution, Shokus Video, 1989.

Dragnet, radio (NBC 1949–1957)

- "The Big Producer" 2/21/1951
- "The Big Hands" ("The Big Ante") 11/22/1951
- "The Big Juvenile Division" ("The Big Juvenile Gang War") 1/17/1952
- "The Big Show" ("The Big Secret") 4/10/1952

  "Heard tonight were" Jack Webb (as Joe Friday), Barton Yarborough (as Ben Romero), Barney Philipps (as Ed Jacobs), and Ben Alexander (as Frank Smith), among others; announcer, Hal Gibney; script by James Moser; technical advice came from the office of Chief W.H. Parker, Los Angeles Police Department; copyright, Charles Michelson 1996; licensed and manufactured by Radio Spirits, Inc., 1996.

LUCILLE BALL

I Love Lucy (CBS 1951–1957)

- "Lucy is Enceinte" 1952
- "Lucy Goes to the Hospital" 1953
- "Lucy and John Wayne" 1955
- "Lucy Visits Grauman's" 1955

    Actors, Lucille Ball, Desi Arnaz, Vivian Vance, William Frawley, among others; producer, Jess Oppenheimer; directed, by William Asher; writers, Jess Oppenheimer, Madelyn Pugh, and Bob Caroll, Jr.; director of photography, Karl Freund; music director, Wilbur Hatch (conducting the Desi Arnaz Orchestra); executive producer, Desi Arnaz; copyright Desilu Productions, Inc.; distribution, CBS/Fox Video.

Other Productions:

- *The Ed Sullivan Show (Toast of the Town*—1948–1971) CBS 1954
  Produced by Marlo Lewis and Ed Sullivan; director, John Wray; copyright, CBS Network Production, 1954; distribution, Shokus Video, 1989.

- *Lucy and Desi, A Home Movie,* Lucie Arnaz 1994
  Hosted by Lucie Arnaz; executive Producers, Lucie Arnaz and Laurence Luckinbill; producer, Don Buford; directed by Lucie Arnaz; special script material, Lonnie Reed; story, Lawrence Luckinbill; supervising editor, Sandra Consentino; cameramen, Jeff Cook, among others; music performed by Desi Arnaz and the Desi Arnaz Orchestra; copyright, Arluck Entertainment, Inc., 1993.

- "Lucille Ball Dies—Wednesday, April 26, 1989," *Nightline,* ABC News, 1989

    Hosted by Jeff Greenfield; copyright, ABC News; packaging and design, copyright, MPI Home Video, 1990.

- *Vintage Commercials: Sixty More Minutes of Classic Television Commercials from the 1950s and 1960s,* vols. 2 and 4, nos. 408 and 432; distribution, Shokus Video, 1989.

EDWARD R. MURROW

See It Now (CBS 1951–1958), *Person to Person* (CBS 1953–1961)

- *Good Night and Good Luck: The Edward R. Murrow Television Collection,* CBS News, 1991

    Vol. 1, "The Best of Person to Person"; hosted by Connie Chung; produced by John Aaron and Jesse Zousmer. Vol. 2, "The Best of See It Now"; hosted by Mike Wallace, (*See It Now* produced and edited by Edward R. Murrow and Fred W. Friendly). Vol. 3, *Harvest of Shame;* hosted by Dan Rather (*Harvest of Shame* produced by David Lowe; director of operations, Palmer Williams; film editor, John Schulz; cameramen, Martin Barnett and Charles Mack; executive producer, Fred W. Friendly; correspondent, Edward R. Murrow; CBS Reports on November 25, 1960). Vol. 4, "The McCarthy Years"; hosted by Walter Cronkite; executive producers, Sam Roberts and Ken Ross; producer, Bernard Birnbaum; written by Sam Roberts and Russ Bensley; camera, Keith Kulin; sound, Bert Canaie; copyright, CBS Inc., 1991; distribution, CBS/Fox Video.

- Additional *See it Now* footage from the Museum of Television and Radio, New York, and from the private archive of J. Fred MacDonald, Chicago.

- Edward R. Murrow, *In the Search of Light: The Broadcasts of Edward R. Murrow, 1938–1961*. Edited with an introduction by Edward Bliss, Jr. (New York: Knopf, 1967).

WALTER CRONKITE

Evening News (CBS 1963–)

- CBS *Evening News*, September 2, 1963, Museum of Television and Radio

- *Cronkite Remembers*, CBS 1996
  A Production of CBS News in Association with Cronkite/Ward and Company; produced by David Browning; editor/producer, Vanessa Procopio; photography, Gregory Andracke and Kevin Cloutier; executive producer, Linda S. Mason; copyright, CBS Inc., 1996; distribution CBS/Fox Video.

- *Vietnam: Chronicle of a War—Narrated by Walter Cronkite*, CBS News 1981
  Hosted by Walter Cronkite; featuring among others Dan Rather, Mike Wallace, Eric Sevaried, Ed Bradley, Charles Collingwood, Bruce Dunning, and Charles Kuralt; copyright, CBS Inc., 1981; distribution, CBS/Fox Video.

- *Man on the Moon: With Walter Cronkite*, CBS News 1989
  Hosted by Dan Rather; featuring Walter Cronkite; produced, directed, and written by Robert Northshield; edited by Jorge J. Garcia; copyright, CBS Inc., 1989; distribution, CBS/Fox Video.

- CBS live broadcast of the moon landing, 1969: footage from the Museum of Television and Radio, New York, and the Museum of Broadcast Communications, Chicago.

MUHAMMAD ALI

- *I Shook Up the World: Clay vs. Liston 1964*, TNT 1964
  Presentation by HBO Sports; original broadcast on Theater Network Television, February 25, 1964; copyright, The Big Fights Inc., 1997; distribution, HBO Home Video.

- *When We Were Kings*, Leon Gast, 1996
  Executive producer, David Sonenberg; co-producers, Leon Gast, David Sonen-berg, and Taylor Hackford; director, Leon Gast; featuring Muhammad Ali, George Foreman, Don King, James Brown, B. B. King, Mobutu Sese Seko (president of Zaire), Spike Lee, Norman Mailor, George Plimpton, and others; edited by Leon Gast and others; cinematography by Maryse Alberti and others; music supervisor, S. McCracken; copyright, DasFilms Ltd., 1996.

- *Champions Forever*, Dimitri Logothetis, 1996
  With footage from *Dinner with the Champs* (produced and directed by Craig N. Glazer and Ron Hamady); directed by Dimitri Logothetis; produced by Nabeel Zahid and Joseph Medawar; writer, Kenneth W. Griswold; edited by Jay Wilson; music by Bebu Silvetti; featuring Muhammad Ali, George Fore-man, Joe Frazier, Ken Norton, Larry Holmes, and Reggie Jackson; camera operators, Doug Froebe and others; copyright, Forever Films, Inc., 1996; dis-tribution, Arrow Film Distributors, Ltd.

- Footage from *Muhammad Ali*, Gemstone Entertainment, 1998
  Narrator Michael Christian; video and sound editor, T.C. Coley; music, Michael McGlory; producer, Chaba Mehes; copyright, Hollywood Video Library, 1988; distribution, UAV Corporation.

- Additional footage from the Museum of Television and Radio, New York.

Bibliography

Abercrombie, Nicholas (1996)   *Television and Society.* Cambridge: Polity Press

Althusser, Louis (1984)   *Essays on Ideology.* London: Verso

Anderson, Benedict (1983)   *Imagined Communities: Reflection on the Origin and Spread of Nationalism.* London: Verso

Arendt, Hannah (1970)   *On Violence.* New York: Harvest Book

Aristotle (1987)   *Physik; Vorlesung über die Natur.* Ed. Hans Günter Zekl, vols. 1–8, Hamburg: Felix Meiner

Bakhtin, Mikhail M. (1984)   *Rabelais and His World.* Trans. Helene Iswolsky, Bloomington: Indiana University Press

(1994)   *The Dialogic Imagination: Four Essays.* Ed. M. Holquist, trans. C. Emerson and M. Holquist. Austin: University of Texas Press

Barkin, Steve (2003)   *American Television News: The Media Marketplace and the Public Interest.* Armonk, New York: M. E. Sharpe

Barnouw, Erik (1974)   *Documentary: A History of the Non-Fiction Film.* New York: Oxford University Press

Barry, Seward A. M. (1997)   *Visual Intelligence: Perception, Image, and Manipulation in Visual Communication.* Albany: State University of New York Press

Barthes, Roland (1974)   *S/Z.* Trans. R. Miller. New York: Hill and Wang

(1977)   *Image-Music-Text.* Trans. Stephen Heath. New York: Hill and Wang

(1988)   "The Advertising Message," in *The Semiotic Challenge.* Trans. Richard Howard. New York: Hill and Wang

(1994)   *Mythologies.* Selected and trans. by Annette Lavers. New York: Hill and Wang

Baudrillard, Jean (1987)   *The Evil Demon of Images.* Sydney: Power Institute of Fine Arts

(1990)   *Revenge of the Crystal: Selected Writings on the
                                Modern Object and its Destiny, 1968–1983.* Ed.
                                and trans. Paul Foss and Julian Pefanis.
                                London: Pluto Press

(2000)   *Simulacra and Simulation.* Trans. Sheila Faria
                                Glaser. Ann Arbor: University of Michigan
                                Press

Baughman, James L. (1997)   *The Republic of Mass Culture: Journalism, Film-
                                making, and Broadcasting in America Since
                                1941.* Baltimore: John Hopkins University
                                Press

Bazin, Germaine (1967)   *The Museum Age.* New York: Universal Press

Benjamin, Walter (1969)   *Illuminations.* Ed. Hannah Arendt, trans. H. Zohn.
                                New York: Schocken Books

Bennett, Tony (1995)   *The Birth of the Museum: History, Theory, Politics.*
                                London: Routledge

Bense, Max (1971)   *Zeichen und Design: Semiotische Ästhetik.* Baden-
                                Baden: Agis

Bentele, Günther (1984)   *Zeichen und Entwicklung. Vorüberlegungen zu
                                einer genetischen Semiotik.* Tübingen: Gunter
                                Narr

Berger, John (1972)   *Ways of Seeing.* London: BBC and Penguin
                                Books

Bertin, Jacques (1983)   *Semiology of Graphics: Diagrams, Networks,
                                Maps.* Trans. William J. Berg. Madison: Univer-
                                sity of Wisconsin Press

Bolvig, Alex ed. (2003)   *History and Images: Towards a New Iconology.*
                                Ed. together with Philip Lindley. Turnhout, Bel-
                                gium: Brepols Publishers

Biere, Bernd Ulrich ed.   *Mündlichkeit und Schriftlichkeit im Fernsehen.* Ed.
(1996)   together with Rudolf Hoberg. Tübingen: Gun-
                                ter Narr

Boddy, William (1990)   *Fifties Television: The Industry and Its Critics.*
                                Urbana: University of Illinois Press

Bourdieu, Pierre (1977)   *Reproduction in Education, Society, and Culture.*
                                Together with Jean-Claude Passeron, trans.
                                Richard Nice. London: Sage Publications

(1984)   *Distinction: A Social Critique of the Judgment of
                                Taste.* Trans. Richard Nice. Cambridge: Har-
                                vard University Press

Braun, Gerhard (1987)   *Grundlagen der visuellen Kommunikation.* Mün-
                                chen: Bruckmann

de Certeau, Michel (1984)   *The Practice of Everyday Life.* Trans. Steven
                                Rendall. Berkeley: University of California Press

Collini, Stefan ed. (1992)   *Interpretation and Overinterpretation.* Cambridge: Cambridge University Press

Curtin, Michael (1995)   *Redeeming the Wasteland: Television Documentary and Cold War Politics.* New Brunswick: Rutgers University Press

Dayan, Daniel (1987)   "Performing Media Events," in James Curran, Anthony Smith, and Pauline Wingate, eds., *Impacts and Influences: Essays on Media Power in the Twentieth Century.* London: Methuen

(1992)   *Media Events: The Live Broadcasting of History.* Cambridge: Harvard University Press

Debord, Guy (1977)   *Society of the Spectacle.* Detroit: Black and Red Books

Derrida, Jacques (1978)   *Of Grammatology.* Trans. Gayatri Chakravorty Spivak. Baltimore: John Hopkins University Press

Doane, Mary Ann (1990)   "Information, Crisis, Catastrophe," in Patricia Mellencamp, ed., *Logics of Television: Essays in Cultural Criticism.* Bloomington: Indiana University Press

Doherty, Thomas (2003)   *Cold War, Cool Medium: Television, McCarthyism, and American Culture.* New York: Columbia University Press

Dondis, Donis A. (1993)   *A Primer of Visual Literacy.* Cambridge: MIT Press

Eco, Umberto (1979)   *A Theory of Semiotics.* Bloomington: Indiana University Press

(1981)   *The Role of the Reader: Explorations in the Semiotics of Texts.* London: Hutchinson

(1986)   *Travels in Hyperreality: Essays.* Trans. William Weaver, "A Helen and Kurt Wolff book." San Diego: Harvest

(1987)   *La struttura assente.* Milano: Tascabili Bompiani

(1990)   *The Limits of Interpretation.* Bloomington: Indiana University Press

Edgerton, Gary R. ed. (2001)   *Television Histories: Shaping Collective Memory in the Media Age.* Lexington: University Press of Kentucky

Elkins, James (1996)   *The Object Stares Back: On the Nature of Seeing.* New York: Simon and Schuster

Ellis, John (1993)   *Visible Fictions.* New York: Routledge

Epstein, Edward Jay (2000)   *News from Nowhere: Television and the News.* New York: Random House

272   *Bibliography*

Ewen, Stuart (1988)   *All Consuming Images: The Politics of Style in Contemporary Culture.* New York: Basic Books

Feldges, Mathias (1970)   "Ein Beispiel für das Weiterbestehen Mittelalterlicher Denkstrukturen in der Barockzeit," in *Wirkendes Wort.* Vol. 20

Fish, Stanley (1980)   *Is There a Text in This Class? The Authority of Interpretive Communities.* Cambridge: Harvard University Press

Fiske, John (1989)   *Reading the Popular.* Boston: Unwin Hyman

(1989)   *Understanding Popular Culture.* Boston: Unwin Hyman

Fleck, Ludwik (1979)   *Genesis and Development of a Scientific Fact.* Trans. Fred Bradley and Thaddeus J. Trenn. Chicago: University of Chicago Press

Fong, Weng (1992)   *Beyond Representation: Chinese Painting and Calligraphy, 8th–14th Century.* New York: Metropolitan Museum of Art

Foucault, Michel (1971)   "Orders of Discourse." Trans. Rupert Swyer, in *Social Science Information* 10, April

(1972)   *The Archaeology of Knowledge and the Discourse on Language.* Trans. A. Sheridan Smith. New York: Dorset Press

(1977)   *Discipline and Punish: The Birth of the Prison.* Trans. A. Sheridan. New York: Pantheon

(1986)   "Of Other Spaces," in *Diacritics*, Spring

(1990)   *The History of Sexuality.* Trans. Robert Hurley, New York: Vintage Books

Gaur, Albertine (1994)   *A History of Calligraphy.* London: British Library

Geertz, Clifford (1973)   *The Interpretation of Culture: Selected Essays.* New York: Basic Books

Gipsrud, Jostein (2002)   *Understanding Media Culture.* London: Arnold

Gitlin, Todd (1987)   *The Sixties: Years of Hope, Days of Rage.* New York: Bantam Books

Gombrich, Ernst H. (1960) *Art and Illusion: A Study in the Psychology of Pictorial Representation.* New York: Bollingen Series

Gómes-Gonzáles, María Á. (2001)   *The Theme-Topic Interface: Evidence from English.* Philadelphia: John Benjamins Publishing Company

Goodman, Nelson (1976)   *Languages of Art: An Approach to the Theory of Symbols.* Indianapolis: Hackett Publishing Company

Gramsci, Antonio (1971)
Selections from the Prison Notebooks. London: Lawrence and Wishart

Habermas, Jürgen (1981)
The Structural Transformation of the Public Sphere: An Inquiry into a Category of Bourgeois Society. Trans. Thomas Burger and Frederick Lawrence. Cambridge: MIT Press

(1984)
The Theory of Communicative Action. Trans. Thomas McCarthy. Boston: Beacon Press

Hallin, Daniel C. (1986)
The Uncensored War: The Media and Vietnam. New York: Oxford University Press

Hanke, Robert (2001)
"*Quantum Leap:* The Postmodern Challenge of Television as History," in Gary R. Edgerton and Peter C. Rollins, eds., *Television Histories: Shaping Collective Memory in the Media Age.* Lexington: University Press of Kentucky

Haug, Wolfgang Fritz (1980)
Warenästhetik und kapitalistische Massenkultur— "Werbung" und "Konsum." Berlin: Argument Verlag

Hayde, Michael J. (2001)
My Name's Friday: The Unauthorized but True Story of Dragnet and the Films of Jack Webb. Nashville: Cumberland House

Hegel, Georg W. F. (1940)
System der Philosophie. Die Wissenschaft der Logik. Ed. H. Glockner. Sämtliche Werke in 20 Bänden. Vol. 8. Stuttgart: Frommann

Hellmann, John (1997)
The Kennedy Obsession: The American Myth of JFK. New York: Columbia University Press

Higgins, Kathleen Marie (2002)
"Television, Realism, and the Distortion of Time," in Ruth Lorand, ed., *Television: Aesthetic Reflections.* New York: Peter Lang

Horowitz, Susan (1997)
Queens of Comedy: Lucille Ball, Phyllis Diller, Carol Burnett, Joan Rivers, and the New Generation of Funny Women. Amsterdam: Gordon and Breach Publishers

Howells, Richard (2003)
Visual Culture. Cambridge: Polity Press

Jakobson, Roman (1962–85)
Selected Writings. The Hague: Mouton

(1990)
"Two Aspects of Language and Two Types of Aphasic Disturbances," in Linda R. Waught and Monique Monville-Burston, eds., *On Language.* Cambridge: Harvard University Press

Jaubert, Alain (1989)
Making People Disappear: An Amazing Chronicle of Photographic Deception. McLean: Pergamon-Brassey's International Defense Publishers

Jay, Martin (1993)
Downcast Eyes: The Denigration of Vision in Twentieth-Century French Thought. Berkeley: University of California Press

Jehle, Peter (1987)   "Zur Herausbildung des Staatstheaters in Frankreich," in *Der innere Staat des Bürgertums; Studien zur Entstehung bürgerlicher Hegemonie-Apparate im 17. und 18. Jahrhundert*. Eds. Herbert Bosch, Peter Jehle, etc. West-Berlin: Argument-Verlag

Jenkins, Henry (1992)   *Textual Poachers: Television Fans and Participatory Culture*. New York: Routledge

Katz, Elihu (1987)   "Performing Media Events," in James Curran, Anthony Smith, and Pauline Wingate, eds., *Impacts and Influences: Essays on Media Power in the Twentieth Century*. London: Methuen

(1992)   *Media Events: The Live Broadcasting of History*. Cambridge: Harvard University Press

Kellner, Douglas (2003)   *Media Spectacle*. New York: Routledge

Kepes, Gyorgy (1944)   *Language of Vision*. Chicago: P. Theobald

Kress, Gunther R. (1996)   *Reading Images: The Grammar of Visual Design*. Together with Theo van Leeuwen. London: Routledge

Kücklich, Julian (2001)   "Auf der Suche nach dem verlorenen Text: Literaturwissenschaften und Computerspiele," in *PhiN Philologie im Netz* (www.phin.de). No. 15

Kuhn, Thomas S. (1962)   *The Structure of Scientific Revolutions*. Chicago: University of Chicago Press

Landay, Lori (1998)   *Madcaps, Screwballs, and Con Women: The Female Trickster in American Culture*. Philadelphia: University of Pennsylvania Press

Latour, Bruno (1993)   *We Have Never Been Modern: Essays in Symmetrical Anthropology*. Trans. Catherine Porter. New York: Harvest Wheatsheaf

(1993)   *La Clef de Berlin, et autres Leçons d'un Amateur de Sciences*. Paris: La Découverte

(1997)   "On Actor-Network Theory: A Few Clarifications," Center for Social Theory and Technology, Keele University

Leeuwen, Theo van (1996)   *Reading Images: The Grammar of Visual Design*. Together with Gunther R. Kress. London: Routledge

Lemert, Charles (2003)   *Muhammad Ali: Trickster in the Culture of Irony*. Cambridge: Polity Press

Leonard, Neil (1962)   *Jazz and the White Americans: The Acceptance of a New Art Form*. Chicago: University of Chicago Press

Lévi-Strauss, Claude (1976)   *Structural Anthropology*. London: Jonathan Cape

Levine, Lawrence W. (1988)   *Highbrow / Lowbrow: The Emergence of Cultural Hierarchy in America.* Cambridge: Harvard University Press

MacDonald, Fred J. (1990)   *One Nation Under Television: The Rise and Decline of Network TV.* Chicago: Nelson Hall Publishers

Makaryk, Irena R. ed. (1993)   *Encyclopedia of Contemporary Literary Theory.* Toronto: University of Toronto Press

Marc, David (1996)   *Democratic Vistas: Television in American Culture.* Philadelphia: University of Pennsylvania Press

Marqusee, Mike (1999)   *Redemption Song: Muhammad Ali and the Spirit of the Sixties.* London: Verso

May, Lary (1980)   *Screening Out the Past: The Birth of Mass Culture and the Motion Picture Industry.* New York: Oxford University Press

McLuhan, Marshall (1964)   *Understanding Media: The Extensions of Man.* New York: Signet

McNeil, Alex (1996)   *Total Television: The Comprehensive Guide to Programming From 1948 to the Present.* New York: Penguin Books

Messaris, Paul (1994)   *Visual Literacy.* Boulder: Westview Press

Metz, Christian (1974)   *Film Language: A Semiotics of the Cinema.* Trans. Michael Taylor. New York: Oxford University Press

(2000)   *Der Imaginäre Signifikant: Psychoanalyse und Kino.* Münster: Nodus Publikationen

Morley, David (1980)   *The "Nationwide" Audience.* London: British Film Institute

(1986)   *Family Television: Cultural Power and Domestic Leisure.* London: Comedia

Morris, Charles (1947)   *Signs, Language, and Behavior.* New York: Prentice-Hall

Murrow, Edward R. (1967)   *In the Search of Light: The Broadcasts of Edward R. Murrow, 1938–1961.* Ed. Edward Bliss, Jr. New York: Knopf

Nöth, Winfried (1990)   *Handbook of Semiotics.* Bloomington: Indiana University Press

(1997)   "Can Pictures Lie?" in Winfried Nöth, ed., *Semiotics of the Media: State of the Art, Projects, and Perspectives.* Berlin: Mouton de Gruyter

Ong, Walter J. (1971)   *Rhetoric, Romance, and Technology: Studies in the Interaction of Expression and Culture.* Ithaca: Cornell University Press

Passeron, Jean-Claude (1977)   *Reproduction in Education, Society, and Culture.* Together with Pierre Bourdieu, trans. Richard Nice. London: Sage Publications

Peirce, Charles S. (1931–58)   *Collected Papers.* Cambridge: Harvard University Press

Persico, Joseph E. (1988)   *Edward R. Murrow: An American Original.* New York: McGraw-Hill

Pomian, Krzysztof (1990)   *Collectors and Curiosities: Paris and Vienna 1500–1800.* Trans. Elizabeth Wiles-Portier. Cambridge: Polity Press

Postman, Neil (1985)   *Amusing Ourselves to Death: Public Discourse in the Age of Show Business.* New York: Penguin Books

Prase, Tilo (1997)   *Das gebrauchte Bild: Bausteine einer Semiotik des Fernsehbildes.* Berlin: Vistas

Racek, Alfred (1983)   *Philosophie der Grenze. Ein Entwurf.* Vienna: Herder

Rostek, Thomas (1994)   *See It Now Confronts McCarthyism: Television Documentary and the Politics of Representation.* Tuscaloosa: University of Alabama Press

Quasthoff, Uta M. (1996)   "Mündliche Kommunikation als Körperliche Kommunikation: Beobachtungen zur Direkten Interaktion und zum Fernsehen," in *Mündlichkeit und Schriftlichkeit im Fernsehen.* Eds. Bernd Ulrich Biere and Rudolf Hoberg, Tübingen: Gunter Narr

Remnick, David (1998)   *King of the World: Muhammad Ali and the Rise of an American Hero.* New York: Vintage Books

Rollins, Richard C. (2001)   "Victoria at Sea: Cold War Epic," in *Television Histories: Shaping Collective Memory in the Media Age.* Eds. Gary R. Edgerton and Peter C. Rollins, Lexington: University Press of Kentucky

Rosen, Philip (2001)   *Change Mummified: Cinema, Historicity, Theory.* Minneapolis: University of Minnesota Press

Rutherford, Paul (1994)   *The New Icons? The Art of Television Advertising.* Toronto: University of Toronto Press

Said, Edward W. (1994)   *Orientalism.* New York: Vintage Books

Saint-Martin, Fernande (1990)   *Semiotics of Visual Language.* Bloomington: Indiana University Press

de Saussure, Ferdinand (1983)   *Course in General Linguistics.* Ed. Roy Harris, trans. Wade Baskin. London: Duckworth

Schmitt, Jean-Claude (2003)   "Images and the Historian," in *History and Images: Towards a New Iconology.* Eds. Alex Bolvig and Philip Lindley. Turnhout, Belgium: Brepols Publishers

Schudson, Michael (1995)   *The Power of News.* Cambridge: Harvard University Press

Scott, Joan W. (1986)   "Gender: A Useful Category of Historical Analysis," in *American Historical Review.* Vol. 91, no. 5, December

Searle, John R. (1969)   *Speech Acts: An Essay in the Philosophy of Language.* Cambridge: Cambridge University Press

Sebeok, Thomas A. (1976)   *Contributions to a Doctrine of Signs.* Bloomington: Indiana University Press

Seiter, Ellen (1992)   "Semiotics, Structuralism, and Television," in Robert C. Allen, ed., *Channels of Discourse, Reassembled: Television and Contemporary Criticism.* Chapel Hill: University of North Carolina Press

Sennett, Richard (1974)   *The Fall of the Public Man.* New York: W.W. Norton and Company

Simmel, Georg (1968)   *The Conflict in Modern Culture and Other Essays.* Trans. Peter K. Etzkorn. New York: Teachers College Press Columbia

Sonesson, Göran (1989)   *Pictorial Concepts.* Lund: Lund University Press

Stark, Steven D. (1998)   *Glued to the Set: The 60 Television Shows and Events That Made Us Who We Are Today.* New York: Delta

Stern, Jane (1992)   *Jane and Michael Stern's Encyclopedia of Pop Culture: An A to Z Guide of Who's Who and What's What, from Aerobics and Bubble Gum to Valley of the Dolls and Moon Unit Zappa.* Together with Michael Stern. New York: HarperPerennial

Sturken, Marita (1997)   *Tangled Memories: The Vietnam War, the AIDS Epidemic, and the Politics of Remembering.* Berkeley: University of California Press

Todorov, Tzvetan (1981)   *Introduction to Poetics.* Trans. Richard Howard. Minneapolis: University of Minneapolis Press

Tomaselli, Keyan (1996)   *Appropriating Images: The Semiotics of Visual Representation.* Hojbjerg: Intervention Press

Tönnies, Ferdinand (1957)   *Community and Society.* Ed. and trans. Charles P. Loomis. East Lansing: Michigan State University Press

Tucholsky, Kurt (1985)   *Gesammelte Werke.* Ed. Mary Gerold Tucholsky and Fritz J. Raddatz. Reinbek bei Hamburg: Rowohlt

Türcke, Christoph (2002)   *Erregte Gesellschaft: Philosophie der Sensation.* München: C. H. Beck

Van Deburg, W. L. (1992)   *New Day in Babylon: The Black Power Movement and American Culture, 1965–1975.* Chicago: University of Chicago Press

Walkowitz, Daniel J. (1998)   "Rescreening the Past: Subversion Narratives and the Politics of History," in Tony Barta, ed., *Screening the Past: Film and the Representation of History.* Westport: Praeger

Walsham, Geoffrey (1997)   "Actor-Network Theory and IS Research: Current Status and Future Prospects," in *Information Systems and Qualitative Research.* Eds. A.S. Lee, J. Liebenau, and J.I. deGross. London: Weinheim

Wellman, Barry (1983)   "Network Analysis: Some Basic Principles," in *Sociological Theory.* Ed. R. Collins. San Francisco: Jossey-Bass, Inc.

Wells, Tom (1994)   *The War Within: America's Battle Over Vietnam.* Foreword by Todd Gitlin. Berkeley: University of California Press

Wiggins, David K. (1997)   *Glory Bound: Black Athletes in a White America.* New York: Syracuse University Press

Wölfflin, Heinrich (1915)   *Kunstgeschichtliche Grundbegriffe: Das Probelm der Stilentwicklung in der neueren Kunst.* München: Bruckmann

Worth, Sol (1981)   "Pictures can't say ain't," in *Studying Visual Communication.* Ed. Larry Gross, Philadelphia: University of Pennsylvania Press

Zelizer, Barbara (1990)   "Where is the Author in American TV News? On the Construction and Presentation of Proximity, Authorship, and Journalistic Authority," in *Semiotica* 80–1/2

Index